Slave Religion

SLAVE RELIGION

The "Invisible Institution"
in the Antebellum South

ALBERT J. RABOTEAU

New York   OXFORD UNIVERSITY PRESS   1978

Library of Congress Cataloging in Publication Data
Raboteau, Albert J   Slave religion.   Includes index.
1.   Afro-Americans—Southern States—Religion.   2.   Slaves—Southern States—Religion.
3.   Southern States—Church history.   I.   Title.
BR563.N4R25   299'.6'0975   78-7275   ISBN 0-19-502438-9

Grateful acknowledgment is made to Présence Africaine for permission
to quote an abridged translation of the poem "Souffles" by Birago Diop
from *Leurres et Lueurs* (Paris: Présence Africaine, 1960).

Printed in the United States of America

To my father, Royal L. Woods
and to the memory of my mother, Mabel S. Woods

It is our duty to proceed from what is near to what is distant, from what is known to that which is less known, to gather the traditions from those who have reported them, to correct them as much as possible and to leave the rest as it is, in order to make our work help anyone who seeks truth and loves wisdom.

ABU'L-RAYHAN MUHAMMAD AL-BIRUNI (973–1050)

Lord! Lord! baby, I hope yo' young fo'ks will never know what slavery is, an' will never suffer as yo' foreparents. O God! God! I'm livin' to tel' de tale to yo', honey. Yes, Jesus, yo've spared me.

MINNIE FULKES, FORMER SLAVE

We are bound to search the intelligible actions of men, for some indications of their inner significance.

THOMAS MERTON

Preface

Until recently, the history of the black Church was a subject largely ignored by historians of religion in America despite the wide recognition that black religious institutions have been the foundation of Afro-American culture. An agency of social control, a source of economic cooperation, an arena for political activity, a sponsor of education, and a refuge in a hostile white world, the black Church has been historically the social center of Afro-American life. One still looks in vain, however, for a major history of Afro-American religion. Valuable pioneering work was done by W.E.B. Du Bois in *The Souls of Black Folks* and *The Negro Church*, both published in 1903; by Carter G. Woodson in his *History of the Negro Church*, published in 1921; and by E. Franklin Frazier, whose 1953 lecture series on black religion was gathered and issued in 1964 as *The Negro Church in America*. However, the field still remains a fertile area for exploration. One of the purposes of this book is to serve as a rough sketch for further, more exhaustive examination of this important subject.[1]

Little enough has been written on the history of the visible institutions of black religion: the independent black denominations and churches. Much less has there been discussion of what might be termed "the invisible institution"—black religion under slavery. Part of the problem has been the assumption that sources for a study of slave religion simply do not exist. Daniel Boorstin

succinctly stated this assumption in the chapter entitled "Invisible
Communities: The Negroes' Churches" in *The Americans: The
National Experience:*

> But . . . organized white churches did not encompass the reli-
> gious life of the Southern Negro. The Negro developed a
> religious life of his own. Much of this life remained unre-
> corded because many of the independent Negro religious
> meetings were illegal, and most of their participants, includ-
> ing sometimes even the preacher, were illiterate. Still we do
> know that such religious meetings were not uncommon, and
> that they became the nucleus, and later the whole organized
> form, of Negro communities. The Negroes' religious life
> thrived in institutions that were often invisible to the white
> masters, and that are barely visible to the historian today.[2]

We should speak of the "invisibility" of slave religion with irony:
it is the neglect of slave sources by historians which has been the
main cause of this invisibility. Studies by John Blassingame, Sterling Stuckey, Lawrence Levine, Eugene Genovese, and others
have demonstrated the fallacy in assuming that slaves left no articulate record of their experience. Blassingame's *The Slave Community* and *Slave Testimony*, Genovese's *Roll, Jordan, Roll,* and
Levine's *Black Culture and Black Consciousness* eloquently prove
that there are indeed ample sources deriving from the slaves
themselves. I have tried to investigate slave narratives, black autobiographies, and black folklore in order to gather, literally out of
the mouths of former slaves, the story of their religious experiences during slavery. Supplementing these sources with the more
traditional ones of travel accounts, missionary reports, and journals of white observers, I have attempted to picture the religion of
American slaves in all its complexity. It has been my special
concern to preserve the texture of the slave testimony and to avoid
forcing the experience reflected in that testimony into any precon-
ceived theoretical framework. I hope that the failings of this narrative will not obscure the wisdom and the rich humanity of the
story that the former slaves had to tell.[3]

What were the origins of black religion in America? What aspects of African religions were retained by the slaves? How did the evangelization and conversion of African slaves to Christianity take place? What was the nature of the religion to which the slave was converted? What, if anything, was distinctive about religion in the slave quarters? These are the general questions that I have attempted to answer.

I am indebted to many people for assistance in the conception and writing of this study. I wish to express my appreciation to Sydney Ahlstrom, who served as adviser for the doctoral dissertation upon which this book is based. I am also grateful to John Blassingame, whose course in Afro-American history was the source of several crucial insights which led to my choice of slave religion as a research topic. My thanks are also due C. Duncan Rice, Wayne Meeks, Charles Davis, James Dittes, Hans Frei, Winthrop Jordan, Lawrence Levine and Sheldon Meyer for their interest and encouragement. Susan Rabiner and Parke Puterbaugh I thank for sensitive and careful editing. To Sylvia Foster I owe thanks for creative assistance in research, and to Margaret Brewton, Teruko Ohashi, and Sylvia Turner for cheerful clerical assistance. Most of all, I am grateful to my wife Katherine for her critical readings and for her confidence that this work would someday be finished.

Contents

Slave Religion

I
The African Heritage

1
The African Diaspora

Hear more often things than beings,
the voice of the fire listening,
hear the voice of the water.
Hear in the wind
the bushes sobbing,
it is the sigh of our forebears.

Those who are dead are never gone:
they are there in the thickening shadow.
The dead are not under the earth:
they are in the tree that rustles,
they are in the wood that groans,
they are in the water that runs,
they are in the water that sleeps,
they are in the hut, they are in the crowd,
the dead are not dead.
. . . .

Those who are dead are never gone,
they are in the breast of the woman,
they are in the child who is wailing
and in the firebrand that flames.
The dead are not under the earth:
they are in the fire that is dying,
they are in the grasses that weep,
they are in the whimpering rocks,
they are in the forest, they are in the house,
the dead are not dead.
. . . .

BIRAGO DIOP

THE ENSLAVEMENT of an estimated ten million Africans over a period of almost four centuries in the Atlantic slave trade was a tragedy of such scope that it is difficult to imagine, much less comprehend.[1] When these Africans were brought to slavery in the mines, plantations, and households of the New World, they were torn away from the political, social, and cultural systems that had ordered their lives. Tribal and linguistic groups were broken up, either on the coasts of Africa or in the slave pens across the Atlantic. Most brutal of all, the exigencies of the slave trade did not allow the preservation of family or kinship ties.

In the New World slave control was based on the eradication of all forms of African culture because of their power to unify the slaves and thus enable them to resist or rebel. Nevertheless, African beliefs and customs persisted and were transmitted by slaves to their descendants. Shaped and modified by a new environment, elements of African folklore, music, language, and religion were transplanted in the New World by the African diaspora. Influenced by colonial European and indigenous native American cultures, aspects of the African heritage have contributed, in greater or lesser degree, to the formation of various Afro-American cultures in the New World. One of the most durable and adaptable constituents of the slave's culture, linking African past with American present, was his religion. It is important to realize, however, that in the Americas the religions of Africa have not been merely preserved as static "Africanisms" or as archaic "retentions." The fact is that they have continued to develop as living traditions putting down new roots in new soil, bearing new fruit as unique hybrids of American origin. African styles of worship, forms of ritual, systems of belief, and fundamental perspectives have remained vital on this side of the Atlantic, not because they were preserved in a "pure" orthodoxy but because they were transformed. Adaptability, based upon respect for spiritual power wherever it originated, accounted for the openness of African religions to syncretism with other religious traditions and for the continuity of a distinctively African religious consciousness. At least in some areas of the Americas, the gods of Africa continued to live—in exile.[2]

African Religious Traditions

Among the Africans who became slaves in the Americas were those, such as the Wolof, Serer, Mandinke, Bambara, Fulani, and Hausa, who were Muslim or at least had been influenced by Islam. The ancient kingdoms of Ghana, Mali, and Songhay had been centers of Muslim influence in the western Sudan. South of the Sahara, along the coasts of "Guinea," and through inland kingdoms, people had been exposed to Islam through trade with North African Muslims, through conquest, through colonization, and through conversion. In fact, the first black Africans with whom white Europeans came into contact on the coast of West Africa were "black Moors" (as distinguished from "tawny Moors," i.e., light-skinned Berbers). In the fifteenth century Portuguese sailors in the service of Prince Henry ventured beyond the Canary Islands and Cape Bojador and sailed along the coast of West Africa in search of trade, wealth, and the legendary Christian king Prester John. In a kind of prologue to the Atlantic slave trade, the Portuguese by the 1440s were capturing Berber and Negro Moors from the coasts of Mauretania and the Senegambia region. According to the Portuguese chronicler Gomes Eannes De Azurara, over nine hundred Africans had been seized and brought to Lisbon as slaves by 1448.[3]

An eighteenth-century traveler observed that while some West African towns had mosques and though some Muslim "Foolas and Mandingoes attend to the ceremonial duties of their religion with such strictness as well might cause Christians to blush," yet "they still entertain a degree of belief in the powers of witchcraft and in those of . . . charms." It is clear that elements of Islam were often mixed with or adapted to forms of traditional African belief.

A case in point is recorded for Dahomey: "Among the *amulets*, or *charms*, the principal is a scrap of parchment containing a sentence of the Koran, which the natives purchase from the Moors who visit the country." As we shall see, Muslim slaves became particularly noted in the New World for the power of their magical charms.[4]

Similarly, it is possible that a few enslaved Africans may have had some contact with Christianity in their homeland. Attempts to establish European Christianity along the coast of West Africa date from the time of Portuguese missionaries in the early sixteenth century. John Barbot, in his account of Guinea, written around 1682, notes that:

> The *Portuguese* missionaries have undergone great labours, and run mighty hazards to convert some of them [Africans in the region of the Gambia] to Christianity, ever since the beginning of the last, and during this century, but with little success: for though some seem to embrace the doctrines, yet many mix it with pagan idolatry and Mahometanism; others are no sooner baptiz'd but they return to their wild natural way of living.[5]

French Capuchins were working on the Gold Coast in 1635 and Portuguese Capuchins were sent out to the kingdom of *Ouwere* in 1683. There were some African converts among the creole societies—made up of mulattoes of Portuguese-African descent—which grew up around the European forts on the coasts of Guinea. The Portuguese had some success in the Kongo where the Mani-Kongo or premier king, Nzinga Mbemba, was converted to Christianity and was baptized as Dom Affonso I (1506–1543). In general, however, the early missionaries had very limited success and did not penetrate the interior. Not until Christianized slaves began to return from Europe and America to Africa in the late eighteenth century did the expansion of Christianity on the West Coast of Africa begin. Christianity was carried further inland by the invasion of European and American missionaries shortly before and contemporary with nineteenth-century colonization. Though Islam—and to a much smaller extent, Christianity—had extended into sub-Saharan Africa, by far the greatest number of those Africans who fell victim to the Atlantic trade came from peoples who held the indigenous and traditional beliefs of their fathers.[6]

Over the four centuries of the Atlantic trade, slaves were seized from many parts of Africa—Central, South, and East—as well as West Africa. The problem of the provenience of American slaves is a difficult one, complicated by the lengthy duration of the trade. Various European and American countries exported and imported slaves at different periods from various points of the African coast, depending on the availability of slaves, the wishes of African slave traders, and other exigencies of the market. As a result, slaves bound for the Americas came from many different nations, tribes, and language groups. Records of the slave ships mention points of embarkation but are often hazy about the original homelands of the human cargo. On this side of the Atlantic, the ethnic names supplied by slave merchants and owners to newly arrived Africans were frequently confused and inexact. Nevertheless, it is clear that a large percentage of American slaves came from West Africa and from the Congo-Angola region. This vast territory stretched along the coast from Senegambia in the northwest to Angola in the southeast; it extended several hundred miles inland, and embraced societies and cultures as diverse as those of the Mandinke, the Yoruba, the Ibo and the Bakongo.[7]

There were, and are, too many significant differences among the religions of various West African peoples, not to mention local variations within any single people, to permit putting them all into a single category. However, similar modes of perception, shared basic principles, and common patterns of ritual were widespread among different West African religions. Beneath the diversity, enough fundamental similarity did exist to allow a general description of the religious heritage of African slaves, with supplementary information concerning particular peoples, such as the Akan, Ewe, Yoruba, Ibo and others, whose influences upon the religions of Afro-Americans have long been noted. It is important to remember also that no single African culture or religion, once transplanted in alien soil, could have remained intact: it was inevitable that the slaves would build *new* societies in the Americas which would be structured in part from their diverse backgrounds in different African societies, in part from the experience of enslavement in a new environment. A common religious heritage then resulted from the blending and assimilation of the many discrete religious heritages of Africans in the New World.[8]

Common to many African societies was belief in a High God, or Supreme Creator of the world and everything in it. It was also commonly believed that this High God, often associated with the sky, was somewhat removed from and uninvolved in the activities of men, especially so when compared with the lesser gods and ancestor-spirits who were actively and constantly concerned with the daily life of the individual and the affairs of society as a whole.[9] Early travelers were quick to note that Africans believed in a High God who transcended ritual relationships with humans. Describing religion on the Slave Coast, William Bosman, a Dutch factor, remarked that the Africans had an "idea of the True God and ascribe to him the Attributes of Almighty, and Omnipresent."

> It is certain that . . . they believe he created the Universe, and therefore vastly preferr him before their Idol-Gods But yet they do not pray to him, or offer any Sacrifices to him; for which they give the following Reasons. God, they say, is too high exalted above us, and too great to condescend so much as to trouble himself or think of Mankind; Wherefore he commits the Government of the World to their Idols; to whom, as the second, third and fourth Persons distant in degree from God, and our appointed lawful Governours, we are obliged to apply ourselves. And in firm Belief of this Opinion they quietly continue.[10]

Occasionally individuals and communities did pray to the High God but sacrifice to him was rare; it was generally the other gods and the spirits of deceased ancestors who received the most attention, since they had been delegated to attend to "the affairs of mankind."[11] Usually, in the traditional religions of West Africa the High God is the parent of the other and lesser gods, who are sometimes seen as mediators between man and God. Among the Yoruba, for example, Olorun is viewed as being above all other gods, and sacrifice to any one of them is concluded in his name. Among other peoples, such as the Ga, there appears to be no overarching High God, but one god who is senior to many, a kind of *primus inter pares*, for each Ga village. The Ibo supreme deity is Chukwu (from *Chi-Uku*, Great Spirit), Chineke the Creator God, who controls rain and fertility and from whom the *chi*, or soul, of a man originates. According to the Bakongo, God (Nzambi) is invisible, the source of rain, seeds, health, and children. From him, *nkisi*, or sacred medicine, which figures importantly in Kongo religious life, receives its power. Nzambi is not sacrificed to but is "called upon in times of sighing and difficulty." Though it would be a mistake to assume that the High God is forgotten or never appealed to, it is nevertheless a fundamental characteristic of West African religious life that the worshiper is most concerned with the lesser gods and spirits.[12]

The lesser divinities or secondary gods are numerous. Some are worshiped generally, others only locally. Among some West African peoples there are pantheons, or groups of gods, associated with natural forces and phenomena. Sky pantheons include the god of thunder, lightning, and rainstorm. The gods of the earth govern fertility and punish wickedness by sending smallpox and other virulent diseases. Water divinities dwell in or are identified with lakes, rivers, and the sea. Still other nature spirits may reside in trees, hills, winds, and animals. European travelers frequently identified African gods with demons or devils and accused Africans of devil worship. Or they mistook the image of the god for the god himself and called them fetish worshipers. However, the representation of the gods as fetishes is a mistake. A fetish, properly speaking, is simply a charm or amulet, and the place or object where the god dwells is properly called a shrine; neither should be confused with the gods themselves. Africans refer to these spirits by various names: the Ashanti know them as *abosom;* the Ewe-speaking Fon of Dahomey name them *vodun;* the Ibo worship them as *alose;* and the Yoruba call them *orisha.*[13] It is these gods who govern the forces of the world and affect the affairs of men for good or ill. The gods may be benevolent or malevolent, as willful and arbitrary as humans. Therefore, people must maintain proper relations with them through dutiful praise, sacrifice, and obedience. Generally speaking, the gods have altars, shrines, and temples dedicated to their worship. Devotees are careful to wear certain colors and to eat certain foods which their particular god favors or conversely, to avoid those colors and foods their god has ruled taboo. The individual personalities of the gods are revealed in myths that establish the relationship of one god to another and define each god's sphere of activity in the world. In these myths much of the cosmology of West African peoples is articulated.[14]

The various cults usually have priests and devotees who are active in their service to the gods. It is the role of the priest to offer worship and proper ritual sacrifice to the gods and to preside at periodic festivals honoring gods and ancestors. In addition, priests often serve as skilled diviners and herbalists. Devotees, known among the Yoruba and the Fon as *iyaworisha* and *vodunsi,* i.e., "wife of the *orisha*" or "wife of the *vodun*" (though there are men devotees as well as women), are initiated into a cult over a more or less lengthy period of training, which involves a novitiate in which the novice "dies," is instructed in the rites of the god, learns a secret language, and finally is "resurrected," to public celebration, as an initiate of the cult. The devotees have become mediums of their gods and upon the occasion of a ritual ceremony they may become possessed. In states of ecstatic trance, described by anthropologists of religion as "spirit possession," the *vodunsi* and *iyaworisha* dance out in mime the character of a god, becoming for a time the god's mouthpiece. Known as "the horse of the god" or "the owner of the god" or "the one mounted by the god," the ecstatic behavior of the possessed is highly stylized and controlled. The identity of the god can be recognized from the dance and demeanor of the possessed devotee. Normally, an individual would become a devotee of the god of his or her mother or father. But occasionally a nonfamilial god may choose an individual for his spouse and will "fight" with that person by sending illness or misfortune until the individual yields and undergoes initiation into the god's cult. Through divination the chosen one discovers the identity of the *orisha* and his will.[15]

Men had to take into account, besides the gods, the power of a "world of spirits." Indeed the religious life of the peoples of the Kongo focused not upon a pantheon but upon a large range of *minkisi*, or sacred medicines, embodying spirits who could harm or cure. If the taboos of the *minkisi* were not observed, these *minkisi* could become malevolent. It was widely believed by West Africans that certain trees, like the iroko, the baobab, and the silk-cotton housed spirits who could grant to supplicants the blessing of fertility.[16]

In the traditional religion of West Africa, the power of the gods and spirits was effectively present in the lives of men, for good or ill, on every level—environmental, individual, social, national, and cosmic. Aspects of reality seen as impersonal from a modern scientific viewpoint were not only personified but personalized, i.e., placed within the context of social relationships. The gods and men related to one another through the mediation of sacrifice, through the mechanism of divination, and through the phenomenon of spirit possession. Widely shared by diverse West African societies were several fundamental beliefs concerning the relationship of the divine to the human; belief in a transcendent, benevolent God, creator and ultimate source of providence; belief in a number of immanent gods, to whom people must sacrifice in order to make life propitious; belief in the power of spirits animating things in nature to affect the welfare of people; belief in priests and others who were expert in practical knowledge of the gods and spirits; belief in spirit possession, in which gods, through their devotees, spoke to men. Certainly not every West African society shared all these beliefs and some societies emphasized different ones more than others. The Yoruba and the Fon, for example, developed a much more highly articulated pantheon than did the Ibo, the Efik, or the Bakongo. Nevertheless, the outline, in most of its parts, holds as a description of the theological perspective of a wide range of West African peoples.[17]

In addition to the gods, a powerful class of spirits in the world of traditional West African religions are the ancestors. Throughout West Africa, the ancestors, both those who died long ago and those of more recent memory, are revered as founders of villages and kinship groups. It is believed that, as custodians of custom and law, the ancestors have the power to intervene in present affairs and, moreover, to grant fertility and health to their descendants, for whom they mediate with the gods. Among the Mende, for example, the "mediator role of the ancestors is assumed to be possible because they are spirit and therefore have ready access to ngewo [God] who is also spirit."[18] Indeed, some gods are the divinized ancestors of sibs, or kinship groups. According to M.J. Field, writing of the Ga, "most people are, in practice, more afraid of offending these [dead forefathers] than of offending the gods, though in theory . . . they give the higher place to the gods."[19] A person neglects the veneration of his ancestors at the risk of sickness, misfortune, even death. If one suffers ill fortune, he might discover in a dream or through divination that an angry ancestor is punishing him for neglecting to offer sacrifice.

It is commonly held that ancestors are born again in their descendants. A resemblance between a grandchild and his deceased grandfather, for example, is proof that the latter has been reincarnated in the former. West African parents turn to diviners to determine which ancestor's spirit has returned in their newborn child. Barrenness is a serious curse, since it prevents the reincarnation of ancestors within their lineage group. Elderly people are respected and revered in part because they preserve the memory of the dead and are closer chronologically to the ancestors.[20]

The ancestors are watchful guardians of the customs of the people. If anyone deviates from them, he or she may be punished.

> The living never forget that they are the trustees of the dead. The continuity of customs must be faithfully preserved. A custom, rite, or ceremony is a link with the dead who instituted it quite as much as it is the right of the god who received it. The dead are always watching to see that the living preserve what their forefathers established. And since the dead have power to bestow either blessing or adversity . . . the welfare of the living is felt to be bound up with the faithful performance of ancient custom.[21]

Because of the powerful position of the ancestors, burial rites become very important. Improper or incomplete funeral rites can interfere with or delay the entrance of the deceased into the spiritual world and may cause his soul to linger about, as a restless and malevolent ghost. Funeral ceremonies are long, complex, and expensive, but it would be a great disgrace for a family not to observe the proper rites, even if they must go into debt to do so. Before a funeral is complete, several customs must be observed: preparation of the body for burial, the wake, interment, "mourning after burial, and later mourning at varying periods." The graves of the deceased of some West African peoples are elaborately decorated with the personal effects of the individuals buried there.[22]

Rites honoring the ancestors vary from the simple private offering of food and drink, a gesture that may occur anytime, to more elaborate public ceremonies such as the *adae* ceremonies held by the Ashanti twice every forty-three days, in which the stools of past clan rulers, representing their spirits, are fed and honored. There are societies, such as the Yoruba *Egungun* society and the Ibo *Mmo* society, that foster the cult of the ancestors. Members of these societies go about masked and ceremonially garbed imitating the dead on certain ritual occasions in order to warn the errant living to mend their ways.[23]

Magic is an integral part of religious life for many African peoples. It is intimately related to medicine in traditional African belief because illness and death are not due to "natural" causes alone but to "spiritual" causes as well. It is the priest-diviner-herbalist, or "root doctor," versed in the use of herbs, barks, leaves, and roots, to whom one goes for a diagnosis of these causes and for prescriptions to ameliorate illness.[24] Prevention, however, remains the best cure. Therefore the use of charms and amulets is widespread. Often called ju-jus, gris-gris, or fetishes in travel accounts, they are believed to bear spiritual power. Talismans protect individuals from illness or witchcraft; charms placed at entryways protect villages, compounds, houses, and fields from thieves, unless the thief has a countercharm powerful enough to negate the force of the protective charm.[25]

Medicine can be used for healing and protection or for harming and killing enemies. A very common method of offensive medicine was described by Bosman: "they cause some Victuals and Drink to be Exorcised by the *Feticheer* or Priest, and scatter it in some place which their Enemy is accustomed to pass; firmly believeing that he who comes to touch this conjured stuff shall certainly dye soon after."[26] Hair cuttings, nail clippings, personal sponges, or anything else that is physically close to a person may be used by experts in medicine, so personal effects must be carefully disposed of lest they fall into an enemy's hands. The use of medicine is especially important in warding off witchcraft, a phenomenon as greatly feared in Africa as it was in Europe and America. It is thought that the witch, usually a woman but occasionally a man, can cause illness and death, often involuntarily, by eating an individual's soul. While the witch is asleep, her spirit leaves her body and flies to a meeting of witches where a soul is consumed. The spirit of the witch may assume the body of an animal in order to travel to meetings, and it is believed that if the animal is killed while bearing the witch's spirit, the sleeping body of the witch will die at the same instant. Witch hunters make a profession of identifying witchcraft and cursing its effects. When a person has been killed by witchcraft, the corpse may force its bearers to lurch back and forth through the town until it stops before the home or the person of the guilty witch. The accused will have to confess guilt or undergo trial by ordeal to prove innocence.[27]

In general, if people want to determine guilt or innocence or to seek the answer to any important question in West Africa they will turn to priest-diviners, who are skilled in reading the fate of individuals and the wills of ancestors or gods by means of simple or elaborate systems of divination. Simpler methods include interpreting omens, reading the entrails of a fowl, or water gazing. More elaborate is the Yoruban *Ifa* system (adapted in Dahomey as *Fa*) of divination. In the *Ifa* system, a *baba-lawo*, "father of mysteries," casts a chain of eight halves of palm nuts or else sixteen separate nuts, and then, reading the pattern of the cast, he marks the permutations on a tray covered with wood dust. Each permutation corresponds to an *odu*, or saying, of which there are two hundred and fifty-six. To each *odu* is attached a number of verses conveying a myth or story that points to the answer of the client's problem.[28]

Religious beliefs are carried into action through ritual. Closely interwoven with the ritual experience of West African peoples is the vibrant pattern of music. Dancing, drumming, and singing play a constant and integral part in the worship of the gods and the ancestors. Among the Yoruba and the Fon, the *orisha* and the *vodun* are called to take possession of their devotees by the songs and the drumming of the cult group, each of the gods having his or her own songs and rhythms. When "mounted" by their gods, the devotees dance to the accompaniment of songs and music the distinctive steps revelatory of their gods. So essential are music and dance to West African religious expression that it is no exaggeration to call them "danced religions."[29]

Thus the religious background of the slaves was a complex system of belief, and in the life of an African community there was a close relationship between the natural and the supernatural, the secular and the sacred. "The heavenly world," in the words of

Pierre Verger, was "not distant . . . and the believer" was "able to speak directly with his gods and benefit from their benevolence."[30] The welfare of the community and of each individual within it derived from the close relationship of man to the gods, the ancestors, and the unseen spirits. The harmony of that relationship was the ground of good; its disruption the source of evil. This religious view of life had been handed down by the forefathers and was "expressed in laws and customs hallowed by time and myth."[31] To what extent did this religious heritage continue to live in the experience of Africans enslaved in a New World?

The Gods in Exile

The gods of Africa were carried in the memories of enslaved Africans across the Atlantic. To be sure, they underwent a sea change. African liturgical seasons, prescribed rituals, traditional myths, and languages of worship were attenuated, replaced, and altered, or lost. Still, much remained, and particularly in Latin America the gods lived on in the beliefs and rituals of the slaves' descendants. *Candomblé* in Brazil, *santeria* in Cuba, *shango* in Trinidad, and *vaudou* in Haiti, all attest to the vitality and durability of African religious perspectives. And it should be emphasized that it is the continuity of perspective that is significant, more so than the fact that the cults of particular African gods, such as Shango or Elegba, have been transmitted to the New World. For new as well as old gods have come to be worshiped by Afro-Americans, but the new, like the old, have been perceived in traditionally African ways.

In Jamaica, for example, where the African gods have not survived by name, the basic theology of West African religions is apparent in two religious groups, the Convince cult and Cumina. The Convince cult, whose members are called Bongo men, traces its roots back to Jamaican maroons (runaway slaves) who fled to the Blue Mountains in eastern Jamaica where they fought against British forces until their independence was recognized by treaty in 1739. The Bible and Christian hymns are important in Convince, but its basic theology, as described by Donald Hogg, is African:

> [Convince] rests on the assumption that men and spirits exist within a single, unified social structure, interact with one another and influence each other's behavior. The principles of cooperation and reciprocity govern the relations between cult members and certain of these spirits. Bongo Men . . . believe that spiritual power is morally neutral—that it can be put to both constructive and malevolent purposes by spirits who have it and by persons who can influence them. It makes little sense, they reason, to propitiate spirits who are neither potentially dangerous nor immediately useful. God and Christ, whom they consider too benevolent to worry about and too remote and otherworldly to be of much practical value, therefore merit little attention from them. Bongo Men focus their concern instead on lesser, more accessible spirits who take an immediate interest in material human affairs and have greater influence upon phenomenal events. They deal exclusively with ghosts . . . [32]

The ghosts that Bongo men venerate most are not those of the recent dead, which lack power, but the strong spirits of African ancestors, slaves, or maroons. To these ghosts Bongo men offer animal sacrifice. And it is these ghosts that take possession of their descendants. Here, as in Africa and elsewhere in Afro-America, the possessing spirit is said to ."mount" and ride his "horse."[33]

In Jamaican Cumina, also termed "African Cumina" and "maroon dance," no African gods, except Shango, the Yoruban god of thunder, are venerated, and yet the African influence on Cumina belief underlies the veneration of three classes of spirits—sky gods, who rank highest; then earthbound gods; and last, ancestors. All three types of spirits possess their mortal followers and can be identified by the African rituals associated with them: by their food preferences, drum rhythms, and style of dancing.[34]

Worship of African gods by name, and in ways remarkably similar to forms of worship in Africa, is characteristic of Afro-

American cults in Brazil, Trinidad, Cuba, and Haiti. In Brazil, slavery was introduced around the middle of the sixteenth century and was not abolished until 1888, although by 1852 the slave trade was being suppressed, with difficulty. Over this period of three centuries slaves were brought at various times from the Western Sudan, Guinea, Angola, Congo, and Mozambique. The Yoruba, Fon, Fanti, Ashanti, Hausa, Tapa, Mandinke, Fulbe, and Bantu peoples were all represented on the slave ships sailing into the Bay of All Saints, Bahia, which for two centuries served as the main port of entry. Among the slaves, traditional African beliefs (and, to a degree, Islam) continued to exist and were syncretized with Portuguese Catholic and Indian beliefs into new Afro-Brazilian forms, which came to be known as *candomblé* in Bahia, as *macumba* in Rio de Janeiro, and as *shango* or *catimbo* in northeastern Brazil.[35]

The *seitas* (sects) of *candomblé* are roughly organized into fictive "nations"—Nago (Yoruba), Gege (from Adja or Fon), and Angola-Congo (Bantu)—representing different African traditions. In Bahia, as in Africa, borrowings between Yoruba and Fon theologies have occurred, and in Brazil Gege and Nago cults have largely fused. The Bantu *seita* has also come under the influence of Yoruban-Dahomean forms. Why this is so is a problem. One theory that attempts to explain the predominance of Yoruban-Dahomean influence is that the majority of Bantu became field hands on rural plantations, whereas the Yoruba and Fon were prized as house servants and so were numerous in the cities, where it was easier to form "nations." Another thesis is that the religion of the Yoruba and the Fon was supported in Africa by highly organized social structures that made them more resistant to European influence in the New World than the less systematized Bantu religions. Very possibly the highly articulated pantheon of Yoruban and Dahomean gods influenced the more magic-oriented traditions of Congo-Angola, particularly since Gege-Nago traditions were fed by continued contact between Bahia and West Africa. However valid these conjectures may be, it is true that the *orisha* and the *vodun* are worshiped in Brazil in essentially the same manner as in Africa.[36]

In *candomblé* the core of ritual is formed around sacrifice, praise, drumming, singing, and possession. Praise and sacrifice are offered to the gods to ensure their favor and blessing. As in Africa, the *orisha* and *vodun* have personal characteristics, particular emblems, sacred foods, feast days, and favorite colors. Priests or priestesses (*paes* or *maes de santo*) have charge of the gods' temples, the conduct of worship, and the training of cult members. Devotees (*filhas* or *filhos de santo*) serve as attendants and, in possessed state, as mediums of the gods. Bahian devotees, sometimes called by the Dahomean term *vodunsi*, are initiated into the service of a god in a novitiate that closely parallels the initiation of *vodunsi* in Dahomey. Possessed by her god, the initiate dresses in the colors of the god, wears or carries the god's emblems, and mimics the character of the god in dance. When the gods enter "the heads" of their devotees in possession, they are greeted with drumming and singing (in African languages in some *seitas*). A significant difference between ceremonial spirit possession in Brazil and Africa is that in Africa a single god has a cult and temple devoted to his or her worship alone, whereas in Bahia, a *seita* includes numerous gods, who may possess their devotees at any one service.[37]

Prominent among the African *orisha* and *vodun* of *candomblé* are Eshu (Legba), messenger of the gods, to whom a special first offering is made at the beginning of ceremonies so that he will open the way, and to ensure that as divine trickster he will not disrupt the proper order and decorum of the service; Ogun, the god of iron and war, the first god after Eshu to be invoked; Oshossi, god of the hunt; Shopona (Sakpata), the earth god who punishes mankind with disease, especially smallpox; Yemoja, "mother of waters," whose offerings are thrown into the sea; Oshun, the African Aphrodite of voluptuous beauty; Shango, god of thunder, whose emblem in Bahia, as in Africa, is the double-edged ax, and whose "thunderstones" are kept on the altars of

Oshe Shango, dance wand for the thundergod. Reprinted, by permission, from Robert Ferris Thompson, *Black Gods and Kings* (Bloomington: Indiana University Press, 1976).

Nago-Gege cult houses. The identities of the gods in Bahia, as explicated in myth and visibly embodied in the gestures and dances of their "horses," closely parallel their traits in Africa. An important exception, which will be discussed later, is the identification of the gods with Catholic saints.[38]

The cults of the major Yoruban and Dahomean gods have also been transplanted in Trinidad, Cuba, and Haiti, but with significant variations and numerous additions. Many of the gods or "powers" worshiped in *shango* are not of African but of Trinidadian origin. Eshu, Ogun, Yemanja, and Shango are worshiped, but the myths attached to the gods in Africa have either disappeared or been replaced by Catholic hagiography in Trinidad. There is an interesting trace of one Yoruban legend about the god Shango. Shango, it is said, has a sibling by the name of Oba Koso (identified with St. Anthony). Among the Yoruba the words *Oba ko so* refer to a legend that Shango, as fourth king of the city-state Oyo, was defeated in battle and in shame left his city and hanged himself. The priests and members of Shango's cult in Africa deny this, and whenever it thunders they claim the divinized Shango is manifesting his power and reiterate the saying *"Oba ko so"* (The king did not hang). In Trinidad this cry of praise has become the name of a new god, Shango's brother.[39]

A combination of fidelity to African religious traditions and divergence from them has also been characteristic of the Afro-Cuban cult of *santeria*. As in *candomblé* and *shango*, Yoruban influence has been significant. Members of the cult refer to themselves as *Lucumi*, from the Yoruban greeting, *"Oluki mi"* (My friend); many of the Yoruban gods, identified with the *santos*, are worshiped; possession by the gods occurs in the African manner; animal sacrifice, the *Ifa* system of divination, Shango's thunderstones, Yoruban *bata* ritual drums, and Yoruban hymns, all figure prominently in *Lucumi* worship.[40] Thunderstones, the neolithic celts familiar in several West African religions, are essential to the rituals of *santeria*, but in Cuba the stones are interpreted differently. According to William Bascom, the "real power of the santos resides in the stones . . . without which no santeria shrine could exist." *Santeros* believe that the most powerful stones were carried from Africa by slaves who had swallowed them. The power of the stones is conferred by "baptism" in a mixture of herbs and blood. By allowing the blood of sacrificial animals to fall upon the stones, the *santos* are fed. If the gods are well fed, in annual ceremonies lasting for three nights, there will be frequent possession, which in turn increases the power of the stones. Charms and beads dedicated to the *santos* receive their power from contact with the stones and from treatment with herbs and blood. Thus, in Cuba, the "concept of the stones (*piedras*) is equivalent not to the Yoruba *okuta* (stone) but to the Yoruba *iponri*, which is the material object which represents the power of a deity and to which its sacrifices are actually presented."[41]

There is, however, an amazingly exact equivalency between the Yoruban and the Afro-Cuban systems of divination, known as *Ifa*. *Lucumi* diviners are called *babalawo* ("father of mysteries") and cast palm nuts (*ikin*) or a chain (*opele*) of seeds just as their Yoruban counterparts do. Bascom has observed that "The same names for the sixteen figures (*odu*) of Ifa are given in the same order as in Nigeria . . . The first verse (*ese Ifa*) of the first *odu* . . . recorded in Yoruba in Ife, was given in Cuba as the first verse of the same *odu*."[42]

The most immediately apparent innovation that *santeria*, *shango*, and *candomblé* have brought to African theological perspectives is the identification of African gods with Catholic saints. Initially the veneration of saints must have provided the slaves with a convenient disguise for secret worship of African gods. Moreover, African religions have traditionally been amenable to accepting the "foreign" gods of neighbors and of enemies. It has not been unusual for one people to integrate the gods of another into their own cult life especially when social changes, such as migration or conquest, required mythic and ritualistic legitimation. Furthermore, Catholic popular piety has long been open to syncretism with "pagan" belief and practice. No fundamental contradiction existed between veneration of the Virgin Mary and the saints in Catholic piety, on the one hand, and devotion to the *orisha* and *vodun* in African religions, on the other. The Portuguese, Spanish, or French colonist appealed to the saints for succor, he lit candles to honor them, knelt before their images, observed their feast days, and trusted them as intermediaries between him and his God. And while, doctrinally, the Holy Trinity was most blessed and alone deserving of all worship, in practice the line between veneration and adoration was frequently crossed in popular devotion to the Virgin and the saints. Catholic notions about the role of Christ, Mary, guardian angels, and patron saints as intercessors with the Father in heaven for men on earth proved quite compatible with African ideas about the intervention of lesser gods in the day-to-day affairs of human life, while the supreme god remained benevolent and providential but distant.

The logic of particular identifications between *orisha* and saint seems to have been based sometimes on the similarity of powers assigned to them. St. Barbara, for example, the protectress against thunder and lightning, was identified in Bahia with Shango, god of thunder and lightning, despite the difference in gender. The malevolent aspect of Eshu-Elegba led to his identification with the devil at Bahia and Trinidad, while in Cuba his role as divine messenger, the "opener of roads," caused him to be matched with St. Peter, "keeper of the keys" to the Kingdom of Heaven. St. Raphael, the archangel who in the Bible heals Tobit, is known in *santeria* as Osanyin, the god of healing, who dispenses cool medicinal leaves.[43]

Other identifications seem to be iconographic, based upon the similarity between emblems of gods and saints. For example, Oshossi, god of the hunt, is known as St. George or as St. Michael the archangel, both traditionally depicted in Christian iconography as warriors with swords in hand. In Cuba, Orunmila, the god of divination, is also called St. Francis, perhaps because Francis is traditionally pictured wearing a rosary, which resembles the *opele* chain used in *Ifa* divination. In Haiti, Damballa-wedo, the rainbow god of Ouidah, symbolized as a serpent, is sometimes identified with Moses because of the miracle of the brazen serpent and sometimes with St. Patrick, pictured driving the snakes from Ireland. In West Africa the birth of twins is looked upon by some peoples with reverence as a sacred occurrence. Known among the Yoruba as Ibeji, the spirits of twins are the object of cults and are represented by twin statuettes. In Bahia and Cuba, the Ibeji, naturally enough, are syncretized with the twin saints Cosmas and Damian, whose feast day in September occasions the offering of the Ibeji's favorite food to the image of the saints. Yemoja, mother of the gods and of the waters, has been syncretized with the Virgin Mary under several of her titles. Correlations are also made between Ogun and St. John the Baptist; Oshun and the Virgin of Cobre (patroness of Cuba); Shopona, lord of smallpox, and St. Lazarus, the beggar covered with sores in the New Testament parable. In Trinidad, according to Herskovits, the names of gods and saints are hyphenated in common usage, e.g., "Ogun-St. Michael," and they are referred to interchangeably when, for instance, a picture of John the Baptist is identified as a picture of Shango.[44]

Correlation of saints with gods is only one aspect of syncretism between Catholic and African forms. Candles, crucifixes, and chromolithographs are blended with rituals associated with African gods. In Trinidadian *shango*, for example, the annual ceremony of the shangoists, which lasts for four nights, "begins with a prayer meeting in which an incense burner, lighted candles, Catholic prayers, original prayers, and the dismissal of Eshu-Satan are the important elements. Ogun-St. Michael is then summoned with one of his drum rhythms . . . Other male powers, followed by the female powers, are then invited."[45] In *candomblé* the drums themselves are offered sacrifice and even baptized in the presence of godparents according to Catholic ritual. Syncretism arises from the fact that "cult members are simultaneously worshipers of the African gods and communicants of the Catholic Church" and see nothing strange about being so.[46] Nevertheless, the notion of syncretism must not be pushed too far. While African gods have been identified with Catholic saints, it is Ogun, for example, who possesses, not St. Michael. And while Catholic liturgical calendars have replaced African ones, on the feast days of the saints the gods are fed with African-style sacrifice. On the deepest levels the parish church and the cult house remain parallel and separate. Even with the addition of Catholic forms, the African provenience of worship in the cult houses is clear. As anthropologist Michel Laguerre has pointed out in reference to Haitian *vaudou*, syncretism between Catholicism and Afro-American cults has largely been a syncretism of material and magic. Blessed objects (candles, pictures, holy water), gestures, and prayers have been appropriated from Catholicism for use in the cults because they are believed to possess magical power. To add the power of Christianity to that of African cults made sense, for "it is better to rely upon two magics instead of one."[47]

Perhaps nowhere in New World slavery did the revolutionary potential of this syncretism between African and Catholic magics emerge as clearly as it did in Haiti. The *Code Noir* of 1685 legislated that all slaves brought to the French possessions in America must receive instruction and baptism within eight days of arrival. Baptism was not difficult but instruction was another matter. Thirty-seven years later, Fr. Jean-Baptiste Labat objected that the slaves used Christianity to disguise their African beliefs: "The Negroes do without a qualm, what the Philistines did; they put Dagon with the Ark and secretly preserve all the superstition of their ancient idolatrous cult alongside the ceremonies of Christianity." In a decree of the Conseil du Cap of 1761 the clergy were still complaining that the slaves were guilty of mingling "the Holy utensils of our religion with profane and idolatrous objects" and of altering "the truths and dogmas of religion."[48]

The preservation of African cults alongside Christianity in Saint-Domingue (as Haiti was formerly called) could not be taken lightly by civil authorities, either. According to an anonymous tract issued in the middle of the eighteenth century,

The dance called at Surinam *Watur mama*, and in our colonies "the water mother," is strictly forbidden to them. They make a great mystery of it, and all that is known of it is that it excites very much their imagination. They become excessively exalted when they meditate a wicked plan. The chief of the plot becomes so ecstatic that he loses consciousness; when he regains consciousness, he claims that his God has spoken to him and has commanded the enterprise, but as they do not worship the same God they hate each other and spy on each other reciprocally, and these plans are almost always denounced.[49]

The comment that the "slaves do not worship the same God" and "hate each other" reflects the divisive effect of the African slaves' diverse origins and suggests the potential threat to the slaveholding regime if a common religion were to help unite them. The point was, as subsequent events would show, well taken.

Religion played a significant role in the early slave revolts led by Macandal and Biassou. Under one rebel leader, Hyacinthe, fifteen thousand slaves went into battle, supported by the belief that their chief had the power to render bullets harmless and confident that if they died on the field they would return to Africa. The revolt led by Boukman in 1791 was inaugurated by an awesome religious ceremony concluded by a blood pact. Though it would be wrong to view the Haitian War of Independence as a religious war, Sidney Mintz is right in stating that "*vaudou* surely played a critical role in the creation of a viable armed resistance by the slaves against the master classes."[50]

Dahomey has commonly been noted as the predominant influence on *vaudou*, but among the slaves who contributed their lives to making Saint-Domingue France's richest colony in the New World were Africans from the whole of West Africa and beyond, from Senegal to Congo. African religious influences upon *vaudou* came from many African nations, a fact commemorated perhaps in the division of the *loa* (gods) into nations, or "ranks," according to origin. Perhaps at one time these divisions actually did correspond to national divergences among the slaves of Saint-Domingue. The two main divisions are the nations of Rada and

Petro. Rada (Allada or Arada in Dahomey) applies to the rites for gods thought to be mainly of Dahomean origin. Petro is conjectured to have originated with an influential eighteenth-century *houngan* (priest), Don Petro. The Petro rank consists of a number of *loa* who are native to Haiti as well as gods from African nations other than Dahomey. There are also subgroups of *loa* named after African nations, such as Ibo, Bambara, and Hausa, or after African areas, such as Congo, Wangol (Angola), and Siniga (Senegal).[51]

Haitians believe in *Gran-Met* (the Supreme Being), but in *vaudou* it is the *loa* who relate actively to human affairs. In Haiti, as in Africa and elsewhere in the Caribbean, possession by the *loa*, or *mystère*, as they are called, is the climax of *vaudou* ritual. When possessing his devotee (*hounsi*), a *loa* is located in the head and is called *mâit tête*. An individual usually gains a *mâit tête* by inheriting him from his family or by being seized and possessed by a "wild" (*bozal*) *loa*, which must first be identified by a *houngan*, or priest-diviner, and then "set" or established by "baptism" in a rite called *lave tête*. Each *loa* has a character manifested by the behavior of the possessed *hounsi*, and within a given area this behavior is so standardized that the *loa* is recognizable. But the style of behavior for a *loa* may vary significantly from area to area. Indeed, *loa* venerated in one district may be totally unknown in another. The unity of *vaudou* as a religion—and the same might be said of other Afro-American cults—lies not in doctrinal or ritual uniformity but in a common and basic African theological perspective.[52]

The preservation of this perspective in Brazil and the Caribbean has frequently been explained by referring to the presence of Catholicism, which, it is argued, tended to reinforce African religious traditions because of its openness to syncretism. There is, as we shall see, some truth in this argument, but the reality is more complex, for there are Afro-*Protestant* cults in the Caribbean as well.

Besides the regular, orthodox Christian denominations, several black Jamaican groups, such as Revival and Pocomania, represent nonorthodox syntheses of Protestant and African beliefs. Among the Jamaican slaves the most successful Christian denomination were the Baptists. First preached in Jamaica in 1787, by George Liele, an ex-slave from Georgia, the Baptist message took hold and was supported by other North American blacks who had emigrated to the British island with their Loyalist owners after the outbreak of the American Revolution. It was not long, however, before independent churches under the direction of Jamaican leaders started to reinterpret Christian doctrine. By the middle of the nineteenth century, African and Baptist beliefs had begun to fuse in the Native Baptist movement, the precursor of present-day Revivalist groups in Jamaica.[53]

In two of these groups, Revival and Pocomania, services culminate in African-style possession. However, it is the Old Testament prophets, the four evangelists of the New Testament, the apostles, the archangels, and the Holy Ghost who take possession of members, not the gods of Africa. Revivalists believe that God the Father created the world and dwells in "highest heaven." He never descends to visit the services nor to possess the believers. Jesus, according to the members of Revival, does visit their services and a "love feast" is held in his memory, but he, like the Father, does not possess. Deceased members, however, may return to possess their relations among the faithful. The choreography of possession movement in Revival is very similar, as we shall see, to the techniques of trance-dance in *vaudou*, *santeria*, *candomblé*, *shango*, and West African cults.[54]

In Trinidad, the Spiritual Baptists, or Shouters, are especially interesting because of their subtle interweaving of African religious customs with a rigidly orthodox Christian creed. Strict Fundamentalists, the Spiritual Baptists subscribe to the five-point platform of the early twentieth-century Fundamentalist movement in the United States. The five points of the fundamentalist platform are biblical inerrancy, authenticity of Gospel miracles, the Virgin Birth, the physical Resurrection of Jesus, and the satisfaction theory of the Atonement. At the same time there are affiliations between Spiritual Baptists and Trinidadian shangoists. Some leaders of *shango* cults mix ritual elements from "Yoruba work" with those of Spiritual Baptist worship; others conduct services in both rites at separate times. Baptism is the crucial event in the religious life of the Shouters. Before receiving baptism, a candidate must first testify to having had a dream or vision, which is tested by the leaders of the church. Up to this point the process of initiation is traditionally Baptist, but then deviation begins. After a candidate presents his dream, he enters upon a period of instruction in which he is given his own special hymn, psalm, and biblical verse to foster reception of the spirit. For some Shouters, there is a further initiation, called "mourning ground," a period of retreat in which the novice travels deeper into the mysteries of faith and is rewarded with new powers. During the period of "mourning," the initiate fasts, abstains from salted food, and refrains from washing. During this time, saints visit the mourner and reveal to him their likes and dislikes, their sacred foods and feast days. Each mourner receives a charism, or power, corresponding to his new role in the life of the church. For each charism a new name, a saint's name, is bestowed upon the novice. He also receives three cloth bands—a "sighting" band and a "study" band which are placed over his eyes, and a "dead" band which is tied around the head and chin. The color of each cloth band symbolizes the charism which the initiate receives. Several features of this mourning ceremony resemble the rites of cult initiation in West Africa. Death-resurrection motifs, fasting and lying quiet, reception of a new role and a new name, color symbolism, and prohibition of salt in food offerings to the gods are all similar features of initiation in West African and Brazilian cults. Moreover, as we shall see in the next chapter, there are intriguing analogies between the "mourning ground" of Spiritual Baptists in Trinidad and the "mourning ground" of black Protestants in the United States.[55] The Revivalist cults of Jamaica and the Spiritual Baptists of Trinidad indicate that in certain contexts Protestantism, like Catholicism, has proved amenable to the continuity of African religious traditions.

African religious influence on Afro-American societies has manifested itself not only in the cult of the gods but also in ancestor worship, magical practices, and ritual-performance style. Veneration of the ancestors must have been all the more poignant for African slaves in the Americas because it had been so closely tied to the land and the kin from whom they had been taken. But the cult of the ancestors, like that of the gods, was not restricted to the soil of Africa. As noted above, the most powerful ghosts venerated in the Convince cult of Jamaica are the African ancestors. In Haiti, at the annual Yam Festival, before any yams are eaten some must be offered to the dead, those recently deceased, those forgotten, and those who never left Africa. In the Bantu-influenced *macumba* cult of Rio de Janeiro cult members become possessed by *pretos velhos*, the spirits of their black ancestors. In Bahia the Yoruban *Egungun* society represents the dead to their descendants as in Nigeria. In the cult houses of São Luiz do Maranhão a feast to honor the dead is celebrated annually (interestingly enough, on the analogous Catholic feast—All Souls Day). Vaudouists occasionally hold *mange-morts*, or feasts for the dead, and commonly place dishes of food for the deceased next to graves and tombs.[56]

Burial rites in Afro-Brazilian and Afro-Caribbean cults, as in West Africa, tend to be long-drawn-out affairs, involving several stages before the burial is complete. It may take months for the spirit of the deceased to be separated from his family, associates, and environs. For example, in some Brazilian cult centers, there is a seven-night ritual called *acheche* for deceased members, during which the ancestor-spirits are asked to welcome the soul of the departed. Occasionally the cult objects formerly used by a member who has died are taken to the coast and placed in the sea to be received by his or her spirit. Similarly, West African burial customs have left traces in present-day services in Jamaica such as the "nine-night ceremony," in which the spirit of the deceased returns on the ninth night after death and takes possession of the leader of the ceremony. Through the possessed leader the "spirit may explain what should be done with his property; or, if the death was not a natural one, it may name the person who was the cause of death; or, if anyone in the family has suffered, or is about to suffer, some trouble or an accident, the cause of the misfortune may be explained." If the burial customs have been carried out properly, then the spirit of the deceased will not trouble the living. But if the funeral was improper or incomplete, the "duppy," or ghost of the dead person, may cause misfortune.[57]

Because it is believed that fatality may be due to unnatural causes such as witchcraft, discovery of the cause of death is of religious, not just medical, concern. If a vaudouist, for instance, were struck down by lightning or smallpox, he would not be allowed a normal burial because, as in Dahomean and Yoruban belief, the deceased would be presumed guilty of an offense which the gods have seen fit to punish by death. The West African custom of carrying the corpse is also commonly employed in the Caribbean in order to determine if a witch was responsible for the death. In Surinam (Dutch Guiana) the coffin-carrying ceremony is used to question the spirit of the deceased about the cause of his death and about the possibility of the deceased having been a witch himself. Priests question the spirit as the coffin is carried on the heads of two bearers. From the movement of the coffin about the village, the priests decipher the spirit's answers to their questions.[58] A similar burial custom was described for Jamaican slave funerals in the early eighteenth century:

> When one is carried out to his Grave, he is attended with a vast Multitude, who conduct his Corpse in something of a ludicrous manner. They sing all the way, and they who bear it on their shoulders, make a Feint of stopping at every Door they pass, pretending that if the deceased Person had received any Injury the Corpse moves towards that House, and that they can't avoid letting it fall to the Ground, when before the Door.[59]

As has been frequently noted, African slaves in many areas of
the New World were convinced that death would free them to
return to Africa. This notion was based not simply upon nostalgia
for the homeland but upon a firm religious belief in reincarnation.
To be properly understood, reincarnation should be placed in the
context of the traditional West African conception of the soul as a
complex entity—that is, the individual has several spiritual com-
ponents. One's personality-soul appears before God after death to
account for its deeds. When a person sleeps, this soul may
wander; dreams are in fact the experiences met by the wandering
soul. Linked with the soul is a shadow which is not immortal and
dies with the body. Each person also possesses a spirit which
serves as moral guide and which is the spirit of God within man.
It returns to God upon death. There is also a guardian spirit,
identified by the Yoruba and the Fon as an ancestor-spirit reincarnated in a descendant. The Yoruba offer sacrifice to the guardian-
spirit to ensure the propitious development of the person's destiny
which the ancestor-spirit has chosen before birth.[60]

Praying to one's guardian angel is a widespread Catholic practice, but the custom has taken on a distinctly African tone among
rural Afro-Brazilians in Maranhão, who believe that everyone has
two spirits, a soul and a guardian angel. While a person sleeps,
the soul may wander from its body. The body, the soul, and the
guardian angel all cast shadows. When the angel's shadow is
visible it is a sign that the angel has been fed by prayer and so is
strong. If a person neglects his guardian angel, it may grow too
weak to protect the soul from the attack of witches, magic, or
natural dangers.[61]

The African complex-soul concept has also been influential in
Dutch Guiana, where it is believed that the spirit of an individual,
his *akra*, should be fed by sacrifice lest it become angry and refuse
to protect the person from evil forces. The *akra*, which is given at
birth, may venture out of the body while a person sleeps, and it
departs at death. A person's shadow may also wander abroad and
may fall prey to witchcraft. After death the *yorka*, or ghost of the

deceased, continues to exist and may be appealed to by relatives for protective aid.[62]

The magical lore of Africa, combined with European and Indian magical customs, figured prominently in the daily lives of the slaves and their descendants. Because magical beliefs tend to be similar worldwide, and because it is the nature of magical thinking to be eclectic, it is rarely possible to speak with certainty about the origins of particular magical practices. Still, it is apparent that the integral connection between magic, medicine, and religion characteristic of many African societies has been replicated in the Afro-American cults of Brazil and the Caribbean. That spirits or powers may be embodied in material objects or charms, and may be manipulated by the knowledgeable to harm people or to protect them, is the basic axiom underlying countless variables of magical technique. Among the Bush Negroes of Surinam each charm has its own taboos that must be obeyed if the charm is to keep its power. Universally it is believed that charms can work for the good of their owners either by defensive protection or by offensive aggression against potential evils, such as witches, sickness, misfortune, or the animosity of others. Evil magic—that is, magic directed by another at you—is a constant possibility and if a person inexplicably falls ill or experiences misfortune he consults a diviner to find out the cause and a *curandeiro* (possibly the same person) to heal by means of magic and medicine combined.[63]

The profession of medicine man or conjurer requires extensive knowledge not only of magical tradition but also of herbal medicine. The professional knowledge of the magician-doctor can be used to create protective or aggressive charms, depending upon the wishes of the client. His knowledge may therefore be a source of danger or of safety. Sorcerers specialize in the "offensive" side of the profession, "harming others at the request of clients, by the use of charms, poisons," and in Jamaican obeah, "shadow catching." The dual potential of magic for help or harm was apparently differentiated in Jamaica into two separate religious systems, obeah and myalism, during the slave period. Obeah, according to early accounts, involved the use of magic for evil. Obeah men caught the duppy, or shadow of a person, in a bowl of water and then stabbed it through the heart or tied it spellbound under a silk-cotton tree. Myalism, on the other hand, was good medicine, an antidote to sorcery and witchcraft. Myal men, or angel men, as they were also called, were skilled herbalists who knew the devices of the obeah men and had the power to release captured duppies. The myal man was also the leader of a cult, which included dancing and possession-trance. As Orlando Patterson has pointed out, obeah and myalism had several important functions in Jamaican slave society: protection against thieves, detection of guilt, and revenge by conjuring or outright poisoning. And obeah, it can be argued, supported rebellion, since "the obeah-man was essential in administering oaths of secrecy, and, in cases, distributing fetishes which were supposed to immunize the insurgents from the arms of the whites."[64]

While the objects used as charms and the prescriptions for their use are limitless, there are some widespread similarities across Afro-American cultures. Grave dirt, hair cuttings, and nail clippings are generally thought of as particularly powerful materials for offensive charms, and crossroads are pointed out as especially strong places for working magic. Chickens with frizzy feathers are adept at scratching up buried charms. And red pepper can be an effective antidote to witchcraft when sprinkled on the skin of a witch who has left it behind to wander. Charms came from everywhere. From Islam: in Brazil, Muslim slaves were known for the power of their talismans, and during the slave revolt of 1835 in Bahia, Muslim slaves wore talismans made of verses from the Koran written in Arabic on scraps of parchment. So noted were the Muslim Mandinke for their magic that the term *mandinga* came to mean magic and *mandingueiros* sorcerers in Brazil, Uruguay, and Argentina. From traditional West African religions: the thunderstones of Shango are particularly effective in healing, according to the devotees of *candomblé* in Bahia. From Catholicism:

Trinidadian *shangoists* believe that during Lent the good powers may be too busy praying to be available for "work," so cult members may be forced to call upon evil powers for help. In Jamaican Cumina the Bible is used as a charm against malignant forces, as are crucifixes, blessed medals, stones, herbs, and leaves. A veritable pharmacopoeia of religious-magical-medicinal objects crowd the sanctuaries of cult houses in Brazil, Haiti, and Cuba. The apparently random justaposition of statues of saints, emblems of gods, and medicinal charms belies a coherent world view of spiritual power, in which religion, magic, and medicine are embraced as one.[65]

Perhaps the most obvious continuity between African and Afro-American religions is the style of performance in ritual action. Drumming, singing, and dancing are essential features of African and Afro-American liturgical expression and are crucial to the ceremonial possession of cult members by their gods. It is the rhythms of the drums which call upon the gods to manifest themselves in *candomblé, shango, vaudou,* and *santeria.* In the cult houses of Bahia the drums themselves are treated with the greatest respect; periodically sacrifices are offered to their spirits, and possessed devotees dance facing the drums and bow to them. In the annual *shango* ceremonies in Trinidad, the drums are of the African type, played in trio. The smallest of the three is called *oumaylee* (the Yoruban term for middle-size drum) and a calabash rattle, resembling the Yoruban *shekere,* is also played. More important, however, than the similarity of particular instruments to African models is the resemblance of function and style. Even in cults to which the drum was forbidden the percussive emphasis and the polyrhythmic character of the music and its functional relation to spirit possession are clear indications of African liturgical influence. Among the Spiritual Baptists of Trinidad, for example, possession by the Holy Spirit occurs not to the beat of drum rhythms but to the sound of "Sankeys," Protestant hymns from the Sankey-Moody hymnal. Beneath the tunes of the Sankeys, however, beats a different musical impulse. At a Shouter service recorded by Frances and

Melville Herskovits, the first few verses of the hymn "Jesus, Lover of My Soul" had barely been sung when suddenly "the singers continuing the melody began to change their rhythms, introducing hand clapping as the tempo became faster, until the hymn was transmuted into a swing idiom which in the proper setting would result in spirit possession." At another ceremony, "the people carrying the melodic line sang slightly faster, while the song-leader and a few others ornamented it with harmonized 'ram-bam-bam, bam, bam, ram-a-bam' simulating drums and making the song irresistible to patting feet and hand-clapping." This hymn with its percussive ornamentation accompanied the testimony of a Shouter who "overcome by the spirit . . . danced on his knees, moving backward and forward in a kind of body-swing."[66]

The phenomenon of possession is the climax of the service in every one of the cults we have noted. Whether the possessing spirit is Shango in *candomblé*, an ancestor in the Convince cult, a spirit in Cumina, or the Holy Spirit in the Shouters' service, the ritual context in which possession occurs and the physiological behavior of the possessed are strikingly uniform. Anthropologist Morton Marks, applying the insights of sociolinguistics to Afro-American song style, has suggested that certain stylistic codes are part of the structure of "performance events" in Afro-American cultures. These codes, he contends, establish a ritual context for possession and are consistent across different Afro-American societies so that it is possible for a Brazilian member of *Umbanda* and a Cuban devotee of *santeria* to recognize immediately when the lead singer of a North American gospel group has "caught a spirit," i.e., become possessed.[67]

On this same point, George Simpson, describing the possession state among Jamaican Revivalists, has noted "muscular movements, particularly of the neck, shoulder, and back muscles" which "are identical with those reported by observers of Haitian *vodun*, Cuban *santeria*, Brazilian *candomblé*, Trinidadian *shango*, and West African cults." He goes on to describe the choreography which facilitates spirit possession in Revival meetings. One of the most common techniques, called "laboring in the spirit," "consists of a counter-clockwise dance around the altar, the 'table,' or the 'seal' (flagpole outside the church) during which evil spirits are trampled underfoot. As the body bends forward breath is expelled, and the participant groans and overbreathes on the upswing. This 'trumping' (also called 'jumping' and 'spiritual dancing') produces dizziness in some persons and thus facilitates the onset of spirit possession." Whatever the validity of Simpson's physiological explanation for the occurrence of the phenomenon, his description of the counterclockwise, hitching dance movement in Revival "trumping" bears a marked resemblance to styles of religious dancing elsewhere in the Caribbean and to nineteenth-century descriptions of the "ring-shout" as performed by freedmen in the southern United States.[68]

When the gods arrive in Brazilian and Caribbean cult houses, they are greeted by song sometimes in African languages or mixtures of Creole and African words. A praise song to Eshu sung in Yoruban by Afro-Bahians makes reference to the god's provocative phallic-style coiffure and to his role as messenger opener-of the road:

> *Ibarabo—o mojuba*
> O great one, I pay obeisance,
> *Iba Koshe omo deko*
> A young child does not confront
> *Elegbara*
> The powerful one;
> *Omojuba*
> I pay obeisance
> *Ileba Eshu lona*
> To Eleba Eshu, who is on the road.
>
> *Odara kolori onego*
> The good one, who has no head for dancing,
> *Sho-sho-sho abe*
> The stubborn knife
> *Kolori eni—ijo*
> Has no head for dancing

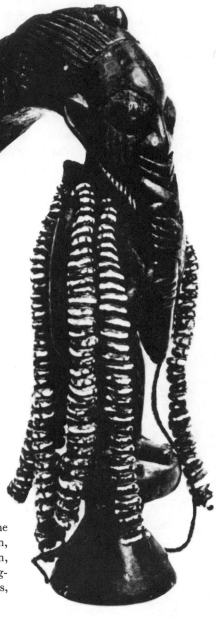

Ogo Elegba, dance wand for the trickster. Reprinted, by permission, from Robert Ferris Thompson, *Black Gods and Kings* (Bloomington: Indiana University Press, 1976).

Eshu tiriri
Eshu the awesome,
Bara abebe
O powerful knife!
Tiriri lona
The Awesome one, on the road.[69]

In addition to oral praise, material sacrifice must be offered to the gods. In *candomblé, vaudou,* and the other cults, ritual sacrifice mediates the relationship between gods and men, as it does in Africa. The unavailability of certain African foods favored by the gods did not lessen the responsibility felt by their devotees to propitiate them with fit offerings in America.

In the cult houses of Haiti, Brazil, Surinam, Jamaica, Trinidad, and Cuba, the gods of Africa have been remembered by the slaves and their descendants—not only remembered but worshipped in exile in ways that have remained vigorously traditional and at the same time creatively adaptive. The reasons for and circumstances surrounding the transmission of African religious perspectives and customs in different Afro-American societies are as varied as the histories of those societies. In the case of Bahia, it has been suggested that the urban environment and continuous contact with West Africa were significant factors in the development of *candomblé.* According to this argument, it was easier for urban slaves, who were under less rigid supervision than plantation slaves and could associate with free blacks, to seek out others of similar ethnic and linguistic background. This process of regroupment was assisted in the early nineteenth century, it seems, by municipal governments that encouraged African-style dances as occasions for slaves to reidentify with their separate tribal origins. As contemporary observers explained, the authorities believed that if the slaves maintained their tribal identities, old animosities would keep them from uniting and would prevent their common experience of oppression from binding them into a rebellious force. The urban religious confraternities, according to Bastide, also aided in the process of regroupment by secretly facilitating the preservation of African languages and religions beliefs. As a result, "the African religions are purer and richer in the large cities than in the rural areas."[70]

The most important factor contributing to the vitality of African religious influence in Brazil was the continuous contact between Bahia and West Africa. As Donald Pierson notes:

> Bahian Negroes long maintained direct contact with the West Coast. Even after the extinction of the slave traffic, vessels regularly plied between Bahia and Lagos, repatriating nostalgic emancipated Negroes and returning with West Coast products much prized by Africans and their descendants in Brazil.[71]

Through continued contact, African myths, rituals, and beliefs in Bahia could be reinforced and "corrected" from their sources by those who had seen how they were used in Africa. To quote Bastide again:

> Certainly, the passage of time eroded in the long run even the most established traditions in the new environment. But trade continually renewed the sources of life by establishing a permanent contact between the early slaves or their children and those newly arrived . . . so that there has been over the course of the entire period of slavery a renewal of religious values as these values tended to weaken.[72]

It is a mistake to view present-day *candomblé*, he continues, as the lineal descendant of ancient cults stretching back continuously into the early days of colonial Brazil. Instead, the *seitas* were organized at a relatively recent date, around the end of the eighteenth century or the beginning of the nineteenth. For example, Pierre Verger has stated that the Casa das Minas of São Luiz do Maranhão was probably founded in 1796 by exiled members of the royal-lineage group from Dahomey. Other cult houses have been traced to slaves seized as contraband after 1815 and freed upon arrival in Brazil. Bastide claims that the *candomblé* of *Engenho Velho* in Bahia was founded by two priestesses of the Shango cult enslaved in the early nineteenth century. "Thus," he concludes, "we ought to depict the religious life of Africans in Brazil as a succession of discontinuous events, of traditions interrupted and recovered, but which nevertheless maintain, from generation to generation, under the most diverse forms possible, the same fidelity to the spirituality or spiritualities of Africa."[73]

Similarly, in Cuba and Trinidad the relatively late importation of significant numbers of Africans in the nineteenth century probably contributed to the formation of *shango* and *santeria*. In Trinidad nearly 7,000 free Africans were imported between 1841 and 1861 to increase the labor force after emancipation had been declared in the British West Indies. Another 8,854 Africans, liberated by the British navy from slavers bound for Cuba and Brazil, were settled in Trinidad between 1834 and 1867. Attempting to explain the Yoruban influence upon Cuban *santeria*, Bascom has theorized that relatively large numbers of Yoruba came to Cuba late in the trade because of the Dahomean wars against Abeokuta and surrounding towns in the nineteenth century and "as the result of the Fulani conquest of Ilorin, Old Oyo" and other Yoruban cities during the 1830s.[74]

Another factor contributing to both the continuity and the reinterpretation of African religious traditions was the existence of societies of maroons, or escaped slaves. Within maroon communities, African traditions had opportunities to develop relatively free from European suppression for various periods of time. It would be a mistake, however, to assume that the maroon societies of Jamaica or Dutch Guiana, for example, were "pure" re-creations of African societies on this side of the Atlantic. The diverse African origins of the maroons necessitated modifications in customs in order to ensure social unity. Moreover, maroon communities were not totally isolated from colonial Europeans. Trade involved contact, and an occasional Christian missionary worked among the maroons. When troops finally conquered the maroon republic of Palmares in Brazil, they found villages with Catholic shrines. Explorers in remote areas of Brazil encountered Indians and mestizos who had learned the rudiments of Christianity from escaped slaves in the eighteenth century. According to Bastide, there were maroons in Surinam who prayed Catholic prayers while facing, Muslim style, the city of Cayenne, and in several Djuka villages the Judaism of the maroons' former masters had influenced their religion.[75]

The historical circumstances, then, in which religious traditions from Africa have been transmitted to New World societies have varied from society to society. Some traditions extend relatively far into the past of colonial slavery; others have died out with the passage of time; and still others have developed out of more recent contact with Africa. Moreover, Afro-American cults have modified traditions and added new ones. Yet, despite discontinuity and innovation, the fundamental religious perspectives of Africa have continued to orient the lives of the descendants of slaves in the New World. Worship of the gods, veneration of the ancestors, African-style drumming and dancing, rites of initiation, priests and priestesses, spirit possession, ritual sacrifice, sacred emblems and taboos, extended funerals, and systems of divination and magic all attest to the living African heritage of black people in Brazil and the Caribbean. When placed in hemispheric perspective, it is clear that the African diaspora in North America was another story altogether. At first glance it would appear, as many have concluded, that the African past of black people in the United States has vanished. Why does the African religious heritage remain so patently vital in some areas of Afro-America and not in others? The continuity or discontinuity of African religious tradition in the United States is the subject of an ongoing debate of basic importance to the study of slave religion.

2
Death of the Gods

Let us rejoice in and adore the wonders of God's infinite love in bringing us from a land semblant of darkness itself, and where the divine light of revelation (being obscured) is in darkness. Here the knowledge of the true God and eternal life are made manifest; but there was nothing in us to recommend us to God . . .

PHYLLIS WHEATLEY

I had always been told from the time I was a small child that I was a Negro of African stock. That it was no disgrace to be a Negro and had it not been for the white folks who brought us over here from Africa as slaves, we would never have been here and would have been much better off.

"AUNT" ADELINE, FORMER SLAVE

I N ONE of her earliest poems
Phyllis Wheatley reflected upon her religious heritage:

'Twas mercy brought me from my *Pagan* land,
Taught my benighted soul to understand
That there's a God, that there's a *Saviour* too . . . [1]

According to B. B. Thatcher, in his *Memoir of Phillis Wheatley*,
the black poet remembered nothing of her African past with the
exception of one ritual, "her mother's custom of *pouring out water
before the sun at his rising.*" Thatcher remarks that this "no doubt,
was a custom of the tribe to which she belonged, and was one of
their religious rites."[2] There were other slaves, however, who
remembered far more of their African past than Phyllis Wheatley
did and who held a different view of their forced migration from
their native lands.

Charles Ball, in the narrative of his life under slavery, recounted
a slave funeral at which he assisted:

> I assisted her and her husband to inter the infant . . . and its
> father buried with it, a small bow and several arrows; a little
> bag of parched meal; a miniature canoe, about a foot long, and
> a little paddle, (with which he said it would cross the ocean to
> his own country) a small stick, with an iron nail, sharpened
> and fastened into one end of it; and a piece of white muslin,
> with several curious and strange figures painted on it in blue
> and red, by which, he said, his relations and countrymen
> would know the infant to be his son, and would receive it
> accordingly, on its arrival amongst them . . . He cut a lock of
> hair from his head, threw it upon the dead infant, and closed
> the grave with his own hands. He then told us the God of his
> country was looking at him, and was pleased with what he
> had done.[3]

According to Ball, the father of the dead infant was a "native of a
country far in the interior of Africa" who claimed to have been a
"priest in his own nation."[4] Of the native Africans among the
slaves, Ball states:

> They are universally of opinion, and this opinion is founded in
> their religion, that after death they shall return to their own
> country, and rejoin their former companions and friends, in
> some happy region . . . [5]

African-born slave Chloe Spear, brought as a child to Boston, like
Phyllis Wheatley, "wished for *death;* supposing that when she
died, she would return to her country and friends." This belief
was derived, according to her biographer, "from a superstitious
tradition of her ancestors, who, she said, supposed that the first
infant born in a family after the decease of a member, was the
same individual come back again."[6]

Nor did all slaves agree that embracing the Christian gospel
meant accepting enslavement as a "providential mercy," as European traveler Fredrika Bremer learned from a conversation with a
"Lucumi" slave on a Florida plantation around 1850:

> 'You have come hither from Africa?' He replied, Yes; that he
> had been smuggled hither from Cuba many years ago. He was
> now overseer on a plantation, and was very well off. He was a
> Christian and seemed pleased to be so. He spoke very sensibly
> and cheerfully, and had a good, open countenance.
> 'You do not wish to return to Africa?' said I. 'Oh yes, Missis;
> oh yes, that I do:' replied he; there I should be still better off.'
> 'But people often kill one another there,' remonstrated I. 'Oh
> but nobody troubles themselves about that. And there are a
> great many good people who live there at peace.' 'But look
> here, my friend,' said Colonel Mac I., who is a strong Calvin-
> ist; 'if you had remained in Africa, you would not have be-
> come a Christian as you are now, and then the devil, in the
> end, would have had you!' The negro laughed, looked down,
> shook his head . . . and at length exclaimed, again looking up
> with an expression of humor and inventive acuteness, 'Now,
> Massa, look'ee here! The Gospel is now being preached over
> the whole of Africa, and if I had remained there, what was to
> hinder me from being one who heard it as well there as here?'
> To this there was no reply to be made, and the . . . negro had
> the last word.[7]

Some slaves, like the ancestor of Leonard Haynes, rejected

Christianity. Recounting a family tradition, Haynes states: "My grandfather of three generations came over from the Gold Coast of Africa and was sold to a Mr. Haynes in Georgia. My grandfather was an African priest. This fact made him hostile to Christian preachers and to the religion of the Christians. Hence, he refused to join with the other slaves in their religious gatherings . . ."[8]

There were, moreover, a few Muslim slaves from Africa who continued, as best they could, to observe the customs of Islam. "Muh gran come from Africa," remarked Rosa Grant of Possum Point, Georgia. "Huh membuh when I wuz a chile seein muh gran Ryna pray. Ebry mawnin at sun-up she kneel on duh flo in uh ruhm an bow obuh an tech uh head tuh duh flo tree time. Den she say a prayuh. I dohn membuh jis wut she say, but one wud she say use tuh make us chillun laugh. I membuh it was 'ashane-gad.' Wen she finish prayin she say 'Ameen, ameen, ameen.' " Similarly, Katie Brown of Sapelo Island, Georgia, was a descendant of Belali Mahomet, a Muslim slave and driver. " . . . Belali an he wife Phoebe pray on duh bead," Katie recounted. "Dey wuz bery puhticluh bout duh time dey pray and dey bery regluh bout duh hour. Wen duh sun come up, wen it straight obuh head an wen it set, das duh time dey pray. Dey bow tuh duh sun and hab lill mat tuh kneel on. Duh beads is on a long string. Belali he pull bead an he say, 'Belambi, Hakabara, Mahamadu.' Phoebe she say, 'Ameen, Ameen.' " Charles Lyell visiting Hopeton Plantation on St. Simon's Island, Georgia, before 1845, encountered "Old Tom," head driver for the plantation, a Foulah who had remained a strict Muslim, though his children and grandchildren had "exchanged the Koran for the Bible." Omar ibn Said, a slave in North Carolina, wrote an autobiographical fragment in Arabic script in 1831 in which he recalled:

> Before I came to the Christian country, my religion was the religion of Mohammed, the Apostle of God—may God have mercy upon him and give him peace! I walked to the mosque before day-break, washed my face and head and hands and feet. I prayed at noon, prayed in the afternoon, prayed at

sunset, prayed in the evening. I gave alms every year . . . I went on pilgrimage to Mecca . . . When I left my country I was thirty-seven years old; I have been in the country of the Christians twenty-four years.

During those twenty-four years Omar had converted to Christianity:

When I was a Mohammadan I prayed thus: 'Thanks be to God, Lord of all worlds, the merciful the gracious, Lord of the day of Judgement, thee we serve, on thee we call for help. Direct us in the right way, the way of those on whom thou hast had mercy, with whom thou hast not been angry and who walk not in error. Amen.'—But now I pray 'Our Father' . . . in the words of our Lord Jesus the Messiah.[9]

According to the Reverend Charles Colcock Jones, "The Mohammedan Africans remaining of the old stock of importations, although accustomed to hear the Gospel preached, have been known to accommodate Christianity to Mohammedanism. 'God,' say they, 'is Allah, and Jesus Christ is Mohammed—the religion is the same, but different countries have different names.' " Some religious customs observed by the slaves seemed to combine African and Christian elements. For example, on the Sea Islands, as Rachel Anderson recalled, at harvest time: "We hab a big feas. All night we shouts an in duh mawnin right at sunrise we pray an bow low tuh duh sun." Alex Anderson described the practice of river baptisms: "Duh preachuh and duh candidates goes down in duh watuh. Den duh preachuh make a prayuh tuh duh ribbuh and duh ribbuh washes duh sin away."[10]

Despite these countervailing examples, it seems that in the United States the experience of Phyllis Wheatley, if not her theological explanation of it, has been the rule rather than the exception. Under British North American slavery, it seems that the African religious heritage was lost. Especially does this appear so when black religion in the United States is compared with the cults of Brazil and the Caribbean. In *candomblé, vaudou, santeria,* and *shango* "the acceptance of Christianity by the African slaves, and its transmission to their descendants, has by no means meant the disappearance of African beliefs or patterns of worship," but to a large extent has led to their continuity in a new "unified system of belief and ritual."[11] Why was the same not true of slaves in the United States? Two conflicting answers have been proposed: one is that African retentions in the United States were negligible because the African was almost totally stripped of his culture by the process of enslavement; and the other, that the slave system did not destroy the slaves' African culture and a considerable number of Africanisms continue to define Afro-American culture in the United States. The foremost advocate of the former position is E. Franklin Frazier; of the latter, Melville J. Herskovits.[12]

The Debate

Herskovits' most complete and most careful statement of his thesis is *The Myth of the Negro Past.* The myth that Herskovits was intent on destroying was the belief that the American Negro had no past except a history of primitive savagery in Africa from which he had been delivered by contact with European civilization in America. For Herskovits the destruction of this myth was not simply a matter of detached scholarship. It also had important practical ramifications in the struggle against racism. To deny that the black American had a culture and history of significance and sophistication in Africa and to suggest that African culture was not advanced enough to endure contact with superior European culture was to imply that Negroes were an inferior people. Furthermore, Herskovits thought it important to recognize the historical relevance of African retentions in order to evaluate cultural differences between white and black Americans in scientific rather than racist terms. Discrepancies between white and black values and behavior were due not to "culture lag," i.e., backwardness on the part of the blacks but to a different cultural background whose roots lay in Africa.[13]

As an anthropologist, Herskovits was interested particularly in the study of culture contact and acculturation. To the debate over African retentions he brought an amazingly broad perspective, informed by extensive field work in Dahomey, Dutch Guiana, Haiti, Trinidad, and, to a lesser degree, Brazil. He studied the "New World Negro" in the light of his research in the slaving area of West Africa where a large number of Afro-Americans originated. In discussing the culture of black people in the United States he insisted that the situation of North American Negroes be placed on a spectrum or continuum with other Afro-American societies. The scale of African retentions stretches from Dutch Guiana with the strongest and most integral examples of African culture, at one end, to the United States with the weakest and most fragmentary evidence of African influence, at the other. Herskovits thought it important to view the United States in comparison with other areas of the hemisphere where Africanisms are apparent in order to discover clues to more subtly disguised African patterns of culture in the United States.[14]

In contrast to Haiti and Brazil, African retentions in the United States cannot be ascribed with any certainty to definite areas of West Africa such as Nigeria or Dahomey. Herskovits compensates for this difficulty by defining West Africa as a single-culture area with an overall similarity and unity despite local differences. He suggests a "base line" of West African culture to serve as a measure for determining Africanisms in the United States; furthermore, within the general culture of West Africa there is a focus, and this focus is religion. Throughout New World Negro cultures the strongest Africanisms are to be found in religion.[15] Herskovits divided the myth of the Negro past into five statements, or submyths, and then proceeded to rebut each statement.

The first myth is: "Negroes are naturally of childlike character, and adjust easily to the most unsatisfactory social situations, which they accept readily and even happily . . . " On the contrary, Herskovits argues, Africans and Afro-Americans are neither childlike nor naive, but have developed a sophisticated world view. A mark of the sophistication of their world view has been a refusal to interpret life in terms of a simplistic dichotomy between good and evil. This world view has allowed them to "adapt to everyday situations of all sorts." Besides, blacks were not content with slavery. Slaves resisted individually and rebelled collectively from the earliest days of slavery in Hispaniola.[16]

The second myth states: "Only the poorer stock of Africa was enslaved, the more intelligent members of the African community raided having been clever enough to elude the slaver's nets." Herskovits answers that the slave trade was not selective of the dregs of African society. There were instances when troublesome rivals who belonged to royal or priestly ranks were sold into slavery by wary rulers attempting to safeguard their thrones. When priests of the water cult in the coastal area of Dahomey, for example, proved intransigent, the conquering king of Abomey solved the problem by selling them into slavery.[17]

"Since," according to the third myth, "the Negroes were brought from all parts of the African continent, spoke diverse languages, represented greatly differing bodies of custom, and, as a matter of policy, were distributed in the New World so as to lose tribal identity, no least common denominator of understanding or behavior could have possibly been worked out by them." Not so, contends Herskovits, since the majority of slaves came from the "areas lying in the coastal belt of West Africa and the Congo." He denies that a large number of slaves were brought from more than two or three hundred miles inland. Within this central slaving area there were two main language groups, Sudanic and Bantu. Within each group distinct dialects had a great deal of similarity in basic structure. Moreover, resemblances between the two large groups do exist. Finally, the slaving regions represented a unified cultural area. Therefore, the separation of tribes during slavery did not create an insurmountable "barrier to the retention of African customs in generalized form, or of their underlying sanctions and values." Slaves from differing tribes had a basis for communication when they "learned words from the language of their masters and poured these into African speech molds."[18] Herskovits goes on to make an even stronger assertion: just as European words were translated into African speech patterns, so European culture was translated into African value and behavior systems. Therefore, "the reasons most often advanced to account for the suppression of Africanisms in the New World turned out to be factors that encouraged their retention."[19] This is an extremely important contention, which will be examined later.

"Even granting," goes myth number four, "enough Negroes of a given tribe had had the opportunity to live together, and that they had the will and ability to continue their customary modes of behavior, the cultures of Africa were so savage and relatively so low in the scale of human civilization that the apparent superiority of European customs as observed in the behavior of their masters would have caused and actually did cause them to give up such aboriginal traditions as they may otherwise have desired to preserve." This belief is based upon a biased ethnology and a simplistic understanding of acculturative process. The culture of West Africa was neither savage nor low and was not automatically overwhelmed by contact with supposedly superior European culture. Africa was an active partner in the acculturative relationship, states Herskovits. However, in the United States, Herskovits admits, African religious behavior had to be reinterpreted "in light of a new theology." Two factors determined the degree of reinterpretation necessary. The first was the intensity of the exposure of slaves to European culture, as determined by the ratio of blacks to whites. The smaller the number of slaves, the more complete was the control of the master; the tighter the supervision, the more intense was the pressure to acculturate. A second factor influenced the slaves to reinterpret African behavior: traditional African openness to the "new and foreign." This characteristic African acceptance was particularly manifest in religion, where "both conquered and conquerors often took over the gods of their opponents." The resilience of slaves' attitudes toward new gods frequently led to "slightly modified African sanctions supporting forms of a given institution that are almost entirely European." In other words, a "principle of disregard for outer form while retaining inner values" is "characteristic of Africans everywhere" and is "the most important single factor making for an understanding of the acculturative situation."[20]

The fifth and final myth is: "The Negro is thus a man without a past." Herskovits asserts that the Negro does indeed have a past, a cultural history which makes him a distinctive participant on the American scene, as distinctive as the Swedish, German, or Irish immigrant. In brief, "the civilizations of Africa, like those of Europe, have contributed to American culture as we know it today."[21]

It is necessary in analyzing Herskovits' thesis and the evidence he adduces in its support to remember that he is attacking a myth. Demythologizers often run the risk of erring on the side of overstatement. This is a fault of which Herskovits is not innocent. Perhaps none took him to task for it more forcefully than the black sociologist E. Franklin Frazier, the foremost spokesman for a position diametrically opposed to Herskovits'. While admitting the existence of African retentions in Latin American and the Caribbean, Frazier denies that African culture was able to survive the conditions of slavery to any significant extent in the United States. He admits that a few individual slaves remembered something of their background in Africa. However, exceptions prove the rule: African traditions and practices did not take root and survive in the United States.

> These isolated instances only tend to show how difficult it was for slaves, who had retained a memory of their African background, to find a congenial milieu in which to perpetuate the old way of life ... The slaves, it seems, had only a vague knowledge of the African background of their parents ... [22]

It is Frazier's position that the process of enslavement and the passing of earlier generations born in Africa destroyed the culture of the slaves. The vacuum thus created was filled by Christianity, which became the new bond of social cohesion. The new world-view which gave meaning to life was Christianity, articulated in the images and stories of the Bible, as accepted by the slaves and celebrated in their spirituals.[23]

Deculturation began, according to Frazier, on the other side of the Atlantic, before the Africans even set foot on the slave ships. The fact that many slaves were captured in intertribal warfare and the demands of the plantation work force ensured that a large percentage of the slave population was young and male. And young males "are poor bearers of the cultural heritage of a people." In the coastal barracoons slaves were mixed together without regard for kinship or tribal ties. The trauma of the Middle Passage further isolated slaves from countrymen who spoke the same language or observed the same traditions.[24]

On this side of the Atlantic the size of the plantation where the slave ended his journey was a significant factor in either allowing for or reducing African cultural retentions. On the larger plantations, where the black population was much larger than the white, there was less opportunity for contact and so the process of acculturation was slow. But, Frazier contends, the majority of slaves in the United States were situated on smaller plantations and farms: "In some of the Upland cotton regions of Alabama, Mississippi, Louisiana, and Arkansas the median number of slaves per holding did not reach twenty, while in regions of general agriculture based mainly upon slave labor in Kentucky, Maryland, Missouri, North Carolina, South Carolina, and Tennessee the median number of slave holdings were even smaller."[25] The process of "seasoning" ("breaking in") new slaves required the prohibition of African languages. "Salt-water" (African-born) Negroes were looked down upon by slaves already used to the ways of plantation America, and social pressure was exerted upon them to learn new customs.[26] Slaves were under continual surveillance and control. On the small farms the slaves worked with their white owners; on larger plantations they toiled under the eye of the driver and overseer. Gatherings of five or more slaves without the presence of a white observer were universally forbidden.

In addition, the mobility of the slave population and the destruction of familial stability due to the internal slave trade made social cohesion an impossibility. Therefore, Frazier concludes, "It is impossible to establish any continuity between African religious practices and the Negro church in the United States."[27] Here the "Negroes were plunged into an alien civilization in which whatever remained of their religious myths and cults had no meaning whatever." African memories were forgotten, African patterns of behavior and attitudes toward the world lost their meaning. Slaves had to develop "new habits and attitudes" in order "to meet new situations."[28]

Frazier takes Herskovits to task for basing his assertions on flimsy evidence. Herskovits had not been able "to refer African survival in the United States to a specific tribe or a definite area." When he argues that the spirit of African belief is preserved under the adoption of European religious forms, Frazier counters that this simply means that the "existence of such survivals cannot be validated on scientific grounds." A case in point is Herskovits' attempt to explain the popularity of the Baptist church among black Americans by reference to water cults in Africa. The Baptists successfully proselytized Negroes, says Frazier, not because they practiced baptism by immersion but because they were energetic proselytizers with strong appeal for lower classes.[29]

Frazier admits that in the "magic and folk beliefs of the rural Negroes in the United States, some African elements have probably been retained." However, he hastens to add, it is a very difficult task to separate African from European folk belief. And as the Afro-Americans "have emerged from the world of the folk" the majority "have sloughed off completely the African heritage."[30]

The debate has been a lasting one. The positions represented by Herskovits and Frazier have continued in one form or another to inform a variety of discussion on black history and culture, including the fields of music, folklore, language, and art. There are those who deny that there is any difference between white and black Americans except color. There are those who ground black identity and black pride upon a reclamation of historical continuity with the African past. There are those who identify black rebellion with the survival of African culture. The ideological conflicts between separatists and integrationists have involved judgments about the survival of African culture in the United States. Commentators on black religious life have been subject to ideological pressures to take a stand in the Herskovits-Frazier debate, understanding that wider implications would derive from their conclusions. Given the implications and emotions involved in the issues, it is a difficult but, for that reason, all the more necessary task to evaluate the evidence with care and open-mindedness, to be aware of one's own preconceptions and not to draw hasty conclusions.

Cases in Point:
Baptism by Immersion and Spirit Possession

The weakest part of Herskovits' argument is his contention that he has found African retentions in the institutional form and theology of certain types of black churches. He is more convincing when he speaks of "patterns of motor behavior" and folk belief, but here, too, he weakens his credibility by overstatement.

Herskovits begins his chapter on "Africanisms in Religious Life" with the following statement:

> Underlying the life of the American Negro is a deep religious bent that is but the manifestation here of a similar drive that, everywhere in Negro societies, makes the supernatural a major focus of interest. The tenability of this position is apparent when it is considered how in an age marked by skepticism, the Negro has held fast to belief. Religion is vital, meaningful, and understandable to the Negro of this country because . . . it is not removed from life, but has been deeply integrated into the daily round. It is because of this, indeed, that everywhere compensation in terms of the supernatural is so immediately acceptable to this underpriviledged folk, and causes them, in contrast to other underprivileged groups elsewhere in the

world, to turn to religion rather than to political action or
other outlets for their frustration.[31]

Arthur Huff Fauset's critique of this generalization is significant,
especially because it has been widely held that black people are
somehow "naturally" religious. Fauset denies statistically that
Afro-Americans are greater churchgoers than other Americans.[32]
As to the importance of the church in the black community, it is a
fact explained by the intransigence of white racism which relegated black control to one social institution, the church. There is
no proof that religion as a compensatory force among the under-
privileged has been more widespread among the black poor than
it has been among the oppressed of other ethnic backgrounds.
Besides, religion has also functioned as a spur to resistance, self-
assertion, and rebellion in black history. Finally, when given the
chance, as for example during the period of Reconstruction,
blacks have turned readily to political action. Herskovits' generalization about the "religious bent characteristic of Negroes everywhere" reveals a characteristic problem in his method: How is
such an assertion to be proved, disproved, or even taken? As an
impressionistic remark it has a certain validity. Religion *has*
played a central role in Afro-American culture in the United
States. But it is a different matter to ground the "scientific" hy-
pothesis that religion forms the focus of black culture in both the
New World and in Africa on the observation that black people
have a "religious bent." The sweeping generalization only seems
to weaken credibility concerning particular examples.

Turning to specific institutional characteristics of the black
churches, Herskovits found Africanisms in the worship of "shouting" churches. Listening to the radio broadcasts of black church
services he concluded that "spirit possession by the Holy Ghost"
inspired "motor behavior that is not European but African."[33]
The rhythmic hand-clapping and antiphonal participation of the
congregation in the sermon, and the theological view in which
"God, Jesus, and the Holy Ghost are all concerned with the

immediate fate of those who worship them," strike Herskovits as "deviations from the practices and beliefs of white Baptists." The *immediacy* of God in the services he heard, the manner in which "the Holy Ghost visits with the minister, taking messages to God from those in need of help," seemed to Herskovits to reflect the African heritage of the worshippers.[34] The theological example is not convincing. A sense of the immediacy of God, of his involvement in daily life is not a deviation from the beliefs of white Baptists or indeed of many other Christians. The role of the Holy Spirit as a messenger seems to be a sermonic conceit that is not foreign to Christian belief.[35] Hand-clapping and congregational response would not be in the least surprising to white holiness and pentecostal church members, nor would "spirit possession."

Perhaps the most frequently attacked example of a specific African survival cited by Herskovits is baptism by immersion which he links to water cults in Nigeria and Dahomey. The strong appeal of the Baptist denomination for Negroes was due partially to the West African religious background, where water cults are extremely important. The Baptists' insistence on immersion was an attractive rite to Africans familiar with water cults because the concept of baptism is one "that any African would find readily understandable." In Africa, Dutch Guiana, and Haiti, possession by water spirits drives the possessed devotee to hurl himself bodily into a stream, pond, or river. Similarly in the baptismal service of rural black Baptists the spirit occasionally falls upon the new Christian emerging from the water, causing him to shout. Therefore, baptism through "the transmutation of belief and behavior under acculturation . . . furnished one of the least difficult transitions to a new form of belief.[36] There are two objections that can be made to Herskovits' comments on baptism by immersion. While Herskovits embraces the principle "that the acculturative process in each locality is to be analyzed in terms of the peculiarities of its own historic past and its own socio-economic present," he violates this principle too frequently by glossing over significant differences.[37] Because he views the whole of Afro-America as a spectrum or continuum, he sometimes blurs important distinctions and argues from an example in one area to an invalid application in another. The applicability of his analogy that just as spirit possession occurs in the water cults in Africa, so is shouting associated with baptism in the United States breaks down upon careful examination. The African devotee is possessed by the god who has replaced his personality and who impels him into the water, the god's own element, whereas the tradition which lies behind baptism by immersion is Judeo-Christian and the descent of the Spirit on this occasion has the warrant of Scripture: " . . . he will baptize with the Holy Spirit."[38]

The second criticism, made by every critic of Herskovits, is that the appeal of the Baptist denomination for Afro-Americans did not derive from their African background but from the attraction of evangelical religion to the slaves. To be fair to Herskovits, it is necessary to point out that he lists several other reasons for the spread of the Baptist denomination among black people: the energy of the Baptist evangelists, the personal emotional appeal of revivalism, the ease with which a Baptist congregation could be founded, the opportunity for even the unlearned to preach. Herskovits clearly saw the African water cults as only part of the explanation.

Furthermore, there is a crucial aspect of Herskovits' argument which often goes ignored in the discussion of slave acculturation: the suggestion that at least some African religious concepts and behavior were not totally dissimilar to certain beliefs and practices charateristic of evangelical Protestantism. Perhaps the religious heritage of American Protestants and the African religious background were not completely antithetical. Culture contact was not in every case culture conflict with either Africa or Europe emerging victorious. The acculturative process was broader and more complex than simple retention or destruction of Africanism. Elements of African behavior and belief could have been modified by contact with European culture and could have merged with it in a new syncretistic form. Conversely, European traits could have been shaped and reinterpreted by the slaves in the light of their African past. On the one hand, the similarity of some traits may make it very difficult or even impossible to separate what is African from what is European in origin; on the other hand, this very commonality might have served to reinforce certain African elements while others withered under severe prohibition and attack. That some elements of African religion survived in the United States not as separate enclaves free of white influence but as aspects hidden under or blended with similar European forms is a thesis worth considering in more detail, especially since there are strong arguments for its validity in the areas of music, folklore, and language. There were two areas of commonality between African and European religion where mutual reinterpretation and syncretism possibly occurred: ecstatic behavior and magical folk-belief.

Ecstatic behavior, in the form of spirit possession, is, as we have seen, central to the liturgy of West African peoples and their descendants in many parts of the New World. Commonly, the rites of worship consist in drumming the rhythms of the gods, singing their songs, creating a setting so that they will come down and "ride" their devotees in states of possession. The possessed takes on the personality of the god, dancing his steps, speaking his words, bearing his emblems, acting out his character in facial expression and bodily gesture.

In the United States slaves and their descendants were not possessed by the gods of their fathers but they did engage in a type of ecstatic behavior called shouting. Is there a relationship between the phenomenon of shouting in black revivalistic churches in the United States and spirit possession in West Africa, South America, and the Caribbean?

Shouting was a common, if sensational, occurrence at the frontier camp meetings. While several accounts of these meetings stressed the slaves' peculiar propensity for shouting, white revivalists also shouted and jerked, barked and laughed a holy laughter as well.[39] Herskovits theorizes that it was the influence of the black participants in the camp meetings that accounted for the pattern of ecstatic behavior which emerged. In support of this contention, he refers to a description by Frederick Morgan Davenport which contrasts ecstatic behavior at a revival in Northern Ireland with one in Kentucky. The account states:

> I wish in closing to call attention to the difference in type of the automatisms of Kentucky and Ulster. In Kentucky the motor automatism, the voluntary muscles in violent action, were the prevailing type, although there were many of the sensory. On the other hand, in Ulster the sensory automatisms, trance, vision, the physical disability and the sinking of muscular energy were the prevailing types, although there were many of the motor. I do not mean that I can explain it.[40]

Davenport and Frazier explained the difference in behavior as a matter of chance. Herskovits thought the difference was due to the influence of the slaves upon the white revivalists in Kentucky. He states that "the tradition of violent possession associated with these meetings is far more African than European, and hence there is reason to hold that, in part at least, it was inspired in the whites by this contact with Negroes."[41] Herskovits supported his contention by referring to the difference between black and white revival services in the twentieth century as described by Hortense Powdermaker in *After Freedom*. At Negro revivals the participants were more active than were white congregations; "greater rhythm and spontaneity" were characteristic of the black revivalists; the black preacher's sermon was more melodic and regular, less halting than the white minister's; black congregations moved less convulsively and more smoothly than their white counterparts. Powdermaker attributed these motor differences to social conditioning, "the repression caused by the interracial situation" which "finds relief in unrestrained religious behavior." Herskovits held that the differences between white and black congregations "in the manifestation of ecstasy and hysteria" served to "underscore the differences between the worship characteristic of the cultures from which the ancestors of these two groups were derived."[42]

Although ecstatic behavior in response to the revivalist preaching of the camp meetings was an experience common to slaves and slaveholders on the frontier of late eighteenth- and early nineteenth-century America, the special responsiveness of the slaves to revivals was noted by several witnesses. One observer remarked: "By no class is a camp meeting hailed with more unmixed delight than by the poor slaves."[43] In 1807 Jesse Lee, a Georgia evangelist, noted: "The first day of the meeting, we had a gentle and comfortable moving of the spirit of the Lord among us; and at night it was much more powerful than before, and the meeting was kept up all night without intermission. However, before day the white people retired, and the meeting was continued by the black people."[44] John Leland noted in 1790 that slaves in Virginia "commonly are more noisy in time of preaching than the whites, and are more subject to bodily exercise, and if they meet with an encouragement in these things, they grow extravagant." In the camp meeting the slaves met with encouragement. The proclivity of the slaves for "bodily exercises" was not due to any innate emotionalism; nor was it totally due to the need of an oppressed class to release pent-up tension. Rather, the slaves tended to express religious emotion in certain patterned types of bodily movement influenced by the African heritage of dance.[45]

Slaves and ex-slaves sought and welcomed the presence of the Spirit, which moved worshipers to shout and dance not only during the special "seasons of revival" but also during regular church services (whenever allowed). Frederick Law Olmsted visited a black church in New Orleans where he experienced firsthand the power of evangelical preaching to arouse ecstatic behavior.

> As soon as I had taken my seat, my attention was attracted by an old negro near me, whom I supposed for some time to be suffering under some nervous complaint; he trembled, his teeth chattered, and his face, at intervals, was convulsed. He soon began to respond aloud to the sentiments of the preacher, in such words as these: "Oh, yes!" and similar expressions could be heard from all parts of the house whenever the

speaker's voice was unusually solemn, or his language and manner eloquent or excited.

Sometimes the outcries and responses were not confined to ejaculations of this kind, but shouts, and groans, terrific shrieks, and indescribable expressions of ecstasy—of pleasure or agony—and even stamping, jumping, and clapping of hands were added . . . I was once surprised to find my own muscles all stretched, as if ready for a struggle—my face glowing, and my feet stamping—have been infected unconsciously. . . . I could not, when my mind reverted to itself, find any connection or meaning in the phrases of the speaker that remained in my memory; and I have no doubt it was his "action" rather than his sentiments, that had given rise to the excitement of the congregation.[46]

After attempting to capture the strong rhythm of the preacher's sermon with each beat marked by the antiphonal response of the congregation, Olmsted went on to describe the effect of the service on one of the worshipers.

The preacher was drawing his sermon to a close . . . when a small old woman, perfectly black, among those in the gallery, suddenly rose, and began dancing and clapping her hands; at first with a slow and measured movement, and then with increasing rapidity, at the same time beginning to shout "ha! ha!" The women about her arose also, and tried to hold her . . . The woman was still shouting and dancing, her head thrown back and rolling from one side to the other. Gradually her shout became indistinct, she threw her arms wildly about instead of clapping her hands, fell back into the arms of her companions, then threw herself forward and embraced those before her, then tossed herself from side to side, gasping, and finally sunk to the floor, where she remained . . . kicking, as if acting a death struggle.[47]

To what extent, if any, did a tradition of African spirit possession influence such ecstatic behavior? There are two issues involved in comparing African spirit possession with the religious behavior of slaves and their descendants in American "shouting" churches. As Erika Bourguignon has succinctly stated:

What is generally spoken of as "spirit possession" actually
involves two distinct aspects, two distinct levels of ethno-
graphic "fact": an observable behavior pattern and a system of
cultural beliefs and interpretations. These, however, in turn
structure expectations and therefore behavior.[48]

In other words, though not separated in fact, there are two aspects which should be distinguished for the sake of clarity in
discussion: the faith context in which the possession experience
occurs and the patterned style of outward response by which the
ecstatic experience is manifest.

On the level of theological interpretation and meaning, African
spirit possession differs significantly from the shouting experience
found in the revivalist tradition of American evangelicalism. In
the central possession cults of the Yoruba and Fon peoples the
devotees are possessed by a god—in the cults of Haiti and Brazil,
by several gods in succession—whose personality displaces that of
the human medium. The advice, commands, gestures, and identity of the god are transmitted through the possessed. Personality
traits of the god are expressed in the patterned action of the
possessed devotee who makes the god present to the cult community. It is believed that the possessed "has been invaded by a
supernatural being and is thus temporarily beyond self-control,
his ego being subordinated to that of the [divine] intruder."[49] The
devotee becomes the carrier of the god, taking up the god's emblems, wearing his sacred colors, tasting his favorite food and
drink. Comparing Haitian vaudouists with Spiritual Baptists
(Shakers) from St. Vincent, Erika Bourguignon distinguishes between African and Protestant forms of spirit possession. "While
the Haitian," she states, "impersonates specific, well-delineated
anthropomorphic entities, with complex personalities and a great
range of possible activities, the Vincentian does not." She adds
that the "Haitian trancer sings and dances, smokes, drinks and
eats," and sometimes "may climb a tree or dive into water" while
possessed. "Most importantly, while the Haitian interacts with
others during his possession trance, with spirits possessing people

and with other human beings, the Vincentian does not." Instead, the Vincentian's attention "is drawn inward to his interaction with the Spirit." Though the Vincentian trancers "participate in a common experience," they do not interact with each other as the Haitians do "from the standpoint of a personal transformation." The "manner of operation" in both experiences, Bourguignon concludes, "is distinct in its formal and in its ideological features."[50] While Bourguignon is specifically comparing Haitian to Vincentian types of spirit possession, her differentiation is applicable to the North American possession experience as well. The context of belief shapes the possession experience and determines the manner in which the experience is interpreted. While there may be similar effects—ego enhancement and catharsis, to name only two—on this level of faith event, there are major differences between spirit possession as it occurs in African and Latin American cults, on the one hand, and the ecstatic shouting experience of United States revivalism, on the other. There is a discontinuity, then, between the African heritage of spirit possession and the black shouting tradition in the United States. The African gods with their myriad characteristics, personalities, and myths do not "mount" their enthusiasts amid the dances, songs, and drum rhythms of worship in the United States. Instead it is the Holy Spirit who fills the converted sinner with a happiness and power that drives him to shout, sing, and sometimes dance.

A different possession belief was held by the slave in North America. One explication of this belief was given by an ex-slave preacher and recorded in *God Struck Me Dead:*

> The old meeting house caught on fire. The spirit was there. Every heart was beating in unison as we turned our minds to God to tell Him of our sorrows here below. God saw our need and came to us. I used to wonder what made people shout but now I don't. There is a joy on the inside and it wells up so strong that we can't keep still. It is fire in the bones. Any time that fire touches a man, he will jump.[51]

It is in the context of action, the patterns of motor behavior

preceding and following the ecstatic experience, that there may be
continuity between African and American forms of spirit possession. While the rhythms of the drums, so important in African
and Latin American cults, were by and large forbidden to the
slave in the United States, hand-clapping, foot-tapping, rhythmic
preaching, hyperventilation, antiphonal (call and response) singing, and dancing are styles of behavior associated with possession
both in Africa and in this country.

The strong emphasis on rhythmic preaching, singing, moving,
and dancing in the religious behavior of the American slaves has
long been noted by observers. Ex-slave Robert Anderson described the patterns of religious expression which he saw in his
youth during slavery:

> The colored people . . . have a peculiar music of their own,
> which is largely a process of rhythm, rather than written music.
> Their music is largely, or was . . . a sort of rhythmical chant. It
> had to do largely with religion and the words adopted to their
> quaint melodies were largely of a religious nature. The stories
> of the Bible were placed into words that would fit the music
> already used by the colored people. While singing these songs,
> the singers and the entire congregation kept time to the music
> by the swaying of their bodies or by the patting of the foot or
> hand. Practically all of their songs were accompanied by a
> motion of some kind . . . the weird and mysterious music of the
> religious ceremonies moved old and young alike in a frenzy of
> religious fervor . . . We also had religious dances, which were
> expressions of the weird, the fantastic, the mysterious, that was
> felt in all our religious ceremonies.[52]

It appears from early accounts that the African tradition of
"danced religion" retained a strong hold on the religious behavior
of the slaves. Rev. Morgan Godwin, who arrived to minister to
Marston Parish in York County, Virginia, in 1665, later wrote of
the religious dancing of the slaves:

> . . . nothing is more barbarous and contrary to Christianity,
> than their . . . *Idolotrous Dances*, and *Revels;* in which they
> usually spend the *Sunday* . . . And here, that I may not be

thought too rashly to impute Idolotry to their *Dances;* my
conjecture is raised upon this ground . . . for that they use
their Dances as a *means* to *procure Rain;* Some of them having
been known to beg this liberty upon the Week Days, in order
thereunto . . . [53]

During the seventeenth and much of the eighteenth century there
was a great deal of indifference, reluctance, and hostility to the
conversion of the slaves. (Not until the successive waves of religious revival known as the Great Awakening began in the 1740s
did incidents of slave conversion occur in any sizable numbers.)
In the face of this religious indifference some forms of African
religious behavior seem to have continued. Rev. John Sharpe
complained in 1712 that even Christianized slaves in New York
"are buried in the Common by those of their country and complexion without the office; on the contrary the Heathenish rites
are performed at the grave by their countrymen . . . "[54] And Alexander Hewatt noted in 1779 that in South Carolina "the negroes
of that country, a few only excepted, are to this day as great
strangers to Christianity, and as much under the influence of
Pagan darkness, idolatry, and superstition, as they were at their
first arrival from Africa . . . " He was particularly disturbed that
Sundays and "Holidays are days of idleness . . . in which the
slaves assemble together in alarming crowds for the purposes of
dancing, feasting and merriment."[55] Later Methodist, Presbyterian, and Baptist revivalists condemned these secular forms of
amusement and taught the slaves that conversion required their
abandonment. While evangelical missionaries prohibited dancing
as sinful, they afforded the slaves a morally sanctioned context for
a sacralized type of dancing in the emotionally charged setting of
the revival. In 1845 Sir Charles Lyell commented on the way in
which slaves, though converted to Christianity, continued to
dance.

Of dancing and music, the Negroes are passionately fond. On
the Hopeton plantation violins have been silenced by the Methodist missionaries . . . At the Methodist prayer-meetings, they

are permitted to move round rapidly in a ring, in which
manoeuvre, I am told, they sometimes contrive to take enough
exercise to serve as a substitute for the dance, it being, in fact,
a kind of spiritual boulanger . . . [56]

The unusual religious behavior of slaves at camp meetings
aroused the disapproval of some Christian evangelists. In a work
entitled *Methodist Error or Friendly Advice to Those Methodists
Who Indulge in Extravagant Religious Emotions and Bodily Exercises* (1819), John Watson complained about the style of musical
behavior of black revivalists in the Philadelphia Conference:

> Here ought to be considered too, a most exceptionable error,
> which has the tolerance at least of the rulers of our camp
> meetings. In the *blacks'* quarter, the coloured people get to-
> gether, and sing for hours together, short scraps of disjointed
> affirmations, pledges, or prayers, lengthened out with long
> repetitious *choruses*. These are all sung in the merry chorus-
> manner of the southern harvest field, or husking-frolic
> method, of the slave blacks; and also very greatly like the
> Indian dances. With every word so sung, they have a sinking
> of one or other leg of the body alternately; producing an audi-
> ble sound of the feet at every step, and as manifest as the steps
> of actual negro dancing in Virginia &c. If some, in the mean-
> time sit, they strike the sounds alternately on each thigh . . .
> the evil is only occasionally condemned and the example has
> already visibly affected the religious manners of some whites.
> From this cause, I have known in some camp meetings from
> 50 to 60 people crowd into one tent, after the public devo-
> tions had closed, and there continue the whole night, singing
> tune after tune, . . . scarce one of which were in our hymn
> books. Some of these from their nature, (having very long
> repetition choruses and short scraps of matter) are actually
> composed as sung and are almost endless.[57]

Besides shedding some light on "the original religious songs of
blacks—as distinguished from the standard Protestant hymns
that they sang—"[58] the account above is significant because it
tends to support the argument that black patterns of behavior
influenced white revivalists at the camp meetings.

Religious dancing and shouting were by no means confined to camp meetings. Olmsted remarked on the regular religious worship of the slaves on one plantation:

> On most of the large rice plantations which I have seen in this vicinity, there is a small chapel, which the negroes call their prayer-house. The owner of one of these told me that, having furnished the prayer-house with seats having a back-rail, his negroes petitioned him to remove it, because it did not leave them *room enough to pray.* It was explained to me that it is their custom, in social worship, to work themselves up to a great pitch of excitement, in which they yell and cry aloud, and, finally shriek and leap up, clapping their hands and dancing, as it is done at heathen festivals. The back-rail they found to seriously impede this exercise.[59]

The religious dance most frequently described was the ring shout of the slaves in the Sea Islands. The ring shout, musicologists agree, is a particularly strong example of African-influenced dance style in the United States. Frazier and others have relegated the ring shout to the Sea Islands, where they admit Africanisms were strong, but there is evidence that the ring shout was a widespread and deeply ingrained practice among slaves in other areas as well. The following passage from A.M.E. Bishop Daniel Alexander Payne's autobiography indicates that he had met with the ring shout in many places a little over a decade after slavery:

> About this time [1878] I attended a "bush meeting" . . . After the sermon they formed a ring, and with coats off sung, clapped their hands and stamped their feet in a most ridiculous and heathenish way. I requested the pastor to go and stop their dancing. At his request they stopped their dancing and clapping of hands, but remained singing and rocking their bodies to and fro. This they did for about fifteen minutes. I then went, and taking their leader by the arm requested him to desist and to sit down and sing in a rational manner. I told him also that it was a heathenish way to worship and disgraceful to themselves, the race, and the Christian name. In that instance they broke up their ring; but would not sit down, and walked sullenly away. After the sermon in the afternoon, having another oppor-

tunity of speaking alone to this young leader of the singing and clapping ring, he said: "Sinners won't get converted unless there is a ring." Said I: "You might sing till you fell down dead, and you would fail to convert a single sinner, because nothing but the Spirit of God and the word of God can convert sinners." He replied: "The Spirit of God works upon people in different ways. At camp-meeting there must be a ring here, a ring there, a ring over yonder, or sinners will not get converted." This was his idea, and it is also that of many others. These "Bands" I have had to encounter in many places . . . To the most thoughtful . . . I usually succeeded in making the "Band" disgusting; but by the ignorant masses . . . it was regarded as the essence of religion.[60]

In the exchange between Payne and the "Band" leader it is significant that the latter found the ring shout necessary for conversion and for the working of the Spirit.

Payne goes on to describe the "ring" of the "Bands," also known as "Fist and Heel Worshippers."

He who could sing loudest and longest led the 'Band,' having his loins girded and a handkerchief in hand with which he kept time, while his feet resounded on the floor like the drumsticks of a bass drum. In some cases it was the custom to begin these dances after every night service and keep it up till midnight, sometimes singing and dancing alternately—a short prayer and a long dance. Someone has even called it the "Voudoo Dance." I have remonstrated with a number of pastors for permitting these practices, which vary somewhat in different localities, but have been invariably met with the response that he could not succeed in restraining them, and an attempt to compel them to cease would simply drive them away from our Church . . . And what is more deplorable, some of our most popular and powerful preachers labor systematically to perpetuate this fanaticism. Such preachers never rest till they create an excitement that consists in shouting, jumping and dancing.[61]

It seems, then, from Payne's account, as well as those of others, that dancing was a crucial part of worship for some slaves and ex-slaves. The label "Voudoo Dance," which Payne records, was not entirely a misnomer. There are close parallels between the style of dancing observed in African and Caribbean cult worship and the style of the American "ring shout." Folklorists John and Alan Lomax who recorded a ring shout in Louisiana in 1934 enumerated the parallels.

> We have seen "shouts" in Louisiana, in Texas, in Georgia and the Bahamas; we have seen vaudou dancing in Haiti; we have read accounts of similar rites in works upon Negro life in other parts of the Western hemisphere. All share basic similarities: (1) the song is "danced" with the whole body, with hands, feet, belly, and hips; (2) the worship is, basically, a dancing-singing phenomenon; (3) the dancers always move counter-clockwise around the ring; (4) the song has the leader-chorus form, with much repetition, with a focus on rhythm rather than on melody, that is, with a form that invites and ultimately enforces cooperative group activity; (5) the song continues to be repeated from sometimes more than an hour, steadily increasing in intensity and gradually accelerating, until a sort of mass hypnosis ensues . . . This shout pattern is demonstrably West African in origin.[62]

George E. Simpson has described the dancing of the Revivalist cult in Jamaica in terms that bear striking resemblance to the American ring shout.

> Halfway through the service the leader may begin to circle counterclockwise the altar, or a table inside the church, or the "seal" in the yard outside the church. The officers and leading members of the church, often up to twenty people, fall in behind him as all of them "labor in the spirit" . . . This "spiritual" dancing is believed to increase the religious understanding of the participants.[63]

There are a number of detailed descriptions of the technique of the ring shout in which African style dance patterns can be noted. W. F. Allen reprinted an account of the shout on the Sea Islands from the *Nation* (May 30, 1867):

> . . . the true "shout" takes place on Sundays or on "praise"-nights through the week, and either in the praise-house or in

some cabin in which a regular religious meeting has been held. Very likely more than half the population of the plantation is gathered together . . . But the benches are pushed back to the wall when the formal meeting is over, and old and young men and women . . . boys . . . young girls barefooted, all stand up in the middle of the floor, and when the 'sperichil' is struck, begin first walking and by-and-by shuffling round, one after the other, in a ring. The foot is hardly taken from the floor, and the progression is mainly due to a jerking, hitching motion, which agitates the entire shouter, and soon brings out streams of perspiration. Sometimes they dance silently, sometimes as they shuffle they sing the chorus of the spiritual, and sometimes the song itself is also sung by the dancers. But most frequently a band, composed of some of the best singers and of tired shouters, stand at the side of the room to 'base' the others, singing the body of the song and clapping their hands together or on the knees. Song and dance alike are extremely energetic, and often, when the shout lasts into the middle of the night, the monotonous thud, thud, thud of the feet prevents sleep within half a mile of the praisehouse . . . It is not unlikely that this remarkable religious ceremony is a relic of some African dance . . . Dancing in the usual way is regarded with great horror by the people of Port Royal, but they enter with infinite zest into the movements of the "shout."[64]

As Harold Courlander wrote: "circular movement, shuffling steps and stamping, postures and gestures, the manner of standing, the way the arms are held out for balance or pressed against the sides, the movements of the shoulder, all are African in conception and derivation."[65] It has even been suggested by Lorenzo Dow Turner that the very word "shout" derives from *saut*, a term used by West African Muslims to denote "dancing or moving around the Kaaba."[66]

The ring form of religious dancing occurred on occasions other than revivals and praise meetings. Funerals, for example, were occasions for dancing and sometimes drumming, at least in the Sea Islands. Rachel Anderson, an elderly Georgia coast resident, recalled: "Use tuh alluz beat duh drums at fewnuls. Right attuh duh pusson die, dey beat um tuh tell duh uddahs bout duh fewnul . . . On duh way tuh duh grabe dey beat duh drum as dey is mahchin long. Wen duh body is put in duh grabe, ebrybody shout roun duh grabe in a succle, singin an prayin."[67] And another old Georgian, Ben Sullivan, stated: "Dey go in a long pruhcession tuh duh buryin' groun. Den dey dance roun in a ring an dey motion wid duh hans. Dey sing duh body tuh duh grabe and den dey let it down an den dey succle roun in duh dance."[68]

In the ring shout and allied patterns of ecstatic behavior, the African heritage of dance found expression in the evangelical religion of the American slaves. To be sure, there are significant differences between the kind of spirit possession found in West Africa and in the shouting experience of American revivalism. Different theological meanings are expressed and experienced in each. But similar patterns of response—rhythmic clapping, ring-dancing, styles of singing, all of which result in or from the state-of-possession trance—reveal the slaves' African religious background. The shout is a convincing example of Herskovits' theory of reinterpretation of African traditions; for the situation of the camp-meeting revival, where enthusiastic and ecstatic religious behavior was encouraged, presented a congenial setting for slaves to merge African patterns of response with Christian interpretations of the experience of spirit possession, an experience shared by both blacks and whites. The Protestant revivalist tradition, accepted by the slaves and their descendants in the United States, proved in this instance to be amenable to the influence of African styles of behavior. Despite the prohibition of dancing as heathenish and sinful, the slaves were able to reinterpret and "sanctify" their African tradition of dance in the "shout."[69] While the North American slaves danced under the impulse of the Spirit of a "new" God, they danced in ways their fathers in Africa would have recognized.

Moreover, the argument, mentioned above, between Bishop Payne and the leader of the ring-shout band hints at a deeper level of reinterpretation. If, as Payne claims, the "ignorant masses" (read "less acculturated") regarded the ring shout "as the essence of religion," and if the shout leader's contention that "without a ring sinners won't get converted" was representative of general belief, the "holy dance" of the shout may very well have been a two-way bridge connecting the core of West African religions—possession by the gods—to the core of evangelical Protestanism—experience of conversion. There are also hints that the process of conversion may have been related in the slaves' minds to the African-style period of initiation into the cults of the gods. Slaves customarily spoke of the period of seeking conversion as "mourning" and thought of it as a time when the sinner should go apart, alone, to a quiet place to struggle with his sins. This period and place of retirement resemble the novitiate of West African and Caribbean cults in two details. Fugitive slave Henry Brown recalled that when his sister "became anxious to have her soul converted" she "shaved the hair from her head, as many of the slaves thought they could not be converted without doing this," a custom similar to initiation rites in Brazil, Trinidad and West Africa. The other similarity may be noted in Samuel Lawton's description of a practice followed in the Sea Islands which resembled the use of cloth bands in the "mourning ground" ceremony of Spiritual Baptists in Trinidad: "Seekers may sometimes be identified by a white cloth or string tied around the head. This is a signal that they are seekin' and all others are to 'leave 'em alon.' "[70]

Ring shouts were also called "running sperichils," a term which suggests a connection with a broader and more inclusive category of religious expression, the Afro-American spirituals. There were several kinds of spirituals—shouts, anthems, and jubilees—serving different occasions and reflecting different moods. Styles ranged from the exciting tempo and rhythmic stamp of the shout to the slow, drawn-out "sorrow songs" which usually come to mind when the spirituals are mentioned. While the lyrics and themes of the spirituals were drawn from Biblical verses and Christian hymns, and although the music and melodies were strongly influenced by the sacred and secular songs of white

Americans, the style in which the slaves sang the spirituals was African.

Frequently, musically literate observers despaired of adequately conveying the style and sounds of the spirituals they had heard. One who tried was Lucy McKim Garrison, who in 1862 wrote of the difficulties involved in her task:

> It is difficult to express the entire character of these Negro ballads by mere musical notes and signs. The odd turns made in the throat, and the curious rhythmic effect produced by single voices chiming in at different irregular intervals, seem almost as impossible to place on the score as the singing of birds or the tones of an AEolian harp.[71]

A later compiler of spirituals complained of a similar problem: "Tones are frequently employed which we have no musical character to represent. Such, for example, is that which I have indicated as nearly as possible by the flat seventh . . . "[72]

The singing style of the slaves, which was influenced by their African heritage, was characterized by a strong emphasis on call and response, polyrhythms, syncopation, ornamentation, slides from one note to another, and repetition. Other stylistic features included body movement, hand-clapping, foot-tapping, and heterophony. This African style of song performance could not be reduced to musical notations, which explains why printed versions do not capture the peculiar flavor of the slave songs, which were consistently labeled "wild," "strangely fascinating," of "peculiar quality," and "barbaric" by white observers.

Despite the African style of singing, the spirituals, like the "running spirituals" or ring shout, were performed in praise of the Christian God.[73] The names and words of the African gods were replaced by Biblical figures and Christian imagery. African style and European hymnody met and became in the spiritual a new, Afro-American song to express the joys and sorrows of the religion which the slaves had made their own.[74]

Another area of religious behavior in which European traditions of slaveholders and African traditions of slaves proved consonant with one another was that of folk belief, the realm of magic, "hoodoo," and "conjure."

Folk Belief: From Vaudou to Conjuring

No discussion of Africanisms in the religious life of black Americans could be complete without reference to voodoo. However, when speaking of voodoo in the United States, as opposed to *vaudou* in Haiti, an important distinction must be made between voodoo as an organized cult and voodoo as a system of magic. Voodoo as a cult flourished until the late nineteenth century, particularly in New Orleans, though it was not confined to that area. From the early days of French Louisiana, the voodoo cult was associated with slaves imported from the French West Indies. Voodoo originated in the religion of Africans, but the most immediate catalyst to the growth of the cult in Louisiana was the emigration of slaves and free blacks from the island of Saint-Domingue at the time of the Haitian Revolution.

Initially the cult and the magical system of voodoo formed an integral whole, but gradually voodoo as an institutionalized cult of ritual worship disintegrated, while its tradition of "root work" persisted in folk beliefs widespread among slaves and their descendants down to the present day. Voodoo priests—and more commonly, priestesses—presided over the cult while building a large clientele for various charms and gris-gris. New Orleans became known as the capital of "root work," and voodoo, or hoodoo, came to be a synonym for conjuring and conjurers apart from the cultic context of its African-Haitian origins.[75]

By all accounts, voodoo in New Orleans was centered upon worship of a snake god. Drumming, dancing, singing, possession, animal sacrifice, eating, and drinking were customary at the ceremonies in Louisiana, as in Haiti and West Africa. In Dahomey the god Damballa (Da) was envisioned as a snake and as the rainbow, principle of fluidity and governor of men's destinies. Particularly in the coastal kingdoms of Arada and Ouidah, conquered by Dahomey in 1724–1727, the cult of the snake god Dangbe was strong. The captives from the Dahomean campaigns against Arada and Ouidah provided a supply of slaves for the West Indian market of the French traders.[76] Louisiana bought her first slaves from the islands of Martinique, Guadeloupe, and Saint-Domingue as early as 1716, when five hundred were imported, followed by three thousand more during the next year. Slaves from the French West Indies continued to enter Louisiana until later prohibitions hindered importation. A decree of the Spanish governor Galvez in 1782 forbade further importation of slaves from the island of Martinique because "these negroes are too much given to voodooism and make the lives of the citizens unsafe." In 1792 slaves from Saint-Domingue were also banned, though some were allowed to enter when their masters were granted asylum at the outbreak of the Haitian Revolution. In 1803 the United States acquired Louisiana and the ban on West Indian slaves was lifted. The largest influx of emigrants from Haiti occurred in 1809, when planters who had fled to Cuba to escape the revolution in Saint-Domingue were forced to emigrate again by France's declaration of war against Spain. It is estimated that New Orleans at that time received about two thousand slaves and an equal number of free people of color. Together with the earlier slave population of Arada or of Dahomean origin this group of Haitian refugees continued to observe the African tradition of *vaudou*.[77]

The few rather sensational accounts of voodoo services in New Orleans give the impression that voodoo was a monolithic snake cult, but there are hints that other *vodun* of the Dahomean pantheon survived besides Damballa, who was known as Damballa Wedo or Li Grand Zombi. One of Robert Tallant's informants, Josephine Green, recalled her mother's account of the time she saw the famous voodoo queen Marie Laveau:

> My ma seen her . . . It was back before the war what they had her wit' the Northerners. My ma heard a noise on Frenchman Street where she lived at and she start to go outside. Her pa say, "Where you goin'? Stay in the house!" She say, "Marie

Laveau is comin' and I gotta see her." She went outside and here come Marie Laveau wit' a big crowd of people followin' her . . . All the people wit' her was hollerin' and screamin', "We is goin' to see Papa Limba! We is goin' to see Papa Limba!" My grandpa go runnin' after my ma then, yellin at her, "You come on in here Eunice! Don't you know Papa Limba is the devil?" But after that my ma find out Papa Limba meant St. Peter, and her pa was jest foolin' her.[78]

Papa Limba is Legba, who in Haiti, as noted above, is frequently identified with St. Peter. The role of St. Peter-Legba is revealed in part of an old voodoo song remembered by another of Tallant's informants, Mary Ellis. The song went:

St. Peter, St. Peter, open the door,
I'm callin' you, come to me!
St. Peter, St. Peter, open the door . . . [79]

Mary Ellis also recounted that "Marie Laveau used to call St. Peter somethin' like "Laba." She called St. Michael "Daniel Blanc," and St. Anthony "Yon Sue." (Agasu?)[80] In her novel *An Angel by Brevet* (1904), Helen Pitkin described several voodoo meetings which, though "written in the form of fiction," were, she claimed, "accurate, being an exact reproduction of what she herself" saw or heard from her servants. In the service there are songs to Liba (St. Peter), Blanc Dani (St. Michael), and Vert Agoussou.[81] (In Dahomey, Agoussou is a god of special significance to the royal line.) Moreover, if Courlander is correct, the vodun Ogun Feraille "survived until recent times in Louisiana as Joe Feraille."[82] It seems, therefore, that along with Damballa Wedo, identified as Blanc Dani, at least Legba, Agoussou, and perhaps Ogun Feraille, were remembered and worshiped in New Orleans in the nineteenth century. As in Haiti, African gods were syncretized with Catholic saints and were associated with certain colors. It is possible that other gods existed in the voodoo pantheon which were not reported by extant sources, and that the outside observers who left accounts saw only the tip of the iceberg of voodoo belief and practice.

Marie Laveau. Reprinted, by permission, from the Collections of the Louisiana State Museum.

The voodoo cult in New Orleans came under the sway of a succession of strong leaders who traded their powers of magic for profit and prestige. By means of charms, amulets, and potions they claimed to predict the future and manipulate the present. Under the strong leadership of priestesses such as Sanite Dede and especially the two Marie Laveaus, mother and daughter, voodoo enjoyed a great deal of influence among the black and white citizens of New Orleans throughout most of the nineteenth century. The long reign of the two Maries stretched from 1830 to the 1880s and included a system of domestic spies among the servant class to keep Marie informed of important secrets. An annual voodoo celebration was held (on St. John's Eve) at Bayou St. John or on the banks of Lake Pontchatrain and the press was occasionally invited.[83]

Behind or apart from all these public aspects were the authentic and secret rituals of the voodoo cult of which very little in the way of description has endured. There are no accounts of New Orleans voodoo services in the eighteenth century, only two of voodoo worship in the early nineteenth century, and one for the late nineteenth century. Apart from newspaper reports which "exposed" the sensational aspects of public voodoo "shows," these three accounts form the basis for almost all descriptions of voodoo worship in New Orleans.[84] Each account mentions the presence of a snake representing the god Li Grand Zombi; drumming, singing, dancing; possession, which usually begins when the priestess comes into contact with the snake god; oracular statements by the possessed priestess and priest; possession of the devotees; the pouring of rum or other liquors as a libation to the god; the spewing of liquor from the mouth of the priest as a form of blessing; Catholic syncretistic elements such as candles, an altar, prayers to the Virgin. All of these elements are characteristic of the Haitian's Afro-Catholic synthesis as well.

By the twentieth century, although voodoo as a cult had been transformed into something different, it had not, however, vanished totally. In the 1930s Zora Neal Hurston underwent initiation into a voodoo cult in New Orleans at the hands of a priest named Turner who claimed to have received his *connaisance* from Marie Laveau herself.[85] It is apparent, however, that the rich pantheon and complex theology of Haitian *vaudou* did not survive in New Orleans voodoo; the panoply of gods was attenuated and the rites of worship corrupted.

The initial popularity of voodoo as an organized cult in New Orleans was in part due to the city's cosmopolitan and permissive atmosphere which lasted even after the American purchase.[86] It would be a mistake, however, to think that the voodoo cult existed only in New Orleans. Mary Owen stated that voodoo dances occurred in Missouri in the late nineteenth century. However, she offers no description of voodoo ritual and most of her article is concerned with voodoo as magic, or, as it was called, hoodoo.[87]

Hoodoo (also known as "conjure" or root work) was a system of magic, divination, and herbalism widespread among the slaves. Since New Orleans was looked upon as the prestigious center of conjuring,[88] the term "voodoo" was extended to conjuring and conjurers throughout the United States regardless of the term's original reference to African-Haitian cults. Hoodoo became the name for a whole area of folklore, the realm of signs, powers, and conjuring.[89] Because magical beliefs and folk superstitions reveal close similarities and parallels worldwide, it is difficult to separate the folk beliefs and practices of African origin from those of European origin. This very similarity, however, may have resulted in a mutual reinforcement and a common interchange of folk beliefs between slave and master. There are, at any rate, a number of hoodoo beliefs which are demonstrably African in origin. These beliefs can be seen, in some cases, to be vestiges of African beliefs removed from their fully intelligible theological and ritual contexts but still remembered. Or, as Herskovits phrased it, "minutiae can persist after the broader lines of ritual procedure and their underlying rationalizations have been lost."[90]

The movement from *vaudou* to hoodoo can serve perhaps as a paradigm of the larger history of African religion in the United

States. The way in which bits of African faith and practice persisted in folk beliefs and customs, though their original meaning had been lost, is evident in the following account from the New Orleans *Times-Democrat* of August 5, 1888. During a thunderstorm elderly Tante Dolores anxiously searched the house for some object. Not finding it, she ran to the yard. According to the article,

> Hither and thither she ran in rapid quest, until at last she stumbled upon the object of her search, no less a thing than an axe for chopping wood . . . a bright expression of joy irradiated her face.

Seizing the ax and raising it over her head, "she made pass after pass in the very face of the rushing current, as if chopping some invisible thing in twain." When the wind suddenly abated she returned to the house in triumph, stating that it never failed her if she "jest got there in time enough."[91]

A similar custom among Mississippi black folk was noted by Puckett:

> . . . foreign to European thought is the Southern Negro custom of going out into the yard and chopping up the ground with an ax when a storm threatens. This is supposed to "cut de storm in two" and so stop it. Others stick a spade in the ground to split the cloud, or simply place an ax in the corner of the house.[92]

The use of the ax as an antidote to the storm is significant, since the sacred emblem of the West African god of thunder and lightning, Shango, is an ax; but equally significant is the fact that the African theological background has disappeared and what remains is a folk custom. There is perhaps a trace of the thunderstones hurled by Shango in the belief, as told to Puckett by an old "conjure doctor" in Mississippi, that "the Indian arrowheads often found in the locality were not made by man at all, but were fashioned by God out of thunder and lightning."[93] It was also a common saying in New Orleans "that when it thunders, *Le Bon Dieu* is rolling his stones."[94]

As seen previously, equestrian imagery is commonly used in Africa and Latin America to describe the relationship between a god and the devotee he mounts and rides in possession. The onset of possession in voodoo rituals in New Orleans was called, according to Castellanos, *monter voudou*.[95] A relic of this imagery can be seen in the term used by blacks in Mississippi for conjurers— "horses."[96]

In Africa and Latin America the seat of possession is often thought to be the head of the devotee. Thus, in Haiti, the *loa* of a deceased person must be removed from the corpse's head. The conjurer in late-nineteenth-century Missouri was said to be one that was "strong in the head."[97] In Africa a charm was regarded as having a spirit of its own and as having taboos which its user had to observe if it were to work. Mary Owen, speaking of a charm owned by Aunt Mymee, remarked that occasionally this "luck ball," worn under the right arm, was given a drink of whiskey. Mymee's charm was called "Lil Mymee," perhaps reflecting a multiple or complex soul concept, similar to the African notion that one's guardian soul has to be fed to keep it strong.[98]

The use of charms and counter charms, to harm or to ward off harm, is an essential trait of conjuring. Materials of great power for "fixing" or conjuring someone are hair and nail clippings, a piece of clothing or personal object belonging to the victim, dirt from a person's footprint, and, especially, grave dirt. Powders, roots, and herbs of various sorts are used to cause or to cure illness, since sudden sickness, physical and mental, is often viewed as the result of being "fixed" by someone who bears ill-will toward the sufferer. This view of misfortune reflects the traditional African perception of illness.

A continuation of African belief may lie behind the statement of Mississippi black folk that the spirit of a tree can speak to men. Indeed, it is not only trees that have spirits; everything does. Ruth Bass writes that an old Mississippi conjuror asked her, "What is in the jimson-weed that cures asthma if it isn't the spirit of the weed? What is that in the buckeye that can drive off rheumatism unless it's spirit?" She adds that he assured her that everything has spirit. To prove this, he said he could take her to a certain spring that was haunted by the ghost of a bucket, and he asked her: "Now if that bucket didn't have a spirit, where did its ghost come from?"[99]

The belief that a person's spirit wanders while the body sleeps was also a part of the lore of African black folk. "Pepul's sperrits wander at night an' effen dey's woke too sudden like de sperrit is likely tuh be left out walkin'."[100] For this reason, it was dangerous to sweep dirt out of the door after sunset lest you sweep out someone's spirit.[101]

African belief in the special power of twins, and of the person born next after twins, lasted in the United States. Loudell Snow interviewed a present-day voodoo practitioner, who explained to him one theory of how she came by her powers.

> I had two brothers, they twins. And I were born behind the twins. Some people believe that twins have the gift, one of 'em. Some people say that I have the gift because I were born behind two twins. But I don't know. I always had the *urge* that I cure anything! I've always felt like that.[102]

While a fully developed cult of the ancestors did not persist in the United States, certain African funerary customs did remain. In Mississippi, for example, it was believed that the spirits of the dead roam on Halloween—a Western belief—but dinners were cooked for these spirits. Ruth Bass reported that "two persons must cook the supper, without speaking and without using salt in any form . . . This food is served on the table with necessary plates and spoons and left all night. Sometime during the night the essence or spirit of the food is eaten by the . . . hungry spirits."[103] Similarly, in the Sea Islands, there were those "sut put a dish uh food out on the poach fuh the spirit, but some of em take cooked food tuh the grave an leave it theah fuh the spirit."[104] The African custom of decorating a grave with the personal belongings of the deceased was also common in the rural South. Cups,

African grave decoration, Congo. Reprinted from *Century Magazine* 41, no. 6 (April 1891): 827.

Afro-American grave decoration, South Carolina. Photograph by Doris Ulmann. Reprinted by permission from the Doris Ulmann Collection, University of Oregon Library.

saucers, bottles, pipes, and other effects were left for the spirit of the deceased; frequently these items were broken or cracked in order to free their spirits and thereby enable them to follow the deceased.[105] Another reason for placing the personal belongings of the deceased on his grave was to "lay the spirit." Sarah Washington, an informant for the Georgia Writers' Project study, *Drums and Shadows*, speculated: "I dohn guess yuh be bodduh much by duh spirits ef yuh gib em a good fewnul an put duh tings wut belong tuh em on top uh duh grave," because the spirits don't have to come back for them. After her former master had died, one of the ex-slaves on Frances Butler Leigh's plantation placed a basin, water, and several towels on his grave, explaining, "If massa's spirit come, I want him see dat old Nanny not forget how he call every morning for water for wash his hands . . . " Frances Butler Leigh records this incident as a mark of respect and affection shown by the former slave for her old master. It might be interpreted as well as an attempt to allay the ghost of the former master once and for all, so that Nanny need not be bothered with him ever again.[106]

Among the black folk of the United States, the West Indies, and West Africa it is commonly held that the crossroads are places of peculiar power for the exercise of evil magic. Another belief common to all three areas is the notion that a chicken with frizzy feathers can scratch up any harmful charms planted in its owner's yard.[107]

Belief in the power of witches to leave their bodies at night and ride their victims was common among black Americans, West Indians, and Africans. It was thought that salt or red pepper sprinkled on the skin of the absent witch would prevent her from reentering her body.[108]

Many Afro-American witchcraft beliefs are European in origin. As such, they are a prime example of an area where there is a fusion of African and European folklore. The capacity of folk beliefs from different peoples to parallel and mutually influence one another makes the enterprise of separating one from another not only difficult but also artificial and speculative. Here, perhaps, is a fitting place to end the search for Africanisms in black religion in the United States.

The resolution of the Herskovits-Frazier debate lies in recognizing the true aspects of both positions. It is not a debate with a winner and a loser, for using differing perspectives, both are right. Herskovits was right in demolishing the myth of the Negro past, in suggesting topics for future research and in demonstrating the mutual influence of cultures in the acculturative process. His theory of reinterpretation as a factor in cultural contact is an advance over the notion that a people's beliefs, values, and behavioral patterns simply disappeared in the face of systematic oppression. He did succeed in demonstrating that elements of African culture survived slavery in the United States. It is true that he sometimes overstated his case. But it is also true that critics have caricatured his position and failed to appreciate some of his subtler arguments.

On the other hand, Frazier was also right. He was right in challenging excesses in Herskovits' argument, in posing the question of African survivals in terms of significance or meaning and in keeping sight of the real differences between Afro-American cultures in the United States and elsewhere in the hemisphere. If he tended to undervalue instances of African survivals in the United States, he did maintain that the new situation was important in influencing slaves to develop a new world view and a new culture. While it is true that Africa influenced black culture in the United States, including black religion, it is also true that African theology and African ritual did not endure to the extent that they did in Cuba, Haiti, and Brazil. In the United States the gods of Africa died.

Why the gods died, why African theology and ritual did not survive here as elsewhere in the New World are questions which impinge on the developing field of study known as comparative slavery, an area which involves ethnography, sociology, economics, demography, and history. A great deal of comparative study remains to be done from the perspectives of all these disciplines. Until such study is more advanced than it is at the present time, only tentative conclusions can be reached about the discrepancy between African retentions in Latin America and the United States.

Hemispheric Perspectives: Differing Contexts

Why have African gods and rituals been able to survive so vigorously in several countries but not in the United States? To answer this question a number of reasons have been suggested. One explanation is that Catholicism was more conducive to the survival of African religion than was Protestanism. Though this explanation is only partial, it has some validity. As noted previously, certain customs of Catholicism proved to be supportive of some practices of African religions among the slaves of the French, Spanish, and Portuguese colonies. In Haiti, Cuba, and Brazil, Catholic devotion to the Blessed Virgin and to the saints offered a rich context for syncretism with the gods of Africa. The use of sacramentals (blessed objects), such as statues, pictures, candles, incense, holy water, rosaries, vestments, and relics, in Catholic ritual was more akin to the spirit of African piety than the sparseness of Puritan America, which held such objects to be idolatrous. Holy days, processions, saints' feasts, days of fast and abstinence were all recognizable to the African who had observed the sacred days, festivals, and food taboos of his gods.

Moreover, the Catholic Church, in Brazil and Cuba, presented the slaves with an institutional mechanism for the preservation of African religion in the organization of religious fraternities. To the extent that religious brotherhoods were organized around groups of slaves from the same or neighboring geographical areas of Africa, they offered an opportunity for regroupment and allowed the slaves and freedmen to preserve particular African customs and, to a limited degree, languages. They also provided a structure for cult organization and a covert setting for syncretisms of African and Catholic devotions. Herbert S. Klein, investigating the brotherhoods in Cuba, reveals their role in preserving African customs:

> . . . the African cofradias [confraternities] played a vital role in the social life of both slaves and freedmen, with their own saints and special functions in various holy marches and carnivals. Usually organized along lines of regional African origins, with its members coming from the same *nacion* . . . these associations were both of a religious and strongly benevolent nature . . . In the great religious processions the Negro cabildos played an increasingly important part. Although outright African fetishes were quickly prohibited from display, the local saints and virgins showed so much influence of African mythology and even of African costume that these displays often tended to perpetuate pre-New World patterns and beliefs.[109]

The nature, then, of Catholic piety with its veneration of saints, use of sacramentals, and organization of religious fraternities among the slaves offered a supportive context for the continuity of African religious elements in recognizable form. In contrast, American Evangelical Protestantism, with its emphasis on biblical preaching, inward conversion, and credible accounts of the signs of grace, was not as conducive to syncretism with African theology and ritual. The contrast between Catholic America and Protestant America as an explanation for African retentions must not be pressed too far, for in Jamaica, for example, Cumina, Pocomania, and Revival groups represent clear syntheses of Protestant and African religions (with some additions from Catholicism). In more subtle form the Spiritual Baptists, or Shouters, of Trinidad also prove the ability of Afro-Americans to continue some African-style customs along with a fundamentalistic Protestanism. Conversely, Afro-Americans in Louisiana were able to preserve only a vestige of the African pantheons and rituals (as far as can be determined), despite the presence of Catholicism during the periods of French and Spanish rule. Even the attenuated voodoo cult in Louisiana owed its strength to the influx of refugees from

Saint-Domingue (now Haiti). It appears that factors other than religious differences must be taken into account.

Demographic factors also determined differences in degrees of African retention in Latin and British America. As both Frazier and Herskovits observed, the ratio of blacks to whites was much greater on the plantations of Latin America than it was on the plantations of the United States. In the tropics large plantations were worked by huge gangs of slaves, but in the United States the large plantation with hundreds of slaves was relatively rare. In the American South, where average slave population was comparatively small, contact between whites and blacks was more frequent than was usual in French, Spanish, and Portuguese colonies or, for that matter, in the British West Indies. Herskovits, using data from U.B. Phillips, summarized this distinction in the following statement:

> In the earliest days, the number of slaves in the U.S. in proportion to their masters was extremely small, and though as time went on thousands and tens of thousands of slaves were brought to satisfy the demands of the southern plantations, nonetheless the Negroes lived in constant association with whites to a degree not found anywhere else in the New World.[110]

As a matter of fact, in the Sea Islands, where the opposite conditions prevailed—a large slave population isolated from contact with white culture—the strongest incidence of African retentions in the United States were found. In comparison with slaves of the Piedmont area, the coastal and Sea Island blacks were far less acculturated to white America until fairly recent times.[111]

In addition, Curtin's census injects a further demographic factor into the discussion of differences between the slave population in the United States and tropical America. The distribution of Africans imported into New World slavery was not uniform throughout the hemisphere. Once again, the United States was unique. Of the total number of 9,566,000 African slaves imported into America from the beginning of the trade to 1861, only about

427,000 went to England's colonies on the North American continent and to the United States. (The figure includes 28,000 imported by French and Spanish Louisiana.) Thus the United States and Canada imported only 4½ percent of the total number of Africans imported into the New World.[112] A clearer picture of this inconsistent distribution emerges when importation figures are linked with the geographical areas of the importing colonies. Using Curtin's figures, C. Vann Woodward states that:

> The islands of the Greater Antilles . . . with an area roughly one third that of Texas, imported nearly six times the slaves landed in the entire territory of the United States. Of these islands, Saint Domingue . . . by 1794, had imported 864,000 or more than twice the total number of the United States. Jamaica had taken in 748,000 by the end of the legal trade in 1808, and Cuba which continued to import Africans for another half century or more, received 702,000. In fact, Cuba took in more after 1808 than the United States received in all.[113]

Brazil, roughtly comparable in size to the continental United States plus Alaska, imported approximately 3,647,000 slaves, eight and a half times the number that the United States received. Thus, comparatively speaking, "the United States was only a marginal recipient of slaves from Africa."[114]

The amazing and as yet unexplained demographic fact, however, is the rate of natural increase of the U.S. slave population. By the time of emancipation in 1865 the number of slaves in the United States had grown to above four million, a figure ten times the number imported from abroad. In contrast, Saint-Domingue, which had imported 864,000 Africans, had by the end of the slave trade and of slavery in 1794 a slave population of 480,000. In 1834 emancipation freed 781,000 slaves in the British West Indies, but 1,665,000 had been imported during the centuries of slavery. Jamaica's freedmen numbered 311,000, though 748,000 Africans had been brought in as slaves. By the end of slavery in the Dutch colonies there was a freed slave population no larger than 20 percent of an estimated half million that had been imported.

Another method of demonstrating the uniqueness of the growth rate of the U.S. slave population is to make a comparison of modern racial statistics. Allowing for the problems involved in the procedure—such as the difficulty in identifying race—it appears that by the mid-twentieth century North America held 31.1 percent of the New World population of African descent, despite the fact that North America accounted for only 4½ percent of the total figure for Africans imported. In comparison, the Caribbean Islands, which had imported 43 percent, accounted for only 20 percent of the Afro-American population by mid-century; and Cuba, with 7.3 percent of the imports held 3 percent of the New World Negro population. Brazil, which had imported the largest number, comprising 38.1 percent, contained 36.6 percent by mid-century.[115]

If Afro-Brazilians had increased at the rate of the U.S. Negro population, they would have totaled 127,645,000 by the mid-twentieth century, twice the number of Afro-Americans estimated for the whole Western hemisphere. Instead the figure was 17,529,000. At the U.S. rate of increase, Afro-Cubans would have numbered 24,570,000 by mid-century rather than the actual 1,224,000.[116]

Thus the slave population of the British continental colonies and the United States had a rate of natural increase unique in the hemisphere. In Brazil and the West Indies the mortality rate of slaves for long periods of slavery exceeded the birth rate by wide margins. Why was this so? Planters in Brazil and the West Indies during some periods of the Atlantic slave trade found it more economical to supply their demand for slaves by importation rather than by encouraging them to reproduce. The cheapness of supply led them to regard slave reproduction with indifference if not hostility. According to Woodward, "Brazilian planters took no pains to balance the sexes among slaves and imported three or four times as many males as females."[117] In the United States the ratio of female to male slaves was nearer parity. The high mortality rate of slaves in Latin America also was due to decimation by tropical diseases, which, of course, were less rampant in more temperate climes. It must be admitted, however, that the reasons so far suggested do not explain adequately the completely atypical growth of the slave population in the United States.

Thus the bulk of the slave population in North America was native-born. In the United States the influx of Africans and of African cultural influence was far less extensive than in the Caribbean and in Brazil. In North America a relatively small number of Africans found themselves enslaved amid a rapidly increasing native-born population whose memories of the African past grew fainter with each passing generation.

The character of the religious milieu, the average number of slaves on plantations, and the number of Africans in the slave population were all factors in the survival or loss of African culture. In the United States all these factors tended to inhibit the survival of African culture and religion. It was not possible to maintain the rites of worship, the priesthood, or the "national" identities which were the vehicles and supports for African theology and cult organization. Nevertheless, even as the gods of Africa gave way to the God of Christianity, the African heritage of singing, dancing, spirit possession, and magic continued to influence Afro-American spirituals, ring shouts, and folk beliefs. That this was so is evidence of the slaves' ability not only to adapt to new contexts but to do so creatively.

II
"The Invisible Institution"

3
Cathechesis and Conversion

Go ye therefore, and teach all nations, baptizing them in the name of the Father, and of the Son, and of the Holy Ghost . . .

MATTHEW 28:19

FROM THE very beginning of the Atlantic slave trade, conversion of the slaves to Christianity was viewed by the emerging nations of Western Christendom as a justification for enslavement of Africans. When Portuguese caravels returned from the coast of West Africa with human booty in the fifteenth century, Gomes Eannes De Azurara, a chronicler of their achievements, observed that "the greater benefit" belonged not to the Portuguese adventurers but to the captive Africans, "for though their bodies were now brought into some subjection, that was a small matter in comparison of their souls, which would now possess true freedom for evermore."[1]

Pangs of guilt over the cruelty inherent in enslaving fellow human beings were assuaged by emphasizing the grace of faith made available to Africans, who otherwise would die as pagans. Azurara's pity was aroused by the tragic scene of a shipload of captives being divided and parceled out to their owners.

> But what heart could be so hard as not to be pierced with piteous feeling to see that company? For some kept their heads low and their faces bathed in tears, looking one upon another; others stood groaning very dolorously, looking up to the height of heaven . . . crying out loudly, as if asking help of the Father of Nature; others struck their faces with the palms of their hands, throwing themselves at full length upon the ground; others made their lamentations in the manner of a dirge, after the custom of their country. And though we could not understand the words of their language, the sound of it right well accorded with the measure of their sadness. But to increase their sufferings . . . those who had charge of the division of the captives . . . began to separate one from another . . . to part fathers from sons, husbands from wives, brothers from brothers. No respect was shown either to friends or relations, but each fell where his lot took him. . . . And you who are so busy in making that division of the captives, look with pity upon such misery; and see how they cling one to the other, so that you can hardly separate them.

Azurara took solace in the fact that these slaves benefited not only spiritually but also materially from contact with Western civilization.

> And so their lot was now quite the contrary of what it had been; since before they had lived in perdition of soul and body; of their souls, in that they were yet pagans, without the clearness and the light of the holy faith; and of their bodies, in that they lived like beasts, without any custom of reasonable beings—for they had no knowledge of bread or wine, and they were without the covering of clothes, or the lodgement of houses; and worse than all, they had no understanding of good, but only knew how to live in bestial sloth.[2]

Azurara's rationalization, stated in mid-fifteenth century, was to be repeated for over four centuries by successive generations of Christian apologists for slavery.

Religious Instruction

England, no less than Spain, Portugal, the Netherlands, and France, proclaimed missionary zeal as an important motive for colonizing the New World. The duty of Christianizing slaves as well as Indians was urged upon the Council for Foreign Plantations by Charles II in 1660. His instructions to the council read in part:

> And you are to consider how such of the Natives or such as are purchased by you from other parts to be servants or slaves may best be invited to the Christian Faith, and be made capable of being baptized thereunto, it being to the honor of our Crowne and of the Protestant Religion that all persons in any of our Dominions should be taught the knowledge of God, and be made acquainted with the misteries of Salvation.[3]

Instructions were sent out from the Crown to colonial governors, such as Culpeper of Virginia in 1682 and Dongan of New York in 1686, to do all within their power to "facilitate and encourage the Conversion of Negroes and Indians" to Christianity.[4] The task was all the more important because England feared that Catholic Spain and France were outstripping her in missionary zeal—a serious weakness in the contest for empire as well as a failure of the Protestant cause.[5]

Despite the widely held justification of slavery as a means of spreading the gospel, and despite proclamations of the duty of Christian colonists to evangelize the heathen, the process of slave conversion was blocked by major obstacles, not the least of which was the antipathy of the colonists themselves. The economic profitability of his slaves, not their Christianization, held top priority for the colonial planter. Writing in 1682, John Barbot noted the indifference of slave owners to their Christian duty:

> ... Christians in America ... especially the Protestants ... take very little care to have their slaves instructed ... as if it were not a positive duty incumbent on them, by the precepts of Christianity. ... There, provided that the slaves can multiply, and work hard for the benefit of their masters, most men are well satisfied without the least thoughts of using their authority and endeavors to promote the good of the souls of those poor wretches.[6]

Morgan Godwin, an English divine who spent several years in Virginia, decried the priorities of the colonists in a sermon published in 1685 with the accusatory title "Trade preferr'd before Religion and Christ made to give place to Mammon."

One of the principal reasons for the refusal of English planters to allow their slaves to receive instructions was the fear that baptism would emancipate their slaves. The notion that if slaves were baptized, "they should, according to the laws of the *British* nation, and the canons of its church" be freed was legally vague but widely believed.[7] Repeatedly, would-be missionaries to the slaves complained that slaveholders refused them permission to catechize their slaves because baptism made it necessary to free them. Thus it seemed that the Christian commission to preach the gospel to all nations ran directly counter to the economic interest of the Christian slave owner. This dilemma was solved by colonial legislation. In 1664 the lower house of Maryland asked the upper house "to draw up an Act obliging negroes to serve *durante vita* . . . for the prevencion of the dammage Masters of such Slaves must susteyne by such Slaves pretending to be Christ[e]ned [;] And soe pleade the lawe of England."[8] By 1706 at least six colonial legislatures had passed acts denying that baptism altered the condition of a slave "as to his bondage or freedome." Virginia's was typical of the statutes enacted in expressing the hope "that diverse masters, freed from this doubt, may more carefully endeavor the propagation of christianity," among their slaves.[9] But there still remained other impediments to the religious instruction of the slaves which were more difficult to remove.

Even after colonial assemblies had declared baptism to be no threat to a planter's legal right to hold Africans in perpetual bondage, the process of religious instruction which had to precede baptism was seen by many slaveholders as an economic detriment. For a slave to be catechized adequately took time. The plantation work schedule gave the slave little leisure for religious instruction. Sunday was the only feasible day for instruction. Yet one of the constant complaints of missionaries was that slaves had to work on the Sabbath either for their masters or, when allotted individual plots, for themselves. A letter to the London secretary of the Society for the Propagation of the Gospel from the Clergy of South Carolina in 1713 complained of "many planters who, to free themselves from the trouble of feeding and clothing their slaves, allow them one day in the week to clear ground, and plant for themselves as much as will clothe and subsist them and their families."[10] The "one day in the week" allowed was usually Sunday. Even when slaves were not forced to work on the Sabbath, finding time for religious instruction was problematic, since the minister had "work enough from the white folk on his hands."[11] Moreover, the slaves frequently used whatever leisure time they had for visiting, dancing, and merriment—activities which seemed to the missionary to be profanations of the Lord's day. Exhorted by missionaries in America and instructed by officials in

London, some governors urged colonial legislatures to pass bills preventing masters from working slaves on Sunday or otherwise blocking their attendance at Sabbath worship.[12] While legislation might have modified a planter's behavior, it did not necessarily alter his attitude against the instruction of slaves.

Masters also objected to slave conversion because they believed that Africans were too "brutish" to be instructed. In part this objection was based on the linguistic and cultural barriers between African-born ("Guinea") slaves and English colonials. Even missionaries despaired of overcoming the linguistic and cultural gap and directed their attention primarily to children and to American-born slaves, who had some facility in English. Toward the end of the seventeenth century Col. Francis Nicholson, governor of Virginia, was instructed by London to recommend to the Virginia Assembly that it pass laws ensuring the education of Indians and Negroes in the Christian faith. The Virginia House of Burgesses replied in 1699 to Nicholson that "the negroes born in this country are generally baptised and brought up in the Christian religion; but for negroes imported hither, the gross bestiality and rudeness of their manners, the variety and strangeness of their languages, and the weakness and shallowness of their minds, render it in a manner impossible to make any progress in their conversion."[13]

Some planters went further than the Virginia legislators and argued that the Africans were incapable of instruction, not only because of cultural differences but because of racial distinctions. The eminent philosopher Bishop Berkeley complained in 1731 about the American colonists that their "ancient antipathy to the Indians . . . together with an irrational contempt for the Blacks, as creatures of another species, who had no right to be instructed or admitted to the sacraments; have proved a main obstacle to the conversion of these poor people."[14] Repeatedly the clergy had to remind their charges that black people were equal to whites in the sight of God. Francis Le Jau, missionary to Goose Creek, South Carolina, reported in 1709 that "Many Masters can't be persuaded that Negroes and Indians are otherwise than Beasts, and use them like such," but "I endeavor to let them know better things."[15] In a letter "To the Masters and Mistresses of Families in the English Plantations Abroad," published in 1727 and distributed by the thousands in the colonies, Edmund Gibson, bishop of London, exhorted colonial slaveholders "to Encourage and Promote the Instruction of their Negroes in the Christian Faith" and "to consider Them, not merely as Slaves, and upon the same Level with Labouring Beasts, but as *Men*-Slaves and *Women*-Slaves, who have the same Frame and Faculties with yourselves, and have Souls capable of being made eternally happy, and Reason and Understanding to receive Instruction in order to it."[16]

Morgan Godwin argued the humanity of slaves on anthropological grounds: "Methinks that the consideration of the shape and figure of our Negroes Bodies, their Limbs and Members, their Voice and Countenance in all things according with other Men's together with their Risibility and Discourse (man's peculiar Faculties) should be sufficient conviction."[17] Cotton Mather, in his tract *The Negro Christianized* (1706), with Puritan thoroughness ranged scriptural verse and logical argument against those who denied the Negro's humanity. "Show your Selves Men," Mather challenged, "and let *Rational Arguments* have their Force upon you, to make you treat, not as *Bruits* but as *Men*, those Rational Creatures whom God has made your *Servants*." Later on in the same tract Mather forcibly argued:

> One Table of the Ten Commandments, has this for the Sum of it; *Thou Shalt Love thy Neighbour as thy Self.* Man, Thy *Negro* is thy *Neighbour.* Twere an Ignorance, unworthy of a Man to imagine otherwise. Yea, if thou dost grant *That God hath made of one Blood, all Nations of men;* he is thy *Brother,* too.

At this point clerical apologists for the slave's humanity began to converge on what the planter saw as dangerous ground. To urge the slave's humanity was one thing; to declare his "equal Right *with other Men, to the* Exercises and Privileges *of Religion*" was another.[18] The danger beneath the arguments for slave conversion which many masters feared was the egalitarianism implicit in Christianity. The most serious obstacle to the missionary's access to the slaves was the slaveholder's vague awareness that a Christian slave would have some claim to fellowship, a claim that threatened the security of the master-slave hierarchy. Even after other fears had been removed by legislation or by argument, unease with the concept of spiritual equality between master and slave caused slave owners to reject the idea of Christianizing their slaves. Peter Kalm, a Swedish traveler in America from 1748–50, perceptively described the masters' fears that Christianity would disrupt their relationship with their slaves:

> It is likewise greatly to be pitied, that the masters of these negroes in most of the English colonies take little care of their spiritual welfare, and let them live on in their Pagan darkness. There are even some, who would be very ill pleased at, and would by all means hinder their negroes from being instructed in the doctrines of Christianity; to this they are partly led by the conceit of its being shameful, to have a spiritual brother or sister among so despicable a people; partly by thinking that they should not be able to keep their negroes so meanly afterwards; and partly through fear of the negroes growing too proud, on seeing themselves upon a level with their masters in religious matters.[19]

A continual complaint of masters was that Christianity would ruin their slaves by making them "saucy," since they would begin to think themselves equal to white folks. Bishop Thomas Secker, in an anniversary sermon preached before the Society for the Propagation of the Gospel (S.P.G.) in 1740 or 1741, diagnosed the basic cause of the planters' opposition: " . . . some, it may be feared, have been averse to their slaves becoming Christians, because, after that, no Pretence will remain for not treating them like Men."[20] Two white parishioners of St. James Church in Goose Creek, South Carolina, expressed their aversion to Christian slaves to Francis Le Jau, their minister. In a letter dated 1711 Le Jau reported: "A few days ago I heard of some strange reasoning of my Neighbors. [W]hat, s[ai]d a Lady Considerable enough in any other respect but in that of sound knowledge; Is it Possible that any of my slaves could go to Heaven, & must I see them there[;]; a young Gent had s[ai]d sometime before that he is resolved never to come to the Holy Table while slaves are Rec[eive]d there."[21]

Slaveholders feared that Christianity would make their slaves not only proud but ungovernable, and even rebellious. The Reverend John Bragg of Saint Ann's Parish in Virginia, for example, complained in 1724 that of the many Negro slaves in his parish very few had been baptized during his fifteen-year tenure, "nor any means used for their Conversion, the owners Generaly not approving thereof, being led away by the notion of their being and becoming worse slaves when Christians."[22] In reply, almost every apologist for the evangelization of the slaves felt obliged to prove that Christianity would actually make better slaves. The answer penned by the bishop of London in 1727 was typical:

> And so far is Christianity from discharging Men from the Duties of the Station and Condition in which it found them, that it lays them under stronger Obligations to perform those Duties with the greatest Diligence and Fidelity; not only from the Fear of Men, but from a Sense of Duty to God, and the Belief and Expectation of a future Account.[23]

Missionaries appealed to the profit motive by pointing out that converted slaves "do better for their Masters profit than formerly, for they are taught to serve out of Christian Love and Duty."[24] The missionaries labored to build a stout wall between spiritual and temporal equality and to uphold the doctrine expressed in an oft-quoted passage: "The Scripture, far from making any Alteration in Civil Rights, expressly directs, that *every Man abide in the Condition wherein he is called, with great Indifference of Mind* concerning outward circumstances."[25] Thus, as Winthrop Jordan has aptly put it, "These clergy men had been forced by the circumstance of racial slavery in America into propagating the Gospel by presenting it as an attractive device for slave control."[26]

The opposition of slaveholders was not the only factor impairing the conversion of slaves; indeed, not all slaveholders opposed conversion. In 1724 William Black, who had labored for sixteen years as minister in Accomako, Virginia, informed the bishop of London that he had baptized about two hundred slaves since his arrival and had leave to "instruct them at their Masters' houses."[27] Ebenezer Taylor, missionary to St. Andrew's Parish in South Carolina from 1711 to 1717, praised the efforts of two of his parishoners:

> Mrs. Haige and Mrs. Edwards, who came lately to this Plantation [Carolina], have taken extra-ordinary pains to instruct a considerble number of Negroes, in the principles of the Christian Religion, and to reclaim and reform them. The wonderful success they met with, in about half a year's time, encouraged me to go and to examine those Negroes, about their Knowledge in Christianity; they declared to me their Faith in the chief articles of our Religion, which they sufficiently explained; they rehearsed by heart, very distinctly, the Creed, the Lord's Prayer, and Ten Commandments; fourteen of them give me so great satisfaction, and were so desirous to be baptized, that I thought it my duty to do it on the last Lord's Day. I doubt not but these Gentlewomen will prepare the rest of them for Baptism in a little time; and I hope the good example of these two Gentlewomen will provoke at least some Masters and Mistresses, to take the same care and pains with their poor Negroes.[28]

Their efforts were indeed extraordinary when compared with the indifference of most masters. Part of the problem was the religious milieu itself. In the Southern colonies, which had the largest concentration of slaves, the religious situation for white colonists was unsettled. Clergy were in short supply. Even in Virginia, where the established Church of England was perhaps on its firmest footing, "in 1701 nearly half of the forty to forty-six parishes containing 40,000 people, were unsupplied with Clergy." Though the colony of Georgia had been divided into eight parishes, by 1769 there were only two churches built and they were a hundred and fifty miles apart. In 1701 "more than one-half of the 7,000 colonists" of South Carolina "(to say nothing of the negroes and Indians) were themselves living regardless of any religion, there being only one Church (at Charleston), no schools and few dissenting teachers of any kind." Samuel Frink, an S.P.G. missionary, said of the religious condition of the Georgia settlers:

> They seem in general to have but very little more knowledge of a Saviour than the aboriginal natives. Many hundreds of poor people, both parents and children, in the interior of the province, have no opportunity of being instructed in the principles of Christianity or even in the being of a God, any further than nature dictates.[29]

In 1724 Hugh Jones reported that North Carolina needed missionaries "not only for the Conversion of the *Indians* and *Baptism of Negroes* there, but for the Christening and Recovery to the Practical Profession of the Gospel great Numbers of English, that have but the bare name of God and Christ; and that too frequently in nothing but vain Swearing, Cursing and imprecations."[30] While ecclesiastical authorities undoubtedly overestimated the danger of Christian Englishmen reverting to paganism in the wilds of the North American frontier, it is true that the Southern colonists were in need of missionaries.

Where ministers were present, they found themselves tending parishes of vast size. Besides long distances to travel, danger from illness and disease, and the unsettled character of colonial life, the Anglican clergy were often dependent upon the local vestry, controlled by the planter class, for their livings and status. The power of the vestry can be seen from the frequent complaints of colonial clergymen that they were refused induction into their livings. One wrote an "Account of the State of the Church in Virginia" for the bishop of London in 1724 in which he outlined the situation: "I have never been inducted into my living. . . . the Parishioners are very defective being . . . adverse from . . . committing themselves solely to the care of one Shepherd, which may be informed from

their . . . dislike of Induction; so that Induction is very little practiced here. . . . That hereby they would reserve to themselves this
handle of restraint on the Ministry, of not being bound to a
Minister . . . lest he should afterwards prove disagreeable to them,
in which case they might the more easily cast him off for another
more suitable to their humour. . . . "[31] Because the closest bishop
was in London, the established church was in no position to
execute its policy with regard to slave conversion in the colonial
South.

A contemporary attempt to determine the religious situation in
the southern colonies, including the extent of instruction among
slaves, was undertaken by the bishop of London in 1724 by
means of a series of "Queries to be Answered by every Minister."
Among the questions was the following: "Are there any Infidels,
bond or free, within your Parish; and what means are used for
their conversion?" Of the written replies extant, thirty clergymen
from Virginia and nineteen from Maryland attempted to inform
the bishop about their efforts on behalf of the slaves. While several
claimed some limited success in instructing slaves and a very few
reported that slave baptisms were common, the majority of the
respondents were significantly vague about accomplishments,
proclaimed intentions of doing better, and offered much more
information about the problems involved in catechizing slaves
than about their own effectiveness. It appears from the responses
to the bishop's questionnaire that the only means used by the
majority of the clergy to convert slaves was Sunday preaching,
coupled with an occasional meeting for catechism lessons and
appeals to masters in instruct their slaves at home, appeals which
too often fell on deaf ears. A typical response was penned by
George Robertson, for thirty years pastor of Bristol Parish, on the
upper part of the James River in Virginia: "I have several times
exhorted their Masters to send such of them as could speak English to Church to be catechised but they would not. Some
masters instruct their Slaves at home and so bring them to baptism, but not many such." John Brunskill, who in 1724 had

ministered to Wilmington Parish in Virginia for over eight years, observed that without legal sanction the ministers' appeals carried little weight: "The Negroes . . . cannot I think, be said to be of any Religion for as there is no law of the Colony obliging their Masters or Owners to instruct them in the principles of Christianity and so they are hardly to be persuaded by the Minister to take so much pains with them, by which means the poor creatures generally live and die without it."[32]

The responses of colonial Maryland and Virginia clergymen to the bishop of London's "Queries" indicate that their commission to catechize the heathen, "bond or free," was severely hampered by the planters' reluctance and outright resistance, by the size of their parishes, by the scarcity of clergy, by linguistic and cultural difficulties with African-born slaves, by the absence of legal support, and by the sheer size of the task. It was clear that something more than ordinary preaching and appeals to masters to instruct their slaves was necessary if slaves were to be brought to Christianity in larger numbers in the colonial South.[33]

The difficulty of persuading slaveholding colonists in Virginia to take an interest in the conversion of their slaves is reflected in an unusual proposal drafted in 1724, a proposal which in effect offered to masters a tax break for instructing their slaves and bringing them to baptism:

> A PROPOSITION for encouraging the Christian Education of Indians, Negroes and Mulatto Children
> It being a duty of Christianity, very much neglected by masters and mistresses of this country to endeavour the good instruction and Education of their Heathen Slaves, in the Christian faith, the said duty being likewise earnestly recommended by his Majesty's Instructions for the facilitating thereof amongst the young slaves that are born among us (the old ones that are imported into the country by reason of their not understanding the Language being much more indocile). It is therefore humbly proposed that every Indian, negro or mulatto child that shall be baptized and afterwards brought to church and publicly catechised by the minister and in church

before the 14th year of his or her age, shall give a distinct
account of the Creed, Lord's Prayer and Ten Commandments
and whose master or mistress shall receive a Certificate from
the minister that he or she hath so done, such Indian, negro or
mulatto child shall be exempted from paying all levies till the
age of 18 years, but whatsoever Indian, negro or mulatto child
shall not be baptized nor give such public account of his or
her faith, nor whose master or mistress receives no such
certificate as aforesaid shall pay levies at the age of 14 years for
it is humbly supposed the advantage of 4 years' difference in
levies will have great effects to this purpose.[34]

In Puritan New England, where religious life was more settled
and where slaves might have come into contact with an environment of strong religious nurture, there were comparatively few
slaves. New Englanders generally shared the attitudes of other
colonists concerning conversion of their slaves. In *Magnalia
Christi* (1702) Cotton Mather found it necessary to criticize those
Puritan slaveholders who "deride, neglect, and oppose all due
means of bringing their poor negroes unto our Lord." New England divines, such as Mather and John Eliot, who was a missionary to Indians as well as to Negroes, complained that the "English
used their Negro's but as their Horses or their *Oxen*, and that so
little care was taken about their immortal Souls."[35] Even though
the *Christian Directory* of the English Puritan theologian Richard
Baxter directed masters to "Make it your chief end in buying and
using slaves to win them to Christ and save their souls," many
New England colonists seemed to be more Yankee than Puritan
in carrying out the duties of their calling as slaveholders. In 1705
the *Athenian Oracle* sarcastically remarked: "Talk to a *Planter* of
the *Soul* of a *Negro* and he'll be apt to tell ye (or at least his
actions speak it loudly) that the body of one of them may be
worth twenty pounds; but the souls of an hundred of them would
not yield him one farthing."[36]

Some efforts were made, however. The first recorded instance
of a slave's baptism in New England occurred in 1641, when,
according to John Winthrop, "a Negro woman belonging to Rev.

Stoughton of Dorchester, Massachusetts, being well approved by divers years experience for sound knowledge and true godliness was received into the Church and baptized." John Eliot volunteered to instruct slaves once a week if masters would only send them to him. Mather organized a Society of Negroes in 1693 which met, with the permission of each slave's master, every Sunday evening. Mather drew up a rule of conduct for the society and on Sunday evenings the slaves heard a sermon and were taught to pray, sing and recite the catechism.[37]

A group of "ministers of the Gospel" petitioned the general court of Massachusetts in May of 1694 to pass a bill denying that baptism bestowed freedom to the slaves, though there is no record that the legislature heeded their memorial. The General Assembly of the Colony of Connecticut was asked to deliberate two issues concerning baptism of slaves in 1738: first, "whether the infant slaves of Christian masters may be baptized in their master's right, provided they suitably promise and engage to bring them up in the ways of religion"; and second, whether the masters were duty-bound to "offer such children [for baptism]" and make the aforesaid promise. The Assembly answered yes to both queries.[38]

In 1773 Rev. Samuel Hopkins of Newport, Rhode Island, hit upon a scheme to evangelize Africa with converted slaves from America. Hopkins persuaded Ezra Stiles to participate in his plan and they successfully sought funding. Two black members of Hopkins' church—one a slave, named Bristol Yamma, the other a freedman, John Quamino—were picked for training under the tutelage of President Witherspoon of the College of New Jersey. The Revolutionary War and Quamino's death in 1779 frustrated this project.[39] Those New England slaves who, like Phillis Wheatley, were regarded as members of the family, were included in family prayers, Bible reading, and religious instruction. One method of instruction consisted in the master or mistress examining a slave about the previous Sabbath's sermon. In New England meetinghouses the slaves listened to sermons segregated in galleries, corners, or rear pews. When black Puritans died they were still segregated from whites in graveyards. Black church members were generally not allowed to participate in church government. It is impossible to speak with accuracy about the number of slaves converted, but the most detailed history of the Negro in colonial New England concludes: "Although relatively larger numbers of slaves may have been Christianized in New England than in the plantation colonies, it is likely that at the end of the colonial era in 1776 a large proportion—possibly a majority—of the slaves in that section were still heathen."[40]

Presbyterian, Baptist and Methodist efforts to convert the slaves were primarily part of the revivalist fervor of the Great Awakening (which will be discussed later). Quakers, despite exhortations from George Fox in 1657 and William Edmundson in 1676 to instruct and educate their slaves, showed no great zeal to do so. Fox, in a tract entitled *Gospel Family Order*, reminded slaveholding Quakers that "Christ died for all . . . for the tawnies and for the blacks as well as for you that are called whites." Fox concluded not only that slaves should be instructed but that masters should "let them go free after a considerable term of years," and with some compensation for their labor.[41] Similarly, Edmundson in an open letter to Friends in America made a connection between spiritual and temporal freedom that most seventeenth-century Christians did not admit:

> And it would be acceptable with God, and answer the witness in all, if you did consider their condition of perpetual slavery, and make their conditions your own, and so fulfill the law of Christ. For perpetual slavery is an aggravation, and an oppression upon the mind, and hath a ground; and Truth is that which works the remedy, and breaks the yoke, and removes the ground. So it would do well to consider that they may feel, see, and partake of your liberty in the gospel of Christ . . . that they may see and know the difference between you and other people, and your self-denial may be known to all.

In a postscript Edmundson asked: "And many of you count it

unlawful to make slaves of the Indians: and if so, then why the Negroes?"[42]

In 1688 a group of Germantown, Pennsylvania, Friends passed a formal remonstrance against slavery to the local meeting. "Is there," they asked, "any [among us] that would be done or handled at this manner? viz., to be sold or made a slave for all the time of his life?"[43] From these tentative beginnings the Quaker antislavery witness grew to loud and forceful denunciations by Friends such as Ralph Sandiford, Benjamin Lay, John Woolman, and Anthony Benezet. However, very few American Negroes became members of the Society of Friends. Part of the explanation for this is that the Friends' antislavery stance denied them access to slaves. Because Quakers had a reputation for condemning slavery, the Virginia Legislature in 1672 forbade Friends to admit Negroes to their meetings. Another reason is the failure of Friends to proselyte slaves or free blacks. It was reported that when it came to religious instruction, Quakers in Delaware left their slaves to "the natural light." The prejudice of some Quakers against black candidates for admission caused the Philadelphia Yearly Meeting in 1796 to incorporate a rule into the Discipline which stated that applications for membership ought henceforth to be received "without respect of persons or color."[44]

English bishops challenged the Protestant colonists to live up to the example of the Catholic missions in evangelizing the Indians and the African slaves. Occasionally a missionary to the British colonies came across slaves who had been baptized by a French, Spanish, or Portuguese missionary. An S.P.G. missionary to South Carolina reported:

> I have in this parish a few negroe slaves and were born and baptized among the Portuguese, but speak very good English. They came to church and are well instructed so as to express a great desire to receive the communion amongst us. I proposed to them to declare openly their adjuring the errors of the Romish Church without which declaration I could not receive them. . . . I require of them their renouncing of those particu-

lar points, the chief of which is praying to the Saints and that they must not return to the Popish Worship in case they shou'd be sent to Medera again.[45]

Slaves in the British colonies of North America were not likely to be exposed to the "errors of the Romish Church" unless they lived in Maryland, the only colony with a sizable Catholic presence. Catholic settlers in Maryland, including Jesuits, owned slaves. The first estimate of the number of Catholic slaves was made in 1785 by John Carroll, superior of the American missions, in his report to Rome on the state of the Church in the United States. Carroll related that there were 15,800 Catholics in Maryland of whom more than three thousand were "slaves of all ages of African origin, called Negroes," and that in Pennslyvania there were about seven thousand Catholics, "very few of whom are negroes." Catholic efforts to convert slaves were debilitated by some of the same difficulties; such as the lack of clergy and the attitudes of slaveholders, faced by the Protestants. At the time of Carroll's report, nineteen priests in Maryland and five in Pennsylvania constituted the entire clergy for the Catholic Church in the United States. Of these twenty-four, two were over the age of seventy and three more were "very near that age." Carroll had heard that there were Catholics scattered in other states "who are utterly deprived of all religious ministry." The Catholic laity came under criticism for failing to instruct their slaves:

> The abuses which have grown among the Catholics are chiefly those which result from unavoidable intercourse with non-Catholics, and the example thence derived: namely . . . among other things a general lack of care in instructing their children and especially the Negro slaves in their religion; as these people are kept constantly at work, so that they rarely hear any instructions from the priest, unless they can spend a short time with one; and most of them are consequently very dull in faith and depraved in morals. It can scarcely be believed how much trouble and care they give the pastor of souls.[46]

Carroll's complaint, except for the sentence accusing non-Catholics of bad example, could have been written by any Protestant cleric.

In the Catholic colony of Louisiana, Bienville's *Code Noir* of 1724 required masters to instruct slaves in the doctrines of the Church. But there is little evidence that the French planters were any more diligent about catechizing slaves than were their English counterparts. In 1724, the very year in which the bishop of London questioned his American clergy about slave instruction, Father Raphael de Luxembourg, superior of the Capuchin missions in Louisiana, reported a number of obstacles to missionary work among the slaves. His report complained of conditions strikingly similar to those described by the Anglican clergy of Virginia. The Indian and Negro mission had been assigned to the Capuchins, but two years after their arrival in Louisiana in 1722 he still did not have missionaries enough to adequately minister to the French, let alone Indians and Negroes. According to Father Raphael, the distance of plantations from missionary stations, the need for boats in order to travel the waterways to those plantations where slaves were most numerous, and, worst of all, the general impiety of masters, some of whom forced slaves to work on Sundays and feast days severely restricted the Capuchin mission to the slaves.[47]

On the other hand, some Louisiana planters did cooperate with the missionaries and at least could not object, as did the English colonists, that baptism necessitated emancipation. It was by no means uncommon for masters and mistresses to stand sponsor for slave baptisms, and parish church registers of the colonial period indicate that baptisms of Negroes and mulattoes were frequent. In the Capuchin missions Holy Saturday and the Vigil of Pentecost were annual occasions for the baptism of large groups of slaves and free blacks. According to John Gillard, records of the St. Louis parish church list as many as seventy-five and a hundred blacks baptized in a single day. But baptism was one thing, instruction another. The very method of large-scale group baptism calls into question the thoroughness of instruction, particularly in the rural areas remote from churches and priests. In 1789 the Spanish government issued orders that planters contribute to support chaplains whose duties would include instruction of slaves upon the plantations. The planters objected that, as it was, there were not enough clergymen to fill the vacancies in the regular parishes, that they could not afford to support chaplains, and that plantations were too far apart for one person to serve as chaplain for several of them. As late as 1823, twenty years after the American acquisition of Louisiana, Father John Mary Odin, later archbishop of New Orleans, complained that still "in Lower Louisiana the French for the most part, do not wish you to speak of instructing their slaves or of giving them the sacraments of matrimony; they are often not even permitted to go to church." It was in the urban settlements that religious instruction for slaves became more feasible than it would be on the plantations for a long time. The stable presence of clergy, even though few in number, the existence of churches, and houses of religious afforded more opportunities for the urban slave to encounter formal religious instruction. In New Orleans, the Ursuline nuns, who arrived in the city in 1727, supplemented the efforts of the few priests to catechize the slaves and the free blacks. It appears that under the leadership of a succession of sisters the Ursuline Convent served as a center for the instruction of black Catholics in New Orleans from 1730 to 1824.[48] Generally, however, the instruction of slaves on the plantations of Catholic Louisiana was obstructed by the same circumstances that hindered the catechesis of slaves on the plantations of Protestant Virginia.

While there were individual clergymen who reprimanded the planters for neglecting the salvation of their servants and who attempted to evangelize slaves when possible, it was not until the organization of the Society for the Propagation of the Gospel in Foreign Parts that an institutional attempt was made to confront the task of slave conversion in English colonial America. The society was founded in London in 1701 as a missionary arm of the

Church of England to minister to the colonists of America and also to instruct the Indians and Negroes. Headed by the bishop of London, the society published tracts and sermons, sent out missionaries and catechists, sought funds in England to help support the missions in the Americas, and even ran a plantation with over 300 slaves in Barbados. Hampered by a lack of men and money, the S.P.G. missionaries had their hands full ministering to the needs of the white settlers. Nevertheless, some missionaries found the time and won the permission of slaveholders to catechize slaves, usually children, but with small success.[49]

Progress in baptizing the slaves was slow, not merely because of the slaveholders' objections but also because of the way in which the process of Christianization was carried out by the missionaries. The Church of England stressed religious instruction in its efforts to convert the slaves. An example of this catechetical method was described by Francis Le Jau in 1710:

> Since it has pleased Almight God to bless me with health I have upon Sundays after our divine service, invited the negroes and Indian slaves to stay for half an hour . . . we begin and end our particular assembly with the Collect *Prevent us O Lord* etc. I teach them the Creed, the Lord's Prayer, and the Commandments. I explain some portion of the catechism. I give them an entire liberty to ask questions. I endeavor to proportion my answers and all my instructions to their want and capacity.[50]

The carefulness with which the Anglican missionary admitted slaves to baptism was exemplified by Le Jau's practice of continuing catechumens on trial for two years. Le Jau explained: "I could easily multiply the number of slaves proselyted to Christianity but I put off their baptism and the receiving some persons to the holy table till we have a good testimony and proof of their life and conversation."[51] The Anglican catechist believed that eventually religious instruction should include teaching the slaves to read. One of the first S.P.G. missionaries sent to the colonies, Samuel Thomas of Goose Creek, South Carolina (Le Jau's predecessor), automatically assumed a connection between Christian initiation and slave literacy when he reported in 1702 that he had taught twenty slaves to read while instructing them in the Christian faith.[52]

The tendency of the S.P.G. to view the religious instruction of slaves as being equivalent to education led it to sponsor (in cooperation with a benevolent society, the Associates of Dr. Bray) several Negro schools in the colonies. The schools established in Charlestown, South Carolina, and New York City proved to be among the more successful. In a letter written in 1740 which proposed the possibility of a Negro school, Alexander Garden, the bishop of London's commissary in South Carolina, suggested that instruction be conducted "by *Negro* Schoolmasters, Home-born, & equally Property as other Slaves, but educated for this Service, & employed in it during their Lives, as the others are in any other Service whatsoever."[53]

Following Garden's advice, the society purchased in 1742 two black teenagers, aged fourteen and fifteen, to be trained as teachers. Both youths, Harry and Andrew, had been baptized as infants. Garden had high praise for one: "He proves of an excellent Genius, & can now (in the Space of eight Months) read N. Testament exceedingly well." "In six more," Garden continued, "he will be thrōly qualified for the intended Service; & by that time, with God's Blessing, I shall have a Schoolhouse ready . . . & everything necessary prepared for his entering upon it here at Charlestown. . . . "[54] Garden's School for Negroes was opened on September 12, 1743, and lasted over twenty years, despite the fact that in 1740 the South Carolina Legislature, in reaction to the Stono Rebellion of 1739, had adopted a strict law against teaching slaves to write.[55] In 1746 Garden informed the society that the school had already trained twenty-eight children and was at that time instructing fifty-five more children during the day and fifteen adults in the evening.[56] The type of education offered can be inferred from Garden's request to the society for the following books: "100 Spelling Books, 50 Testaments, 50 Bibles, and 50 Psalters with Common Prayer."[57]

The aim of the Charlestown Negro school was stated clearly by Commissary Garden in his letter of 1740:

> As among us Religious Instruction usually descends from Parents to Children, so among them it must at first ascend from Children to Parents, or from young to Old.
>
> They are as 'twere a Nation within a Nation. In all County Settlements, they live in contiguous Houses and often 2, 3, or 4 Familys of them in one House, Slightly partitioned into so many Apartments. They labour together and converse almost wholly among themselves, so that if once their children could but read the Bible to them, and other Tracts of Instruction of Evenings & other spare Times, specially Sundays; would bring in at least a Dawning of the blessed Light amongst them; and which as a Sett or two of these children grew up to Men and Women, would gradually diffuse and increase into open Day.

Obviously, this was a scenario that would take a long while to develop, yet Garden optimistically predicted that if "this method of Instructing the Young Slaves continued, in this or any other Colony, but for the Space of Twenty Years, the Knowledge of the Gospel 'mong the Slaves of such Colony . . . (excepting those newly Imported) would not be much inferior to that of the lower sort of white People."[58] The Charlestown school experiment lasted until 1764, when Harry, the teacher, died. Andrew had "proved a profligate" and Garden had died in 1756.[59] Even when the school was successfully operating, its significance was more an example of a valiant effort than a statistically effective way of converting a "nation within a nation." Richard Clarke, Garden's successor as commissary, placed the school in perspective when he reported to the society in 1755 that the Negro school was well attended but that there was a lamentable negligence on the part of white people with regard to Negro education: there was not "so much as one Civil Establishment in the Colony for the Christian Instruction of 50,000 Negro Slaves."[60]

Under the auspices of the S.P.G., Elias Neau, a lay catechist, instituted a school in New York City in 1704 for catechizing

Negroes. By July of 1707 Neau was able to report over a hundred pupils and the next year more than two hundred. Neau's methods consisted of going "from house to house, persuading the owners to send their slaves every Monday, Wednesday, and Friday at 4 P.M. to his house where he [taught] them the Lord's Prayer in English, and gradually [led] up to the Creed and Catechism." Of the slaves who came, "many who could not read, could yet by Memory repeat the History of the Creation of the World, the Flood, the giving of the Law, the Birth, Miracles and Crucifixion of our Lord, and the chief Articles and Doctrines of Christianity." In 1720 Neau's school had eighty-four students, consisting of thirty-five women and forty-nine men. Four of the women were free; the remaining eighty persons were slaves owned by fifty-one different slaveholders. Thirty-nine had been baptized and six were communicants.[61] The existence of the school was threatened in the aftermath of a slave insurrection in 1712 but managed to survive Neau's death in 1722 and lasted until the War of Independence.

The S.P.G. and the Associates of Dr. Bray also supported a lay catechist to instruct Negroes in Georgia after slaves were legally admitted to the colony in 1749. The catechist, Joseph Ottolenghe, an Italian-born convert from Judaism, landed at Savannah in 1751 and quickly announced a program of instruction. He proposed to hold meetings for slaves three times a week, on Sunday, Tuesday, and Thursday evenings after the day's work was done. Reporting to the Associates a few months after his arrival, Ottolenghe described his teaching methods:

> When we meet, I make them go to Prayers with me, having composed for that Purpose a few Prayers, suitable (I hope) to the Occasion. Having thus recommended our Selves to the Protection of Heaven . . . I instruct them to read, that they may be able in Time to comfort themselves in reading the Book of God. After this is done, I make them to repeat the Lords Prayer & the Belief, [Creed] & a short portion of the Catechism, explaining to them in as easie & Familiar a man-

ner as I can the Meaning of what they repeat, & before I part
with them, I make a Discourse to them on the Being of a
God, or the Life & Death of our adorable Redeemer, or upon
some Event or Story, taken out of the Bible, suitable to the
Discourse in Hand . . . [62]

Contending with the usual problems—vehement objections
from some planters who alleged "a Slave is ten times worse when
a Xn, than in his State of Paganism," inability to communicate
with African slaves, irregular attendance—Ottolenghe nevertheless reported "good Success" by the summer of 1752. In 1759 his
work for the Associates and the S.P.G. was terminated. Whatever
success Ottolenghe could claim was at best limited. The draw-
backs of the Associates' method, namely, founding schools for
educating Negroes, were all too clear to Rev. Bartholomew Zouberbuhler, the rector of Christ Church in Savannah. Writing to
the Secretary of the Associates in 1758, Zouberbuhler argued for
the necessity of itinerant catechists to work among the slaves
where they were—on widely scattered plantations:

I have once proposed the erecting of a Publick School, But
from the Observations I have since made, particularly on the
labours of Mr. Ottolenghe, who whilst he acted in the Capacity of School Master & Catechist discharged his Duty with
great Care & Diligence, I am now of Opinion that such a
foundation is not only too limited but also attended with many
Inconveniences. This Province is as yet but thinly inhabited,
consequently such a School can only reach a few adjoining
Neighbours, & there are but few Masters who will spare their
Negroes capable of any service to be taught in the Day
Time . . . The best & most effectual Method then of delivering these poor Creatures out of their Darkness & to make
them Pertakers of the Light of the Gospel, is, to attend them
at their respective Habitations . . . instructing them in the
Fundamental Truths of Christianity. And if two or three Men
properly qualified would undertake to be itinerant Catechists
or Schoolmasters. They might be dispersed 2 or 3 Months in
One District & the same Time in another & thereby compass
the whole Colony."[63]

Thus Zouberbuhler recognized, as did the Methodists of a slightly later period, the advantages of itinerancy in spreading the Gospel in the sparsely settled areas of the various American frontiers. Not until over seventy years later, when the plantation mission was propagated as an ideal, would the concept of carrying Christian instruction to the slaves on the plantations win widespread attention and effective organization.

The Church of England was not alone in thinking of conversion as a process of religious nurture which involved teaching the slaves. (In Woodson's phrase, this was a "Religion *with* Letters.") Colonial Protestants, whether Anglican, Puritan, Baptist, or Quaker, thought the Catholic emphasis on the efficacy of the sacraments ex opere operato was mechanistic and magical. The Reformed emphasis on an individual's relationship to God, on searching the Scriptures, and on discerning the workings of grace within one's heart tended to de-emphasize the mediative role of the sacraments. The importance of the scriptural word—and the sermonic words which explicated it—encouraged literacy and religious learning. Until the wave of revivals known as the Great Awakening reminded American Protestants of the importance of the conversion *experience*, becoming Christian was seen as a process of careful nurture and slow growth.[64]

The history of the religious instruction of slaves involved three parties: planters, missionaries, and slaves. The slaves' response to evangelization varied, but it was always conditioned by the circumstances of slavery. There was something peculiar about the way African slaves were evangelized in America. Traditionally, "preaching the gospel to all nations" meant that the Christian disciple was sent *out* with the gospel *to* the pagans. In America the reverse was the case: the pagan slave was brought to a Christian disciple who was frequently reluctant to instruct him in the gospel. The irony of that situation bore practical implications for the interrelationships between master, missionary, and slave.

It is clear from the reports of S.P.G. missionaries that they had little success with African-born slaves. Sharp distinctions were drawn between imported, or "Guinea," Negroes and American, or "native-born," slaves. Frequently the former never learned English well enough to understand catechesis. The bishop of London lamented this communication gap in a pastoral letter of 1727 in which he stated that "they are *utter strangers to our language and we to theirs;* and the gift of tongues being now ceased, there is no means left of instructing them in the doctrines of the Christian religion." The bishop encouraged his charges not to despair, however, for he had been informed that "many of the Negroes who are grown persons when they came over, do of themselves attain so much of our language as enables them to understand and to be understood, in things which concern the ordinary business of life." The bishop failed to understand that the degree of fluency in English necessary for an African slave to "get by" in the "ordinary business" of plantation life may not have been high enough to carry him very far in listening to an explanation of Christian doctrine. A catechist in New York had difficulties with slaves who were "bashful because, as yet, they pronounced the English language very poorly."[65]

Not all slaves who could understand religious instruction were eager to accept Christianity. William Tibbs, of St. Paul's Parish, Baltimore County, Maryland, reported in 1724 that he had baptized and taught some slaves but that most refused instruction. Some masters revealed to a missionary in Santee, South Carolina, that when slaves became Christian "all other slaves do laugh at them."[66] Bishop Secker suggested to the S.P.G. in a sermon, delivered in 1741, two reasons for the aversion of some slaves to Christianity—"the Fondness they have for their old Heathenish Rites, and the strong Prejudice they must have against Teachers from among those, whom they serve so unwillingly." The bishop concluded, "it cannot be wondered, if the Progress made in their Conversion prove but slow."[67]

Missionaries in the field complained that the "wicked life of Christians" was an obstacle impeding the conversion of the infidel.[68] And the slaves themselves were not insensitive to the hypocrisy of masters. Rev. Francis Varnod, minister to St. George's Parish in South Carolina, observed in 1724 that the slaves were "also sensible that as we are Christians, we do not act accordingly, upon which account a negro boy about 14 who has never been instructed, being blamed by his mistress (as she was going to church) for some things he had done amiss, was heard to say, My mistress can curse and go to church. . . . "[69] The brutality endemic to slavery gave the slaves much to be "scandalized" about. Francis Le Jau objected to "a very severe act" passed by the South Carolina Legislature in 1712 which threatened runaway slaves with mutilation and, for frequent violations, death.[70]

One missionary, who took the time to inquire, discovered that a pagan slave's theology bore some resemblance to his own:

> I find that some of our negro-pagans have a notion of God and of a Devil, and dismal apprehensions of apparitions. Of a God that disposes absolutely to all things. For asking one day a negro-pagan woman how she happened to be made a slave, [she] replied that God would have it so and she could not help it. I heard another saying the same thing on account of the death of her husband. And a Devil . . . who leads them to do mischief, and betrays them, whereby they are found out by their masters and punished.[71]

The slaveholders' charge that religious instruction made slaves more intractable was not without foundation. George Ross, minister of Emmanuel Church in New Castle, Delaware, explained that one reason for the "general indifference" of even churchgoing planters to the instruction of their slaves was "the untoward haughty behaviour of those Negroes who have been admitted into the Fellowship of Christ's Religion." Rev. Philip Reading, who began his work at Apoquinimick, Pennsylvania, in 1746 wished "that the slaves themselves by their rebellious behaviour after baptism, had not given too much cause for such prejudices." Rev. James Whetmore, who succeeded Elias Neau as catechist in 1723, observed that "some [slaves] have under pretence of going to Catechizing, taken opportunity to absent from their Masters service many days." Rev. Charles Martyn, of South Carolina, complained that some baptized slaves "became lazy and proud, entertaining too high an opinion of themselves, and neglecting their daily labour."[72]

The hard-to-suppress belief that baptism resulted in manumission was not restricted to slave masters. Le Jau found it necessary to draw up a declaration which adult slaves had to accept before he would baptize them. Candidates for baptism were required to assent to the following:

> You declare in the presence of God and before this Congregation that you do not ask for the holy baptism out of any design to free yourself from the Duty and Obedience that you owe to your Master while you live, but merely for the good of Your Soul and to partake of the Graces and Blessings promised to the members of the Church of Jesus Christ.[73]

That this was no public relations ploy for the benefit of the masters was demonstrated by a slave conspiracy aroused over this very issue of baptism and freedom. On June 28, 1729, Rev. James Blair, official representative of the bishop of London in Virginia, wrote his superior that

> I doubt not some of the Negroes are sincere Converts, but the far greater part of them little mind the serious part, only are in hopes that they will meet with so much the more respect, and that some time or other Christianity will help them to their freedom.

Two years later Blair announced that his suspicions had been confirmed: " . . . notwithstanding all the precautions which the ministers took to assure them that baptism did not alter their servitude, the negroes fed themselves with a secret fancy that it did, and that the King designed that all Christians should be made free. And when they saw that baptism did not change their status they grew angry and saucy, and met in the nighttime in great numbers and talked of rising." The threat of rebellion was squelched by patrols, whipping, and the execution of four conspirators.[74]

The clerical argument that Christianity made slaves more docile was weakened in South Carolina in 1725, when some slaves who had embraced Christianity participated in "secret poisonings and bloody insurrection." Rev. Richard Ludlam complained that thus they had "returned . . . the greatest of evils for the greatest good."[75] Rev. William Cotes, of St. George's Parish in Dorchester, South Carolina, interviewed a Christian slave condemned to death in 1751 for her part in poisoning slaveholders:

> One of Col. Blake's [slaves], who had been baptized, told me, that notwithstanding what was alleged against her, she hoped to be saved, because she believed in Christ (a vague phrase much in use among our sectaries).

Arguing with her antinomian view of faith, Cotes "endeavored to show her the true import and meaning thereof, and at last she made some kind of confession, and desired to be remembered in our prayers."[76]

The slaves' response to instruction and to reading was not always what the missionaries (and the masters) had hoped. Rev. Le Jau described in a letter a disturbing incident:

> The best scholar of all the negroes in my parish and a very sober and honest liver, through his learning was like to create some confusion among all the negroes in this country. He had a book wherein he read some description of the several judgements that chastise men because of their sins in these latter days, that description made an impression upon his spirit, and he told his master abruptly there would be a dismal time and the moon would be turned into blood, and there would be dearth of darkness and went away . . . but when he spoke these few words to his master, some negro overheard a part, and it was publicly blazed abroad that an angel came and spoke to the man. He had seen a hand that gave him a book; he had heard voices, seen fires, etc. As I had opportunities I took care to undeceive those who asked me about it. . . . [77]

Le Jau had no way of predicting it, but apocalyptic imagery was to have an unsettling effect among Christian slaves for a long time to come.

Other converted slaves, however, were found to "behave themselves very well, and do better for their master's profit than formerly." Le Jau had baptized some slaves who could be trusted to "Instruct one another" since they were "zealous, honest," and "read well." Significantly, Le Jau added, "and by them I am inform'd when there is any disorder among their fellows slaves that it may be remedyed."[78] Even after a slave had been catechized, baptized, and sometimes married in the Church, there remained a peculiar dimension to his Christian life—his slave condition. The strictures of that state often led to practical problems such as those which puzzled Rev. Adam Dickie of Drysdale Parish, in Virginia. Writing the bishop of London in 1732, Dickie inquired whether married slaves belonging to two different masters should be considered as separated if one master moved away or sold one of the slaves, "they being Effectually Separated as by Death, not of Choice but necessity." Furthermore, should slaves be allowed to stand as sponsors at baptisms for each other's children, since few white people were willing to do so? Finally, should Christian slaves be allowed all the Christian privileges, such as the churching of mothers after childbirth?[79] The last two questions reveal the limits which slave staus could place on Christian fellowship. The first of Dickie's questions presented a problem which was not to be solved until emancipation, namely, how to maintain the permanence of Christian marriage within a social system which recognized no such thing for slaves. Thus, the missionary could advise the baptized slave that the "Christian Religion does not allow plurality of wives, nor any changing of them" and demand that "you promise truly to keep the Wife you now have til Death does part you." But frequently neither he nor the slave had the final say about keeping or breaking the promise.[80]

During the first century and a half of slavery in the United States, only a small minority of slaves received instruction in the

Christian faith. The objections of slaveholders; the unsettled state of religion in the Southern colonies, which held the great majority of the slave population; the paucity of missionaries to catechize slaves; linguistic and cultural barriers between Africans and Europeans; the very way in which conversion was generally perceived—as catechesis, a time-consuming process of religious instruction—all these factors ensured that Christianity touched most slaves indirectly if at all. There were, however, a few slaves who did accept Christianity and were baptized into the Church under Anglican, Puritan, Baptist, Quaker, and Moravian (a very few) auspices. Some attained full if not equal communion with their white fellow Christians.

Whatever the lack of numerical effectiveness, the religious instruction of slaves during the colonial period still had a significant impact on the lives of many slaves, missionaries, and masters. What was involved in the slave's acceptance of Christianity, as all three parties to the interchange—missionaries, slaveholders, and slaves—dimly realized, was the slow process by which "Africans became New Negroes." A generational process, analogous (but by no means identical) to that of other immigrant groups, it involved complex social and psychological adaptation on the part of both black slaves and white colonists. Adapting to the foreign culture of the Europeans meant for the Africans not the total abandonment of their own cosmologies but, rather, a process of integrating the new into the old, of interpreting the unfamiliar by reference to the familiar. Catechesis moved in two directions. The slaves were taught the prayers, doctrines, and rites of Christianity, but as the missionaries realized, the slaves had to somehow understand the meaning of Christian belief and ritual if instruction was to become more than mere parroting. And here the whites had only limited control. For the slaves brought their cultural past to the task of translating and interpreting the doctrinal words and ritual gestures of Christianity. Therefore the meaning which the missionary wished the slaves to receive and the meaning which the slaves actually found (or, better, made) were not the same.

The "inaccuracy" of the slaves' translation of Christianity would be a cause of concern to missionaries for a long time to come.

Because there is only sparse slave testimony from the colonial period, historians can only speculate about the ways in which slaves during that period interpreted Christianity to fit the world views inherited from their African past. It is important to observe that on a very general level African religions and Christianity (Protestant as well as Catholic) shared some important beliefs. A basic Christian doctrine which would not have seemed foreign to most Africans was belief in God, the Father, Supreme Creator of the world and all within it. The divine sonship of Jesus and the divinity of the third person of the Trinity, the Holy Spirit, would have also seemed intelligible to many Africans accustomed to a plurality of divinities. That there were only three divine persons and that Jesus was the only begotten Son of the Father would have seemed too limited a pantheon to some Africans. The notion of an afterlife where the evil suffer and the good prosper and the concept of sin as wrongdoing deserving of divine anger and punishment were also held in many African societies, though the doctrine of man's depravity as a result of original sin would have been repugnant to most. That adoration and prayer were owed by man to a god would have seemed obvious to Africans, for whom the essence of piety consisted in propitiating gods and ancestors. Most centrally, the absence from Christian ritual of drumming, dancing, sacrifice, and possession would have been keenly felt by most Africans. The differences between Protestant Christianity and African religious belief were, of course, much more numerous and much more important than the similarities, but there were enough similarities to make it possible for slaves to find some common ground between the beliefs of their ancestors and those of the white Christians. The theory that African acceptance of Christianity required the adoption of a totally alien world view needs therefore to be modified.[81]

Colonial legislation and clerical declaration to the contrary, the

religious instruction of the slaves had implications beyond the
spiritual—implications which would be revealed more fully in the
tumult of revivalist preaching under the impact of the conversion
experience. But even before that storm of revival broke, a beginning had been made. As one historian felicitously expressed it:
"The complete cycle of a sacramental progression from baptism to
burial, with the special training of each successive step between,
including the learning of the white man's language, might not be
a legal emancipation, but was, nevertheless, a participation in the
white man's folk ways amounting to something like tribal adoption."[82] Though adoption on both sides was incomplete, the way
had been opened for a kind of stepbrotherhood which would
occasionally result in situations of religious reciprocity. The impact of revivalism and the experience of conversion would, for a
time at least, increase the visibility of the egalitarian implications
within Christianity.

Revival and Conversion

The Great Awakening represented "the dawning of the new day"
in the history of the conversion of slaves to Christianity.[83] In what
might be termed the preliminary "showers of grace" before the
deluge of the Awakening, Jonathan Edwards noted that the
Northampton, Massachusetts, revival of 1734–36 was affecting
black churchgoers as well as whites: "There are several Negroes
who, from what was seen in them and what is discernable in them
since, appear to have been truly born again in the late remarkable
season."[84] When the full tide of the Great Awakening swept over
the colonies, beginning in 1740, blacks were among those lifted
to new heights of religious excitement. Whitefield, Tennent, and
other revivalists noted with satisfaction the presence of black
people swelling the crowds who flocked to hear their powerful
message of salvation. Whitefield recounted an occasion in Philadelphia in 1740 when "near fifty negroes came to give me thanks
for what God had done to their souls."[85] In a letter to Whitefield,

Tennent described the result of his preaching in Charlestown, Massachusetts: "multitudes were awakened, and several had received great consolation, especially among the young people, children and Negroes."[86] An Anglican clergyman in Salem, Massachusetts, reacted with disdain to the effects of the revival: "So great has been the enthusiasm created by Wesley and Whitefield and Tennent, that people talk of nothing but, 'renovating, regeneration, conviction and conversion . . . ' Even children 8–13 assemble in bodies preaching and praying, nay the very Servants and Slaves pretend to extraordinary inspiration, and under the veil thereof cherish their idle dispositions and in lieu of dutifully minding their respective businesses run rambling about to utter enthusiastic nonsense."[87] Active participation by Negroes, as exhorters, in the fervor of the Awakening was one of the charges leveled against the revival by critics like Charles Chauncy: " . . . chiefly indeed young *Persons*, sometimes *Lads*, or rather *Boys:* Nay, *Women* and *Girls*, yea *Negroes*, have taken upon them to do the Business of Preachers."[88]

In the Southern colonies the revival impulse continued to smolder and to flare up sporadically under the preaching of evangelical ministers. Pro-revival, or New Light, Presbyterians, as well as pro-revival, or Separate, Baptists and Methodists continued the work of the revival moving west with the frontier into the Old Southwest, where the conflagration would begin anew at the turn of the century in the camp meeting revivals of Kentucky and Tennessee.[89]

Presbyterian Samuel Davies, a leading New Light and future president of the College of New Jersey (Princeton), began his ministry to seven congregations in Hanover County, Virginia, in 1748. Along with his fellow New Light colleagues, John Todd and John Wright, Davies experienced considerable success in his efforts to evangelize Negroes. Davies reportedly "had the pleasure of seeing 40 of them around the table of the Lord, all of whom made a credible profession of Christianity, and several of them gave unusual evidence of sincerity, and he believed that more than

1,000 Negroes attended on his ministry at the different places where he alternately officiated." In 1757 Davies wrote: "What little success I have lately had, has been chiefly among the extremes of Gentlemen and Negroes. Indeed, God has been remarkably working among the latter. I have baptized about 150 adults; and at the last sacramental solemnity, I had the pleasure of seeing the table *graced* with about 60 black faces. They generally behave well as far as I can hear, though there are some instances of apostacy among them."[90] Davies, with the respect for education characteristic of Presbyterians, emphasized the need for teaching the slaves to read, and had hoped to compose "a book with the combined purpose of teaching reading and Christianity"—a project never completed. The evangelical heart of Davies' message to the slaves, however, was not so much instruction as the experience of conversion, as can be seen from his advice to prospective black converts:

> You will say perhaps 'other negroes are baptized; and why not I?' But, consider some other negroes have been in great trouble about their souls; their hearts have been broken for sin; they have accepted Christ as their only Saviour; and are Christians indeed; and when you are such, it will be time enough for you to be baptized.[91]

Davies' criteria for baptism demanded more than learning the Lord's Prayer, the Apostles' Creed and memorizing parts of the catechism. He faced little opposition from slaveholders and could boast that slaves "are freely allowed to attend upon my ministry, and some time my private instructions, even by such masters as have no religion at all, or are Bigots to the Established church."[92]

More than the Presbyterians, the Separate Baptists and the Methodists reaped a revival harvest of black and white members in the South. By the end of the century these two denominations were in the ascendancy in the South. Slaves and free blacks were among those swelling the Baptist and Methodist ranks. Methodist itinerants frequently commented on the presence of blacks in their congregations. Joseph Pilmore wrote to Wesley in 1770 that "the number of blacks that attend the preaching affects me much." A revival from 1773 to 1776 under Devereux Jarratt, which covered fourteen counties of Virginia and two of North Carolina, was attended by "hundreds on Negroes . . . with tears streaming down their faces." One evangelist reported that "the chapel was full of white and black"; another that "in general the white people were within the chapel and the black people without." Moved by Freeborn Garretson's preaching in Maryland, "hundreds both white and black expressed their love of Jesus." Thomas Rankin figured that in 1777 Methodists in the colonies included "many hundreds of Negroes . . . convinced of sin, and many of them happy in the love of God."[93]

In 1786, the first year in which Methodists distinguished white and black members in their records, there were 1,890 black members out of a total membership of 18,791. By 1790 the number of black Methodists had increased to 11,682, and in 1797 the black membership stood at 12,215, or almost one-fourth of the total Methodist membership. The majority of black Methodists in 1797 were located in three states: Maryland, with 5,106; Virginia, with 2,490; and North Carolina, with 2,071. South Carolina followed with 890, while Georgia had 148.[94]

Unlike the Methodists, Baptists kept sparse records, so it is difficult to gauge accurately the extent of their black membership, particularly during the early period of their expansion. One estimate is that in 1793 the black Baptist membership was about one-fourth the total membership of 73,471, or between 18,000 and 19,000. William Warren Sweet stated that there were 17,644 black Baptists in the South in 1795. According to Charles Colcock Jones, the black membership of the Baptists increased from about 18,000 in 1793 to about 40,000 in 1813.[95] While these figures are probably inflated, there is no doubt that the growth in black as well as white membership among the Baptists and Methodists was astounding. The main spur to this growth was the religious fervor of revival. For example, Baptists in the Savannah, Georgia, area, through "frequent and extensive" revivals, "especially among the coloured population," in 1812 "received by baptism about fifteen hundred persons."[96]

The revivalist impulse of the Great Awakening broke out anew on the frontier in 1800. The Great Western Revival, inaugurated by the Gaspar River and Cane Ridge camp meetings in Kentucky, embraced blacks, who eagerly participated in the tumultuous exercises which became characteristic of frontier revivalism. The camp meeting proved to be a powerful instrument for accelerating the pace of slave conversions.

The increase in conversions of Negroes under the impact of revivalism was due to several factors. The evangelical religion spread by the revivalists initiated a religious renaissance in the South as a somnolent religious consciousness was awakened by revivalist preachers. The revival itself became a means of church extension for Presbyterians and, particularly, for Methodists and Baptists. The mobility of the Methodist circuit rider and the local autonomy of the Baptist preacher were suited to the needs and conditions of the rural South. In the heat of religious fervor, planters became less indifferent about their own religious involvement and, potentially, about that of their slaves.

The individualistic emphasis of revivalism, with its intense concentration on inward conversion, fostered an inclusiveness which could border on egalitarianism. Evangelicals did not hesitate to preach the necessity of conversion to racially mixed congregations. Revivalist preachers had little doubt—indeed they were enthusiastic—about the capacity of slaves to share the experience of conversion.

Stressing the conversion experience instead of the process of religious instruction made Christianity more accessible to illiterate slaves and slaveholders alike. Evangelicals were as concerned as Anglicans about observing the rules of Christian conduct after conversion, but it was the *experience* of conviction, repentance, and regeneration which occupied the attention of the former. While the Anglican clergyman tended to be didactic and moralistic, the Methodist or Baptist exhorter visualized and personalized the drama of sin and salvation, of damnation and election. The Anglican usually taught the slaves the Ten Commandments, the Apostles' Creed and the Lord's Prayer; the revivalist preacher helped them to feel the weight of sin, to imagine the threats of Hell, and to accept Christ as their only Savior. The enthusiasm of the camp meeting, as excessive as it seemed to some churchmen, was triggered by the personal, emotional appeal of the preacher and supported by the common response of members of his congregation. The revivalists tended, moreover, to minimize complex explanations of doctrine. The heightened emphasis on conversion left little room for elaborate catechesis. The plain doctrine and heavy emotion of revivalist sermons appealed as much to the black slave as to the white farmer. The experience of John Thompson, born as a slave in Maryland in 1812, is illustrative:

> My mistress and her family were all Episcopalians. The nearest church was five miles from our plantation, and there was no Methodist church nearer than ten miles. So we went to the Episcopal church, but always came home as we went, for the preaching was above our comprehension, so that we could understand but little that was said. But soon the Methodist religion was brought among us, and preached in a manner so plain that the way faring man, though a fool, could not err therein. This new doctrine produced great consternation among the slaveholders. It was something which they could not understand. It brought glad tidings to the poor bondman; it bound up the broken-hearted; it opened the prison doors to them that were bound, and let the captive go free. As soon as it got among the slaves, it spread from plantation to plantation, until it reached ours, where there were but few who did not experience religion.[97]

The Baptists and Methodists did not insist on a well-educated clergy. A converted heart and a gifted tongue were more important than the amount of theological training received. If a converted slave showed talent for exhorting, he exhorted, and not only to black audiences. The tendency of evangelical religion to level the souls of all men before God became manifest when awakened blacks preached to unconverted whites. In 1766 an S.P.G. missionary named Barnett in Brunswick, Virginia, was disturbed because "New light baptists are very numerous in the southern parts of this parish—The most illiterate among them are their Teachers even Negroes speak in their Meetings."[98] During the 1780s a slave named Lewis preached to crowds as large as four hundred in Westmoreland County, Virginia, "on the theme of the state man was in by nature, urging that his hearers must not remain in an unconverted state but come and accept Christ by faith. . . . " Harry Hosier or "Black Harry" traveled with Methodist ministers Asbury, Coke, Garretson, and Whatcoat and was reportedly an excellent preacher. After the resignation in 1792 of its pastor, the mixed congregation of the Portsmouth, Virginia, Baptist Church "employed Josiah (or Jacob) Bishop, a black man of considerable talents to preach for them." The Portsmouth congregation thought so much of Bishop that it purchased his freedom and that of his family.[99] In that same year the Roanoke (Virginia) Association purchased a slave named Simon and set him free to exercise his gifts because they thought "him ordained of God to preach the Gospel." Another black man, William Lemon, pastored a white Baptist church in Gloucester County, Virginia, at the turn of the century. A color-conscious Baptist historian explained that Lemon, "though not white, as to his natural complexion, had been purified and made white, in a better sense."[100]

In 1798 a free Negro, Joseph Willis, who was a duly licensed Baptist preacher, began his work in southwest Mississippi. In 1804 he moved to Louisiana and in 1812 formed that state's first Baptist church at Bayou Chicot, where he served as pastor. He helped to organize several other churches in the area, and in 1818, when the Louisiana Baptist Association was organized, "Father" Willis was its first moderator.[101]

In Lexington, Kentucky, a slave named "Old Captain" gathered a church in 1801 which eventually included over three hundred black members. When he sought ordination the South

Kentucky Association "did not consider it proper to ordain him, in form," though they were willing to give him "the right hand of Christian affection and directed him to go on in the name of their Common Master." Captain proceeded without ordination to examine and baptize those who came to him.[102] John Chavis, another free black, was appointed by the Presbyterian General Assembly in 1801 to work in Virginia and North Carolina "as a missionary among people of his own color." Licensed to preach, Chavis did not confine his ministry to Negroes. In 1808 he opened a school in Raleigh, North Carolina, for the instruction of white children by day and black children at night. In 1832 Chavis was barred from preaching by a North Carolina law which forbade slaves and free Negroes to exhort or preach in public.[103] "Uncle" Jack, an African-born slave and a Baptist convert, preached in Nottoway County, Virginia, in 1792. Jack impressed some white church members enough to make them purchase his freedom and settle him on a farm. Jack continued to preach for forty years and had the satisfaction of converting his former master's son.[104] Henry Evans, a free man and shoemaker by trade, was licensed as a local preacher by the Methodists toward the end of the eighteenth century. Evans was responsible for "the planting of Methodism" in Fayetteville, North Carolina. Originally preaching to black people only, he attracted the attention of some prominent whites, and ironically "the white portion of [his] congregation increased till the negroes were crowded out of their seats." Evans was displaced by a white minister but continued as an assistant in the church he founded until his death in 1810.[105]

The occasional preaching of black preachers to white congregations is of less significance for slave conversions than the fact that black preachers, licensed or not, preached to slaves. Baptist minister Edmund Botsford of Welsh Neck, South Carolina, noted with pleasure that during a revival in 1790 several black members of his congregation did "go to the plantations, and preach to their own colour on Lord's-day evenings, and at other times when we have no services in the meeting-house."[106] More than any other denomination the Baptists gave leeway to their black members to preach. One historian of the Baptists lauded the anonymous but effective ministry of black preachers: " . . . among the African Baptists in the Southern states there are a multitude of preachers and exhorters whose names do not appear on the minutes of the associations. They preach principally on the plantations to those of their own color, and their preaching though broken and illiterate, is in many cases highly useful." Black ministers were active in the cities as well. One outstanding example was the biracial First Baptist Church of Richmond, Virginia, "which had a large slave membership" and "at one time included five Negro preachers and seven black exhorters."[107]

Until several state legislatures passed laws restricting Negroes from preaching, the Baptist churches licensed and ordained black men who felt the call to preach after they demonstrated their gifts and evidenced their faith before a committee of the church. Slave preachers were allowed to preach only with permission from their owners and normally were restricted to the area of the local parish. The duties of black preachers included conducting funerals and sanctifying marriages for slaves.[108]

Among the Methodists many black men served as lay preachers. As such, they could not celebrate the sacraments but were allowed to preach and to discipline black members within a restricted locale. Even when the practice was illegal, the Methodists sent out black assistants with their itinerant preachers in a few instances. William Capers, of South Carolina, recalled sending out eight black preachers to work with the slaves in 1811, though it was forbidden by civil and ecclesiastical law. Methodists skirted legal restrictions against black preachers by simply licensing them as exhorters. Strictly speaking, exhorters were assistants, but black exhorters were in fact known to act as pastors of their own people.[109] The importance of these early black preachers in the conversion of slaves to Christianity has not been sufficiently appreciated. Emerging in the latter half of the eighteenth and the early decades of the nineteenth centuries, they acted as crucial mediators between Christian belief and the experiential world of the slaves. In effect they were helping to shape the development of a bicultural synthesis, an Afro-American culture, by nurturing the birth of Christian communities among blacks, slave and free. In this sense the sociologist Robert Park was right when he commented that "with the appearance of these men, the Negroes in America ceased to be a mission people. At least from this time on, the movement went on of its own momentum, more and more largely under the direction of Negro leaders. Little Negro congregations, under the leadership of Negro preachers, sprang up wherever they were tolerated. Often they were suppressed, more often they were privately encouraged. Not infrequently they met in secret." In at least two towns, Petersburg, Virginia, and Savannah, Georgia, black Baptists organized churches *before* white Baptists did so.[110]

The swarming of black converts into Baptist and Methodist churches led to mixed, though segregated, congregations. Negroes usually sat in galleries or in back pews. It was not unusual for the black membership in a church to far exceed that of the whites. When Negroes became too numerous, separate services were held for them, or sometimes, particularly in cities, white members withdrew, leaving black members to form a separate church. Usually these splits were amicable. Generally, slaves in rural areas attended church, if they attended at all, with whites, and the church was under white control. Blacks in towns and cities enjoyed more frequent "*access to religious privileges.*"[111] A few African Baptist churches sprang up, some before 1800, which were independent to the extent that they called their own pastors and officers, joined local Baptist associations with white churches, and sent black delegates to associational meetings. Much of the early autonomy of these separate black churches was short-lived. By the 1820s black churches were under the supervision of white pastors. The shift in situations was reflected by two decisions, made thirty-four years apart, by the same Virginia Baptist organization. In 1794 the Portsmouth Association discussed the question: "Is it agreeable to the Word of God to send a free black man a delegate to the Ass'n?" And answered: "We can see nothing wrong in this. A church may send any one it chooses." In 1828 the Portsmouth Association ruled that "whereas the constitution of independent and colored churches, in this state, and their representation in this body, involves a point of great delicacy," black churches must be represented in the association "through white men."[112] There were cases, however, where the control of white pastors over black churches was nominal. The white minister in charge of the black Baptist Elam Church, in Charles City, Virginia, thought his duty fulfilled after he had "sat in the most comfortable seat to be had, listened to sermons by some of the colored brothers, drew his one dollar for attendance, enjoyed a good dinner such as colored people can cook, and quietly sauntered back to his . . . home."[113]

Though the separate black church was primarily an urban phenomenon, it drew upon surrounding rural areas for its membership, which consisted of both free and slave blacks. Some black churches were not created by segregation from previously biracial congregations but, rather, arose independently from the start. Such a church was the African Baptist Church of Williamsburg, Virginia, which flourished despite initial attempts to stamp it out. The origins of this early black church were described in 1810:

> This church is composed almost, if not altogether, of people of colour. Moses, a black man, first preached among them and was often taken up and whipped, for holding meetings. Afterwards Gowan, who called himself Gowan Pamphlet, . . . became popular among the blacks, and began to baptize, as well as to preach. It seems, the association had advised that no person of colour should be allowed to preach, on the pain of excommunication; against this regulation, many of the blacks were rebellious, and continued still to hold meetings. Some were excluded, and among this number was Gowan. . . . Continuing still to preach and many professing faith under his ministry, not being in connexion with any church himself, he formed a kind of church out of some who had been baptized,

who, sitting with him, received such as offered themselves;
Gowan baptized them, and was moreover appointed their pastor; some of them knowing how to write, a churchbook was
kept; they increased to a large number; so that in the year
1791, when the Dover association was holden . . . they petitioned for admittance into the association, stating their number to be about five hundred. The association received them,
so far, as to appoint persons to visit them and set things in
order. These, making a favourable report, they were received,
and have associated ever since.[114]

The distinction of being the first separate black church in the
South (and the North), however, belonged to the Baptist church
founded between 1773 and 1775 in Silver Bluff, South Carolina,
across the Savannah River from Georgia. The importance of the
Silver Bluff Church lies not only in its chronological priority but
in its role as mother church of several far-flung Baptist missions.
This church owed its beginning to the preaching of a white Baptist minister named Palmer who preached to the slaves of one
George Galphin at Silver Bluff. David George, George's wife,
Jesse Galphin (or Jesse Peter), and five other slaves were converted and baptized by Palmer at Galphin's mill. These eight
formed the nucleus of the Silver Bluff Church. David George had
a talent for exhorting and was appointed to the office of elder on
the recommendation of Palmer. When the American Revolution
began, white ministers were no longer allowed to attend the
slaves "lest they should furnish . . . too much knowledge"—about
Governor Dunmore's proclamation freeing all slaves who would
support the British. Due to the lack of a regular minister, David
George assumed the responsibility and "continued preaching . . .
till the church . . . encreased to thirty or more, and till the British
came to the city Savannah and took it." The British occupation of
the city in 1778 disrupted the Silver Bluff Church. Galphin, a
patriot, decided to flee, and his slaves took refuge in Savannah
behind British lines. When American forces reclaimed the area,
David George elected to gain his freedom by emigrating to Nova
Scotia in 1782. There he preached to other black emigrés and

founded a Baptist church at Shelburne. In 1792 George migrated again, this time with a colony of blacks to Sierra Leone, where he planted yet another Baptist church.[115]

George Liele, a childhood friend of David George, had been converted by the preaching of a white Baptist minister, Matthew Moore, around 1773, and he began to preach a few years later in the area of Silver Bluff. When the British evacuated their forces from Savannah, Liele left the country for Jamaica, where in 1784 he organized at Kingston the first Baptist church on the island with "four brethren from America." Soon Liele's "preaching took very good effect with the poorer sort, especially the slaves," and by 1791 there were "nigh three hundred and fifty members," including a few white people. In a letter to the editor of the English *Baptist Annual Register*, Liele recounted his endeavors with a trace of justifiable pride:

> I have deacons and elders, a few; and teachers of small congregations in the town and country, where convenience suits them to come together; and I am pastor. I preach twice on the Lord's Day, in the forenoon and afternoon, and twice in the week, and have not been absent six Sabbath days since I formed the church in this country. I receive nothing for my services; I preach, baptize, administer the Lord's Supper, and travel from one place to another to publish the gospel and to settle church affairs, all freely.[116]

Meanwhile the Silver Bluff Church had reorganized under the ministry of Jesse Galphin, one of its eight founders. He also supplied "three or four other places in the country, where he [preached] alternately." According to a contemporary's description: "His countenance is grave, his voice charming, his delivery good, nor is he a novice in the mysteries of the kingdom." The membership of the church had grown to around sixty by 1793, when it appears that the congregation, having long since outgrown Galphin's mill, moved to Augusta, Georgia, twelve miles from Silver Bluff, and formed the First African Baptist Church of that city.[117]

George Liele, before he sailed for Jamaica in 1782, had converted a slave named Andrew Bryan (by preaching on John 3:7, "Ye must be born again"). After Liele's departure Bryan began to exhort blacks and whites. When he and a few followers started gathering in a suburb of Savannah for worship, they were harassed by white citizens, "as it was at a time that a number of blacks had absconded, and some had been taken away by the British." Andrew Bryan and his brother Sampson were hauled before the city magistrates for punishment. "These, with many others, were twice imprisoned, and about *fifty* were severely whipped, particularly *Andrew, who was cut, and bled abundantly.*" Reportedly, Andrew "told his persecutors that he rejoiced not only to be whipped, but *would freely suffer death for the cause of Jesus Christ.*" Finally, the parallels to the Acts of the Apostles must have become too embarrassing to local officials, who examined and released them with permission to resume their worship, but only between sunrise and sunset. Andrew's master permitted the congregation to use his barn at Brampton, three miles outside of town, as a meeting place. In 1788 the white Baptist minister, Abraham Marshall, accompanied by Jesse Galphin, visited the Brampton congregation, examined and baptized about forty people, and licensed Andrew Bryan to preach. After his master's death Andrew obtained his freedom and eventually owned eight slaves himself, "for whose education and happiness" he provided.[118]

In 1790 Bryan's church numbered 225 full communicants and about 350 converts, "many of whom" did not have their masters' permission to be baptized. By 1800 Bryan was able to inform Rippon that his church was no longer persecuted but met "in the presence, and with the approbation and encouragement of many of the white people." An occasional white minister served as guest preacher in this First African Baptist Church of Savannah. It was estimated that "fifty of Andrew's church" were able to read, "but only three can write." Bryan was assisted by his brother Sampson, who had remained a slave. Andrew Marshall, Bryan's nephew, succeeded him as pastor of the First African Church. In

Andrew Bryan. Reprinted from E. K. Love, *History of the First African Baptist Church* (Savannah, Ga., 1888).

1803 a Second African Church was organized from members of the First, and a few years later a Third came into being. Both of the new churches were led by black pastors.[119]

As mentioned earlier, African Baptist churches also came into existence by separating from white congregations. The Gillfield Baptist Church of Petersburg, Virginia, was originally part of a mixed congregation with a black majority. Located outside of Petersburg, the original church moved into town between 1788 and 1809 and in the process split along racial lines. In 1810 the newly formed Gillfield Church with 270 black members was admitted to the Portsmouth Association.[120]

The independence of black churches and black ministers in the South was always threatened by restrictions. It was not only the civil authority which curtailed the ministry of black preachers. Officers of the Baptist Church in Cedar Spring, South Carolina, for example, decided in 1804 to allow brother Titus, "to sing, pray and exhort in public, and appoint meetings in the vicinity of the church," with the understanding that "all his acting . . . be in Subordination to his master, and that his master council him in particular cases as his prudence may dictate." Titus was suspended a few months later for behavior contrary to the committee's stipulation. The realities of slavery continually circumscribed the religious authority of Southern blacks, slave or free.[121]

Fear of slave rebellions haunted Southern whites and hindered attempts to convert the slaves, for the same egalitarian tendencies within revivalism which helped to bring the slave to conversion, could, if pushed too far, deny him access to religion—as the Methodists quickly discovered. The founders and early leaders of Methodism—John Wesley, Francis Asbury, and Thomas Coke—were opposed to slavery. In 1780 a conference of seventeen Methodist divines at Baltimore took up the question of slavery, cognizant of the rapid growth of Methodism in the American South. The conference decided that traveling preachers who held slaves had to promise to set them free and declared that "slavery is contrary to the laws of God, man, and nature—hurtful to society; contrary to the dictates of conscience and pure religion, and doing that which we would not others should do to us and ours." These declarations proved less than effective, and other conferences in 1783 and 1784 had to broach the subject again. A definitive stand was taken at the Christmas Conference of 1784, when it was determined once and for all "to extirpate this abomination from among us." Any member who failed to comply with rules for emancipation was given twelve months to either withdraw or be excluded from Methodist societies; slaveholders were to be admitted to membership only after they had signed emancipation papers. Brethren in Virginia, however, were given special consideration due to "their peculiar circumstances," and were allowed two years to comply. Buying and selling slaves for any reason except to free them was banned. That these rules were going to be very difficult to execute became immediately clear from the experience of Thomas Coke in Virginia. When he preached against slavery in 1785, Coke was threatened by a mob and was served with indictments in two counties. One irate woman offered a crowd fifty pounds to give Coke one hundred lashes. Later that same year the Baltimore Conference suspended the rules against slavery, because, as Coke stated: "We thought it prudent to suspend the minute concerning slavery, on account of the great opposition that has been given it, our work being in too infantile a state to push things to extremity." Though the conference reiterated its principle, "We do hold in deepest abhorrence the practice of slavery; and shall not cease to seek its destruction by all wise and prudent means," in fact it had to admit failure.[122]

In 1798 Bishop Francis Asbury complained about slavery to his Journal: ". . . my mind is much pained. O! to be dependent on slaveholders is in part to be a slave and I was free born. I am brought to conclude that slavery will exist in Virginia perhaps for ages; there is not a sufficient sense of religion nor of liberty to destroy it; Methodists, Baptists, Presbyterians, in the highest flights of rapturous piety, still maintain and defend it." Eleven years later he was lamenting the fact that the antislavery reputation of the Methodists was keeping them from gaining access to the slaves:

> We are defrauded of great numbers by the pains that are taken to keep the blacks from us; their masters are afraid of the influence of our principles. Would not an *amelioration* in the condition and treatment of slaves have produced more practical good to the poor Africans, than any attempt at their *emancipation*? The state of society, unhappily does not admit of

this: besides, the blacks are deprived of the means of instruction; who will take the pains to lead them into the ways of salvation, and watch over them that they may not stray, but the Methodists? Well; now their masters will not let them come to hear us.

The answer to Asbury's dilemma of conscience was at hand: Emphasize the results of the slave's conversion! "Our tabernacle is crowded again: the minds of the people are strangely changed; and the indignation excited against us is overpast: the people see and confess that the slaves are made better by religion; and wonder to hear the poor Africans pray and exhort."[123] There were Baptists and Presbyterians who also opposed slavery, but because their witness was not institutionally promulgated, as were those of the Methodists and the Friends, their denominations did not "arouse the ire of slaveholders" to the extent that the latter two did.[124]

The egalitarian trend in evangelicalism which drove some Methodists, Baptists, and Presbyterians to condemn slavery foundered on the intransigency of that institution in the South. Those evangelicals who had condemned slavery found themselves defending slave conversion for making slaves "better," which was easily transposed into making "better slaves." Baptists, Methodists, and Presbyterians appointed black "watchmen" or "overseers" to observe the behavior of slave members and report those in need of discipline. Slave members were subject to the discipline of the congregation, and sometimes the discipline extended to "upholding the institution of slavery itself." For example, the Gillfield Baptist Church of Petersburg, Virginia, a separate black church, more than once expelled slave members for running away from their masters! The sight of a separate black congregation disciplining slaves for breaking the slave code must surely have appealed to slaveholders.[125]

However, slaveholders were not easily convinced that religion always supported slave docility, for there was ample proof that

Christianity was a two-edged sword. A common form of slave rebelliousness was the act of running away. It is clear from advertisements for runaway slaves that religious conversion did not make all slaves "better." One disgruntled slave owner complained in the *Virginia Gazette* of Williamsburg, March 26, 1767, that his escaped slave woman Hannah "pretends much to the religion the Negroes of late have practised." Thomas Jones, advertising for his escaped slave Sam in *The Maryland Journal and Baltimore Advertiser* of June 14, 1793, warned: "HE WAS RAISED IN A FAMILY OF RELIGIOUS PERSONS, COMMONLY CALLED METHODISTS, AND HAS LIVED WITH SOME OF THEM FOR YEARS PAST, ON TERMS OF PERFECT EQUALITY; the refusal to continue him on these terms, the subscriber is instructed, has given him offence, and is the sole cause of his absconding. . . . HE HAS BEEN IN THE USE OF INSTRUCTING AND EXHORTING HIS FELLOW CREATURES OF ALL COLORS IN MATTERS OF RELIGIOUS DUTY. . . ." From Jones's point of view, his slave had been ruined from imbibing Methodist notions of equality; from Sam's point of view, spiritual freedom had carried over to the temporal order. Sam's case was not an isolated one. In *The Maryland Gazette*, January 4, 1798, James Brice advertised for "a negro man named JEM," twenty-eight years old, an artisan who "IS OR PRETENDS TO BE OF THE SOCIETY OF METHODISTS, HE CONSTANTLY ATTENDED THE MEETINGS, AND AT TIMES EXHORTED HIMSELF. . . ." From the same paper, September 4, 1800, edition, Thomas Gibbs of Queene Anne County advertised for his slave Jacob, thirty-five years of age, and revealed "HE PROFESSES TO BE A METHODIST, AND HAS BEEN IN THE PRACTICE OF PREACHING OF NIGHTS." Finally, Hugh Drummond, in the same paper, advertised a runaway slave, Dick, about forty, "HE IS A METHODIST PREACHER."[126]

A different kind of rebellious act took place in King William County, Virginia, in 1789. An appeal to the governor from the county sheriff stated that Methodists and Baptists had been meeting after dark several times a week with slaves in attendance. When "paterrolers" tried to arrest the slaves at one of these gatherings they were attacked and thrown out of a window. The sheriff requested state assistance in restoring law and order.[127]

In 1800 an event occurred which had a widespread effect on white fear of slave insurrection and on reaction against slave conversion—Gabriel's Rebellion, a slave insurrection planned against Richmond, Virginia. Religion played a role in the attitudes and discussions of the rebels. "Preachings," or religious meetings, served as occasions for the recruitment of slaves and for plotting and organizing the insurrection. Gabriel's brother Martin, one of the plot's leaders, was known as a preacher. He used the Bible to argue that their plans would succeed even against superior numbers. In one discussion of the rebellion Martin contended that "their cause was similar to the Israelites," and that in the Bible God had promised "five of you shall conquer an hundred & a hundred a thousand of our enemies." Significantly, African religious beliefs were also referred to in the conspiracy. One organizer, George Smith, proposed that he travel to the "pipeing tree" to enlist the "Outlandish people" (born outside this country) who had the ability "to deal with Witches and Wizards, and thus [would be] useful in Armies to tell when any calamity was about to befall them." The testimony of a captured insurrectionist that all whites were to be massacred, except Quakers, Methodists, and Frenchmen, who "were to be spared on account . . . of their being friendly to liberty," hardly helped the cause of Methodism (or Quakerism) among Virginia slave holders.[128] Reactionary laws were quick to follow news of the plot. South Carolina passed a law that same year which forbade Negroes to assemble, even with whites present, between sunset and sunrise, "for the purpose of mental instruction or religious worship." Virginia passed a similar law two years later. Both laws had to be amended, due to pressure from "religious societies," so that nothing in them should "prevent masters taking their slaves to places of religious worship conducted by a regularly ordained or licensed white minister."[129]

Rebellion and docility were not the only alternatives for the relationship between master and slave. Evangelical religion supported both, but it also fostered a more subtle relationship, that of religious reciprocity. When white sinners were awakened by black exhorters, when masters were converted by the singing, shouting, and praying of their slaves, when white congregations were pastored by black preachers, the logical extreme of revivalistic religion was reached. Certainly these incidents were rare, but that they occurred at all indicates the manner in which religious reciprocity was able to bend the seemingly inflexible positions of master and slave.

The revivalism of the Great Awakening, spread over time and space by evangelical preachers, created the conditions for large-scale conversion of the slaves. By revitalizing the religious piety of the South, the Awakening(s) stirred an interest in conversion which was turned toward the slaves. By heavily emphasizing the inward conversion experience, the Awakening tended to de-emphasize the outward status of men, and to cause black and white alike to *feel* personally that Christ had died for them as individuals. Evangelical religion had a universalistic dimension which encouraged preaching to all men, embracing rich and poor, free and slave. The emotionalism and plain doctrine of revivalist preaching appealed to the masses, including slaves. Black exhorters and ministers were licensed to preach and did preach the gospel of spiritual freedom to slaves, who were sometimes gathered into their own black churches. Negroes, slave and free, attended revival meetings or Sabbath services and joined Methodist and Baptist churches in numbers not seen before. The very fact that there were increasing numbers of black Christians undermined the old notion among whites that evangelization of the slaves was impossible or anomalous. Still, there was widespread opposition on the part of slaveholders, especially during periods of reaction to acts of rebellion by Christian slaves.

Demographic and cultural factors, as well as the revivalist phenomenon, helped to increase the chances of slave conversion by the end of the eighteenth and the beginning of the nineteenth centuries. In spite of the fact that between 1780 and 1810 "about as many Africans" were "brought into the United States . . . as during the previous hundred and sixty years of the U.S. involvement in the slave trade," the growth in "countryborn" slaves "was by far more significant."[130] The increasing numbers of second-, third-, and even fourth-generation slaves born and raised in America meant that the linguistic and cultural barriers of earlier days were no longer so overwhelming. Moreover, as noted in the last chapter, there were situations which allowed for cultural adjustment and reinterpretation. The powerful emotionalism, ecstatic behavior, and congregational response of the revival were amenable to the African religious heritage of the slaves, and forms of African dance and song remained in the shout and spirituals of Afro-American converts to evangelical Protestantism. In addition, the slaves' rich heritage of folk belief and folk expression was not destroyed but was augmented by conversion.

The majority of slaves, however, remained only minimally touched by Christianity by the second decade of the nineteenth century. Presbyterian minister Charles Colcock Jones, a leading advocate of the mission to the slaves and an early historian of the religious instruction of Negroes, evaluated efforts to convert slaves during the period 1790–1820: "On the whole . . . but a minority of the Negroes, and that a small one, attended regularly the house of God, and taking them as a class, their religious instruction was extensively and most seriously neglected." Jones gave a clue as to the class of slaves most likely to be converted: "Growing up under the eyes and in the families of owners, they became more attached to them, were identified in their households and accompanied them to church."[131] The slaves who had most opportunity to become church members were household servants, slave artisans, and urban slaves. Slaves in remote rural areas had less opportunity to attend church, which did not mean, however, that they were totally ignorant of Christianity. Slaves could have heard the rudiments of Christianity without regularly attending church. Jones's mention of religious instruction and church membership are significant because they suggest the limits of revivalism. The critics of revivalist enthusiasm had admitted that a "season of awakening" produced a large number of converts, but they questioned the depth and sincerity of these conversions. When the revival ended, many recent converts "backslid." At issue was the perennial alternation in Christianity between revival and "declension." Revivals by their very nature are temporary and sporadic. Peak experiences of religious fervor may reoccur, but they are not constant. After revival comes church organization; after conversion comes religious nurture. Conversion experience and religious instruction, the experiental and the noetic, are complementary in the Christian life. The revivalist impulse helped to bring slaves to conversion in large numbers. Jones and others realized that the next step was missionary outreach. It was necessary to bring religious instruction onto the plantation. Now that the soil was prepared by the intermittent showers of revival, and the seed planted by evangelical preaching, what was most needed to gain a bountiful harvest was systematic, institutional effort—which was exactly what the plantation mission was designed to supply.

4
The Rule of Gospel Order

Servants, be obedient to them that are your masters according to the flesh, with fear and trembling, in singleness of your heart, as unto Christ; Not with eyeservice, as menpleasers; but as the servants of Christ, doing the will of God from the heart; With good will doing service, as to the Lord, and not to men: Knowing that whatsoever good thing any man doeth, the same shall he receive of the Lord, whether he be bond or free. And, ye masters, do the same things unto them, forebearing threatening: knowing that your Master also is in heaven; neither is there respect of persons with him.

EPHESIANS 6:5–9

THE INTENSE emphasis upon

conversion, which was the primary characteristic of evangelical, revivalistic Protestantism, tended to level all men before God as sinners in need of salvation. This tendency opened the way for black converts to participate actively in the religious culture of the new nation as exhorters, preachers, and even founders of churches, and created occasions of mutual religious influence across racial boundaries whereby blacks converted whites and whites converted blacks in the heat of revival fervor. This egalitarian tendency could push, as it did in the case of early Methodism, toward the condemnation of slavery as inconsistent with the gospel of Jesus. However, very few white Christians in the South were willing to be pushed that far. Increasingly, slavery was not only accepted as an economic fact of life, but defended as a positive good, sanctioned by Scripture and capable of producing a Christian social order based on the observance of mutual duty, slave to master and master to slave. It was the ideal of the antebellum plantation mission to create such a rule of gospel order by convincing slaves and masters that their salvation depended upon it.

Plantation Missions

The closing years of the eighteenth and the early decades of the nineteenth centuries witnessed an unprecedented spread of Christianity among Afro-Americans, slave and free.

Although the numbers of black Christians, particularly among the Baptists and Methodists, increased rapidly, and while those slaves living in or close to towns and cities had opportunities to attend church with their masters, and even in rare instances to worship at independent black churches, the great majority of rural slaves remained outside the reach of the institutional church. In the 1830s and 1840s some Southern churchmen became increasingly concerned about this neglect and determined to remedy it. In 1834 Charles Colcock Jones, one of the leading pro-

ponents for the establishment of plantation missions, explained
why more needed to be done:

> It is true they [slaves] have access to the house of God on the
> Sabbath; but it is also true that even where the privilege is
> within their reach, a minority only, (and frequently a very
> small one) embrace it. There are multitudes of districts in the
> South and Southwest, in which the churches cannot contain
> one-tenth of the Negro population; besides others in which
> there are no churches at all. It must be remembered also that
> in many of those churches there is preaching only once a
> fortnight, or once a month, and then perhaps only one ser-
> mon. To say that they fare as well as their masters does not
> settle the point; for great numbers of masters have very few or
> no religious privileges at all.[1]

The distance of many plantations from churches meant that it was
not possible to reach numerous plantations through ordinary pastoral care. It was necessary to carry the gospel to slaves at home.
Planters had generally become accustomed to the idea that slaves
should be converted, but mere passive permission was not
enough. An aggressive program of plantation missions was
needed to bring the slaves under Church care. Missionaries were
required who could devote at least part-time energy to improving
religious conditions for slaves. Monetary support for plantation
missions was to come from denominational missionary societies,
from local churches, and from slaveholders. It was recommended
that one church or a single planter associate with others to share
the expense of paying a missionary and building a mission station
or chapel.[2]

In the antebellum South the plantation mission was widely
propagated as an ideal whose time had come. Techniques similar
to those used by Bible, Temperance, Tract, and other reform
societies were employed to raise Southern Christian consciousness
about the cause of plantation missions. Addresses before planter
associations, printed sermons and essays, committee reports and
resolutions of clerical bodies, meetings of concerned clergy and
laymen, annual reports of associations, interdenominational cooper-

ation, and networks of correspondence were all devoted to spreading the message. Through the circulation of pamphlets and papers, plantation missions were brought to the attention of thousands. Religious journals such as *The Gospel Messenger* (Episcopal) of Charleston, *The Christian Index* (Baptist), and *The Southern Christian Advocate* (Methodist), to name only three, gave favorable coverage and editiorial support to missions for slaves. *The Charleston Observer* (Presbyterian) even ran a series in 1834 on the "Biographies of Servants mentioned in the Scripture: with Questions and Answers," as a practical aid to the religious instruction of slaves.[3]

Pamphlets with such titles as "Detail of a Plan for the Moral Improvement of Negroes on Plantations," "Pastoral Letter . . . on the Duty of Affording Religious Instruction to those in Bondage," and "The Colored Man's Help, or the Planter's Catechism" were published and distributed widely. A Baptist State Convention actually sponsored a contest for the best essay on the topic "Conversion of the slaves," which was won by Holland N. McTyeire with a paper entitled "The Duties of Christian Masters to Their Servants." The aim of most of this literature was succinctly described in a pamphlet published in 1823 by an Episcopal clergyman from South Carolina: "to show from the Scriptures of the Old and New Testament, that slavery is not forbidden by the Divine Law: and at the same time to prove the necessity of giving religious instruction to our Negroes." These attempts to mold public opinion in favor of plantation missions were evaluated optimistically by Jones: "As an evidence of the increase of feeling and effort on the subject of the religious instruction of the colored population we state, that *more has been published and circulated* on the general subject, within the last two years [1833–34] than in ten or twenty years' preceding . . . ."[4] Various denominational bodies frequently urged support for plantation missions in official resolutions. Not only churchmen but also laymen spoke out for religious instruction of the Negro. The prominent planters Charles Cotesworth Pinckney, Edward R. Laurens, and Whitemarsh B. Seabrook, in 1829, 1832, and 1834, respectively, stressed the benefits of a Christian slave population before South Carolina agricultural societies.[5]

Writing pamphlets and making speeches for the plantation missions did not exhaust the efforts of proponents of the cause. Missionary societies and associations were actually founded. In 1830 the Missionary Society of the South Carolina Conference was founded as an auxiliary branch of the Missionary Society of the Methodist Episcopal Church under William Capers, superintendent of missions and, later, bishop. In 1830–31 two associations of Georgia planters were formed for the religious instruction of slaves. One of these, in Liberty County, Georgia, became famous. Formed by the Midway Congregational Church, pastored by Robert Quarterman, and the local Baptist church, under Samuel Spry Law, the Liberty County Association, with Presbyterian Jones as missionary, served as a model plantation mission.[6] In the association's twelve annual reports, printed and distributed in pamphlet form throughout the slave states, planters and clergy could read of the practical programs and experience of a working mission. The annual reports served also as a clearinghouse for information about the mission activities of Baptists, Methodists, Presbyterians, and Episcopalians throughout the South by publishing progress reports and letters from as far away as Louisiana, Tennessee, and Arkansas. The geographical center of the plantation mission movement was lowland South Carolina and Georgia. Letters printed in the Liberty County Association Reports indicate that there was growing interest but much less concrete achievement in other areas of the South. Methodists seemed the most active, but the efforts of smaller churches, such as the Moravians and German Lutherans, were duly noted. It was hoped that example would move the inactive to missionary zeal.

The conversion of slaves occupied an important place on the agendas of denominational meetings and sometimes was the topic for whole conferences. In 1839 an assembly of Presbyterians from the slave states met to consider religious instruction of slaves. In

Charles Colcock Jones. Reprinted, by permission, from the Joseph Jones
Collection, Special Collections Division, Tulane University Library,
New Orleans.

1845 a meeting was held at Charleston which was attended by some of the most prominent planters and ministers of the state. A circular had been sent out in preparation for the meeting asking interested parties in all the Southern states what was being done in their areas for slave conversion. The *Proceedings* of the three-day meeting as well as answers to the circular were published. Aiming to mold public opinion, slaveholders were exhorted in the *Proceedings* to realize that a "moral agency . . . gains strength by action. The efforts of masters to afford religious instruction to their negroes, will act upon others, and react upon themselves."[7]

Charles Colcock Jones, the leading theoretician and chief publicist of the plantation mission, tried to portray the movement as part of the national fervor for reform which was articulated institutionally in the interlocking group of benevolent societies known corporately as the United Evangelical Front. In Jones's view, in the interdenominational efforts to make America holy by means of home and foreign mission societies, Bible and tract societies, and temperance and Sabbath School societies, the urgent need of the heathen slaves at home to have the Gospel preached to them should not be neglected. But as Jones himself was well aware, the practical realities of slave control and the maintenance of the institution of slavery against abolitionist attack made it impossible for the plantation mission to take its place as simply one more tide in the flood of evangelical reform. Jones was too much the realist not to admit "the very strong objections of Southern States" to the "formation of associations or societies on an extensive scale embracing States, or even the whole United States, with central boards, appointing agents for the collection of funds and forming auxiliaries, employing and appointing ministers and missionaries, disbursing monies, in a word assuming the entire control of the great work." Instead, the plantation mission, if it was to be practical, had to proceed by "*local* associations . . . formed by the people interested, on the ground itself which they propose to occupy."[8] Reform or no reform, first and last the plantation mission had to prove that it represented no threat to slavery, the South's peculiar institution.

Looming in the background of antebellum discussions of religious instruction of the slaves was the growing abolitionist fervor in the North and the growing sectional controversy within the churches themselves. The abolitionist movement created ambivalence in Southern thought about the instruction of slaves. On the one hand, the fear that abolitionist literature would incite slave rebellions tended to have a chilling effect on any kind of instruction for slaves. On the other hand, abolitionist arguments against slavery challenged proslavery apologists to push slave evangelization as one of the strongest proofs that slavery was a positive good. The detrimental effect of the abolition crusade on the plantation mission was strongly resented by missionaries like Jones:

> ... the excitement in the free States on the *civil* condition of the Negroes manifested itself in petitions to Congress, in the circulation of inflammatory publications, and other measures equally and as justly obnoxious to the South; all of which had a disastrous influence on the success of the work we were attempting to do. The effect of the excitement was to turn off the attention of the South from the *religious* to the *civil* condition of the people in question; and from the salvation of the soul, to the defence and presevation of political rights .... A tenderness was begotten in the public mind on the whole subject, and every movement touching the improvement of the Negroes was watched .... The result was, to arrest in many places efforts happily begun and successfully prosecuted for the religious instruction of the Negroes. It was considered best to disband schools and discontinue meetings, at least for a season; the formation of societies and the action of ecclesiastical bodies, in some degree ceased.[9]

The distribution in the South of revolutionary manifestos, such as David Walker's *Appeal*, aroused a distrust of all missionaries and colporteurs coming into the South "for the purpose of establishing tract, temperance, Bible and all societies of that kind." The *Southern Religious Telegraph* of Virginia had been running a series of articles on Christianizing the slaves, but when the public became alarmed about antislavery agitation, the editor announced:

"At the suggestion of some of our fellow citizens, who regard the discussion of the religious instruction of slaves inexpedient at this time, we cheerfully comply with their wishes, and will discontinue for the present the publication of articles on the subject."[10] It was a settled policy for the Liberty County Association that non-Southerners were welcome visitors to the mission stations, but they were not allowed to address or preach to the slaves. Abolitionist attacks gave renewed credence to the notion that "religious instruction tends to the dissolution of the relations of society as now constituted . . . and . . . will . . . lead to insubordination." The Missionary Society of the Methodist Conference of South Carolina in 1841 found it expedient to end a report with the following disclaimer: "So to preach this Gospel . . . is the great object, and, we repeat it, the *sole* object of our ministrations among the blacks. This object attained, we find the terminus of our anxieties and toils, of our preaching and prayers."[11]

Nevertheless, the impact of abolitionism as a detrimental force on the slave missions should not be overstressed. In some areas reaction was short-lived, and affected public discussion more perhaps than private action. The Presbyterian Synod of South Carolina and Georgia remarked in 1835 that "the religious instruction of our slave population, entirely suspended in some parts of the country, through the lamentable interference of abolition fanatics has proceded with almost unabated diligence and steadiness of purpose through the length and breadth of our synod."[12]

Moreover, the abolitionists' arguments against slavery served as a challenge which leaders of the plantation-mission cause accepted. If slavery was to be defended as a positive good, slaves must be Christianized and master-slave relations regularized by the Gospel. As early as 1829 C. C. Pinckney told South Carolina planters that it was important to gain the "advantage in argument over . . . our Northern Brethren" by improving the religious state of the slaves.[13] *The Fifth Annual Report* of the Liberty County Association frankly acknowledged the abolitionists' challenge:

One of their repeated charges is, that we do not afford religious instruction to the Negroes; nor have they failed to paint
up our deliquences in the strongest colors, and to pervert our
publications on the subject, designed to arouse ourselves to
duty; to the support of their own exaggerated statements.—
To this it may briefly be replied, that they themselves have
greatly retarded this work . . . .[14]

Schisms over slavery among the Methodist and Baptist
churches resulted in the formation of the Methodist Episcopal
Church, South, in 1844 and the Southern Baptist Convention in
1845, and created greater urgency among Southern churchs to
convert the slaves. At the debates over slavery in the General
Conference of the Methodist Church, William Capers had forcefully argued that if the Church took action against slavery, Southern ministers would be kept from contact with slaves and they
would be lost to the Church. Once the Church had split over
slavery, it became incumbent upon Southern churchmen to live
up to the ideals for which they had seceded.[15]

The schisms relieved some of the anxiety among slaveholders
that the churches were sympathetic to abolitionism. As Methodist
bishop John Early reported to the editor of the *Southern Christian
Advocate* in 1856, "until the Church was divided between North
and South," planters "were opposed to the Methodist ministry"
among their slaves "because of the constant agitation on the subject
of slavery."[16] The pronouncements of Southern clergymen were
also reassuring. The Baptist State Convention of Alabama, for
example, adopted a resolution strongly condemning abolitionists:

We regard with feelings of strong disapprobation the proceedings of such fanatics, believing that their efforts are inconsistent with the gospel of Christ; are calculated to oppress the
slave, to arm the assassin to shed the blood of good people in
our state, and to alienate the people in one state from those in
another, thereby endangering the peace and permanency of
our happy republic.[17]

A more positive approach was taken by the Liberty County
Association:

We should protect ourselves by Law, as far as possible, from the Circulation of Incendiary publications, and from the teachings of incendiary Agents; and then should we *look at home*, and enter upon such a discharge of our Duty to the Negroes, as will meet the approbation of God and our consciences, and commend ourselves to the consciences of other men. One important step towards a discharge of our duty in the most effectual manner, we believe to be, a general and judicious system of religious instruction . . . . *No means will so effectually counteract evil influences, and open up our way to the proper improvement of our colored population, as a judicious system of religious instruction.* [18]

No doubt the plantation missions existed before there was abolitionist pressure and would have continued without it, but the criticism leveled at Southern churches by Northern ones made them more sensitive about their duty to instruct slaves.

The "judicious system of religious instruction," referred to above, was a practical method consisting of several procedures deemed prudent and appropriate for Southern circumstances. The first step was regular preaching to the slaves on the Sabbath with sermons geared to their "level of understanding." Secondly, a lecture was to be held once a week during the evening, or if that proved impractical, one or two plantation meetings could be held for slaves in connection with regular pastoral visitations of white church members. The master and his family were urged to go to religious meetings attended by their slaves in order to give a good example and to create a sense of Christian community. Thirdly, Sabbath schools should be organized for children, youths, and adults. Fourthly, instruction was to be by the oral method. Antiliteracy laws for slaves ensured that missionaries instructed slaves in a "religion without letters," as Woodson called it. Jones rather defensively claimed that "The amount of religious Knowledge which may be communicated *orally*, can be conceived of by those only, who have made the experiment." The oral method required that the teacher first pose questions, state the answers, and then ask the class to repeat question and answer until both were memorized. After that, the teacher would ask each pupil in turn to answer a question. Several catechisms had been specially prepared for teaching slaves. Two of the most popular were Capers' *A Short Catechism for the Use of the Colored Members on Trial of the Methodist Episcopal Church in South Carolina* (1832) and Jones's *A Catechism for Colored Persons* (1834), though sometimes regular catechisms were employed. (Jones's *Catechism* proved so popular that it was eventually translated into Armenian and Chinese for use in the foreign mission field.)[19] The oral method of instruction also created a demand for collections of homilies, such as that of Episcopalian bishop Meade, *Sermons, Dialogues and Narratives for Servants, To Be Read to Them in Families* (1836). Audiovisual aids, such as hymns and Scripture cards—illustrations of Bible stories with texts, questions, and answers printed on the back—were also used.

Fifthly, "stated seasons for gathering together all colored members" of the church were strongly recommended. These gatherings were of prime importance, since, as Jones complained, "whatever pains may be taken to instruct candidates for church membership, the almost universal practice is to leave them to themselves after they become members and no further efforts are made to advance them in knowledge." This was a fatal error, since the slaves required "as much instruction *after* admission to the church as *before*," according to the missionary. Finally, no plantation meeting should ever be held without the knowledge and express consent of the owner or manager of the place.[20]

According to the plantation missionaries, their judicious methods of instruction would improve the morals of the slaves and would make them more honest and reliable. Jones's *Catechism* enjoined slaves

> to count their Masters 'worthy of all honour,' as those whom God has placed over them in this world; 'with all fear,' they are to be 'subject to them' and obey them in all *things*, possible and lawful, with good will and endeavour to *please them well*, . . . and let Servants serve their masters as faithfully be-

hind their backs as before their faces. God is present to see, if
their masters are not.[21]

As masters were well aware, there was no insurance that slaves
would take this lesson to heart. The memories of two slave revolts, led by black men who claimed religious validation for their
cause, made slaveholders wary of missionaries' assurances about
the tranquilizing effect of Christianity upon slaves.

A majority of the slaves executed for conspiring to revolt in
Charleston, South Carolina, in 1822 were members of the city's
African Methodist Church. Two of the conspirators were class
leaders, and several witnesses implicated Morris Brown, pastor of
the church and later assistant bishop to Richard Allen. It was
alleged that Denmark Vesey, the plot's leader, used scriptural
texts to win supporters for the insurrection. One conspirator confessed that Vesey "read in the Bible where God commanded, that
all should be cut off, both men, women and children, and said . . .
it was no sin for us to do so, for the Lord had commanded us to
do it."[22] Vesey, an ex-slave, who had purchased his own freedom
(with the proceeds from a lottery), read his Bible and found in it
that slavery was wrong. According to a deposition against Vesey,
"His general conversation was about religion which he would
apply to slavery, as for instance, he would speak of the creation of
the world, in which he would say all men had equal rights, blacks
as well as whites,—all his religious remarks were mingled with
slavery." Another leader of the conspiracy was "Gullah" Jack
Pritchard, frequently referred to by the slave conspirators as "the
little man who can't be killed, shot or taken." Gullah Jack, who
combined membership in the African Methodist Church with the
practice of conjure, promised the conspirators that his charms
would make them invulnerable. Thus, as Vincent Harding has
observed, the Vesey Conspiracy had the best of both religious
worlds, the doctrinal sanction of Scripture and the practical protection of conjure.[23]

In 1831 the bloodiest slave revolt in U.S. history took place in

Southampton, Virginia, under the leadership of Nat Turner, who had the reputation of being a seer, a prophet, and a preacher. Upon capture Turner was questioned about his motives. He answered that in 1826 he had received power to command the clouds, that he could cure disease by imposition of his hands, and that he had been directed to act by an omen from God.[24]

To counteract the damage done to the cause of slave instruction in the minds of white Southerners by reports of the Vesey and Turner revolts, plantation missionaries maintained that religious fanaticism and false teachings were to blame. Slaves who had been correctly instructed would never have followed such false prophets. As proof of this assertion, Jones offered the example of a "truly religious" Negro:

> I shall never forget the remark of a venerable colored preacher made with reference to the South Hampton tragedy. With his eyes filled with tears, and his whole manner indicating the deepest emotion, said he, 'Sir, it is the Gospel that we ignorant and wicked people need. If you will give us the Gospel it will do more for the obedience of servants and the peace of the community than all your guards, and guns, and bayonets.' This same Christian minister, on receiving a packet of inflammatory pamphlets through the Post-office . . . immediately called upon the Mayor of the City and delivered them into his hands.[25]

Which image of slave religion was the true one: that of Nat Turner, prophet and rebel, or that of Jones's "good Negro preacher"? The plantation missionaries worked long and hard to ensure that it was the latter.

Supporters of the missions reiterated their contention that Christianity would regularize and pacify relations between slaves and masters. To attain this end, plantation missionaries attempted to convince masters that they had duties toward their slaves. Masters and, particularly, mistresses were urged to take an active part in catechizing their slaves by reading sermons to them, including them in family prayers, and teaching them in Sabbath schools. More than instruction was necessary; it was important to build a relationship between master and slave consonant with Christianity. Religion, it was argued, must influence the owner's whole treatment of his slaves, physical as well as spiritual:

> It is the duty of Masters to *provide* for their Servants, both old and young, good houses, comfortable clothing, wholesome and abundant food; to take care of them when old, and infirm and crippled and useless; nurse them carefully in their sickness, and in nothing let them suffer, so far as their means will bear them out; and *keep their families together*. It is their duty to protect their Servants, from abuse or ill-treatment, and have justice done them when they are wronged.[26]

An ideal for plantation life was preached to slaveholders. Slaves were to be allowed opportunities "to make themselves comfortable and to accumulate money." A plot for gardening or for raising livestock would benefit both slave and owner for the "greater the interest which they have at stake on the plantation, the greater security for their good behavior, and the greater prospect of their moral improvement." Such missionaries as Jones and Capers who were slaveholders themselves predicted that "religious instruction of the Negroes will *promote our own morality and religion*," for when "one class rises, so will the other; the two are so intimately associated they are apt to rise or fall together; to benefit servants, evangelize the masters; to benefit masters, evangelize the servants." Ideally, the aim of the plantation mission was to create a "biracial community" of Christian masters and slaves. Pragmatically, it was suggested at the Charleston Meeting of 1845 "that where every good motive may be wanting, a regard to *self-interest* should lead every planter to give his people instruction.[27]

The missionary's ideal picture of a Christianized master-slave relationship contributed to the Southern myth of the benevolent, planter-patriarch presiding benignly over his happy black folks. In reality it was realized no more frequently than most religious ideals. Even economic self-interest was not always enough to bar capricious acts of cruelty in a system where one man had autocratic control over another. Numerous cases perversely proved that "gettin' religion" made the master treat his slaves more strictly and thus, from the slaves' point of view, worse. Frederick Douglass in his *Narrative* sarcastically portrayed the ill effects of religious conversion upon the personality of his master, Thomas Auld. And there is a great deal of supporting testimony from less famous ex-slaves, who announced their preference for "unconverted" masters. Former slave Mrs. Joseph Smith explained to the American Freedman's Inquiry Commission in 1863 why she thought Christian slaveholders "were the hardest masters."

> Well, it is something like this—the Christians will oppress you more. For instance, the biggest dinner must be got on Sunday. Now, everybody that has got common sense knows that Sunday is a day of rest. And if you do the least thing in the world that they don't like, they will mark it down against you, and Monday you have got to take a whipping. Now, the card-player and horse-racer won't be there to trouble you. They will eat their breakfast in the morning and feed their dogs, and then be off, and you won't see them again till night. I would rather be with a card-player or sportsman, by half, than a Christian.[28]

Before the same commission Isaac Throgmorton testified:

> I believe the people that were not religious treated their slaves better than those who were religious. A religious man will believe whatever the overseer says, and he has the control of the hands in the field. Whatever he says is law and gospel. If he says 'John has acted impudent,' the master will come round and say, 'Chastise him for it,' and the overseer will give him two or three hundred lashes. Then, in the next place, they don't feed nor clothe their slaves as well as the irreligious man. There was one Mr. Anderson, a preacher who married a girl who had slaves, and after that, he quit preaching pretty much, and drove his slaves very hard. He couldn't see anything but cotton bales . . . If pork was selling at a high price, all the slaves would get from the religious man would be three pounds a week, while the man that couldn't be so religious would give them four pounds.[29]

As Throgmorton's testimony attests, the virtues of thrift and careful management as exercised by a religious-minded slaveholder might very well mean hard times for his slaves.

Incidents of Christian slaveholders, including clergymen, brutalizing their slaves abound in the narratives of former slaves. Susan Boggs, ex-slave from Virgina, for example, recalled, "the man that baptized me had a colored woman tied up in his yard to whip when he got home, that very Sunday and her mother belonged to that same church. We had to sit and hear him preach and her mother was in church hearing him preach." She concluded, "I didn't see any difference between the slaveholders who had religion and those who had not . . . " Similar examples of the cruelty of pious slave masters could be multiplied indefinitely.[30] The blatant hypocrisy of white Christians was a fact of life to slaves, a fact undoubtedly discussed and deplored in the quarters. "I'd say old master treated us slaves bad," recalled Carey Davenport of Walker County, Texas, "and there was one thing I couldn't understand, 'cause he was 'ligious and every Sunday mornin' everybody had to git ready and go for prayer. I never could understand his 'ligion, 'cause sometimes he git up off his knees and befo' we git out the house he cuss us out."[31] The ideal of the patriarchal master, his rule tempered by Christian benevolence, was for many slaves an ironic fiction. An interview with a South Carolina freedman, which was reported from Port Royal in 1863 by a Northern white journalist, Charles Nordhoff, illustrates the basis for the slave's ironic view of their masters' Christian virtue:

> For a people living under a patriarchal system, they display a singular dislike to the patriarchs. I find the testimony universal, that the masters were 'mean.' All were not cruel, but all were hard taskmasters, so their former subjects say. 'Dey's all mean alike,' said one man, when closely questioned. Now there was one Fripps, a planter on one of the islands, of whom the blacks habitually speak as 'good Mr. Fripps.' 'Come now, Sam,' said the questioner, 'there was good Mr. Fripps, he

could not have been mean.' 'Yes, sah, he bad to his people
same as any of 'em.' 'Why do you call him good Mr. Fripps,
then?' 'Oh!' said Sam, 'dat no tell he good to we; call him
good 'cause he good Metodis' man—he sing and pray loud on
Sundys.'[32]

Whether the master was good or bad, benevolent or cruel, the
institution of slavery itself frequently made the ideal seem unat-
tainable. One well-intentioned planter, for example, complained:
"When I instruct my people they presume upon it, and almost in
proportion to my attention to them is my trouble with them. If I
have occasion to correct one of them, immediately he absents
himself from meeting, and there ends religious instruction with
him." In 1829 plantation owners petitioned the South Carolina
Methodist Conference for special preachers for their slaves on the
grounds that the "relationship between *Master* and *slave* made
void the best efforts of the most pious owners in Christianizing
them." Wary slaveholders warned that "if you gave a nigger an
inch he would take an ell" and that granting religious privileges
to slaves was to open a Pandora's box of troublesome claims. The
attitude of a good many masters was probably represented by the
statement of one Mississippi slaveholder to the effect "that there
was no difference in the market value of sinners and saints." Finally, there were those who were certain that "fiddling and dancing made the largest crops of cotton, and nigger religion led to
secret combinations and dangerous insurrections."[33]

While Jones, Capers, and other spokesmen for the plantation
mission consistently reiterated the distinction between temporal
and spiritual equality, there remained among slaveholders, even
those generally favorable to slave conversion, a lingering suspicion
that the two could not be as clearly segregated as the missionaries
claimed. In brief, they objected "that religious instruction tends to
the dissolution of the relations of society as now constituted;
and . . . that it will really do the people no good, but lead to
insubordination."[34] They felt that Christian fellowship between
master and slave, unless very carefully regulated, would corrode

the proper social hierarchy—the essential inferiority of blacks and superiority of whites—upon which the system rested. Slave conversion had to be measured by the rule of slave control, and a plantation manager would be dangerously remiss if he allowed anyone other than himself to do the measuring. So thought Whitemarsh B. Seabrook, a prominent South Carolina planter who accepted the value of religious instruction of slaves but who also fretted about fuzzy proposals delivered by idealistic missionaries without sufficient regard for the safeguards necessary to protect "domestic policy." In his capacity as president of the Agricultural Society of St. John's Colleton, Seabrook delivered an address on the *Management of Slaves*, published in 1834, in which he castigated those missionaries who, "in their *behavior* and *teachings*, apply the same rules to the black as the white man: Thereby laying the foundation for opinions inimical to the peace of the State, and hence to the cause of Christ itself." Seabrook detected in the missionaries' activities in regard to the slaves a "levelling tendency" which had to be condemned immediately and in no uncertain terms. This tendency toward leveling resulted from too idealistic a view of slave conversion: "Impelled by the paramount injunction to watch over the souls of the destitute," the missionaries, according to Seabrook, "having that isolated principle in view are, at this moment; pursuing a course of conduct in reference to our coloured population which may terminate in habits of irremediable insubordination." Challenging the mission ideal, Seabrook cynically observed that the "spectacle, of about three hundred thousand slaves under 'the care of the Church' of South Carolina, preparing themselves 'with prayer and fasting,' to receive the admonitions and precepts of the Saviour, is one of those fairy sketches educed from the exuberance of an erratic fancy."[35]

After vehemently denying that slaves should be "acquainted with the whole Bible," or every doctrine therein, Seabrook argued that it was "absolutely necessary" for them to become "intimately acquainted" with "the prominent portions of Scripture which shew the duties of servants and the rights of masters."

Moreover, any attempt to make the religious knowledge of slaves "co-extensive with that of their owners" was sheer lunacy. It was entirely sufficient if the slave was "informed on points essential to his salvation." Indeed, many servants had been "irretrievably ruined," he asserted, "by a false conception on the part of the owner or teacher of the duties which Christianity enjoins." Criticizing two of the more widely accepted programs for the religious instruction of the slaves, those drafted by Charles Colcock Jones and Thomas S. Clay in 1833, Seabrook attacked the suggestion that "the slaveholder and his family should officiate as teachers to their own people" as impractical, and predicted that the scene of white South Carolinians "reading and explaining the Bible and conversing with their servants on the subject of the soul's immortality" would surely signal that the "reign of fanaticism and misrule will have commenced."[36]

Even more threatening to a sane "domestic policy" was the existence of black preachers, lecturers, and catechists, who "have been the instruments of positive evils to society; apparent good they might have rendered; of real benefit they never have been to any one," as the precedents of 1822 and 1831 effectively demonstrated. Seabrook's objection to black clergymen and black catechists followed logically from his distrust of religious leveling: "The South are not, and I trust never will be prepared to establish among our servants a system of ecclesiastical preferment. They cannot allow any slave or free negro to assume an authority and influence, in derogation of the right, which, in this community, should be the exclusive property of the whites." In his enthusiasm to stamp out any suggestion of religious equality between blacks and whites, Seabrook totally rejected the seemingly innocuous practice of adapting a part of every sermon to the "intellectual wants" of the slaves, and even objected to the custom of lining out a few verses of the hymns so that the slaves might more readily join in the services. Both techniques he judged anathema as devices of the levelers.[37]

Certainly, most plantation missionaries would have considered

Seabrook's views to be alarmist in the extreme. And yet, over-stated as his position may have been, it did point up a very real problem: the difficult, if not impossible, task of ensuring that the egalitarian tendencies of Christian instruction would remain safely within the boundaries of slave management. Labor as they might, the missionaries could not yoke together the goals of slave instruc-tion and slave control into a stable and permanent union. Inherent in the recognition of the slave's claims to humanity and even more in the assertion of his *right* to Christian instruction was, as Sea-brook astutely recognized, an implicit threat, even though muted, to the practice of slave control and management. The threat came closer to being explicit when some masters admitted that they had been converted to a more spiritual view of their slaves. Seabrook's worst fear would have been confirmed, for example, by the slave-holder who pledged, "I will never put obstructions between man and his God; thinking it a matter of conscience, and every man, white or black has a right to pursue a course to suit himself."[38]

Plantation missionaries asserted that the discipline of the church was a useful means of reminding slaves of their duties toward their masters. And so it was. But once in a while it worked to remind masters of their duties toward their slaves. In 1820 the Hephzibah Baptist Church in East Feliciana Parish, Louisiana, "took up the conduct of Br. Wilm West for whipping his black brother; the church considered there was no cause for his doing so and he was excluded for the same by the church." The Frederiksburg Baptist Church in Virginia charged one of its members "Bro. Wingfield with Ill Treatment of a Servant Girl" in July 1846. After a committee had been appointed to investi-gate the charge, Wingfield admitted that he had "whipped the girl indiscreatly." Concern for the slaves' religious state led the Dover Baptist Association of Virginia to protest in 1850 against the law forbidding slave literacy. The association resolved "to use all proper means to procure such a modification of the laws as would remove all restraints from the prudent exertion to teach the African race to read the Bible and instruct them in those things

William Capers. Reprinted from William Pope Harrison, *The Gospel Among the Slaves* (Nashville, 1893).

which belong to their everlasting weal." Incidents like these were few and far between, but the fact that they occurred at all indicates that the ideal of reciprocal Christian duties had some power to arbitrate if not to ameliorate the relationship of master and slave. The suggestion that masters had any *duties* toward their slaves, was, as Eugene Genovese has pointed out, a significant admission affecting the theoretical framework of the slave system. It was a concession which slaves were quick to grab hold of, insist upon, and extend. Similarly, the qualification that Jones added to his description of the slaves' duties toward their masters—that slaves ought to "obey them in all *things* possible and lawful"—was important in that it made conditional and relative the absolute authority of the master. If a slave was obliged to obey only the lawful commands of his master, a door, no matter how small the space, had been left ajar for the slave's own judgment and will to be vindicated if they came into conflict with his master's.[39]

The antebellum plantation missionary faced, besides these ideological challenges, the usual practical difficulties which hampered his predecessors: too few ministers, inadequate facilities, and lack of money. Concerning financial difficulties Holland N. McTyeire commented bitingly, "It is this necessity of taking poor men's money to preach to rich men's Negroes that keeps the treasury of the Missionary Society low." A report of the Missionary Society of the Methodist Episcopal Church in 1841 described a few other difficulties encountered by missionaries, particularly in the lowland coastal regions where they were most active:

> In no portion of our work are our missionaries called to endure greater privations or make greater sacrifices of health and life, than in these missions among the slaves, many of which are located in sections of the Southern country which are proverbially sickly, and under the fatal influence of a climate which few white men are capable of enduring even for a single year.

Capers confirmed that a missionary acted as "a servant of slaves literally—treated as inferior by the proprietors, as hardly equal to the overseers, half starved sometimes, suffocated with smoke, sick with the stench of dirty cabins & as-dirty negroes, sleepless from the stings of . . . musquitoes and all in the very centre . . . of the kingdom of disease," all for the privilege of being called a "nigger preacher."[40]

Yet the task inspired some to missionary zeal. "My heart was filled with gratitude and thankfulness to God," exclaimed one South Carolina missionary, "for the great privilege of being an honored instrument in his hand of carrying the gospel to those who had never heard it before although they were in my own native land." Another missionary confessed simply: "I was pleased with the idea of preaching the gospel to the poor."[41]

In all the reports, resolutions, minutes, sermons, and speeches devoted to the plantation-mission cause, several kinds of motives were expressed by planters and missionaries. The desire to evangelize the poor, the desire to make slaves docile, the desire to create a model plantation, and the desire to defend slavery against abolitionist attacks were all reasons for supporting plantation missions. In addition, it has been suggested, there was another reason moving laymen and clergy alike, although this reason remained largely unexpressed. Not only was Christianization of the slaves a rationale for slavery, but it was, as it had been from the beginning, a balm for the occasional eruptions of Christian conscience disturbed by the notion that maybe slavery was wrong. Donald G. Mathews has aptly described this unconscious motivation:

> The conversion of his slave would . . . please a Christian slaveholder who was concerned with the state of their souls, and who might even have had some secret misgivings about owning them. If Negroes could not be trusted with the gospel, Christianity might be "at war" with slavery, but if they became true Christians within the structures of Southern society, they would be living proof of God's favor, and conscience might be satisfied. After all, the Church had said that the master's first duty was to provide for the salvation of his servants.[42]

In moments of doubt about his own salvation, the slaveholder perhaps found some compensation in zeal for the conversion of his slaves. Moreover, as the *North Carolina Christian Advocate* of December 15, 1859, argued, the Southern Christian conscience was caught in a bind: "Everybody who believes in religion at all, admits that it is the duty of Christians to give religious instruction to the slave population of the Southern States. To deny the safety and propriety of preaching the Gospel to the negroes, is either to abandon Christianity, or to admit that slavery is condemned by it."[43]

The effectiveness of the antebellum plantation mission is difficult to measure. Undoubtedly, the publicity generated by sponsors of the mission contributed to an increased awareness of their cause as a current issue in Southern society. As the century wore on into the decade of the 1850s, institutional efforts were increased. However, the resolutions of some clerical bodies remained simply that. For example, in 1834 an impressive-sounding "Kentucky Union for the moral and religious improvement of the colored race" was formed as "a union of several denominations of christians in the State." Five years later, according to the chairman of the Union's executive committee, the "Union had not accomplished much," despite ten vice presidents and a seven-man executive committee. The opposite was true of the Liberty County Georgia Association, which was an effective organization for catechizing slaves, though its successes were dwarfed by the size of the black population in the area where it worked.[44]

In the field of plantation missions the Southern Methodists proved to be the most active, although Baptists, Presbyterians, and Episcopalians also increased their efforts toward slave conversion. From 1846 to 1861 the Methodist Episcopal Church, South, is said to have raised its black membership from 118,904 to 209,836. Methodist contributions to plantation missions grew from about $80,000 in 1845 to $236,000 in 1861. However, Methodist claims to increased membership due to mission work must be viewed with caution. It has been pointed out that "The apparent rapid growth of missions, compared to that of the regular work, was not as impressive as it appears . . . many city churches put their Negroes into missions, thus swelling the mission statistics without any actual growth in Church membership." It has been estimated that between the years 1845 and 1860 the black membership of the Baptist Church increased from 200,000 to 400,000.[45] But figures of church membership are not generally noted for their accuracy. It should be remembered also that church membership is not the only measure of evangelization. Undoubtedly, many slaves learned the tenets of Christianity, accepted them, and attended church, without actually appearing on the official rolls of any church. In 1857 the white Methodist minister, John Dixon Long, described the class of slaves most likely to be so enrolled, "such as are owned by the less extensive slaveholders and farmers . . . have no overseer, live in the kitchen, mingle with the master's family, eat the same kind of food . . . Their children are raised with their master's children, play with them, and nurse them . . . A strong attachment frequently exists between them and their masters and mistresses. From this class we derive most of our church members . . . " (Significantly Long adds: "Notwithstanding the superior physical condition of this class of slaves, they are generally more unhappy and restless than the more degraded classes. Their superior advantages only serve as a lamp to show them their degradation.")[46]

How did slaves respond to plantation missions? For some, the novelty of religious instruction exerted an appeal. Other slaves met the missionary's instruction with arguments he did not expect. Novice missionaries were forewarned:

> He who carries the Gospel to them . . . discovers deism, skepticism, universalism . . . all the strong objections against the truth of God; objections which he may perhaps have considered peculiar only to the cultivated minds . . . of *critics* and *philosophers*![47]

Some slaves resented the message of docility preached by the missionaries and rejected it out of hand as "white man's religion."

Still another attitude toward religious practice was expressed by those slaves who complained that they were too weary to attend church, and that it was "hard for them to serve their earthly and heavenly master too."[48] And, of course, there were slaves who found meaning in the message spread by plantation missionaries, accepted it on faith and tried their best to incorporate it in their lives.

It is important to realize that slaves learned about Christianity not only from whites but from other slaves as well. Some slave children received their first instruction in Christianity from parents, kinfolk, or elder slaves. According to Jones, "The Negroes on plantations sometimes appoint one of their number, commonly the old woman who minds the children during the day to teach them to say their prayers, repeat a little catechism and a few hymns, every evening."[49] Slave preachers, licensed and unlicensed, black exhorters, and church-appointed watchmen—or "overseers," as they were also called—instructed their fellow slaves in the rudiments of Christianity, nurtured their religious development, and brought them to conversion in some cases without the active involvement of white missionaries or masters. Then, too, it was in the nature of Protestant evangelicalism to de-emphasize the role of mediators between the person and God. As Luther Jackson perceptively observed: "Experimental religion by its very nature is an inward, subjective, experience so that the slave who was convinced of sin in his own heart might seek baptism and church membership without the intervention of any white Christians whatsoever."[50] At the core of this piety was the Reformation insight that salvation was based not on external observance and personal merit, nor on the intercession of church and clergy, but on the relationship of the individual to the sovereign will of God. With this view of the religious life the person inevitably turned inward and searched his or her own heart to discern the workings of God's Spirit there.

Coupled with the notion that ultimate authority rested on God's Word as expressed in the Bible, the stress on inner personal experience encouraged individual autonomy in matters of religious conscience, an autonomy difficult to control, as the fissiparous tendencies of Protestantism have frequently shown. Among the evangelical churches the Baptists, in particular, institutionalized the spirit of Gospel freedom by insisting upon the autonomy of each congregation. Black Protestants, as well as whites, imbibed this spirit of religious freedom, and proved, to the extent possible, not at all reluctant about deciding their own religious affairs. Baptists, precisely because of their independent church polity, offered more opportunity than any other denomination for black members to exercise a measure of control over their church life. In some mixed churches committees of black members were constituted in order to oversee the church order of black members. These committees listened to applicants relate their religious experience and heard the replies of those members charged with breach of discipline. They were usually restricted to an advisory role, as their recommendations had to be approved by the general church meeting. Still, committees of "the brethern in black," meeti. g once a month, conducting business, and reporting their recommendations to the general meeting, gave to black church members experience in church governance, and so laid a foundation upon which freedmen would rapdily build their own independent churches after emancipation.[51]

Long before that day, however, as discussed earlier, both slaves and free blacks in some towns of the South had already begun to exercise control over religious organizations. The early independence of black churches and preachers had been curtailed in law and in fact by the reaction of Southern whites to slave conspiracies and to abolitionist agitation. By 1832 some separate African Baptist churches wre required to merge with white churches. The African Baptist Church at Williamsburg, Virginia, was closed, and slave members at Elam Baptist in Charles City were transferred by their owners to a church under white control.[52] Despite harassment and legal restriction, there were black churches and black preachers who managed, now and then to

successfully evade limits to their autonomy. Decried as a dangerous anomaly by some Southern whites, black congregations—a
few led by black pastors—not only survived but even thrived. In
1845 the Baptist Sunbury Association of Georgia had 4,444
black members (and 495 whites) served by seven black churches
with four ordained black ministers and at least one more black
member licensed to preach. In Virginia several African church
choirs gave concerts and organized fairs to raise funds for their
churches. Black churches engaged in benevolent activities as well.
According to one traveler, "In 1853, fifteen thousand dollars were
contributed by five thousand slaves in Charleston, to benevolent
objects." One benevolent cause which black Christians took up
was the foreign missions. As early as 1815 the Richmond African
Baptist Missionary Society was formed, and in 1821 two members of the society, Lott Carey and Colin Teague, were sent as
missionaries to Liberia. In 1843 the slaves of J. Grimke Drayton
of South Carolina "planted in their own time, a *missionary* crop"
which netted sixteen dollars for "the extension of the gospel."
Another benevolent cause sponsored by black churches was self-
help. The Gillfield Baptist Church, in Petersburg, Virginia, received a "petition of a member from a sister church for funds with
which to buy her self and her children"—a common request. By
the time of emancipation there were black churches in the South
with histories that extended back fifty—and in a few cases, seventy-five—years.[53]

For slaves, either in mixed or in separate black churches, to
participate in the organization, leadership, and governance of
church structures was perceived as "imprudent," and attempts
were made to carefully limit black participation. Surely it was
inconsistent, argued the more thoroughgoing defenders of slavery,
to allow blacks such authority. As Charles Cotesworth Pinkney
declared before the Charleston Agricultural Society in 1829, the
exercise of religious prerogatives opened to slaves a sphere of
freedom from white control. "We look upon the habit of Negro
preaching as a wide-spreading evil; not because a black man can-

not be a good one, but . . . because they acquire an influence independent of the owner, and not subject to his control; . . . when they have possessed this power, they have been known to make an improper use of it."[54] By active if limited participation in the institutional life of the church, black preachers and church members seized opportunities to publicly express their views and to direct themselves. The problem with including slaves in church fellowship was that it was difficult to control their efforts toward autonomy, particularly when the churches stressed an inner, personal, experiential approach to religion and thus encouraged individualism. The difficulty was augmented by the participatory character of church government which did not, among evangelical Protestants, depend solely upon the clergy but involved the voices and votes of individual members of the congregation in such important matters as "calling" ministers, electing representatives to meetings of larger church bodies, disciplining fellow members, and admitting new ones. There were, then, two conflicting tendencies in the biracial religious context: one encouraged black independence; the other, white control.

The Limits of Christian Fellowship

An essential part of church life for white and black church members was the ordering of personal behavior and social relationships according to the moral precepts of the Bible. It was the serious responsibility of the congregation as a whole, and of each member as well, to keep watchful care over the daily activities of the brothers and sisters. Meetings were held regularly, usually quarterly or monthly, to discuss and adjudicate breaches of church discipline. At these meetings church members were reported or reported themselves for un-Christian conduct; committees were appointed to investigate disputes between the brethren; those accused were given opportunity to answer charges made against them; letters of "dismission" were granted and denied; unrepentant offenders were suspended or expelled; the repentant were readmitted into church fellowship; and minutes were kept of the proceedings. Sins for which members, white and black, could expect to be disciplined ranged from lying and backbiting to drunkenness and adultery. It was in the context of this disciplined "watch care" that the ideal fellowship of covenanted believers was to be built and preserved. It was in this context also that the white and black members of mixed churches in the antebellum South struggled with the tension between Christian fellowship and the system of slavery. Fellowship required that all church members be treated alike; slavery demanded that black members, even the free, be treated differently.[55]

One of the more touchy areas of potential conflict between fellowship and slavery was the problem of the mistreatment of slaves. Did the rule of Gospel order extend to the means used by masters to control their slaves? In theory the answer was, of course, yes, but in practice it was a difficult issue. When, for example, the Baptist Dover Association of Virginia was questioned in 1796, "Is there no restriction on believing masters in the chastisement of their servants?" its response was: "There is no doubt but masters may, and sometimes do exercise an unreasonable authority; but as it is very difficult, and perhaps impossible to fix a certain rule in these cases, we think the churches should take notice of such as they may think improper and deal with the transgressor, as they would with offenders in other crimes."[56] The Mississippi Baptist Association, meeting in session in October 1808, received a similar query: "What steps would be most advisable to take with members of our society whose treatment to their slaves is unscriptural?" Their answer was as general as that of the Virginia Dover Association: "We recommend to the several churches belonging to our connection to take notice of any improper treatment of their members toward their slaves and deal with them in brotherly love according to the rule of the gospel."[57] It was a problematic issue for a very basic reason: to permit a slave to bring an accusation of misconduct against a white member was to contradict in the Church the civil order where slave testimony against whites was legally unacceptable.

Even if a slave owner was accused of abusing a slave by a white church brother, it remained a sensitive issue: How was one to judge when discipline had become abuse? That such accusations occurred at all indicates the way in which church discipline could potentially complicate the slave-master relationship and how that relationship could in turn complicate church discipline. The peace of more than one antebellum congregation was disturbed by charges and countercharges about slave disobedience and slave-owner brutality. When the Forks of Elkhorn Baptist Church in Kentucky held its monthly church conference on the second Saturday of January 1806, Brother Palmer brought before the church a complaint against Brother Stephens and his wife "for not dealing with Nancy their Negroe Woman and bringing her before the Church and for putting her in Irons." Brother Stephens was acquitted of the charge. A second charge was brought against Sister Stephens "for giving their Negroe Woman the lye." Sister Stephens was acquitted of both charges. But Brother Palmer and the slave member Nancy didn't let the matter rest there: on the second Saturday of April 1806 Palmer once again "brought a complaint against Bro. Stephens and Wife for not leeting [sic] Nancy come to see her Child . . . ." This time Sister Stephens countered with a complaint against Nancy for falsely reporting that "Bro. Stephens said he would give her a hundred stripes and every Six stripes dip the Cow hide in Salt and Water—And saying while she was in Irons she suffered every day for [want of] Fire, Victuals and Water—And for saying when ever she and the Children fell out they would not hear her, but believe the Children and whip her . . . ." Decision on the charges was delayed until the next meeting, at which time Brother Stephens and Sister Stephens were once more acquitted. Nancy was found guilty and excluded from church fellowship.[58] Though she failed, it is interesting that Nancy attempted to seek recourse for her problems with her master and mistress in the church. Evidently she had to do so indirectly, through a white spokesman, Brother Palmer, who voiced her accusations for her. Even so, she apparently had reason to hope that the church would intervene on her behalf or at the very least serve as a forum for her complaint. (One can only wonder if she succeeded in embarrassing Brother Stephens and Sister Stephens, and at what cost.) The church, after all, did take up her charge instead of dismissing it out of hand. More research into the minute books of antebellum congregations will be necessary before we can accurately estimate how frequently or infrequently slaves sought redress for maltreatment by appealing to church discipline.[59]

Another area of conflict between the Gospel and slavery which some congregations struggled to solve was the vexing problem of slave marriage. How could the church define breaches of the marital relation by slaves separated from their husbands and wives because of sale? Was it adultery for them to take up with another while their former spouses were still alive? In 1805 the Sandy Creek Baptist Association of North Carolina received a query from the Bear Creek church asking for some guidance in this matter: "What do we consider as a valid marriage between black people; and if any marriage be valid, is it in our fellowship to part them on any occasion?" The association put off an answer until 1808, when the question was placed before the delegates again. They answered that slaves were validly married "When they come together in their former and general custom, having no [other] companion. Owners of slaves should use all reasonable and lawful means to prevent them from being separated. To effect this, they should put themselves to some inconvenience, in buying, selling, or exchanging, to keep them together. Both moral obligation and humanity demand it."[60]

The practical problem in judging the marital status of slaves is evident in the indecision of the Virginia Portsmouth Baptist Association, which took up the issue in 1792 and again in 1793. "Is it lawful and agreeable to the Word of God, for a black Man servant, (or Slave) who has been Married, and his Wife removed from him a great distance, without his or her consent to marry another Woman during her Life or not?" After much debate it was agreed that the question be withdrawn and that a committee of three brethren substitute a rephrased query. The amended question read: "What ought Churches to do with Members in their Communion, who shall either directly, or indirectly separate married Slaves, who are come together according to the custom as Man and Wife?" After another prolonged debate the question "was thought by a Majority to be so difficult, that no answer could be given it."[61]

On the local level, individual congregations had to come up with an answer, difficult though it might be, particularly since the charge of adultery was such a serious one. In November 1790 the Flat River Primitive Baptist Church of Person County, North Carolina, took up the case of "Negro Sam," who had come "before the church, in consequence of a letter sent from Bro. Davidson concerning his [Sam's] wife who belonged to said Davidson, and was carryed by him to South Carolina, and . . . has got another husband." Sympathetically the church decided "this being a trying case where a man and wife is parted by their owners, who being in bondage cannot help themselves, as such we have come to this conclusion that it shall not brake fellowship with us if Sam should git another wife."[62] When Charles, another of the slave members of the Flat River Church, "was accused of taking two different women as his wives," the church meeting in conference in September 1792 appointed a committee to inquire into the charge. Charles apparently had been moved a distance from his old wife and claimed that he took a new one because he was "prevented . . . from going after the one he left." The committee found that Charles's story was contradicted by two white men who claimed that they prevented him from going to see his old wife *after* he had taken another one. Upon their testimony the church agreed in October to "give Charles up as an heathen man or publican." In November Charles complained that "the report upon which he was turn'd out was not right," and the church appointed a different committee to reopen his case. In January 1793 Charles's complaint was judged "well founded." Although vindicated of the charge of adultery, Charles was accused of drunkenness and so had to remain under excommunication until he gave satisfaction.[63]

The same Flat River Church was exercised again in July 1795 over the issue of slave marriage, but this time the issue involved a white member. The request of Brother Henry Lyon for a letter of "dismission" "was objected to on account of his being about to carry his negro women away from their husbands." Because the circumstances were unclear, "with respect to the lawfulness of their coming together" [slave marriages], the case was postponed until the next meeting, which was spent almost entirely in debating the matter. After a good deal of argument about which the record is unfortunately silent, "the church without the concurrence of the minister and one other member" agreed to grant Lyon a letter of dismission. Five years later, however, Lyon got his comeuppance; after the church received a report from Tennessee that he was leading a disorderly life, keeping a tavern with a billiard table and running a dancing school, he was excommunicated "as a heathen man or publican." Why these offenses were viewed more severely by the church than the parting of two women from their husbands is a question not raised in the church minute book.[64]

An appreciation of the turmoil caused by the issue of slave marriage in a congregation seriously concerned about Gospel ordinances can be gained by reading the minute books of the Welsh Neck Baptist Church of South Carolina. The problem of plural marriages among slave members had plagued the church for several years, and in January 1829 it was brought to a head by the request for a letter of dismission by a slave called Dicey. The church decided to refuse Dicey's request because she had taken a husband in Mississippi when her master removed her there, though she already had a husband in South Carolina. During the discussion of Dicey's case "it was ascertained that a number of the coloured members were implicated on the subject of Double Marriages, & some since they had become members of the Church."

All told, ten slave members, some of long standing, were involved. Meeting to consider what action to take, the church "felt particularly embarrassed in regard to the old members, who had been received & held in fellowship by our Fathers in the Church." The troubled congregation decided to postpone decision. The next day, after his sermon, the pastor proposed that the church remain after service to consider several resolutions he had drawn up to deal with the problem.[65] An honest and poignant statement of the difficulty facing a church torn between sympathy for slave members and the prohibitions of the Bible, the minister's resolutions are worth quoting extensively:

> It has been found, upon examination, into the state of our coloured members, that some of them had long been living with a second Companion in the familiar intercourse of husband or Wife; after having separated from one or more that were still living & in the same neighborhood. In some of these instances they had a number of Children. The Church feel greatly embarrased, on account of this unhappy state of things & are still not perfectly satisfied as to what they ought to determine in relation to them. However after much Prayerful searching of the Holy Scriptures; & seeking to God for direction: *It is Resolved.* 1st that great deference is due to the memory of the Fathers of the Church; & we cherish such respect for their Opinions & Conduct, that we dare not, without the most express warrant from the Word of God, reverse what they had deliberately done. Therefore since the Church was given to us in this condition; & we lived Years together with the persons above alluded to in Christian Union; We think it now a less evil to retain them in fellowship than to disown them for a wrong, that probably was not known by the Church at the time of their reception; & not viewed by themselves in a Scriptural point of light, as the most of them are bound servants; & have not been taught to read the Sacred Word. 2nd. But as we know that many of the younger members have been better instructed in the nature & perpetuity of the Marriage obligations; while we would neither reverse the doings of our Venerable Elijahs, nor dictate to posterity; We resolve for ourselves to instruct, reprove, & labour with any,

who have knowingly departed from the Gospel rule; & their Covenant engagements & if possible correct the wrong; or exclude them from our connection. 3rd. That Servants, separated by their owners, & removed to too great a distance to visit each other, may be considered as virtually dead to each other; & therefore at liberty to take a second Companion, in the life time of the first; as the act of separation was not their own voluntary choice; but the will of those, who had legal control over them. These resolutions being read & considered were Unanimously adopted. In Conformity with the last resolution a letter of dismission was granted to Dicey . . . .[66]

It is significant that a major reason for the congregation's decision to overlook the slave members' "adulterous" unions was the fact that those involved had been living in regular church fellowship for a long time, in some cases for as many as twenty years. The third resolution, by equating involuntary separation with death, presented a solution to the problem which took account of the realities of the slave situation. But for all its realism, the solution is in effect one more indication of the extent to which the churches accommodated the social system rather than attempting to change it. It is apparent that the Welsh Neck and other churches were sincerely troubled by the issue of slave marriage, but what is puzzling about their efforts to solve the problem is the failure of the churches to petition for the legal recognition of slave marriage. Even though the appeal almost certainly would have proved fruitless, the fact that it was not even considered by the churches demonstrated the limits of Christian fellowship.

Another area of potential conflict between institutional church life and the restrictiveness of slavery was the active participation of slaves as exhorters, deacons, and preachers. A few, as noted above, exercised their ministry in separate black churches, which managed to preserve a surprising degree of autonomy even while weathering times of proscription. The "pioneer black preachers" of the late eighteenth century were succeeded in the 1830s by a second generation. The majority of the black preachers and separate black churches were Baptist, which helps to explain why the

Baptists attracted as many black members as they did. Baptists simply offered more opportunity for black participation than any other denomination, as noted in 1842 by Charles Colcock Jones: "There are more Negro communicants, and more churches regularly constituted, exclusively of Negroes, with their own regular houses of public worship, and with ordained Negro preachers, attached to this denomination than to any other in the United States. . . . Perhaps in most of the chief towns in the South there are [Baptist] houses of public worship erected for the Negroes alone . . . ."[67] The labors of the vast majority of these preachers, whether they ministered to their black brethren in racially mixed or separate churches, were recorded sparsely, if at all. But now and then glimpses of individual black clergymen and black churches emerge from the records of churches and associations in various areas of the South.

Baptist associations, from Virginia and Georgia in the East to Kentucky and Louisiana in the West, included black churches, sometimes pastored by black men, and listed not infrequently as among the largest churches in the association. The black Gillfield Baptist Church of Petersburg, Virginia, admitted to the Portsmouth Association in 1810, had grown by 1821 into the largest church of the association, with a membership of 441, more than twice the number of the next largest. Frequently represented in its earlier years in the associational meetings by Israel Decoudry, a free black of West Indian origin, and by other free black members, Gillfield was pastored by white ministers and was gradually subjected to tighter and tighter restrictions by the Portsmouth Association, which attempted in 1829 to make it consolidate with the white Market Street Church of Petersburg. The Gillfield congregation resisted this attempt to disband it, but did accede to the association's decision that it be represented through white delegates from the Market Street Church. In 1838, however, the Gillfield Church tried to persuade the association to allow it to be represented once again by delegates from its own congregation, but the request was denied.[68] The actions of Gillfield and other black churches indicate that separate black churches resisted to the extent possible, given their precarious status, the attempts of associations to constrict their sphere of autonomy.

An incident in the history of the First African Church of Savannah, Georgia, is particularly instructive about the limitations white-controlled associations placed upon black churches and about the ability of black congregations to find ways to protect their partial independence. The First African Church, as noted above, was formed in the midst of severe persecution by a slave named Andrew Bryan and was organized into a church on January 20, 1788. Bryan pastored the church and lived to see its congregation increase to over four hundred members, and two daughter churches, the Second African and the Ogeechee, or Third African, emerged from it.

In 1815 Andrew Marshall, Bryan's nephew, became pastor of the First African Church of Savannah, and by 1830 his congregation numbered 2,417.[69] A man of exceptional energy and strong personality, Marshall was at the center of a controversy which threatened the continued existence of his church. Alexander Campbell, upon visiting Savannah, was permitted by Marshall to preach from the pulpit of the First African Church. Upset by Campbell's "new doctrines," especially after Marshall gave the impression that he believed in them, some members of the church, led by Deacon Adam Johnson, objected. Contention rapidly escalated to division and violence, with Marshall and the majority of the congregation breaking away from the church and leaving it in the hands of Johnson and his supporters. When the controversy came to the attention of the Sunbury Baptist Association in 1832, a committee was appointed to investigate, and promptly recommended not only that Marshall be silenced for heterodoxy and schism, but also that the First African Church "on account of its corrupt state be considered as dissolved" and reconstituted as a branch of the white Baptist Church. The association went so far as to recommend that the Second African and all African churches in the area constitute themselves as branches of white Baptist churches and, finally, appointed a committee to transmit this last resolution to the state legislature and the mayor of Savannah "with explanatory remarks." In 1833 the association concluded: "this Association, having undoubted testimony of Andrew Marshall's holding the sentiments avowed by Alexander Campbell, now declares him, and all his followers, to have thrown themselves out of the fellowship of the Churches of this Association."[70]

Ecclesiastically, the association, according to Baptist policy, had no juridical power over individual churches. Church government belonged, in theory, to each church. But in actuality the slave codes gave white associations a great deal of control over black churches. The mechanism of control was described by James Simms, in his history of the First African Church of Savannah: "under the then existing laws of the State of Georgia our white brethren were held somewhat responsible for our good conduct, and . . . they came and sat in the conferences or any other meetings when they thought it necessary, and the courts of jurisdiction would not give our colored ministers a license to preach or officiate in the ordinances of the Church unless they were endorsed by two or more white Baptist ministers."[71] Furthermore, the land on which the church stood, purchased in 1797 by Andrew Bryan, could legally be held only under a system of perpetual trusteeship by whites. Fellowship with the white members of the association, then, was politically necessary if black churches were to survive as separate bodies.

In January 1833 the First African Church responded to the resolutions of the Sunbury Association by apparently agreeing to place itself under the control of the white Savannah Baptist Church. The African Church, however, set down certain conditions which the white church would have to observe, and the first of these conditions affirmed in effect the fundamental autonomy of the black church:

> We propose to come under the supervision of a committee of your own body, provided you will receive us on the terms and

conditions following: 1st. That we be independent in our meetings; that is, that we receive and dismiss our own members, and elect and dismiss our own officers, and finally, manage our own concerns independently; however with this restriction—in case any measure is taken by us which shall seem to militate against our good standing as a church of Christ we shall submit it to a committee of five members, whom we shall choose out of the Baptist Church in Savannah, [white] whose counsel we bind ourselves to follow, provided it be not contrary to the precepts of the Gospel.[72]

There followed four more resolutions, none of them seriously restricting the self-determination ensured in the first. This was obviously a far cry from the expressed wish of the Sunbury Association that the African church be dissolved and reconstituted as part of the white church. Yet the crucial test was the status of Andrew Marshall. Late in January 1833 a committee from the white Savannah Baptist Church advised the First African Church "that Andrew Marshall should not go into the pulpit and preach, nor administer the ordinance of baptism, nor the Lord's supper," but there was no objection to his leading prayers, exhorting, "making pastoral visits, marrying, attending funerals and extending the right hand of fellowship."[73] However, one month later, the white church was informed that the "officers of the First African Church stated that it had called Andrew C. Marshall to be its pastor, and that they had thought it best for him to resume his pastoral duties . . . " The white committee (excepting one member, whose support Marshall had gained) refused to countenance this flagrant disregard of its instruction that Marshall not be allowed to resume his pastoral charge, and it appealed to the white trustees of First African and to the city authorities to shut down the African Church.[74] Significantly, the committee closed its letter to the trustees with the following sentiment: "We appeal to you not only as a Christian but as a large property holder to aid us in checking false doctrine among our slaves." In its letter to the mayor of Savannah the committee portrayed Marshall as "a designing man, seeking only his own aggrandisement and the love of power, even

Andrew Marshall. Reprinted from E. K. Love, *History of the First African Baptist Church* (Savannah, Ga., 1888).

at the expense of the peace and happiness of his own people." The committee admitted that "the majority of the church appear determined to go with Marshall at all hazards," and explained, "he has them so completely under his control that they are ready on all occasions to sanction his mandates, whether right or wrong." As if that were not a large enough red flag to wave before the eyes of the mayor, the committee made sure the implications were clear: "The individuals composing the First African Church are in part the property of our citizens, and it is for them, if they feel any interest in their everlasting or temporal welfare, to interpose and save them from the baneful influence of a designing man."[75]

There is no record that the mayor responded; the civil authorities did not shut down the church. The trustees did answer, but not exactly as the committee had expected. Writing on behalf of the trustees of the First African Church, John Williamson attacked the right of the committee to interfere in the affairs of an independent Baptist church, defended Andrew Marshall against unproven charges of heresy, and upheld the religious privileges "of a large number of our fellow beings . . . which are guaranteed to them by the laws of our State, by the word of God, and by every principle of kindness which ought to be a prominent feature in the behavior of all those who profess the Gospel." Williamson declared, "I consider it incumbent on me, in connection with the other Trustees, *to see the church kept open* in order to afford Andrew C. Marshall, and the church of which he is pastor, the privilege of worshipping God to the best of their knowledge."[76]

In 1835 and 1836 the First African Church applied for readmission to the Sunbury Association. It was denied both times. Finally in 1837 "Andrew Marshall having made full renunciation of holding the peculiar sentiments of Alexander Campbell with which he has been charged," the First African Church was readmitted, with a membership of 1,263. Expelled in 1832 with Marshall as pastor and delegate, the church returned five years later with Marshall still as pastor and delegate.[77] During the five years of turmoil, Marshall had survived challenges to his authority from deacons within his congregation and from white authorities without. The First African Church had tactfully but firmly resisted the advice and warnings of the Savannah Church committee and had kept the pastor the majority of its membership wanted. That Marshall and his congregation maneuvered successfully through several years of political struggle was due to their determination, initiative, and astuteness. That they had any space within which to maneuver was due to the Baptist principle that the church is its own government.

The separate black Baptist churches in New Orleans also benefited from their denomination's tradition of guarding congregational independence. In 1857 Mayor Waterman of New Orleans revoked "all permission heretofore given for Divine Services in Colored Churches." Members of the African churches immediately met in order to make some arrangement with the white churches, an arrangement which would, according to the minutes of the First African Church, "enable the Colored people to occupy their House of Worship again." After several meetings a plan which served the purpose was developed and agreed upon "with the white brethren." The agreement included eight provisions, of which the most important was the first: "Each Colored Church is constituted a Branch of the [white] Coliseum Place Baptist Church. Each, however, will retain its distinct and separate existence as 'First African Baptist Church,' 'Second African Baptist Church,' . . . " The pastor of the white church was to be the pastor of each of the black churches, but he would, "with the advice and consent" of a committee of black elders, "nominate the preachers who are to occupy the pulpits of the several colored churches." Although the white church's Committee on Discipline was constituted "the directing power over the colored churches," a board of officers chosen by the black churches would "be the managing and discipline committee of each colored church," and church and conference meetings would be held as before, once a month. It seems clear that what the African churches gave up with one hand they mostly took back with the other. While the agreement did create an overarching structure of white supervision, within that structure the black congregations still kept control of their institutions. The plan worked; the mayor approved it and allowed the black churches to continue meeting under the new provisions.[78]

If extended to blacks the principle of religious freedom obviously could cause conflict with the practical necessities of slave control as formulated most fully in the slave codes. Because of their commitment to this principle, a group of white Baptists petitioned the Georgia legislature in 1863 to repeal a section of the new legal code which prohibited "any church, society or other body or any persons to grant any license or other authority to any slave or free person of color, to preach, or exhort, or otherwise officiate in church matters." The petition, composed by Rev. H. H. Tucker, a former professor at Mercer College in Macon, Georgia, was an unusual document. Certainly, it went too far in its defense of religious liberty for blacks to have been representative of general white sentiment on the issue. However, it does articulate one pole of this particular dichotomy in Southern society, a dichotomy which black churches and black preachers sometimes worked to their advantage. Prohibiting blacks from obtaining licenses to preach was an obnoxious and impious statute, according to the Baptist petitioners,

> because it trespasses upon the rights of conscience, and is a violation of religious liberty. To say nothing of the sacred rights of the black to preach, exhort or pray, if God called and commanded him to do either. Cases might arise in which we might feel it our duty as Baptists to license a man of color to preach or otherwise officiate in church matters. To grant such license would then be a part of our religion. But the Code of Georgia forbids our acting according to the dictates of our own consciences . . . Our religion is a matter between us and our God, with which no power on earth has a right to interfere. Soul-liberty is the rightful heritage of all God's moral creatures. Not over the religion of the slave has civil authority any power, nor yet has it over that of the citizen.

But aside from . . . its attempted despotism over the conscience of men, the most objectionable feature of all in the obnoxious section is its heaven-daring impiety. It trespasses not
only on the rights of men, but on the rights of God. It dictates
to the Almighty on what color his preachers shall be. The
great majority of the human race are of dark complexion. If
one of these among us is called by the great Head of the
Church to minister in holy things, the Code of Georgia forbids obedience. It stops the preaching of the everlasting gospel on the ground of a police regulation . . . . It allows Jehovah to have ministers of a certain complexion and no other,
and so exacting and rigid are these regulations imposed on the
Almighty, that they not only forbid his having preachers such
as he may choose, but also prescribe that none shall even
exhort, or in any way whatever officiate in church matters,
unless they be approved by this self-exalted and heaven-defy-
ing tribunal.[79]

The impact of this petition on the legislature's decision is not
known, but the disputed section of the new code was repealed,
leaving in effect, however, the old statute which required that a
court give its permission before a slave could be licensed to
preach.

It is significant that black preachers, some slave and some free,
continued to be licensed and that separate black churches continued to be organized despite periodic harassment by civil and ecclesiastical authorities, because these actions represent an area of
institutional freedom and self-governance for slaves. To be sure,
the exercise of this freedom was frequently modified by white
supervision, but it was nevertheless real. In various sections of the
antebellum South, black churches over the years kept gathering
members. Mainly, town churches, they drew slaves from both
town and country, swelling in size to hundreds and in a few
instances, thousands of members. In some areas of the South the
"rise of the black church" was not a post- but a pre-emancipation
phenomenon. The earliest black Baptist churches, as noted earlier, were founded in Virginia and Georgia. The Williamsburg
Church, founded by the black preachers Gowan Pamphlet and

Moses in the 1780s, had grown into one of the largest churches in the Dover Association by 1830, only to be closed and disbanded in the wake of reaction to the Southampton insurrection in 1831. Reorganized before 1843, the congregation numbered 305 in 1851 and 505 by 1860. By far the largest church in the Dover Association, however, was the First African Church of Richmond, formed in 1841 from the mixed First Baptist Church, where black members had outnumbered whites four to one for many years. Pastored by a leading white minister, Robert Ryland, president of Richmond College, the First African of Richmond numbered 2,056 members in 1843 and 3,260 in 1860. By that date second, third, and fourth African Baptist churches had been organized in Richmond. Not until emmancipation was any of these churches pastored by black men. First African received its first black pastor in 1866, when Ryland was succeeded by a former slave, James Henry Holmes, who had served as a deacon of the church since 1855. A Northern visitor to Richmond in 1865 commented on the ability of the black leadership emerging from these African churches: "Never have I attended committee meetings more dignified and to the point than the many we have appointed with the leading men in the colored churches . . . . I saw the first black man in a Richmond pulpit and heard from him a sermon that lifted me up to heights my spirit seldom reaches."[80]

The largest church in the Portsmouth Baptist Association of Virginia was the First African of Petersburg, which in 1851 reported a membership of 1,635, followed closely by the black Gillfield Church, also of Petersburg, with a membership of 1,361. The origins of both churches stretched back into the late eighteenth century.[81]

In Georgia the Sunbury Association was unparalleled for the number and size of its separate black churches. By the 1850s the First African of Savannah was the largest of thirteen black Baptist churches located in the Savannah area. Besides Andrew Marshall, there were five black pastors—John Cox, Guy McQueen, Garrison Fraser, Moses Golphin, and Kelly Low—and at least seven additional black preachers. The Savannah African churches, as described by one visitor in 1850, were "large, old but very decent buildings . . . every Sabbath, as well as some week day evenings, well filled with colored people." The aggregate number of members listed for the First, Second, and Third churches in that year was about 2,400. The regular pattern of Sunday worship consisted of three services, an early-morning prayer meeting, preaching at 10 A.M. and again at 3 P.M., and commemoration of the Lord's Supper every three months.[82] The First African of Savannah, under Marshall, become a tourist attraction for visitors to the city, and descriptions of services there were sketched by two European visitors, Fredrika Bremer and Charles Lyell. Aside from its mildly patronizing tone, Lyell's description is worth quoting for the rare glimpse it allows of the inside of an antebellum black church:

> [In 1846] I attended afternoon service in a Baptist church at Savannah, in which I found that I was the only white man, the congregation consisting of about 600 negroes, of various shades, most of them very dark. As soon as I entered I was shown to a seat reserved for strangers, near the preacher. First the congregation all joined, both men and women, very harmoniously in a hymn, most of them having evidently good ears for music, and good voices. The singing was followed by prayers, not read, but delivered without notes by a negro of pure African blood, a gray-headed, venerable-looking man, with a fine sonorous voice, named Marshall. He, as I learnt afterwards, had the reputation of being one of their best preachers, and he concluded by addressing to them a sermon, also without notes, in good style, and for the most part in good English; so much so, as to make me doubt whether a few ungrammatical phrases in the negro idiom might not have been purposely introduced for the sake of bringing the subject home to their family thoughts. He got very successfully through one flight about the gloom of the valley of the shadow of death, and speaking of the probationary state of a pious man left for a while to his own guidance, and when in danger of failing saved by the grace of God, he compared it to an eagle teaching her newly fledged offspring to fly, by carrying

it up high into the air, then dropping it, and, if she sees it
falling to the earth, darting with the speed of lightning to save
it before it reaches the ground. Whether any eagles really
teach their young to fly in this manner, I leave the ornitholo-
gist to decide; but when described in animated and pictur-
esque language, yet by no means inflated, the imagery was
well calculated to keep the attention of his hearers awake. He
also inculcated some good practical maxims of morality, and
told them they were to look to a future state of rewards and
punishments in which God would deal impartially with 'the
poor and the rich, the black man and the white.'[83]

"To see a body of African origin, who had joined one of the
denominations of Christians, and built a church for themselves—
who had elected a pastor of their own race, and secured him an
annual salary, from whom they were listening to a good sermon
scarcely, if at all, below the average standard of the compositions
of white ministers—to hear the whole service respectably, and the
singing admirably performed," made a strong impression upon
Lyell and caused him to revise his estimate of the "capabilities of
the negroes" to make progress in "civilization." From a perspective different from Lyell's, the really important lesson to be drawn
from the achievements of Marshall and his congregation is not
that they were capable of assimilating the Christian religion but
that they were able, "even in a part of a slave state, where they
outnumber[ed] the whites," to control their own institution, to
receive and dismiss their own, to listen to the preaching of one of
their own. In black churches, like the First African of Savannah,
one sees the institutional formation and spiritual nurture of an
"*imperium in imperio*," to use the term of a contemporary white
observer, i.e. a "nation within a nation."[84]

Black preachers and separate black churches were not
confined to the Southeastern seaboard states; they extended into
western areas of the South as well. In Alabama, black churches
were listed by some Baptist associations as early as 1820. The
African Huntsville Church, pastored by William Harris, a free
black, united with the Flint River Baptist Association in 1821,

when its membership stood at seventy-six. By 1840 the same church numbered 265 and was the largest Baptist church in the state. The African Cottonfort, also a member of the Flint River Association after 1830, had about 130 members in 1840 and was pastored for years by a slave named Lewis. Before emancipation, Mobile had three black Baptist churches, all with large congregations. Two slave preachers who gained some notoriety among Alabama Baptists were Caesar Blackwell and Doc Phillips. The former was owned by the famous Baptist itinerant James McLemore. After Blackwell's owner died, the Alabama Baptist Association bought and freed the slave to preach to his people. Phillips was active in the Tuskegee area and participated in associational meetings.[85]

In Mississippi black members outnumbered whites by a five-to-one margin in the Union Baptist Association. In 1846 the largest church in this association was the Natchez Baptist Church, which included 442 members, 62 white and 380 black. In the same association Clear Creek Church had 154 members in 1846, of whom only 15 were white, and Grand Gulf Church listed 107 black members out of a total 113. In the Central Baptist Association black members constituted more than one-half of the association. In several locales black churches were constituted separately. One of the largest was Rose Hill Church at Natchez, which was formed by the black members of the mixed Wall Street Church and housed in a church built with contributions from both black and white members. Though legally still part of the Wall Street Church, the black congregation met for worship in their new building and were preached to by an unlicensed slave exhorter, Randle Pollard.[86]

In Louisiana the elderly black preacher Joseph Willis was succeeded by his grandson Daniel Willis, who was ordained by the Louisiana Baptist Association in 1849 as assistant pastor of Occupy Church in Rapides Parish. Another free black preacher, Henry Adams, pastored Mount Lebanon, a mixed church in Bienville parish, from 1837 to 1839 and then moved to Louis-

ville, Kentucky, where he served as pastor of the city's First Colored Baptist Church for over thirty years. Licensed to work among black people by the Grand Cane Association in 1856, John Jones was frequently invited to preach before white congregations in Shreveport. In New Orleans several African Churches were organized and led by black men before emancipation, beginning in 1826 when the First African Baptist Church was founded under the pastoral care of Asa Goldsbury.[87]

Antebellum black churches arose and prospered especially in the border states. The First African Church of Lexington, Kentucky, gathered by Old Captain in 1801, chose Loudon Ferrill, a former slave from Hanover county, Virginia, to succeed the founder as pastor in 1824. During Ferrill's thirty-two-year term of service the membership of the church grew from 280 to 1,820, the largest of any church in Kentucky. The First Colored Church of Louisville, with Henry Adams as minister, numbered 644 in 1845 and was the largest church in the Long Run Baptist Association. By 1860 Kentucky had seventeen separate black churches with an aggregate membership of 5,737. George W. Dupee, who was to be a leading figure in the organization of black Baptist churches, associations, and a monthly journal, began his ministerial career while still a slave. Licensed to preach in 1846, he was ordained pastor of the black Baptist church in Georgetown in 1851, though he remained a slave until permitted to purchase his freedom after 1856. In Missouri the First African Baptist Church of St. Louis grew out of a Sabbath school for Negroes opened in 1818 and was constituted a separate church in 1822. In 1827 the congregation called John Berry Meachum to be its pastor. Meachum, a carpenter and cooper by trade, had purchased his own freedom and that of his wife, children, and twenty more slaves. In 1835 Meachum was reputedly worth about $25,000. His church prospered as well, and grew from a membership of 220 in 1835 to 648 in 1851. The church included a large Sabbath school and a temperance society. A second black Baptist church was formed in St. Louis in 1847 and was pastored until 1862 by another

Richard Allen. Reprinted from James A. Handy, *Scraps of African Methodist Episcopal History* (Philadelphia, n.d.).

Daniel Coker. Reprinted from James A. Handy, *Scraps of African Methodist Episcopal History* (Philadelphia, n.d.).

black preacher, J. R. Anderson, who had been educated and taught a trade in the Alton, Illinois, printing shop of Elijah P. Lovejoy, the celebrated martyr of the abolitionist cause. In Nashville, Tennessee, 500 black members withdrew from the First Baptist Church in 1847 in order to hold separate services. In 1849 Nelson G. Merry, the former sexton of the white church, was ordained as the first black pastor of the new church.[88]

The structure of Baptist organization was more amenable to the existence of black churches and black preachers than was the system of government of any other denomination. Besides the Baptists, the Methodists were the only other denomination to license black preachers with any frequency. And among the Methodists, also, a very few black churches were founded in the antebellum South. African Methodist churches arose in Baltimore, Charleston, and New Orleans. In Maryland, with a large free black population, Baltimore was one of the centers of the separatist movement among black Methodists which led to the creation of the African Methodist Episcopal Church. Led by Daniel Coker, black Methodists from Baltimore joined with delegates from Philadelphia under Richard Allen in 1816 to form the connection. While the location of the A.M.E. church in Maryland was urban and its leadership free, the slaves within Baltimore and in the rural environs were included in the church's care. The formation of the A.M.E. connection was to prove important to slaves further south as well.[89]

In Charleston, South Carolina, the number of slaves and free blacks in the Methodist society totaled about four thousand in 1815. Up to that year the black members had been allowed their own separate quarterly conference, with their own preachers and class leaders in charge of financial and disciplinary affairs. Upon the discovery of some financial irregularities, the white Preacher in Charge ordered the black officers to hand over all collections to the stewards and to conduct church trials only in his presence. The black leaders resented this intrusion, and when their separate quarterly conference was abolished, the black membership began to move in secret to form their own church. Two members of the African society, including Morris Brown, were sent to Philadelphia, where they were ordained by Bishop Richard Allen and commissioned to return to Charleston to organize an A.M.E. church. When the white trustees of the Charleston Bethel Church insisted upon erecting a hearse house on the burial lot used by the black members, the incident served as the catalyst for open schism. "At one fell swoop," as one contemporary observer described it, "nearly every leader delivered up his class papers, and four thousand three hundred and sixty-seven of the members withdrew." The seceders erected a building and formed the African Church of Charleston, with Morris Brown as pastor. In 1822 the African Church was suppressed by the civil authorities after the discovery of the Vesey plot. Even the church building was ordered demolished. Morris Brown was spirited North, and separate African Methodism was not revived until A.M.E. missionaries returned to Charleston after the war.[90]

Four black Methodist churches had been founded in the city of New Orleans before 1860. According to one estimate, the four had a combined membership of 1,700 and held property worth $10,600. Three of these congregations had slave preachers who served their people under the supervision of white ministers. The fourth congregation decided in 1848 to affiliate with the African Methodist Episcopal Church and sent Charles Doughty to the Indiana Conference of the A.M.E. Church to petition for that privilege. Doughty, already licensed as a local preacher by the M.E. Church, South, was ordained a deacon and sent back to take charge of the Louisiana Mission, subsequently named St. James A.M.E. Church. Fredrika Bremer visited a class meeting in one of the African Methodist Churches of New Orleans in 1851 and later published a vivid description of the intensity of the exhorters and the ecstatic behavior of the members. In St. Louis black Methodists led by two free blacks, Jonathan Duncan and George Spears, built a small church for "African Methodists" around 1823 or 1824. The pulpit of the

Morris Brown. Reprinted from James A. Handy, *Scraps of African Methodist Episcopal History* (Philadelphia, n.d.).

African Church, however, was filled by the pastors of the white "Old First" church.[91]

While the hierarchical structure of Methodism severely limited the possibility of black members organizing their own churches under their own black preachers, the Methodist churches before and after 1845 included large numbers of black members in the regular stations and circuits, as well as in missions, and regularly licensed black men as exhorters and local preachers. Just as some Baptist associations included black delegates, Methodist quarterly conferences admitted black exhorters and preachers. Yet, if John Dixon Long, himself a Methodist minister, is right, when their licenses came up for renewal annually they had "no voice in voting for one another, or for others." "Thus," he concluded, " even in the midst of their brethren, they are made to feel that they are not one in Christ Jesus."[92]

Among other denominations in the antebellum South—Presbyterian, Lutheran, Disciples, Episcopalian, Moravian—black ministers were extremely rare or nonexistent. The Presbyterians did license George M. Erskine, a slave, in east Tennessee in 1818. Erskine bought his freedom and that of his wife and seven children and went to Africa as a missionary. In 1846 Harrison W. Ellis, a former slave whose freedom had been purchased by several churches in Mississippi and Alabama, was licensed and ordained by the Presbytery of Tuscaloosa. The next year he was sent to Liberia as a missionary by the Presbyterian Board of Foreign Missions. A free black, Hiram Revels, later to win fame as U.S. senator from Mississippi, left the A.M.E. Church and organized a black Presbyterian congregation of almost a hundred members in St. Louis in 1855, but the church did not last. As a recent historian of Presbyterians in the South has remarked about black Presbyterian ministers: "An exceptional Negro minister here and there only proved the rule. The ministry of Presbyterians to the Negroes in the South was carried on almost exclusively by whites." The same comment minus the "almost" applies to the Disciples of Christ, the Lutherans, Episcopalians, and Moravians.[93]

Although the instances were rare, in the licensed ministry and in black churches, slaves had channels—public, institutional ones at that—for autonomous control of religious organizations. Certainly these channels were frequently restricted and sometimes completely blocked, but black congregations, slave and free, struggled to keep them open. Aided by the impulse to respect the independence of the individual relationship between man and God's will, and especially by the Baptist articulation of the autonomy of each congregation, black preachers and black churches were able to excercise a degree of authority, power, and self-government denied them in other areas of life by the system of slave control. In the middle of the conflict between two social values—the practical necessity of slave control and the ideal of religious freedom—slaves sometimes discovered that they could take advantage of the confusion and act as if the Gospel of Christian fellowship included them after all.

In mixed churches, too, there was tension between fellowship and slave status. It affected seating patterns, the distribution of communion, the application of church ordinances, and participation in church meetings, but most important, it affected the experience of being Christian. This tension revealed the irreducible gap between the slave's religion and that of his master. The slave knew that no matter how sincerely religious his master might be, his religion did not countenance the freedom of his slave. This was, after all was said and done, *the* limit to Christian fellowship. The division went deep; it extended as far as the interpretation of the Bible and the understanding of the Gospel. The dichotomy between black and white experiences of Christianity was recognized belatedly by a white Methodist minister who had preached in 1862 to black Methodists as pastor of Bethel Church in Charleston.

> There were near fourteen hundred colored communicants. . . .
> [Their] service was always thronged—galleries, lower floor,
> chancel, pulpit, steps and all. . . . The preacher could not
> complain of any deadly space between himself and congrega-
> tion. He was positively breast up to his people, with no possi-

ble loss of . . . rapport. Though ignorant of it at the time, he remembers now the cause of the enthusiasm under his deliverances [about] the 'law of liberty' and 'freedom from Egyptian bondage.' What was figurative they interpreted literally. He thought of but one ending of the war; they quite another. He remembers the sixty-eight Psalm as affording numerous texts for their delectation, e.g., 'Let God arise, let his enemies be scattered'; His 'march through the wilderness'; 'The Chariots of God are twenty thousand'; 'The hill of God is as the hill of Basham'; and especially, 'Though ye have lain among the pots, yet shall ye be as the wings of a dove covered with silver, and her feathers with yellow gold' . . . It is mortifying now to think that his comprehension was not equal to the African intellect. All he thought about was relief from the servitude of sin, and freedom from the bondage of the devil. . . . But they interpreted it literally in the good time coming, which of course could not but make their ebony complexion attractive, very.[94]

What the preacher is describing is the end of a long process, spanning almost two hundred and fifty years, by which slaves came to accept the Gospel of Christianity and at the same time made it their own. It is important to remember that it was a dual process. The slaves did not simply become Christians; they creatively fashioned a Christian tradition to fit their own peculiar experience of enslavement in America.

Church membership is one index—a rather stringent one—to the influence of Christianity upon the life of the slave. Du Bois quoted a figure of 468,000 black church members in the South in 1859. Within forty years after emancipation, however, a black population of 8.3 million contained 2.7 million church members.[95] This astounding figure sheds some light on the extent to which slaves had adopted Christianity in the antebellum South. When missionaries from the free black churches of the North came South in the wake of Union armies to minister to the freedmen, they found a significant community of Christians among the ex-slaves. They found ex-slaves who knew not only the tenets of Christianity but also some of the finer points of doctrine and church polity. They encountered freedmen who already had the experience of forming their own congregations and of pastoring their own people. Most important, they found an extensive religious life among the ex-slaves which had never been totally encompassed by the institutional church. This "invisible institution" was the folk religion of the slave community.

5
Religious Life in the Slave Community

He have been wid us, Jesus,
He still wid us, Jesus,
He will be wid us, Jesus
Be wid us to the end.

SLAVE SPIRITUAL

BY THE EVE of the Civil War, Christianity had pervaded the slave community. The vast majority of slaves were American-born, and the cultural and linguistic barriers which had impeded the evangelization of earlier generations of African-born slaves were generally no longer a problem. The widespread opposition of the planters to the catechizing of slaves had been largely dissipated by the efforts of the churches and missionaries of the South. Not all slaves were Christian, nor were all those who accepted Christianity members of a church, but the doctrines, symbols, and vision of life preached by Christianity were familiar to most. During the closing decades of the antebellum period the so-called invisible institution of slave Christianity came to maturity. The religious life of slaves in the late antebellum period is well documented by sources from the slaves themselves.

At first glance it seems strange to refer to the religion of the slaves as an invisible institution, for independent black churches with slave members did exist in the South before emancipation. In racially mixed churches it was not uncommon for slaves to outnumber masters in attendance at Sunday services. But the religious experience of the slaves was by no means fully contained in the visible structures of the institutional church. From the abundant testimony of fugitive and freed slaves it is clear that the slave community had an extensive religious life of its own, hidden from the eyes of the master. In the secrecy of the quarters or the seclusion of the brush arbors ("hush harbors") the slaves made Christianity truly their own.

The religion of the slaves was both institutional and noninstitutional, visible and invisible, formally organized and spontaneously adapted. Regular Sunday worship in the local church was paralleled by illicit, or at least informal, prayer meetings on weeknights in the slave cabins. Preachers licensed by the church and hired by the master were supplemented by slave preachers licensed only by the spirit. Texts from the Bible which most slaves could not read were explicated by verses from the spirituals. Slaves forbidden by masters to attend church or, in some cases, even to pray risked floggings to attend secret gatherings to worship God.

His own experience of the "invisible institution" was recalled by former slave Wash Wilson:

> When de niggers go round singin' 'Steal Away to Jesus,' dat mean dere gwine be a 'ligious meetin' dat night. De masters . . . didn't like dem 'ligious meetin's, so us natcherly slips off at night, down in de bottoms or somewhere. Sometimes us sing and pray all night.[1]

Into that all-night singing and praying the slaves poured the sufferings and needs of their days. Like "Steal Away" and the rest of the spirituals, Christianity was fitted by the slave community to its own particular experience. At the same time the symbols, myths, and values of Judeo-Christian tradition helped form the slave community's image of itself.

"Steal Away"

Slaves frequently were moved to hold their own religious meetings out of disgust for the vitiated Gospel preached by their masters' preachers. Sermons urging slaves to be obedient and docile were repeated ad nauseam. The type of sermon to which he and other slaves were constantly subjected was paraphrased by Frank Roberson:

> You slaves will go to heaven if you are good, but don't ever think that you will be close to your mistress and master. No! No! there will be a wall between you; but there will be holes in it that will permit you to look out and see your mistress when she passes by. If you want to sit behind this wall, you must do the language of the text 'Obey your masters.'[2]

Another former slave, Charlie Van Dyke, bitterly complained: "Church was what they called it but all that preacher talked about was for us slaves to obey our masters and not to lie and steal.

Nothing about Jesus, was ever said and the overseer stood there to see the preacher talked as he wanted him to talk." Consequently, even a black preacher "would get up and repeat everything that the white preacher had said, because he was afraid to say anything different."³

For more authentic Christian preaching the slaves had to turn elsewhere. Lucretia Alexander explained what slaves did when they grew tired of the white folks' preacher:

> The preacher came and . . . He'd just say, 'Serve your masters. Don't steal your master's turkey. Don't steal your master's chickens. Don't steal your master's hawgs. Don't steal your master's meat. Do whatsomever your master tells you to do.' Same old thing all the time. My father would have church in dwelling houses and they had to whisper. . . . Sometimes they would have church at his house. That would be when they would want a real meetin' with some real preachin'. . . . They used to sing their songs in a whisper and pray in a whisper. That was a prayer-meeting from house to house once or twice—once or twice a week.⁴

Slaves faced severe punishment if caught attending secret prayer meetings. Moses Grandy reported that his brother-in-law Isaac, a slave preacher, "was flogged, and his back pickled" for preaching at a clandestine service in the woods. His listeners were flogged and "forced to tell who else was there." Grandy claimed that slaves were often flogged "if they are found singing or praying at home." Gus Clark reported: "My Boss didn' 'low us to go to church, er to pray er sing. Iffen he ketched us prayin' er singin' he whupped us. . . . He didn' care fer nothin' 'cept farmin.' " According to another ex-slave, "the white folks would come in when the colored people would have prayer meeting, and whip every one of them. Most of them thought that when colored people were praying it was against them. For they would catch them praying for God to lift things out of their way and the white folks would *lift them*." Henry Bibb was threatened with five hundred lashes on the naked back for attending a prayer meeting conducted by slaves on a neighboring plantation, because he had no permission to do so. The master who threatened Bibb with this punishment was, incidentally, a deacon of the local Baptist church. Charlotte Martin asserted that "her oldest brother was whipped to death for taking part in one of the religious ceremonies." Despite the danger, slaves continued to hold their own religious gatherings because, as Grandy stated, "they like their own meetings better." There the slaves could pray and sing as they desired. They were willing to risk threats of floggings at the hands of their earthly masters in order to worship their "Divine Master" as they saw fit.[5]

Slaves devised several techniques to avoid detection of their meetings. One practice was to meet in secluded places—woods, gullies, ravines, and thickets (aptly called "hush harbors"). Kalvin Woods remembered preaching to other slaves and singing and praying while huddled behind quilts and rags, which had been thoroughly wetted "to keep the sound of their voices from penetrating the air" and then hung up "in the form of a little room," or tabernacle. On one Louisiana plantation, when "the slaves would steal away into the woods at night and hold services," they "would form a circle on their knees around the speaker who would also be on his knees. He would bend forward and speak into or over a vessel of water to drown the sound. If anyone became animated and cried out, the others would quickly stop the noise by placing their hands over the offender's mouth." When slaves got "happy an' shout[ed]" in their cabins, "couldn't nobody hyar 'em," according to George Young, "'caze dey didn't make no fuss on de dirt flo'," but just in case, "one stan' in de do' an' watch." The most common device for preserving secrecy was an iron pot or kettle turned upside down to catch the sound. The pot was usually placed in the middle of the cabin floor or at the doorstep, then slightly propped up to hold the sound of the praying and singing from escaping. A variation was to pray or sing softly "with heads together around" the "kettle to deaden the sound." Clara Young recalled, "When dark come, de men folks would hang up a wash pot, bottom upwards, in de little brush church house us had, so's it would catch de noise and de overseer wouldn't hear us singin' and shoutin'." According to one account, slaves used the overturned pot to cover the sound of more worldly amusements too: "They would have dances sometimes and turn a pot upside down right in front of the door. They said that would keep the sound from going outside."[6]

Whether the pots were strictly functional or also served some symbolic purpose is not clear. The symbolic element is suggested by Patsy Hyde, former slave in Tennessee, who claimed that slaves "would tek dere ole iron cookin' pots en turn dem upside down on de groun' neah dere cabins ter keep dere white folks fun herein' w'at dey waz sayin'. Dey claimed dat hit showed dat Gawd waz wid dem." The origin of this custom also remains unclear. When asked about the custom, one ex-slave replied, "I don't know where they learned to do that. I kinda think the lord put them things in their minds to do for themselves, just like he helps us Christians in other ways. Don't you think so?" One theory has been advanced which explains the slaves' use of the pot as a remnant of African custom. Sidney Mintz has offered an interesting suggestion: "One is entitled to wonder whether a washtub that 'catches' sound, rather than producing it, may not represent some kind of religious symbolic inversion on the part of a religious group—particularly since the suppression of drumming by the masters was a common feature of Afro-American history." He explains further: this is perhaps "a case in which some original symbolic or instrumental commitment has outlived its original circumstantial significance. Rather than disappearing however, that commitment is somehow transmitted and preserved." Whatever the origin of this folk custom, the widespread belief among slaves was that the pots worked.[7] The need for secrecy even dictated that children keep quiet about what went on in the slave quarters. "My master used to ask us children," recalled one former slave, " 'Do your folks pray at night?' We said 'No' cause our folks had told us what to say. But the Lord have mercy, there was plenty of that going on. They'd pray, 'Lord, deliver us from under bondage.' "⁸

Looking back at these secret and risky religious gatherings, an ex-slave declared, "Meetings back there meant more than they do now. Then everybody's heart was in tune, and when they called on God they made heaven ring. It was more than just Sunday meeting and then no godliness for a week. They would steal off to the fields and in the thickets and there . . . they called on God out of heavy hearts." Truly communal, these meetings, as Hannah Lowery noted, needed no preacher because "everyone was so anxious to have a word to say that a preacher did not have a chance. All of them would sing and pray."⁹ A description of a secret prayer meeting was recorded by Peter Randolph, who was a slave in Prince George County, Virginia, until he was freed in 1847:

> Not being allowed to hold meetings on the plantation, the slaves assemble in the swamp, out of reach of the patrols. They have an understanding among themselves as to the time and place of getting together. This is often done by the first one arriving breaking boughs from the trees, and bending them in the direction of the selected spot. Arrangements are then made for conducting the exercises. They first ask each other how they feel, the state of their minds, etc. The male members then select a certain space, in separate groups, for the division of the meeting. Preaching . . . by the brethren, then praying and singing all around, until they generally feel quite happy. The speaker usually commences by calling himself unworthy, and talks very slowly, until feeling the spirit, he grows excited, and in a short time, there fall to the ground twenty or thirty men and women under its influence . . .

Randolph went on to elucidate the importance of these gatherings for the life of the slave community:

> The slave forgets all his sufferings, except to remind others of the trials during the past week, exclaiming: 'Thank God, I shall not live here always!' Then they pass from one to another, shaking hands, and bidding each other farewell. . . . As they separate, they sing a parting hymn of praise.¹⁰

Prayer, preaching, song, communal support, and especially "feeling the spirit" refreshed the slaves and consoled them in their times of distress. By imagining their lives in the context of a different future they gained hope in the present.

The contrast between present pain and future relief formed the matter of slave prayer and song. From his memory of slavery, Anderson Edwards cited a song which starkly combined suffering and hope.

> We prayed a lot to be free and the Lord done heered us. We didn't have no song books and the Lord done give us our songs and when we sing them at night it jus' whispering so nobody hear us. One went like this:
>
> > My knee bones am aching,
> > My body's rackin' with pain,
> > I 'lieve I'm a chile of God,
> > And this ain't my home,
> > 'Cause Heaven's my aim.[11]

Slaves sought consolation in the future, but they also found it in the present. Exhausted from a day of work that stretched from "day clean" to after sundown, the slaves sometimes found tangible relief in prayer, as Richard Caruthers attested: "Us niggers used to have a prayin' ground down in the hollow and sometime we come out of the field . . . scorchin' and burnin' up with nothin' to eat, and we wants to ask the good Lawd to have mercy. . . . We takes a pine torch . . . and goes down in the hollow to pray. Some gits so joyous they starts to holler loud and we has to stop up they mouth. I see niggers git so full of the Lawd and so happy they draps unconscious."[12]

Freedom was frequently the object of prayer. According to Laura Ambromson, "Some believed they'd git freedom and others didn't. They had places they met and prayed for freedom." Others were certain it would come. "I've heard them pray for freedom," declared another former slave. "I thought it was foolishness then, but the old time folks always felt they was to be free. It must have been something 'vealed unto 'em." Mingo White remembered: "Somehow or yuther us had a instinct dat we was goin' to be free," and "when de day's wuk was done de slaves would be foun' . . . in dere cabins prayin' for de Lawd to free dem lack he did chillun of Is'ael." Andrew Moss revealed that his mother would retreat to her private praying ground, "a ole twisted thick-rooted muscadine bush," where she prayed for the deliverance of the slaves. George Womble, former slave from Georgia, recalled that "slaves would go to the woods at night where they sang and prayed" and some used to say, "I know that some day we'll be free and if we die before that time our children will live to see it." The father of Jacob Stroyer, before his family went to bed, would pray that "the time which he predicted would come, that is, the time of freedom when . . . the children would be [their] own masters and mistresses." Forbidden to pray for liberation, slaves stole away at night and prayed inside "cane thickets . . . for deliverance."[13]

Secrecy was characteristic of only part of the slave community's religious life. Many slaveholders granted their slaves permission to attend church, and some openly encouraged religious meetings among the slaves. Baptisms, marriages, and funerals were allowed to slaves on some plantations with whites observing and occasionally participating. Annual revival meetings were social occasions for blacks as well as for whites. Masters were known to enjoy the singing, praying, and preaching of their slaves. Nevertheless, at the core of the slaves' religion was a private place, represented by the cabin room, the overturned pot, the prayin' ground, and the "hush harbor." This place the slave kept his own. For no matter how religious the master might be, the slave knew that the master's religion did not countenance prayers for his slaves' freedom in this world.

The Seasons of Religious Life

The religious format varied from plantation to plantation for the slaves. Former slave John Brown depicted two extremes:

Sunday was a great day around the plantation. The fields was forgotten, the light chores was hurried through, and everybody got ready for the church meeting. It was out of the doors, in the yard . . . Master John's wife would start the meeting with a prayer and then would come the singing—the old timey songs. But the white folks on the next plantation would lick their slaves for trying to do like we did. No praying there, and no singing.[14]

Some masters did not allow their slaves to go to church and ridiculed the notion of religion for slaves because they refused to believe that Negroes had souls. Others forbade their slaves to attend church because, as an ex-slave explained, "White folks 'fraid the niggers git to thinkin' they was free, if they had churches 'n things." Refusal to grant a slave permission to participate in religious meetings was also a means of punishment or a result of capricious malice on the part of the master or overseer. On the other hand, many slave owners did permit—some even required —their slaves to worship on the Sabbath, either at the local church or at meetings conducted on the plantation by white ministers or slave preachers.[15] On those plantations where slaves enjoyed religious privileges the slave community was able to openly celebrate the religious side of its folk culture. The Reverend Greene gave a detailed description of religion in the quarters to interviewers from Fisk University:

At night, especially in the summertime, after everybody had eaten supper, it was a common thing for us to sit outside. The old folks would get together and talk until bedtime. Sometimes somebody would start humming an old hymn, and then the next-door neighbor would pick it up. In this way it would finally get around to every house, and then the music started. Soon everybody would be gathered together, and such singing! It wouldn't be long before some of the slaves got happy and started to shouting. . . . [16]

A similar picture of evening prayer meetings was rendered by Robert Anderson:

We would gather out in the open on summer nights, gather around a big bonfire, to keep the mosquitoes away, and listen to our preachers preach sometimes half the night. There would be singing and testifying and shouting. Usually when we had these meetings there would be people there from other plantations, and sometimes there would be white visitors who would stand on the outside of the circle and listen to our services.

Sunday prayer meetings in the quarters could, if allowed to, last all day. The emotional power of these meetings left a deep impression on Mose Hursey, who many years later vividly recalled them:

On Sundays they had meetin', sometimes at our house, sometimes at 'nother house. . . . They'd preach and pray and sing—shout, too. I heard them git up with a powerful force of the spirit, clappin' they hands and walkin' round the place. They'd shout, 'I got the glory. I got that old time 'ligion in my heart.' I seen some powerful 'figurations of the spirit in them days.[17]

Nor were white visitors to the slave meetings immune to their emotional impact. Despite her criticism that a prayer she heard offered at one meeting was meaningless, Mary Boykin Chesnut admitted she was deeply moved nonetheless:

Jim Nelson, the driver . . . was asked to lead in prayer. He became wildly excited, on his knees, facing us with his eyes shut. He clapped his hands at the end of every sentence, and his voice rose to the pitch of a shrill shriek, yet was strangely clear and musical, occasionally in a plaintive minor key that went to your heart. Sometimes it rang out like a trumpet. I wept bitterly. . . . The Negroes sobbed and shouted and swayed backward and forward, some with aprons to their eyes, most of them clapping their hands and responding in shrill tones: 'Yes, God!' 'Jesus!' 'Savior!' 'Bless de Lord, amen,' etc. It was a little too exciting for me I would very much have liked to shout, too. Jim Nelson when he rose from his knees trembled and shook as one in a palsy, and from his

eyes you could see the ecstasy had not left him yet. He could
not stand at all, and sank back on his bench.

Some whites found the slaves' ways of worship humorous; many
others went "to hear the colored ones sing and praise God," as
John Thompson observed, "and were often much affected by
their simple but earnest devotion."[18]

In the evenings, after work, while religious slaves met to pray,
sing, and shout, other sounds also rang out in the slave cabins.
Apparently, the traditional conflict between sacred and secular
music in Afro-American culture was alive even then, as the ante-
cedents of gospel and blues clashed in the quarters. Harry Smith's
recollection could only hint at the riot of sound:

> After eating, often preaching and prayer meetings by some of
> the old folks in some of the cabins and in others fiddles would
> ring out. It was a scene never to be forgotten, as the old chris-
> tians sing and pray until four in the morning, while at the other
> cabins many would be patting, singing and dancing.[19]

To the religious slaves, fiddling, dancing, and secular music were
the devil's work. According to John Thompson, when a master
on one plantation wished to halt a revival among his slaves he
shrewdly hired a slave named Martin who was a talented fiddler.
Thompson reported that the plan succeeded: "what the whip
failed to accomplish, the fiddle completed, for it is no easy matter
to drive a soul from God by cruelty, when it may easily be drawn
away by worldly pleasures." The backsliding was temporary,
however, since Martin left with his fiddle when his term of hire
expired and the revival of Christianity sprang up anew.[20] The
only form of "dancing" allowed to the converted was the movement which occurred in prayer meetings under the influence of
the holy spirit, as in the ring shout.

Morally sanctioned enjoyments were to be found at Sunday
church service and revival meetings which were occasions for so-
cializing, news gathering, and picnicking as well as for prayer.
Robert Anderson acknowledged that "I always liked to go to

church for I always found some of the colored folks from the other plantations that I could visit with for a little while before church started." Another former slave recalled, "The young folks would ride in wagons to and from church and have a big time singing songs n' things." For most field hands Sunday was a holiday when they could wear their better clothes to church, "the onliest place off the farm we ever went," recalled one. Olmsted observed a Sabbath worship service in which the slaves were more neatly dressed than the poor whites present. Some slaveholders took pride in showing how well "their people" dressed at Sunday service. Slaves themselves were fond of dressing up on Sunday and, if allowed to earn a little money, would add to their Sunday wardrobe. For example, Tom Singleton, former slave from Georgia, recalled that as a slave he was allowed to hire out his time at night to cut wood and fix fences for neighboring whites. "With the money they paid me," he admitted, "I bought Sunday shoes and a Sunday coat, because I was a Nigger what always did like to look good on Sunday." The pleasure of dressing up no doubt added to the specialness of the day and expressed in small measure the slaves' sense of proper dignity, of that value which they called "being quality folks." "Looking good" at Sabbath and revival services also had a special purpose for the younger slaves, since these were potential occasions for courting. Another opportunity for asserting one's dignity came when the collection plate was passed. It was not unusual for slaves to add their contributions from money they had earned selling the produce of their own garden patches.[21]

When slaves from neighboring plantations were allowed to congregate for worship, visiting and fellowship added an almost festive dimension to the service. Julia Francis Daniels, a slave on a Georgia plantation remembered: "We'd ask niggers from other farms and I used to say, 'I like meetin' jus' as good as I like a party.' " Camp meetings were also "big times." "When de crops was laid by and most of de hardest wuk of de year done up, den was camp meetin' time, 'long in de last of July and sometimes in August," reminisced Robert Shepherd. "Det was when us had de biggest times of all. Dey had great big long tables and jus' every-thing good t'eat." According to Charlie Aarons: "there would be camp meetings held and the slaves from all the surrounding plan-tations would attend, going . . . in these large wagons . . . They then would have a jolly time along the way, singing and calling to one another, and making friends."[22]

Sundays and revival meetings were not the only respites from work anticipated by the slaves. Christmas was the most festive holiday of all. Generally, the slaves received three to six days off to celebrate the Christmas season and were permitted to visit family and friends on neighboring plantations. On Christmas day it was customary for slaves to greet the master's family with cries of "Christmas gift, Christmas gift," to which the whites were obliged to respond with a small gift, perhaps tobacco for the men, ribbons for the women, ginger cakes for the children, and some special tokens for favorite slaves. Drams of whiskey, bowls of eggnog and other spirits were freely distributed, and a special Christmas supper was prepared for the quarters as well as for the big house. The slaves dressed in the best clothes they could gather in anticipation of the supper and the visiting and merry-making which followed. Then, as now, Christmas was more a holiday than a holy day. Feasting, drinking, and dancing were the order of the day and must have sorely tempted the more religious slaves. As Adeline Jackson recalled, "Everything lively at Christ-mas time, dances wid fiddlers, pattin' and stick rattlin', but when I jined de church, I quit dancin'," She allowed that the fiddlers, dancers and patters were "all nothin' but sinners, I wuz too, but we sho' had a good time." Christmas season did give the religious slave time to hold prayer meetings, to preach and to pray. Yet "many of the strict members of the church who did not dance," Jacob Stroyer asserted, "would be forced to do it to please their masters." At any rate, slaves whether religious or not looked for-ward to Christmas as an all-too-short break from plantation rou-tine. With the arrival of New Year's the celebration ended, and another year of work faced the slaves.[23]

Of course, many slaves cared not at all about church, revival meetings, or prayer services, would not go if they could, and resented being forced to attend. Nonreligious slaves spent Sundays in hunting, fishing, marble shooting, storytelling, or simply resting when allowed. Not all slaves appreciated the opportunity to attend church. "On Sunday after workin' hard all de week dey would lay down to sleep and be so tired; soon ez yo' sleep, de overseer would come an' wake you up an' make you go to church," complained Margrett Nickerson. Some reprobate and ingenious slaves even rationalized a way to dance on the Sabbath: "The cabins were mostly made of logs and there were large cracks in them" through which the sunlight filtered, "so on Sunday mornings when they were dancing and did not want to stop" they filled "up the cracks with old rags. The idea was that it would not be Sunday inside if they kept the sun out, and thus they would not desecrate the Sabbath." Sunday also served as market day for those slaves who were allotted individual plots to produce vegetables or poultry for their own use.[24]

The camp meeting had its nonreligious attractions. John Anderson, who courted his wife, Maria, at a camp meeting, remarked: "Many slaves who have no religion, go to camp meetings that they may be merry, for there is much whiskey sold at these gatherings, and the people drink and play at cards while others attend to religion." While some slaves were allowed holidays to attend camp meetings, others took advantage of the time to enjoy "dances, raffles, cock-fights, foot-races, and other amusements . . ."[25]

Although religious slaves enjoyed the fellowship and excitement of church services and revival meetings, their enjoyment was marred by the shadow of white control. When they attended church, slaves often felt inhibited by the presence of whites, so they preferred to worship at a separate service by themselves. As Sarah Fitzpatrick, a slave in Alabama, explained:

> "Niggers" commence ta wanna go to church by de'selves, even ef dey had ta meet in de white church. So white fo'ks have deir service in de mornin' an' "Niggers" have deirs in de

evenin', a'ter dey clean up, wash de dishes, an' look a'ter
ever'thing. . . . Ya' see "Niggers" lack ta shout a whole lot an'
wid de white fo'ks al' round 'em, dey couldn't shout jes' lack
dey want to.

Slaves assembled separately at the camp meetings, as one white
observer explained, so they could enjoy the "freedom in speaking,
singing, shouting, and praying they could not enjoy in the presence of their masters." This freedom of expression was circumscribed, however, by the attendance of some whites at slave
church services to ensure that nothing occurred which could be
contrued as subversive of the system. Moreover, to attend separate services, slaves needed written passes from their masters
which stated the time when the slave had to return home. A slave
who stayed too late at meeting risked a beating from the "padde-
rollers" [patrols] or his master. The slaves' enjoyment of religious
"privileges" was diminished by those masters who forced them to
attend prayer service whether they wanted to or not. Sometimes
moments of religious celebration were interrupted by the cruel
realities of slavery. James Smith related one such incident which
took place at a revival he attended. A slave named Nancy Merrill
was converted; the next day of the meeting someone came to the
church door seeking the new convert. It was a "slave trader, who
had bought her during the day from her mistress! As soon as she
went to the door, he seized and bound her, and then took her off
to her cabin home to get her two boys he had bought also." That
this was not an isolated incident is suggested by Moses Roper,
who accompanied his slave-trading master to "many such meetings," where there was "a fruitful season for the drover" who
caried on a profitable traffic with the slave owners attending the
revival. Roper claimed this was a practice "common to Baptists
and Methodists."[26] Nevertheless, Sunday services, Christmas seasons, annual revival meetings, and especially the slaves' own evening prayer meetings in the quarters were times of refreshment and
renewal amid the routine toil of the slave life.

Religion not only added some moments of brightness to the

day-to-day life of the slave community, but it also provided special rituals to mark the important events of life by means of baptisms, weddings, and funerals. Baptism, the central Christian symbol of spiritual death, rebirth, and initiation was a memorable occasion for the slaves. Accompanied by song, shouting, and ecstatic behavior, baptism—especially for Baptists—was perhaps the most dramatic ritual in the slave's religious life. "De biggest meetin' house crowds was when dey had baptizin'," noted a former Georgia slave. "Dey dammed up de crick on Sadday so as it would be deep enough on Sunday . . . At dem baptizin's dere was all sorts of shoutin', and dey would sing *Roll, Jordan, Roll, De Livin' Waters,* and *Lord, I'se Comin' Home.*" Dressed in white robes and attended by the "brothers and sisters," the candidates proceeded "amidst singing and praises" to the local pond or creek, symbol of the river Jordan, where, according to Baptist practice, each was "ducked" by the preacher. Sometimes the newly regenerate came up from the baptismal waters shouting for joy at being made new in the Lord.[27] Presbyterians, Methodists, and Episcopalians did not go down to the waters of baptism to be "ducked," but were "sprinkled" instead. Though less dramatically stated, the symbolism of death and rebirth still pertained: "Except a man be born again, he cannot see the kingdom of God" (John 3:3). For the newly baptized a major change had occurred, an event which they believed transformed them and which they would remember for the rest of their lives. Recollecting the baptism of his mother, Isaiah Jeffries has left a description which conveys something of the excitement and the sense of new beginning which "baptizings" brought to many slaves:

> When I got to be a big boy, my Ma got religion at de Camp meeting at El-Bethel. She shouted and sung fer three days, going all over de plantation and de neighboring ones, inviting her friends to come to see her baptized and shouting and praying fer dem. She went around to all de people dat she had done wrong and begged dere forgiveness. She sent fer dem dat had wronged her, and told dem dat she was born again and a new

> woman, and dat she would forgive dem. She wanted everybody
> dat was not saved to go up wid her. . . . My Ma took me wid
> her to see her baptized, and I was so happy dat I sung and
> shouted wid her. All de niggers joined in singing.[28]

Occasionally, especially after revivals, there would occur mass
baptisms of large numbers of slaves. The manager of one Florida
plantation, for example, wrote the owner, "There was forty one
41 of your Negroes Baptised Last Sunday in the Canall above the
Bridge . . . the largest Negroe meeting I ever saw . . . " The excitement of "baptizings" attracted slaves from all around. Charlie
Hudson claimed "if there was a baptizing inside of ten miles
around from where us lived, us didn't miss it. Us knowed how to
walk and went to git the pleasure."[29]

The wedding ceremony was meant to solemnize and publicly
announce the union, in love, of two individuals—and here lay the
terrible irony—which was to last for life, a union which God had
made and no man was to break asunder. For slave weddings, no
matter what form they took, could not escape the threat inherent
in slavery, a threat which contradicted the very notion of Christian marriage: the constant possibility of separation by sale. Unre-
cognized by law, the most stable slave marriages were all too
fragile in their dependence upon the will of the slaveholder. As
Lunsford Lane noted of his own marriage, "In May, 1828, I was
bound as fast in wedlock as a slave can be. God may at any time
sunder that band in a freeman; either master may do the same at
pleasure in a slave." Despite this contingency the unions of slave
couples were celebrated by wedding ceremonials of some kind on
many plantations. The most frequent method of marrying two
slaves was the custom of jumping the broomstick. One of several
variations of the ritual was described by William Davis: "Dey lays
de brooms on de floor and de woman put her broom front de man
and he put he broom front de woman. Dey face one 'nother and
step 'cross de brooms at de same time to each other and takes hold
of hands and dat marry dem." Another variation was to hold the

broomstick a foot off the ground and then require the bride and groom one after the other to jump over it backwards. William Wells Brown asserted that "this custom had as binding force with negroes, as if they had been joined by a clergyman; the difference being the one was not so high-toned as the other. Yet, it must be admitted that the blacks always preferred being married by a clergyman."³⁰

Some slave weddings were performed according to Christian ritual by ministers, either white or black. Minerva Davis proudly stated that when her parents married, their master "had a white preacher to read out of a book to them. They didn't jump over no broom . . . " There were slaves, particularly favorite or prominent ones—cooks, butlers, maids—who were treated to elaborate weddings by the white folks. A mistress of a Louisiana plantation, Priscilla Bond, described a wedding of this type in her diary:

> Had a wedding here tonight. Two of the servants got married. . . . The bride looked quite nice dressed in white. I made her turban of white swiss pink tarlatan and orange blossoms. They were married at the gallery. The moon shone beautifully. They afterwards adjourned to the 'hospital' where they enjoyed a 'ball.' . . . The groom had on a suite of black, white gloves and tall beaver. The bride was dressed in white swiss, pink trimmings and white gloves. The bridesmaid and groom's man were dressed to correspond.

At the opposite pole, there were slaveholders who merely told their slaves they were married without further ado. Occasionally the broomstick ceremony was combined with the regular marriage rite at the slaves' request so that "they felt more married."³¹

"The slaves . . . in regard to marriage . . . try to make it as near lawful as they can," commented escaped slave John Warren. After emancipation some slaves felt the desire to regularize already long-standing marriages. Bongy Jackson enjoyed the rare privilege of attending her parents' wedding: "During slavery, us niggers just jumped the broom wit' the master's consent. After the Cibil War, soon's they got a little piece of money they got a preacher and had a real weddin'. My ma dressed like a bride an' all, an' she done already had nine children by my pa. All us kids was there an' we sure had a fine time." With or without preacher or license, some slaves viewed marriage as permanent and formed lasting relationships. James Curry and his wife were refused permission to marry, and even though they dared not risk any ceremony, they knew they were married and that their marriage was binding, Curry insisted, because "God married us." Others, "since they had no law to bind them to one woman . . . could have as many as they pleased by mutual agreement," observed Jacob Stroyer. The slaves held "different opinions about plurality of wives as have the most educated and refined among the whites."[32]

Like weddings, funeral services for slaves required permission, which was not always given. When Samuel Andrew's father died, his body "was driven in an ox-cart to a hole that had been dug, put in it and covered up"; his wife and children were not allowed "to stop work to attend the funeral." On the other hand, Isaam Morgan recalled that on his plantation "De slaves had dere own special graveyard an' us'd make de coffins raght on de place dar. When someone died, he was taken in a ox cart to de grave, wid all de slaves a-walkin' 'long behine de cart singin' de spirituals." Frequently slave funerals were held at night, when work stoppage was no problem. According to witnesses, these night funerals were impressive, solemn, and eerie ceremonies. The procession from the quarters to the grave site lit by pine-knot torches, the "wild" mournful strains of the hymns, the prayers of the slave preacher, the graves marked with posts and, as in Africa, decorated with the broken belongings of the deceased, all formed a dramatic backdrop for the slave community's farewell to one of its members. Mixed with the sadness was consolation. For some the deceased had returned home to Guinea, for others to heaven, "where bondage is never known." When permission could be obtained, fellows from neighboring farms attended, and when it couldn't they might steal away to pay last respects.[33]

It was not unusual for the funeral sermon to be separated from the burial by several days, weeks, and even months. Sometimes several funerals were preached at once. Charles Raymond, a white minister, noticed that slave funerals were usually preached on Sundays and explained that "there was no immediate chronological connection between the death and the funeral; and no necessary allusion in the sermon to the life, death, or virtues of the departed." Former slave Paul Smith testified "later on dey had de funeral sermon preached in church, maybe six months atter de buryin'. De white folkses had all deir funeral sermons preached at de time of buryin'." John Dixon Long, commenting on this time lag between burial and funeral observances, noted that "unless the funeral is preached," whether the deceased was sinner or saint, "there is no peace of mind to his friends."[34] It is difficult to say whether this practice reflected an African system of multiple funerals or was simply a necessity dictated by the uncertainty of permission and the lack of time available to the slaves to attend such services.

Funerals were the last in a cycle of ceremonies during the life of a slave. Sunday worship, prayer meetings, revivals, Christmas, "baptizing," weddings, funerals, all came and went, alternating like the seasons of the year, from day to day, from week to week, from month to month, in the life of the plantation. To the slaves these services and celebrations were special times, counteracting the monotony of life in slavery. Furthermore, the slaves asserted repeatedly in these seasons of celebration that their lives were special, their lives had dignity, their lives had meaning beyond the definitions set by slavery. In their meetings slaves enjoyed fellowship, exchanged mutual consolation, and gave voice to individual concerns. And here, too, some slaves found the place to exercise their talents for leadership.

Slave Preachers

Presiding over slave baptisms, funerals, and weddings was the slave preacher, leader of the slaves' religious life and an influential

figure in the slave community. Usually illiterate, the slave preacher often had native wit and unusual eloquence. Licensed or unlicensed, with or without permission, preachers held prayer meetings, preached and ministered in a very difficult situation. Carefully watched and viewed with suspicion, the preacher had to
straddle the conflict between the demands of conscience and the
orders of the masters. As one former slave put it, "Back there they
were harder on preachers than they were on anybody else. They
thought preachers were ruining the colored people." Anderson
Edwards reflected on the difficulty he experienced as a slave preacher in Texas:

> I been preachin' the Gospel and farmin' since slavery time. . . .
> When I starts preachin' I couldn't read or write and had to
> preach what massa told me and he say tell them niggers iffen
> they obeys the massa they goes to Heaven but I knowed
> there's something better for them, but daren't tell them 'cept
> on the sly. That I done lots. I tell 'em iffen they keeps prayin'
> the Lord will set 'em free.[35]

The slave preacher who verged too close on a gospel of equality
within earshot of whites was in trouble. Sarah Ford told how "one
day Uncle Lew preachin' and he say, 'De Lawd make everyone to
come in unity and on de level, both white and black.' When
Massa Charles hears 'bout it, he don't like it none, and de next
mornin' old Uncle Jake git Uncle Lew and put him out in de
field with de rest." Henry Clay Bruce retold the story of an old
preacher named Uncle Tom Ewing, "who was praying on one
occasion, after the close of his sermon, in the church near Jacob
Vennable's place . . . The old fellow got warmed up, and used the
words 'Free indeed, free from work, free from the white folks, free
from everything.' After the meeting closed, Jacob Vennable, who
sat in front of the pulpit, took Tom to task and threatened to have
his license revoked if he ever used such language in public."
Bruce concluded: "I heard Uncle Tom preach and pray many
times after the above described occurrence, but never heard him
use the words quoted above." Uncle Lew and Uncle Tom got off

light; Rev. R. S. Sorrick, a slave preacher in Washington County, Maryland, was placed in prison in 1841 for three months and eight days "for preaching the gospel to my colored brethren."[36]

By comparison with other slaves, some preachers were privileged characters. One former slave, from Alabama, remarked that "Nigger preachers in dem times wuz mighty-nigh free." Amanda McCray declared that the preacher on her plantation, though a slave, was exempt from hard manual labor. Conscious of his own importance, he went about "all dressed up" in frock coat and "store bought shoes." As long as he didn't interfere with other slaves' work he was allowed to hold services whenever he wished, and frequently he traveled to neighboring places to conduct prayer meetings. It was from the preacher, this relatively mobile and privileged slave, that the rest "first heard of the Civil War." During the war he offered whispered prayers for the success of the Union Army. Another former slave recalled: "I saw a preacher in Mississippi carry on a revival and he had persuaded the white man's son to go, and he professed and they would let him have meetings any time, 'cause that white man's son professed under him."[37] James L. Smith reported that he was able to exercise a busy ministry while still a slave:

I had a meeting appointed at a freedwoman's house . . . I left home about seven o'clock on Saturday evening, and arrived there about ten; we immediately commenced the meeting and continued it till about daylight . . . After breakfast we went two miles further, and held another meeting till late in the afternoon, then closed and started for home reaching there some time during the night. I was very much fatigued . . . so much so that I was not able to work the next day.[38]

Most slave preachers were hampered by illiteracy in a religion that placed such importance on the written word of the Bible. White folks would sometimes read a biblical verse for the preacher, and he would proceed to preach from it to his fellow slaves. William Pease, a fugitive from slavery in Tennessee, complained that the minister on his plantation, the slave driver, was "as ignorant as the rest of the slaves . . . knew nothing at all of the book and did not know enough to preach." There were slave preachers, however, who learned on the sly the rudiments of reading. After a friend had taught him the alphabet, Peter Randolph taught himself to read the Bible while in slavery. London, the head cooper on Frances Kemble's plantation, had secretly "obtained some little knowledge of reading, and was able to read "prayers and the Bible to his fellow-slaves." When asked how he learned to read, London replied evasively, "Well missis me learn . . . me try . . . me 'spose Heaven help me." Sam Johnson, slave preacher on a South Carolina plantation, learned to read from his master's young son. The boy's parents had forbidden him to drink tea or coffee which he liked. Sam, who was also the butler, supplied him with both in exchange for reading and writing lessons, from which he learned enough to be able to read the Bible.[39]

Yet illiteracy did not necessarily prevent eloquent preaching. As one former slave claimed, "My grandfather was a preacher and didn't know *A* from *B*. He could preach." And Louis Fowler remembered that the slave "preacherman" back on the Georgia plantation "am not educated, but can he preach a pow'ful sermon. O Lawd! He am inspire from de Lawd and he preached from his heartfelt." Clara Young testified about the power of the slave preacher:

> De preacher I liked de best was named Mathew Ewing. He was a comely nigger, black as night, and he sure could read out of his hand. He never learned no real readin' and writin' but he sure knowed his Bible and would hold his hand out and make like he was readin' and preach de purtiest preachin' you ever heard.[40]

Several observers noted that slaves preferred their own preachers. Anthony Dawson exclaimed: "Mostly we had white preachers, but when we had a black preacher that was heaven!" A white minister remarked in 1863 that "the 'colored brethren' are so much preferred *as preachers*. When in the pulpit there is a wonderful sympathy between the speaker and his audience. . . .

This sympathetic influence seems the result of a . . . peculiar experience. None but a negro can so preach as fully to arouse, excite, and transport the negro."[41]

Vivid imagery and dramatic delivery were characteristic of the slave preacher's sermons. Speaking of their abilities in general, a white traveler observed somewhat critically, "they acquire a remarkable memory of words, phrases, and forms; a curious sort of poetic talent is developed, and a habit is obtained of rhapsodizing and exciting furious emotions . . . " David Macrae, another traveler, who listened to ex-slave preachers shortly after the Civil War, acknowledged: "Some of the most vivid reproductions of Scripture narrative I have ever listened to were from the lips of such men, who might with proper training have been orators."[42] Missionaries to the freedmen were frequently amazed at the wisdom and eloquence of the black preachers recently released from slavery. "What wonderful preachers these blacks are!" exclaimed one correspondent from Georgia to the editor of the *American Missionary*:

> I listened to a remarkable sermon or talk a few evenings since. The preacher spoke of the need of atonement for sin. "Bullocks c'dn't do it, heifers c'dn't do it, de blood of doves c'dn't do it—but up in heaven, for thousan and thousan of years, the Son was saying to the Father, 'Put up a soul, put up a soul. Prepare me a body, an I will go an meet Justice on Calvary's brow!" He was so dramatic. In describing the crucifixion he said: "I see the sun when she turned herself black. I see the stars a fallin from the sky, and them old Herods comin out of their graves and goin about the city, an they knew 'twas the Lord of Glory."[43]

George Hepworth, a war correspondent, was similarly impressed by a slave he heard preach behind the Union lines:

> The moment I looked at him, I saw that he was no common man. He had a full forehead, a tall commanding figure. . . . I remember, too, some of his phrases: they were very beautiful, and were epic in grandeur. He spoke of '*the rugged wood of the cross*,' whereto the Saviour was nailed; and, after describing

that scene with as much power as I have ever known an orator
to exhibit, he reached the climax, when he pictured the earth-
quake which rent the veil of the temple, with this extremely
beautiful expression: 'And, my friends, *the earth was unable to
endure the tremendous sacrilege, and trembled.*' He held his
rude audience with most perfect control; subdued them, excited them, and, in fact, did what he pleased with them."[44]

Attempting to analyze the preaching of Uncle Robert, a slave in
Beaufort, North Carolina, a white missionary noted, "In his sermons there is often a clearness of statement, an earnestness of
address, a sublimity and splendor of imagery, together with a
deep pathos, which give his public addresses great power." As a
result, "many who affect to despise the negro, want to hear Uncle
Robert when it is announced that he is to preach."[45] A.M.
French, writing of the "Colored Ambassadors" at Port Royal,
touched upon the reasons which the slave preachers themselves
gave for their authority:

> The real spiritual benefit of these poor Colored people, instru-
> mentally, seems to have been mostly derived from a sort of
> local preachers, Colored, and mostly slaves, but of deep spiri-
> tual experience, sound sense, and capacity to state Scripture
> facts, narratives, and doctrines, far better than most, who feed
> upon commentaries. True, the most of them could not read,
> still, some of them line hymns from memory with great accu-
> racy, and fervor, and repeat Scripture most appropriately, and
> correctly. Their teaching shows clearly that it is God in the
> soul, that makes the religious teacher. One is amazed at their
> correctness and power. They say: "God tell me 'you go teach
> de people what I tell you; I shall prosper you; I teach you in
> de heart.' "[46]

The style of the folk sermon, shared by black and white evangelicals, was built on a formulaic structure based on phrases,
verses, and whole passages the preacher knew by heart. Characterized by repetition, parallellisms, dramatic use of voice and gesture, and a whole range of oratorical devices, the sermon began
with normal conversational prose, then built to a rhythmic ca-

dence, regularly marked by the exclamations of the congregation, and climaxed in a tonal chant accompanied by shouting, singing, and ecstatic behavior. The preacher, who needed considerable skill to master this art, acknowledged not his own craft but, rather, the power of the spirit which struck him and "set him on fire." The dynamic pattern of call and response between preacher and people was vital to the progression of the sermon, and unless the spirit roused the congregation to move and shout, the sermon was essentially unsuccessful.[47]

A highly visible figure in the community, the preacher occupied a position of esteem and authority and undoubtedly developed a reputation which could form the basis for folk tales. The prestige of the role attracted some characters to the ministry who furnished the prototypes of the rascal jackleg preacher. Perhaps the genre of black-preacher tales began during slavery. For some the call to preach might have been a call to status and privilege, but for the majority it was the command of God to spread the Gospel. One former slave explained his calling in simple and eloquent words which epitomized the ideal of the preacher's vocation:

> Yer see I am a preacher. De Lord call me once when I was workin'. . . . He call me and told me, in imagination, you know, that he wanted me to preach. I told him I didn't know enough—that I was ig'nant, and the folks would laugh at me. But he drew me on and I prayed. I prayed out in the woods, and every time I tried to get up from my knees He would draw me down again. An' at last a great light came down sudden to me, a light as big as the moon, an' struck me hard on the head and on each shoulder and on the bress, here and here and here . . . And den same time warm was in around my heart, and I felt that the Book was there. An' my tongue was untied, and I preach ever since and is not afraid. I can't read de Book, but I has it here, I has de text, and de meanin', and I speaks as well as I can, and de congregation takes what the Lord gives me.[48]

The preacher was not the only figure of religious influence in the quarters. The conjurer was the preacher's chief rival for au-

thority of a supernatural kind. Witches possessed a negative kind
of power to frighten. Elder slaves, who had earned respect because of their wisdom or vision acted as spiritual mentors to their
fellows. Frederick Douglass, for example, as a boy frequently
sought the counsel of Uncle Charles Lawson, whom he called his
spiritual father and "chief instructor in religious matters." Lawson
taught Douglass "that the Lord had great work for me to do. . . .
When I would tell him, 'I am a slave, and a slave for life, how can
I do anything?' he would quietly answer, 'The *Lord* can make you
free . . . ' " Sinda, an elderly slave woman on Frances Kemble's
plantation, exerted considerable religious influence among the
slaves as a prophetess until she damaged her credibility by predicting an imminent end to the world. On the Sea Islands in 1864
Laura Towne encountered Maum Katie "an old African woman,
who remembers worshipping her own gods in Africa." Over a
century old, she was a " 'spiritual mother,' a fortune-teller or,
rather, prophetess, and a woman of tremendous influence over her
spiritual children." The "watchman" was also an important religious leader on the plantation. His duties included advising on
spiritual matters, opening and leading prayer meetings, counsel-
ing "mourners," sinners seeking conversion, and generally setting
Christian example for the slaves.[49]

Much discussion has focused on the question, Were the slave
preachers a force for accommodation to the *status quo* or a force
for the exercise of slave autonomy? On the one hand, the slave
preacher was criticized by former slaves as the "mouthpiece of the
masters." On the other hand, some slave preachers preached and
spoke of freedom in secret. The weight of slave testimony suggests that the slaves knew and understood the restrictions under
which the slave preacher labored, and that they accepted his authority not because it came from the master but because it came
from God. They respected him because he was the messenger of
the Gospel, one who preached the word of God with power and
authority, indeed with a power which sometimes humbled white
folk and frequently uplifted slaves. For a black man and a slave to

stand and preach with eloquence, skill, and wisdom was in itself a sign of ability and talent which slavery's restrictiveness could frustrate but never completely stifle.

Bible Christians

The sermons of the slave preacher were based upon the Bible. Indeed the biblical orientation of slave religion was one of its central characteristics. Stories, characters, and images from both Old and New Testaments pervaded the preaching, praying, and singing of the slaves. Keenly aware of their inability to read the Scriptures, many slaves came to view education with a religious awe and bitterly resented the slaveholders' ban on reading. "Dey jus' beat 'em up bad when dey cotched 'em studyin' readin' and writin'," recalled William McWhorter. "Folks did tell 'bout some of de owners dat cut off one finger evvy time dey cotch a slave tryin' to git larnin'. How-some-ever, dere was some Niggers dat wanted larnin' so bad dey would slip out at night and meet in a deep gully whar dey would study by de light of light'ood torchers; but one thing sho, dey better not let no white folks find out 'bout it, and if dey was lucky 'nough 'til dey larned to read de Bible, dey kept it a close secret." The thirst of slaves for religious education led them to sneak lessons whenever they found a teacher. W. L. Bost reflected upon reading, religion, and revelation:

> Us poor niggers never allowed to learn anything. All the readin' they ever hear was when they was carried through the big Bible. The massa say that keep the slaves in they places. They was one nigger boy . . . who was terrible smart. He learn to read and write. He take other colored children out in the fields and teach 'em about the Bible, but they forget it before the next Sunday. . . . The white folks feared for niggers to get any religion and education, but I reckin somethin' inside just told us about God and that there was a better place hereafter.[50]

Slaves were distrustful of the white folks' interpretation of the Scriptures and wanted to be able to search them for themselves.

The reverence which they held for the Bible moved many ex-slaves to flock to schools set up by missionaries after freedom came. Woodson's statement, "Negroes . . . almost worshiped the Bible, and their anxiety to read it was their greatest incentive to learn," is not an exaggeration. One visitor to a night school for freedmen in Beaufort, North Carolina, learned from the teacher the story of a fugitive slave "who carried a big Bible about with her through the woods and swamps." Though she was unable to read, she "had got her old mistress to turn down the leaves at the verses she knew by heart, and often she would sit down in the woods and open the big Bible at these verses, and repeat them aloud, and find strength and consolation." Another slave, who was a nurse for her master's family, had been taught by one of the children to spell the name of Jesus and to recognize it in the text. It became her devotion "to take the Bible and search for the name," but since "she had no idea in what parts of the Bible it was to be found" she would open the book at random and "travel with her finger along line after line, and page after page" until she found "Jesus." Harriet Ware, missionary in Port Royal, noted in 1862 the freed slaves' almost superstitious regard for letters. Observing a funeral, she noticed: "As we drew near to the grave we heard all the children singing their A,B,C, through and through again, as they stood waiting round the grave for the rest to assemble . . . Each child has his school-book or picture book . . . in his hand,—another proof that they consider their lessons as in some sort religious exercises."[51]

There were slaves who did learn to read. Some planters, ignoring the law or customs prohibiting slave literacy, did not hinder their slaves' efforts to learn. Sir Charles Lyell on his second visit to the American South discovered that some of the planters in Glynn County, Georgia, "have of late permitted the distribution of Bibles among their slaves," and he noted that "they who were unable to read were as anxious to possess them as those who could." Olmsted came across a plantation in northern Mississippi where the owner took pride in the fact that his slaves could read:

"there ent one of my niggers but what can read; read good too—better'n I can at any rate." "How did they learn?" "Taught themselves. I b'lieve there was one on 'em that I bought, that could read, and he taught all the rest." According to the planter, his slaves preferred religious books, which they purchased from peddlers. A few slaves—Frederick Douglass and Elijah Marrs among them—learned to read from friendly whites, especially children. John C. Becton, former slave in North Carolina, explained: "When the white children studied their lessons I studied with them. When they wrote in the sand I wrote in the sand too. The white children, and not the marster or mistress, is where I got started in learnin' to read and write."[52]

Illiteracy proved less of an obstacle to knowledge of the Bible than might be thought, for biblical stories became part of the oral tradition of the slaves. Oral instructions and Sunday School lessons were committed to memory. As one missionary to the slaves reported: "To those who are ignorant of letters, *their memory is their book*. . . . In a recent examination of one of the schools, I was forcibly struck with their remembrance of *passages of Scripture*. Those questions which turned upon and called for passages of Scripture, the scholars answered more readily than any other." William H. Heard, former slave and, later, bishop in the A.M.E. Church, recalled: "In . . . Sunday School we were taught the Bible and the Catechism, and committed much to memory by having the same repeated to us in the Sunday School, and then some member of the white family carried this out during the week; so that there were those of us who could repeat whole Psalms and chapter after chapter in the shorter Catechism." The Reverend S. G. Whiton, missionary to the freedman of Fortress Monroe, Virginia, in 1866, was amazed by one of his students, Uncle Peter, who was very familiar with the Bible even though he read poorly. "His memory," explained Whiton, "is remarkable, and he can repeat a great many chapters entire. This morning, among others, he repeated the first chapter of Matthew, hardly making a single mistake in that long list of genealogies."[53]

Because they were unable to read the Bible, some slaves believed that God revealed his word to them directly, in their hearts. "De Master teaches we poor coloured folk in dat way," claimed one elderly freedwoman, "for we hasn't edication, and we can't read His bressed word for ourselves." A missionary to the contrabands (fugitive slaves behind Union lines) at Beaufort, South Carolina, heard the same belief expressed by another freedwoman: " 'Oh! I don't know nothing! I can't read a word. But, oh! I read Jesus in my heart, just as you read him in de book'; and drawing her forefingers across the other palm, as if tracing a line: 'I read and read him here in my heart just as you read him in de Bible. O, . . . my God! I got Him! I hold him here all de time! He stay with me!' " Several ex-slaves claimed that they recognized verses read to them from the Bible because they had heard them before in visions they had experienced during slavery. Some slaves apparently espoused a doctrine of enthusiasm which stressed direct inspiration from God rather than the revelation contained in the pages of the Bible. Susan H. Clark noticed this emphasis on personal revelation among the freedmen with whom she worked at Fortress Monroe. "The Bible being so long a sealed book to them, they believed that God revealed everything that pertained to their salvation, without reference to the Bible or its teaching. They think no one should read the Bible until after conversion—that it is *then* a guide. Some say it is written on their hearts, and that is all they want."[54]

It is not surprising that the uses to which slaveholders had put the Bible would lead some slaves to distinguish their own experiential Christianity from the "Bible Christianity" of their masters. As one observer noted of ex-slave church members in Virginia: they "were quite alarmed . . . that those who were concerned for their soul's salvation should attempt to look for instruction or comfort from the Bible. They wanted to see their children and friends get religion as they did. *They* fell under the mighty power of God, and after mourning many days, and then came out shouting, for an angel, they said, told them their sins were forgiven.

They said their masters and families were Bible Christians, and they did not want to be like them."

Unable to read the Bible for themselves and skeptical of their masters' interpretation of it, most slaves learned the message of the Christian Gospel and translated it into songs in terms of their own experience. As John Dixon Long observed, "Many of them could state the cardinal doctrines of the Gospel in the language of song."[55] It was in the spirituals, above all, that the characters, themes, and lessons of the Bible became dramatically real and took on special meaning for the slaves.

Slave Spirituals

Drawing from the Bible, Protestant hymns, sermons, and African styles of singing and dancing, the slaves fashioned a religious music which expressed their faith in "moving, immediate, colloquial, and, often, magnificently dramatic terms."[56] The argument over the relative importance of European versus African influence on the development of the slave spirituals has demonstrated that these songs, like all folk songs, are hybrids, born of mutual influence and reciprocal borrowing between traditions. As noted in Chapter 2, the discussion of African and Anglo-American musical contributions to the spirituals has been long and sometimes heated, but more important for interpreting the meaning of the spirituals is an appreciation of the context, social and religious, in which the spirituals were performed, as well as an insight into the extraordinary power of these songs to shape the experience and the conscious identity of a people.

Spirituals are too often seen simply as words and notes printed on a page. What must be recognized is that they emerged as communal songs, heard, felt, sung and often danced with hand-clapping, foot-stamping, head-shaking excitement. It was at the prayer or praise meeting that the spiritual was sung in its full communal and liturgical setting. Slave preacher James L. Smith offered a glimpse of this setting: "The way in which we worshipped is almost indescribable. The singing was accompanied by a certain ecstasy of motion, clapping of hands, tossing of heads, which would continue without cessation about half an hour; one would lead off in a kind of recitative style, others joining in the chorus. The old house partook of the ecstasy; it rang with their jubilant shouts, and shook in all its joints."[57] Writing after slavery, but discussing a tradition that stretched back beyond emancipation, Harris Barrett, of Hampton Institute, also attempted to picture the spirituals in their original context:

> Those who have never heard these songs in their native setting can have no conception of the influence they exert upon the people. I have sat in a gathering where everything was as quiet and placid as a lake on a summer day, where the preacher strove in vain to awaken an interest; I have heard a brother or a sister start one of these spirituals, slowly and monotonously; I have seen the congregation irresistibly drawn to take up the refrain; I have seen the entire body gradually worked up from one degree of emotion to another until, like a turbulent, angry sea, men and women, to the accompaniment of the singing, and with shouting, moaning, and clapping of hands, surged and swayed to and fro. I have seen men and women at these times look and express themselves as if they were conversing with their Lord and Master, with their hands in His . . . [58]

In response to a question about the way in which spirituals were created, one ex-slave from Kentucky claimed that they were formed out of traditional African tunes and songs with which the slaves were familiar. Then she went on to describe another part of the process by which spirituals came to be—the moments of religious excitement when the slaves' emotions spontaneously broke out in moaning, praying, singing and shouting, the ecstatic expressions of religious fervor:

> Us ole heads use ter make 'em on de spurn of de moment, after we wressle wid de Spirit and come thoo. But the tunes was brung from Africa by our grandaddies. Dey was jis 'miliar song . . . dey calls 'em spirituals, case de Holy Spirit done

revealed 'em to 'em. Some say Moss Jesus taught 'em, and I's
seed 'em start in meetin'. We'd all be at the 'prayer house' de
Lord's Day, and de white preacher he'd splain de word and
read whar Ezekiel done say—
>Dry bones gwine ter lib again.
And, honey, de Lord would come a-shining thoo dem pages
and revive dis ole nigger's heart, and I'd jump up dar and den
and holler and shout and sing and pat, and dey would all
cotch de words . . . and dey's all take it up and keep at it, and
keep a-addin to it and den it would be a spiritual.[59]

To fully understand these slave songs, then, the reader of spirituals must try to imagine them as performed. The verses of some
spirituals take on new meaning when one realizes that spirituals
were not only *sung* in the fields or at prayer and worship services
but were *shouted*—that is, danced in the ring shout—with the
result that the lyrics of the songs were acted out or dramatized by
the band of shouters. The shout would start with a leader calling
out a verse of a spiritual while the shouters responded by walking
around in a circle. When the singers who stood outside the ring
took up the chorus, the shout proper would begin with the ring
band shuffling rapidly to the beat announced by the hand-clapping and foot-tapping of the chorus of singers who were said then
to be "basing" the shouters. Here is an example of the lyrics of a
spiritual:

(*Chorus*)   O shout, O shout, O shout away,
>And don't you mind,
>And glory, glory, glory in my soul!

(*Verse*)   And when 'twas night I thought 'twas day,
>I thought I'd pray my soul a-way,
>And glory, glory, glory in my soul!

It may contribute significantly to the reader's appreciation of the
song if he visualizes it as an all-night shout, literally creating the
experience it describes: "shouting until the glory in my soul
turned night into day."[60]

In the creation as well as the performance of the spirituals, spontaneity, variety, and communal interchange were essential characteristics. The interplay between individual and group participation in the formation of the spirituals was illustrated by one freedman when asked about the origin of a song:

> I'll tell you; it's dis way. My master call me up and order me a short peck of corn and a hundred lash. My friends see it and is sorry for me. When dey come to de praise meetin' dat night dey sing about it. Some's very good singers and know how; and dey work it in you know; till dey git it right; and dat's de way.[61]

The flexible, improvisational structure of the spirituals gave them the capacity to fit an individual slave's specific experience into the consciousness of the group. One person's sorrow or joy became everyone's through song. Singing the spirituals was therefore both an intensely personal and vividly communal experience in which an individual received consolation for sorrow and gained a heightening of joy because his experience was shared. Perhaps in the very structure of many spirituals one can see articulated this notion of communal support. In the pattern of overlapping call and response an individual would extemporize the verses, freely interjecting new ones from other spirituals. Frequently, before he was finished, everyone else would be repeating a chorus familiar to all. This pattern may be seen as a metaphor for the individual believer's relationship to the community. His changing daily experience, like the verses improvised by the leader, was "based" by the constancy of his Christian community. This symbolism is especially powerful in the ring shout when the individual shouter stood outside himself, literally in ecstasy, transcending time and place as the rhythms of the chorus were repeatedly beat out with hands, feet, and body in the constant shuffle of the ring.

To say that the spontaneity and fluidity of the spirituals permitted the slaves to make reference to individual incidents is not to assert—as some have—that the spirituals were coded protest songs. Certainly, there were spirituals that were used to announce secret meetings or to warn of the overseer's approach. But the relevance of most spirituals to the situation of slavery was both more ambiguous and more profound. Because the spirituals were open formally and thematically to change, a spiritual in one situation might mean one thing and in another something else, without negating its earlier meaning. A particular verse might have a particular significance for a person at one time and not at another. It is a common experience for people to refer to a widely circulated and well-known song as "our song" because it seems a particularly apt comment on some situation in their own lives. In the same way, one former slave recalled that although "her" song, "I Heard the Voice of Jesus Say," came from a hymnbook, it was her song because "It just suited me when I was praying to the Lord to have mercy on me for my sins."[62] It is not necessary, then, to believe that the line "I am bound for the land of Canaan" always meant going North to escape from slavery, even though that is exactly what the line signified for Frederick Douglass and his fellows while they plotted to escape.

A keen observer might have detected in our repeated singing of

O Canaan, sweet Canaan,
I am bound for the land of Canaan,

something more than a hope of reaching heaven. We meant to reach the *North*, and the North was our Canaan.

I thought I heard them say
There were lions in the way;
I don't expect to stay
Much longer here.
Run to Jesus, shun the danger.
I don't expect to stay
Much longer here,

was a favorite air, and had a double meaning. On the lips of some it meant the expectation of a speedy summons to a world of spirits, but on the lips of our company it simply meant a

speedy pilgrimage to a free state, and deliverance from all the
evils and dangers of slavery.[63]

This was clearly a case where a spiritual with a generally accepted
meaning was applied to a specific situation by Douglass and his
company in order to bolster their courage and strengthen their
camaraderie.

Religious images, such as freedom, were ambiguous. To some
slaves they undoubtedly meant freedom from physical as well as
spiritual bondage. At certain times one meaning probably had
more urgency than the other. Whites frightened by the possibility
of slave insurrection were suspicious of ambiguity in the spirituals, as slaves in Georgetown, South Carolina, discovered when, at
the beginning of the Civil War, they were jailed for singing:

> We'll soon be free,
> We'll soon be free,
> We'll soon be free,
>   When de Lord will call us home.
> My brudder, how long,
> My brudder, how long,
> My brudder, how long,
>   'Fore we done sufferin' here?
> It won't be long (*thrice*)
>   'Fore de Lord will call us home. . . .
> We'll soon be free (*thrice*)
>   When Jesus sets me free.
> We'll fight for liberty (*thrice*)
>   When de Lord will call us home.

Thomas Wentworth Higginson, who collected spirituals from
black troops during the Civil War explained " 'De Lord will call
us home' was evidently thought to be a symbolical verse; for, as a
little drummer-boy explained to me, showing all his white teeth
as he sat in the moonlight by the door of my tent, 'Day tink *de
Lord* mean for say *de Yankees.*' " Higginson concluded that "suspicion in this case was unfounded," but one wonders if he noted the
ambiguity of the drummer boy's smile.[64] William Sinclair, whose
early childhood was spent in slavery in Georgetown, South Caro-

lina, claimed that when slave owners forbade the slaves to sing "One of these days I shall be free/ When Christ the Lord shall set me free," they "hoodwinked the master class by humming the music of this particular song, while the words echoed and re-echoed deep down in their hearts with perhaps greater effect than if they had been spoken."[65]

By the end of the war once ambiguous references to freedom and slavery had become clear. One traveler heard freedmen singing these verses, adopted "sometimes during the war":

> Oh! Fader Abraham
> Go down into Dixie's land
> Tell Jeff Davis
> To let my people go.
> Down in de house of bondage
> Dey have watch and waited long,
> De oppressor's heel is heavy,
> De oppressor's arm is strong.
> Oh, Fader Abraham.[66]

Booker T. Washington, recalling his last days in slavery, made a similar point about the ambiguity of the religious imagery in spirituals:

> As the great day [of emancipation] grew nearer, there was more singing in the slave quarters than usual. It was bolder, had more ring, and lasted later into the night. Most of the verses of the plantation songs had some reference to freedom. True, they had sung those same verses before, but they had been careful to explain that the "freedom" in these songs referred to the next world, and had no connection with life in this world. Now they gradually threw off the mask; and were not afraid to let it be known that the "freedom" in their songs meant freedom of the body in this world.[67]

The spirituals, then, were capable of communicating on more than one level of meaning. Indeed it would have been strange had they not, since much of the verbal art of West Africans and many of the folk tales of their American descendants were characterized by indirect, veiled social comment and criticism, a technique appropriately described as "hitting a straight lick with a crooked stick."[68]

Important though it is to recognize that the spirituals sometimes expressed the slaves' desire for freedom in this world as well as in the next, it is at least as important to understand the profound connection between the other world and this world in the religious consciousness of the slaves. Categorizing sacred and secular elements is of limited usefulness in discussing the spirituals because the slaves, following African and biblical tradition, believed that the supernatural continually impinged on the natural, that divine action constantly took place within the lives of men, in the past, present and future. It was precisely at the worship and praise services in which the spirituals were so important that the contact between God and man became real for the slaves.

In the spirituals, as Lawrence Levine has persuasively argued, a sense of sacred time operated, in which the present was extended backwards so that characters, scenes, and events from the Old and New Testaments became dramatically alive and present.[69] As a result, the slaves' identification with the children of Israel took on an immediacy and intensity which would be difficult to exaggerate. The slaves' religious community reached out through space and time to include Jacob, Moses, Joshua, Noah, Daniel, the heroes whose faith had been tested of old. From the New Testament they remembered "weeping Mary," "sinking Peter," and "doubting Thomas," again noting the trials of faith through which these "true believers" had passed: Mary weeping in the garden because she did not know where Jesus' body had been taken, until he appeared to her in his risen glory; Thomas doubting that Jesus had risen until Jesus appeared to him and said, "Blessed are those who have not seen, yet believed"; Peter sinking beneath the waves of the Sea of Galilee because he was weak in faith, until Jesus, walking upon the water, reached out to save him. These were the models, the analogues, reminding the slaves to hold on to their faith despite grief, doubt, and fear.

Identification with the children of Israel was, of course, a significant theme for white Americans, too. From the beginnings of colonization, white Christians had identified the journey across the Atlantic to the New World as the exodus of a new Israel from the bondage of Europe into the promised land of milk and honey. For the black Christian, as Vincent Harding has observed, the imagery was reversed: the Middle Passage had brought his people to Egypt land, where they suffered bondage under Pharaoh. White Christians saw themselves as a new Israel; slaves identified themselves as the old. Certainly, a great deal of the imagery and even the verses which occur in the slave spirituals occur in the white revivalist spirituals also.[70] Particularly, to those poor whites who knew suffering, hardship, and oppression these images must have meant much the same as they did to slaves. But oppression was not slavery. The slaves' historical identity as a unique people was peculiarly their own. In the spirituals the slaves affirmed and reaffirmed that identity religiously as they suffered and celebrated their journey from slavery to freedom.

Like many Christians before and after, the slaves found in the journey an archetypal symbol for the progress of the Christian life. It is no surprise to find that numerous texts of the spirituals dramatize episodes along the path which begins with conversion "down in that lonesome valley" and ends in salvation "across the river Jordan, on Canaan's bright shore." And since the spirituals were songs of praise and worship, they were meant not only to narrate the Christians' pilgrimage but to exhort, instruct, and help move them on the way. The first step on the way was for the sinner to turn and, convicted of sin, repent. To exhort the sinner, and to renew the fervor of the converted as well, the spirituals attested to the comforts to be found in religion.

> O walk Jordan long road,
> And religion so sweet,
> O religion is good for anything,
> And religion so sweet.
> Religion make you happy.
> Religion gib me patience.

> O member, get religion
> I long time been a-huntin'
> I seekin' for my fortune.
> O I gwine to meet my Savior.
> Gwine to tell him 'bout my trials . . . [71]

The invitation to "get religion" was sometimes directly personal,
as in "The Heavenly Road":

> You may talk of my name as much as you please,
>   And carry my name abroad,
> But I really do believe I'm a child of God
>   As I walk in de heavenly road.
> O, won't you go wid me? (*Thrice*)
>   For to keep our garments clean.
> O Satan is a mighty busy ole man,
>   And roll rocks in my way;
> But Jesus is my bosom friend,
>   And roll 'em out of de way.
> O, won't you go wid me? (*Thrice*)
>   For to keep our garments clean.
>
> Come, my brudder, if you never did pray,
>   I hope you may pray to-night;
> For I really believe I'm a child of God
>   As I walk in de heavenly road.
> O, won't you, etc.[72]

The exhortation to repent could also be dramatically urgent:

> Turn sinner, turn today, Turn sinner, turn O! (*Twice*)
> Turn, O sinner, de worl' da gwine, Turn, sinner, turn O! (*Twice*)
> Wait not for tomorrow's sun, Turn sinner, turn O! (*Twice*)
> Tomorrow's sun will sure to shine, Turn sinner, turn O! (*Twice*)
> The sun may shine, but on your grave, Turn sinner, turn O!
> While de lamp hold out to burn, Turn, sinner, turn O!
> De wile' sinner may return, Turn, sinner, turn O![73]

In the slave spirituals which have come down to us, references
to hellfire and damnation are not common, but they did occur.

One fragment of this threatening approach to sinners was recorded by a traveler shortly after the end of the war:

> A negro lad who sang me a weird hymn in which the follow-
> ing verse occurred,
>
>> You'd better mind how you fool with Christ
>> In a moment you'll be as cold as ice,
>
> paused, and said, "I saw six converted on that verse."[74]

"Down in the Valley," a spiritual collected by Higginson, com-
bines images of divine mercy and apocalyptic judgment to persuade the sinner to seek conversion, and adds a note of urgency
by repeating "Who will rise and go with me?"

> We'll run and never tire,
> We'l run and never tire,
> We'll run and never tire,
>> Jesus set poor sinners free.
> Way down in de valley,
>> Who will rise and go with me?
> You've heern talk of Jesus
>> Who set poor sinners free.
>
> De lightnin' and de flashin'
> De lightnin' and de flashin',
> De lightnin' and de flashin',
>> Jesus set poor sinners free.
> I can't stand the fire. (*Thrice*)
>> Jesus set poor sinners free,
> De green trees a-flamin' (*Thrice*)
>> Jesus set poor sinners free,
>>> Way down in de valley,
>>>> Who will rise and go with me?
>> You've heern talk of Jesus
>> Who set poor sinners free.[75]

"Going down into the lonesome valley" was a difficult passage
that each sin-laden "mourner" had to experience before "comin'
through" to conversion.

My sister, you want to get religion?
Go down in de Lonesome Valley,
My brudder, you want to git religion,
Go down in the Lonesome Valley.

(*Chorus*)
Go down in de Lonesome Valley,
Go down in de Lonesome Valley, my Lord,
Go down in de Lonesome Valley,
To meet my Jesus dere![76]

The figurative lonesome valley took on literal shape as the troubled sinner wandered the woods, the marshes, and other deserted places, seeking to find release from the burden of sin:

O where d'ye tink I fin' 'em?
I fin' 'em, Lord, in de grave-yard.
I fin' 'em in de boggy mire.

It was in the wilderness, as the Bible so often illustrated, that one waited for the Lord.[77]

Jesus call you. Go in de wilderness,
Go in de wilderness, go in de wilderness,
Jesus call you. Go in de wilderness
To wait upon de Lord,
Go wait upon de Lord,
Go wait upon de Lord,
Go wait upon de Lord, my God,
He take away de sins of de world.
Jesus a-waitin'. Go in de wilderness,
Go, etc.
All dem chil'en go in de wilderness
To wait upon de Lord.[78]

From those who had already "come through," the anxious "mourner" could expect encouragement:

Hunt till you find him, Hallelujah,
And a-huntin' for de Lord

> When I was a mourner jus' like you,
> I want to go to heaven when I die,
> I fast and I prayed till I came thro',
> For I want to go to heaven when I die.
> O my soul! O my soul!
> I want to go to heaven when I die.[79]

In the Old Testament story of Jacob wrestling all night with an angel, the slaves found a striking metaphor for the sinner's struggle with his soul. The scene was vividly recalled by one former slave, "Preachers used to get up and preach and call moaners up to the moaner's bench. They would all kneel down and sometimes they would lay down on the floor, and the Christians would sing:

> Rassal Jacob, rassal as you did in the days of old,
> Gonna rassal all night til broad day light
> And ask God to bless my soul."[80]

At the revival and prayer meetings, Christian members were willing to sing and pray over "mourners" all night long to help them come through to the Lord.

(Chorus)   I hold my brudder wid a tremblin' han',
            I would not let him go.
            Wrastl' on, Jacob, Jacob, day is a-breaking,
            Wrastl' on, Jacob, Oh Lord I would not let him go.

(Verses)   I will not let you go, my Lord.
            Fisherman Peter out at sea
            He fish all night and he fish all day
            He catch no fish, but he catch some soul.
            Jacob hang from a tremblin' limb.[81]

Once a "mourner" had come through he was baptized into Christian fellowhip, among the band of "true believers" and "valiant soldiers" of the Lord. But the journey had just begun; there was still "Jordan's long road" to walk, as one spiritual taught:

De rough, rocky road what Moses done travel,
I's bound to carry my soul to de Lawd;
It's a mighty rocky road but I mos' done travel,
And I's bound to carry my soul to de Lawd.[82]

Yonder's my old mudder,
        Been a-waggin' at de hill so long
It's about time she'll cross over;
        Get home bimeby.
Keep prayin', I do believe
        We're a long time waggin' o'er de crossin'.
Keep prayin', I do believe
        We'll get home to heaven bimeby.

Bendin' knees a-achin', Body racked wid pain,
        I wish I was a child of God,
I'd git home bimeby.
        Keep prayin', I do believe
We're a long time waggin' o' de crossin.'
        Keep prayin', I do believe
We'll git home to heaven bimebye.[83]

The spirituals urged the weary slaves to follow the example set by others who had traveled the road before:

All dem Mount Zion member
dey have many ups and downs;
But cross come or no come,
        for to hold out to the end.
Hold out to the end,
        hold out to the end,
It is my 'termination for to hold out to the end.[84]

In the face of temptation to backslide, the Christian slaves exhorted one another to perservere until the end.

O brothers, don't get weary
O brothers, don't get weary
O brothers, don't get weary
We're waiting for the Lord
We'll land on Canaan's shore,

We'll land on Canaan's shore,
When we land on Canaan's shore,
We'll meet forever more.[85]

What makes ole Satan follow me so?
Satan got nuttin' 't all fur to do wid me.
    Tiddy [Sister] Rosa, hold your light!
    Brudder Tony, hold you light!
All de member, hold bright light
    On Canaan's shore.[86]

Alluding to the New Testament parable of the ten wise and ten
foolish virgins, these verses advised the members to be vigilant:

Brudder, keep your lamp trimmin' and a-burnin',
Keep your lamp trimmin' and a-burnin',
Keep your lamp trimmin' and a-burnin',
    For dis world most done
So keep your lamp, etc.
    Dis world most done.[87]

The Christian had to be vigilant against the snares of "Ole Cappen Satan," who seems in the slave spirituals to be more a malevolent trickster than a fearful demon:

Ole Satan toss a ball at me.
Him tink de ball would hit my soul.
De ball for hell and 1 for heaven.
What make ole Satan hate me so?
Because he got me once and he let me go.

O, Satan is a liar, and he conjure too,
And if you don't mind, he'll conjure you.

When I get dar, Cappen Satan was dar
Says, young man, young man, dere's no use for pray,
For Jesus is dead, and God gone away,
And I made him out a liar, and I went my way.

O Satan is a mighty busy ole man,
    And roll rocks in my way;

> But Jesus is my bosom friend,
> And roll 'em out of de way.[88]

In the religious consciousness of the slaves, as revealed by the spirituals, the most serious spiritual problem was not the battle versus "ole Satan" but the inner turmoil of a "trebbled spirit."

> I am a-trouble in de mind,
> O I am a-trouble in de mind,
> I ask my Lord what shall I do,
> I am a-trouble in de mind.
> I'm a-trouble in de mind,
> What you doubt for:
> I'm a-trouble in de mind.[89]

One former slave recalled: "I remember seeing my old mother spinning with tears running down her cheeks, crying about her brother who was sold and carried to Arkansas. She would sing,

> "Oh my good Lord, go low in the valley to pray,
> To ease my troubling mind."[90]

Although the conversion experience had already brought the Christian through the lonesome valley, in a wider sense he was traveling there still. For all of life was a valley of tears, a road of suffering and sorrow, weariness and toil. It is difficult to believe that a slave sang of suffering and toil without reference to his life in slavery. The spirituals did that and more. They also presented the slave's reflections on the human condition, which masters had to endure as well as slaves. In attempting to make sense out of their individual lives, the slaves—as numerous commentators on the spirituals have noted—found meaning in their religion. The meaning was not so much an answer to the problem of suffering as the acceptance of the sorrow and the joy inherent in the human condition and an affirmation that life in itself was valuable. This act of affirmation as expressed in the spirituals sometimes led to verses of jarring contrast where suffering and Gospel joy were juxtaposed:

> Wish I'd died when I was a baby,
> O lord rock a' jubilee,
> Wish I'd died.

and

> Nobody knows de trouble I see
> Nobody knows but Jesus,
> Nobody knows de trouble I've had
> Glory hallelu!

Perhaps, the spirituals' most eloquent image of life's alternation between sadness and joy occurs in the verses of "Nobody Knows the Trouble I've Had."

> One morning I was walking down,
> I saw some berries hanging down,
> I pick de berry and I suck de juice,
> Just as sweet as the honey in de comb.
> Sometimes I'm up, sometimes I'm down
> Sometimes I'm almost on de groun'.[91]

In the face of this world's trials the slaves asserted their trust in the providence of God:

> Jehoviah, Hallelujah, De Lord is perwide [provide]
> Jehoviah, Hallelujah, De Lord is perwide
> De foxes have a hole, an' de birdies have a nest,
> De Son of Man he hanno where to lay de weary head.[92]

In their oppression the slaves found it natural to identify with the sufferings of Jesus, who was depicted in the spirituals as an ever-present and intimate friend:

> He have been wid us, Jesus,
> He still wid us, Jesus
> He will be wid us, Jesus,
> Be wid us to the end.

> In de mornin' when I rise,
> Tell my Jesus huddy [howdy] oh;
> I wash my hands in de mornin' glory,
> Tell my Jesus huddy, oh.

The closeness of Jesus was felt, according to one former Georgia
slave, Mary Gladdys, especially at the all-night prayer meetings
when each member would be touched by the spirit of Jesus "just
before day."

> Jest befo' day, I feels 'im. Jest befo' day, I feels 'im.
> My sister, I feels 'im. My sister, I feels 'im.
> All night long I've been feelin' 'im.
> Jest befo' day, I feels 'im. Jest befo' day, I feels 'im.
> The sperit, I feels 'im. The sperit, I feels 'im![93]

The slaves took note that, when on earth, Jesus had used his
power to assist the lowly:

> (*Chorus*) Walk (Ride) in, kind Saviour (King Jesus),
> No man can hinder me!
> Walk in, sweet Jesus,
> No man can hinder me!
> See what wonder Jesus done,
> O no man can hinder me!
>
> (*Verses*) Jesus make de dumb to speak.
> Jesus make de cripple walk.
> Jesus give de blind his sight.
> Jesus do most anything.
> Rise [Raise] poor Lajarush, from de tomb[94]

The slaves sang of the power of the Lord to deliver them just as
he had delivered his people of old.

> O my Lord delivered Daniel
> O why not deliver me too?[95]

But final deliverance from the troubles of the world would only
come with death. For only then would they be "done wid de
trouble o' de world." One of the most beautiful of all the spirituals
reflects the desire for peace and tranquillity in the final rest, when
the body and its cares are laid in the grave.

> I know moon-rise, I know star-rise
> Lay dis body down.

I walk in de moonlight, I walk in de starlight,
To lay dis body down.
I'll walk in de graveyard, I'll walk through de graveyard,
To lay dis body down
I'll lie in de grave and stretch out my arms;
Lay dis body down.
I go to de judgement in de evenin' of de day,
When I lay dis body down;
And my soul and your soul will meet in de day
When I lay dis body down.[96]

Death was the passage to freedom where

Dere's no rain to wet you,
    O, yes, I want to go home.
Dere's no sun to burn you,
    O, yes, I want to go home,
O, push along, believers,
    O, yes, etc.
Dere's no whips a-crackin',
    O, yes, etc.
O, push along, my brudder,
    O, yes, etc.
Where dere's no stormy weather,
    O, yes, etc.
Dere's no tribulation,
    O, yes, etc.[97]

Death, as the slaves knew all too well, was a capricious figure, striking at will:

Oh Deat' he is a little man
And he goes from do' to do'
He kill some souls and he wounded some,
And he lef' some souls to pray

Therefore, a well-prepared death was a blessing:

I want to die like-a Jesus die,
    And he die wid a free good will,
I lay out in de grave and I stretches out ee arms,
    Do, Lord, remember me.[98]

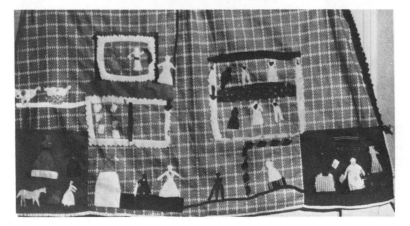

Slave's apron depicting souls enroute to Heaven or Hell. Yalobusha
County, Mississippi. Photograph by Eudora Welty. Reprinted by per-
mission of Eudora Welty and Mississippi Department of Archives and
History.

But most frequently Death was, in the spirituals, the River Jordan, the last river to cross before reaching Canaan, the promised
home for which the weary travelers had toiled so long.

In Heaven, or the New Jerusalem, parents, relatives, and
friends would meet again—a devout hope for slaves who had seen
parents, sisters, brothers, and children sold away with no chance
of reunion in this world. Jacob Stroyer described the departure of
a group of slaves sold South and the song which accompanied the
parting scene:

> . . . those who were going did not expect to see their friends
> again. While passing along many of the negroe's left their
> master's fields and joined us . . . some were yelling and wring-
> ing their hands, while others were singing little hymns that
> they had been accustomed to for the consolation of those that
> were going away, such as:

> When we all meet in heaven,
> There is no parting there;

When we all meet in heaven,
There is parting no more.[99]

As the community of Christian slaves shuffled around the ring of the shout, they literally embodied a vision of heaven and their own presence there:

> O walk 'em easy round de heaven
> Walk 'em easy round de heaven
> Dat all de people may join de band
> Walk 'em easy round de heaven. (*Thrice*)
> O shout glory till 'em join dat band!

Heaven would be a social band where one could walk and talk with Jesus, Mary, and the heroes in the Bible whose stories were so familiar. Heaven would be a Sabbath without end, one long day of everlasting rest.[100]

Christian slaves delighted in imagining the future happiness of heaven. In doing so, they added to their imaginative life symbols by which they expanded the horizons of their present. The vision of the future had an additional effect on the present because the end of time would bring not only glory but Judgment. The eschatological imagery of the book of Revelation had a powerful impact upon the imagination of the slaves, as revealed by spirituals like this one:

(*Chorus*)   And de moon will turn to blood (*Thrice*)
                    In dat day, O-yoy [a sort of prolonged wail] my soul!
                 And de moon will turn to blood in dat day.

(*Verses*)   And you'll see de stars a-fallin'.
                 And de world will be on fire.
                 And you'll hear de saints a-singin.
                 And de Lord will say to de sheep.
                 For to go to Him right hand;
                 But de goats must go to de left.[101]

Even so consoling an image of the afterlife as "Rock o' my soul in de bosom of Abraham" includes this warning of Judgment:

He toted the young lambs in his bosom (*thrice*)
And leave the old sheep alone.

In that "great gettin' up morning," "when the stars begin to fall," Jesus, that "mighty man," will come again on his milk-white horse, to judge the living and the dead, "wid a rainbow on his shoulder." No doubt, white was the color of a large number of the goats sent to the left and of the "old sheep" abandoned to Hell.[102] The faithful Christian ("true believer") need not fear and might sing, as did one confident band of slaves:

I meet my soul at de bar of God
I heerd a mighty lumber
Hit was my sin fell down to hell
Jes' like a clap er thunder.
    Run home believer: oh, run home believer!
    Run home, believer, run home.[103]

Images of the Bible, from Genesis to Revelation filled the hymns and spirituals which the slaves sang in church, in the fields, and in the quarters. Themes and events from the Old and New Testaments were used by the slaves to interpret their own experience by measuring it against a wider system of meaning. Simultaneously, the biblical symbols were translated in the light of the slaves' own day-to-day experiences. For the vast majority of slaves who could not read, hymns and spirituals were their channel to the word of God.

The moods of the spirituals were many—sad, triumphant, resigned, expectant, serious, and light. The "sorrow song" aspect of the slave spirituals has been so stressed that it is sometimes forgotten that the slaves' religion embraced a lighter side. Indeed, spirituals and shouts were performed for social occasions—on holidays, at weddings and celebrations—in effect replacing the secular songs and dances which the converted slaves refused to perform. For example, freedmen on the Butler plantation in Georgia found nothing strange about shouting for the construction of a new barn, in thanksgiving for a good harvest, and even to celebrate their former mistress's birthday![104]

Principally, however, the spirituals were the soul of communal worship in the quarters. Merging with prayers and sermons, the spirituals focused the consciousness of the worshiping community upon the common bond of their faith. Frequently the spirituals made mention of individual members present, either by name— "Sister Tilda, Brother Tony," etc—or by description—"the stranger over there in the corner"—in effect including all in the experience of mutual exhortation and support. In the fellowship of the meeting, the spirituals articulated the slaves' vision of "a new heaven and a new earth," and as the spirit started working and the shouting broke out, vision became real in ecstasy. And for a time, at least, the sorrow and toil of the individual's life were assuaged and given meaning.

In addition to spirituals and hymns, slaves expressed their religious feelings in prayers and stories. Shortly after the war, David Macrae, a Scottish traveler observed: "The pious negroes delight in prayer; and the women, at some of their religious meetings, are as free to lead as the men. Their prayers are full of fire, and often exceedingly vivid and impressive." He went on to give several examples. "Here was one, offered by Sister Nancy Brooks at a camp meeting in Poplar Springs":

> Oh Father Almighty, O Sweet Jesus, most gloriful King, will you be so pleased as to come dis way and put your eye on dese yere mourners? O sweet Jesus, ain't you de Daniel God? Didn't you deliber de tree chill'un from de firy furnis? Didn't you hear Jonah cry from de belly ob de whale? Oh, if dere be one seeking mourner here dis afternoon, if dere be one sinking Peter, if dere be one weeping Mary, if dere be one doubting Thomas, won't you be so pleased to come and deliber them? Won't you mount your gospel horse an' ride roun' de souls of dese yere mourners, and say, 'Go in peace and sin no more'? Won't you be so pleased to come wid de love in one han' and de fan in de odder han' to fan away doubts? Won't you be so pleased to shake dese yere souls over hell, and not let 'em fall in?[105]

A missionary at Fortress Monroe recorded these prayers in 1866: "O, Lord! please to hist the diamond winders of hebben, an'

shake out dy table-cloth, and let a few crumbs fall among us."
"[O]pen de diamond winders, lay back de lovely curtains, an' take
a peep into dis world of sin an' sorrer." Some other examples have
a surprising kind of witty aptness: "Lord, when we'se done
chawin' all de hard bones, and when we'se done swallerin' all de
bitter pills, take us home to thyself." "We come to Thee like
empty pitchers *widout any bottom*, to ask if it be Thy will to fill
poor we wid Thy love."[106]

A down-to-earth familiarity and whimsy appear in the treatment of religious themes in some verses of the spirituals and in
some of the ex-slaves' prayers. The same light humor occurs in
religious tales. For example, Ella Kelly remembered a story told
her by her father about partridges and the Savior:

> My pappy allowed de reason pa'tridges couldn't fly over trees
> was: One day de Savior was a-riding long on a colt to de
> Mount of Olive Trees, and de drove flewed up, make sich a
> fuss they scared de colt and he run away wid him. De marster
> put a cuss on de pa'tridges for dat, and ever since, they can't
> fly over tree tops.[107]

In 1901 W. E. B. Du Bois wrote a classic essay, "Faith of the
Fathers," in which he distinguished the three characteristics of the
slaves' religion as being the preacher, the music, and the frenzy or
shouting. He might well have added a fourth characteristic, the
conversion experience.[108] The experience of conversion was essential in the religious life of the slaves. For the only path to
salvation lay through that "lonesome valley" wherein the
"seekers" underwent conversion, an experience which they treasured as one of the peak moments in their lives.

The Conversion Experience

The typical conversion experience was preceded by a period of
anxiety over one's salvation which lasted for days or even weeks.
Elijah Marrs grew anxious about the state of his soul when he

heard his father discussing religion with a preacher. Anthony Burns' conversion was preceded by his agitated reaction to Millerite predictions of the end of time and to an epidemic of scarlet fever in his neighborhood. Josiah Henson, at the age of eighteen, was struck by the words of a sermon he heard, "Jesus Christ, the Son of God, tasted death for every man; for the high, for the low, for the rich, for the poor, the bond, the free, the negro in his chains, the man in gold and diamonds." Henson recalled, "I stood and heard it. It touched my heart and I cried out: 'I wonder if Jesus Christ died for me.' "[109]

The normal context for sinners to become seekers was the mourners' bench, or anxious seat, at prayer meetings and revivals. But some were suddenly moved when alone in the woods or fields. One former slave remembered: "I went to the mourners' bench, and people was storming and screaming. And you know I couldn't pray in that; so I went back home, and when I was all by myself, I prayed . . . I found the Lord all by myself." Feelings of sadness or loneliness were sometimes associated with the onset of conversion, as in the case of one ex-slave, who recalled: "God started on me when I was a little boy. I used to grieve a lot over my mother. She had been sold away from me and taken a long way off. One evening . . . I was walking along thinking about Mama and crying. Then a voice spoke to me and said 'Blessed art thou.' " Another account of a conversion began "after my husband had died . . . I felt awfully burdened down"; and still another seeker prayed, "Lord I have neither father or mother."[110]

Conversion experiences, by their very nature, are intensely personal, inward, and individual events. Yet the social and cultural background of the individual does shape the categories and constructs employed in thinking and speaking about the most private experiences. While there is variety in the conversion experiences recounted by former slaves, there is also a great deal of similarity. Between the classically orthodox conversion account of George Liele and the more visionary experiences described by the anonymous folk interviewed in God Struck Me Dead there are close parallels in structures and patterns of experience. Of his conversion Liele wrote:

> ... the Rev. Mr. Matthew Moore, one Sabbath afternoon, as I stood with curiosity to here him ... unfolded all my dark views, opened my best behaviour and good works to me, which I thought I was to be saved by, and I was convinced that I was not in the way to heaven, but in the way to hell. This state I laboured under for the space of five or six months. The more I heard or read, the more I [felt that I] was condemned as a sinner before God; till at length I was brought to perceive that my life hung by a slender thread, and if it was the will of God to cut me off at that time, I was sure I should be found in hell, as sure as God was in heaven. I saw my condemnation in my own heart, and I found no way wherein I could escape the damnation of hell, only through the merits of my dying Lord and Savior Jesus Christ ...

Abandoning himself to prayer, Liele found relief and "felt such love and joy as my tongue was not able to express. After this I declared before the congregation of believers the work which God had done for my soul, and the same minister, the Rev. Matthew Moore, baptized me . . . "[111]

The basic pattern discernible in Liele's experience and generally in those recounted by others consists of a tripartite movement—first a feeling of sinfulness, then a vision of damnation, and finally an experience of acceptance by God and being reborn or made new. The essential dynamic of the conversion is an inward, experiential realization of the doctrines of human depravity, divine sovereignty, and unconditional election made vividly apparent to the imagination and the emotions. Professed doctrine becomes internally real. The inner self recognizes that "Jesus died for *me*." In the words of a former slave: "Wisdom in the heart is unlike wisdom in the mind." Others speak of the experience as "God beginning to work on the main altar of the heart."[112]

"Nobody can talk about the religion of God unless they've had a religious experience in it," claimed one former slave. Some slaves' conversion experiences were accompanied by visions and trances. The similarity of images that recur in the visions suggests the influence of the Bible—particularly Revelation—the folk sermons, the lyrics of the spirituals, and a store of tradition created by "experience meetings" during which conversion accounts were told. According to Charles Raymond, writing in 1863:

> 'Experience Meetings' . . . are usually held as preparatory to the negro's 'joining the church' upon a public profession of religion. In attending such meetings in different neighborhoods, from Louisiana to Virginia, I have always found the same prominent features delineated. So invariable has been the recurrence of ideas, phrases, and descriptions that one is puzzled in accounting for the uniformity. . . . These experiences when analyzed readily resolve themselves into the different gradations of feeling expressed by the words, awakening, conviction, pardon, . . . The great load and pressure, corresponding to the state known . . . as *awakening*, is always located by a significant gesture as being felt in the region of the diaphram. The second stage, that of *conviction*, is expressed by the pit and flame, and the imminent danger of helpless destruction. The pardon and deliverance by Christ, under the form of a palpable, bodily rescue, succeeded by a state of ineffable physical delight.

The tangible, or "sensuous," nature of the slaves' conversion experiences was disconcerting to Raymond. A boy named Julius described his vision: " . . . den I went to hebben, and dere I see de Lord Jesus, *a sittin' behind de door an' a reading his Bible*." When asked to describe her feelings upon conversion, Sally declared: "I feel, Sah, *jus like I had a fiddle in my belly*." Another slave claimed that in his vision "I could feel the darkness [of Hell] with my hands."[113]

As described by the former slaves interviewed in *God Struck Me Dead*, the conversion experience is usually inaugurated by a feeling of heaviness or sadness, the weight of sinfulness. Sometimes the individual feels ill and cannot eat or drink. In this condition the sinner hears a voice warning him of his state. His condition worsens, he falls into a trance or dream in which he sees himself dead, while another self, an inner or "little" self, cries for mercy. The sinner sees a vivid image of Hell and realizes that he is destined for eternal damnation. He hangs over the deep pit suspended by a single thread. Satan may appear and threaten to knock him down or to loose hellhounds to pursue him. Suddenly a mediator appears in the form of an angel or a mysterious "little man." An emissary from God, the mediator reassures the frightened sinner and leads him to a vision of heaven, which frequently appears as the gleaming New Jerusalem or as a peaceful pasture full of grazing sheep. Taken up into the presence of God, the person learns that he is not damned but saved and, as one of the elect, receives from God a commission to lead a holy life and to preach the Gospel. Awakened, the convert is overwhelmed with a sudden feeling of being totally renewed. Filled with joy, he cannot resist shouting. Struck by the spirit "from head to foot," he feels a "burning in the heart and bones" which drives him to speak. The rest of the convert's life is marked by his conversion experience. The date it occurred is almost always noted. One of the elect, he now has the responsibility to evangelize others. "Ever since that day I have been preaching the gospel and am not a bit tired. I can tell anyone about God in the darkest hour of midnight for it is written on my heart. Amen." Not only is the convert renewed, but everything around him seems blessed and holy. He is filled with compassion and love for every living thing. "I ran to an elm tree and tried to put my arms around it. Never had I felt such a love before. It just looked like I loved everything and everybody." "The eyes of my mind were open, and I saw things as I never did before . . . "[114]

It is not possible to judge how common such visionary conversion experiences were. Certainly, the majority of those slaves who believed, like the majority of believers at any time, had less intense religious experiences. In the words of one former slave:

> My religion means as much to me as anyone else, but I have not had . . . a chance to see any kind of funny forms or anything like that . . . This is my religion . . . 'Repent, believe,

and be baptized, and you shall be saved.' That is my religion,
and I believe it will take me to heaven . . . I have seen nothing
nor heard nothing but only felt the spirit in my soul, and I
believe that will save me when I come to die.[115]

Yet at the center of the evangelical Protestant tradition, the tradition which slaves increasingly made their own, stood the experience of conversion.[116]

Not all slaves, however, accepted evangelical Protestantism. As noted in Chapter 2, some slaves rejected Christianity and preserved their traditional African beliefs or their belief in Islam. Other slaves accepted Christianity of a different type—Catholicism. Relatively few slaves, mainly concentrated in southern Louisiana and Maryland, were Roman Catholics. According to a generous estimate, the number of black Catholics, free and slave, at the time of emancipation was one hundred thousand. The situation of Catholicism among Louisiana's black population at the end of the Civil War was summarized by Roger Baudier, a historian of Catholicism in Louisiana:

Some effort had been made in Louisiana for the evangelization
of the Negroes, particularly by the religious orders of
women . . . However, the slave state made this work all but
impossible. . . . Many attempts were made to give instructions
on the plantations, but this was extremely difficult. Some of the
parish priests also gave attention to this work. All of this, however, was spasmodic and unorganized. There was always present the prejudices of slave owners . . . Negroes were freely admitted to Catholic Churches and to the Sacraments; but even in
this there was some opposition, though the clergy resisted any
interference with the practice of their religion by the slaves. . . .
Baptism of slave children was very generally practiced . . . in
some parishes the practice being generally followed of baptizing many in a group on Holy Saturday and the Vigil of Pentecost. As a whole, however, the work of evangelization was
certainly far from what it should have been.[117]

It was a fact that Catholicism, "for many Negroes in
Louisiana . . . meant little more than baptism into a religion in

which they had insufficient instruction." The Church was more successful with the urban "colored Creole" population of French-speaking free blacks, whose culture was consciously Catholic and distinct from English-speaking "American blacks" who were Protestant. An important distinction between the religious experience of black Protestants and black Catholics was described by Elizabeth Ross Hite: "We was all supposed to be Catholics on our place, but lots didn't like that 'ligion. We used to hide behind some bricks and hold church ourselves. You see, the Catholic preachers from France wouldn't let us shout, and the Law done said you gotta shout if you want to be saved. That's in the Bible." An elderly slave from Virginia who had been sold and moved to Louisiana forty years previously told the traveler Olmsted that he had become Catholic, but remarked wistfully, "Oh Sar, they don't have no meetin' o' no kind round here."[118]

Prayer meetings, shouting, and spirituals—the staples of black Protestantism—were foreign to the experience of black Catholics. On the one hand, Protestantism denied the slaves the ritual use of sacred objects and devotion to the saints which were so readily adaptable to syncretism with African ritual and theology. On the other, the formal structure of the Catholic Mass, with each gesture and genuflection governed by rubric, did not allow the bodily participation and ecstatic behavior so common to Protestant services and so reminiscent of African patterns of dance and possession. Neither the Bible nor the sermon played as important a role in Catholic piety as in Protestant worship. The Catholic view of the priest as a sacral figure, ordained primarily to officiate at the holy sacrifice, differed significantly from the Protestant notion of the minister as preacher of the Word. The sacral character and the necessity of meticulous training in liturgical gesture and language—Latin being obligatory—made it impossible for a Catholic layman to assume the role of priest, in contrast to the relative ease with which a Baptist, for example, could become a preacher. As a result, the status, authority, and influence of the black Protestant minister were not duplicated among black Catholics. Augustus Tolton, born a slave in Hannibal, Missouri, the first black priest to serve in the United States, was ordained in Rome in 1888.[119] The first black priest to be ordained in the United States, Charles Randolph Uncles, S.S.J. (Josephite), was ordained by Cardinal Gibbons in Baltimore, Maryland, in 1891.

Contrary to Protestant custom, many Catholic churches did not practice segregation in worship. Antebellum visitors to St. Louis Cathedral in New Orleans, for example, noted the fact of integrated congregations. According to Harrison Trexler, in his study of slavery in Missouri, it was very common among the French settlers of that state "for the white mistress to stand as sponsor for the black babe at its baptism, or for the slave mother to act as godmother to the master's child."[120] The experience of Pierre Landry, a Louisiana slave, is illustrative of the power of Catholic ritual to remove, at least temporarily, distinctions of race:

> My early religious training was in the Roman Catholic Church at Donaldsonville. I was prepared for first communion in a large class of both white and colored youths. The sacrament was administered on an Easter Sunday morning, and I shall never forget the impressiveness of the services of that day. The august presence of the bishop who confirmed the class was to me typical of extraordinary grandeur and power, and when it came to my turn to kiss the signet ring of His Grace, the jewel appeared to me as a blazing torch in which were reflected the burning candles of the resplendent altar.[121]

However, segregation did occur in Catholic churches, and religious orders generally practiced racial exclusion down into the twentieth century. During the antebellum period two congregations of black nuns were founded: the Oblate Sisters of Providence in Baltimore, in 1829, and the Sisters of the Holy Family in New Orleans, in 1842. Of the religious orders of men, one exception to the custom of racial exclusion was the Josephites, founded in England in 1866. They began their mission to American Negroes in 1871, and began to accept black candidates in 1888.[122] Paradoxically, the inclusion of black Catholics within the parish

Sister of the Holy Family, New Orleans, Reprinted from
Harper's New Monthly Magazine 74 (January 1887): 200.

structure did not permit the exercise of leadership and control enjoyed by some Protestant blacks in their segregated and quasi-independent churches.

Nevertheless, there were slaves as well as free blacks who found deep meaning in the centuries-old rituals of Catholicism and centered their piety upon the Mass, the sacraments and personal devotion to the Virgin and the saints. Those slaves who lived in cities with a strong Catholic presence, such as Baltimore and New Orleans, or who were owned by Catholic religious orders had the greatest opportunity to practice their Catholicism. After the Civil War, Protestant missionaries to the South were seriously concerned that Catholicism was making extensive gains among the freedmen. Their fears proved groundless, as the Catholic Church required most of its manpower and resources to face the renewed waves of European Catholic immigration in the late nineteenth century. Though interested, the Catholic hierarchy was able to do little in the way of missions to the freedmen. Not until the twentieth century would black people in North America turn to Catholicism in significant numbers.[123] The predominant religious tradition, then, among slaves and their descendants in the United States was evangelical Protestantism. The strongest other religious force in the quarters was not Catholicism but conjure, which was pervasive throughout all regions of the South and influential on most plantations, whether Catholic or Protestant.

Conjure

A rich tradition of folk belief and practice, including conjure, herbalism, ghost lore, witchcraft, and fortune-telling, flourished in the slave quarters. The power of the supernatural impinged on the daily lives of slaves and affected their relationships with one another and with the world around them. Like Christianity, conjure was a system of belief, a way of perceiving the world which placed people in the context of another world no less "real" than the ordinary one. Many slaves, and whites as well, knew the world of conjure to be real because they had experienced its power. In part, conjure was a theory which made sense of the mysterious and inexplicable occurrences of life. Duncan Gaines, former Virginia slave, described this explanatory function of conjure when he recalled that during slave times "there was much talk of 'hoodooism' and anyone ill for a long time without getting relief from herb medicine was thought to be 'fixed' or suffering from some sin that his father had committed."[124] The concept of suffering for the guilt of the father is biblical; the concept of being victimized by a "fix" is conjure. Both attempt to locate the cause of irrational suffering. Among Africans and their descendants in America illness which did not respond to natural medicines and the sudden, unpredictable occurrence of misfortune were the result of another's animosity. Slaves believed adversity was due not to blind fate or mere happenstance but to the ill will of someone working through a conjurer.

Not only was conjure a theory for explaining the mystery of evil, but it was also a practice for doing something about it. Because the conjure doctor had the power to "fix" and to remove "fixes," to harm and to cure, it was possible to locate the source of misfortune and control it. Therefore the conjurer, as a man of power—and supernatural power at that—enjoyed a measure of authority in the slave community directly proportional to belief in his power. Variously known as root doctor, hoodoo doctor, twofacer, and wangateur (from *oanga*-charm), he was respected and feared by those blacks and whites who had implicit faith in his power. Conjurers cultivated an aura of mystery which lent credibility to their reputations as men familiar with supernatural lore. Distinctive features, such as "red eyes" and "blue gums," unusual dress, and the accoutrements of his trade—a crooked cane, charms, and conjure bag—all were outward manifestations of the root worker's special expertise. The ultimate source of the conjurer's power was either God or the devil. Being born the seventh son of a seventh son or being born with a caul also were seen as sources of power. In addition, it was believed that the lore of conjure could be passed on from teacher to pupil.[125]

Conjurers were said to be two-faced or two-handed because they could do "left-handed work"—"charm" a person—or "right-handed" work—counteract a charm. Conjurers employed to do left-handed work used both direct and indirect methods. A substance, perhaps a root or a toad's head, could be ground into powder and then mixed or dissolved in the food or drink of the intended victim. The substance used sometimes was poisonous. It would be interesting to know how many cases of slaves poisoning their masters involved conjure.[126] The indirect approach was to place the charm near the victim where contact or at least proximity would transmit the harm intended. A charm, also known as hand, trick, toby, mojo, and gris-gris, might lurk anywhere—under the doorstep, inside a mattress, out in the yard, or alongside a path the victim was sure to take. Tricks placed by the roadside could even distinguish their targets from other passersby if hair from the victim or dirt from his footprint was wrapped up in the charm.[127]

A virtual job summary of conjure was detailed by Rosanha Frazier, ex-slave born in Mississippi, who blamed her loss of sight upon a "hoodoo-nigger."

> Dey powder up de rattle offen de snake and tie it up in de little old rag bag and dey do devilment with it. Dey git old scorpion and make bad medicine. Dey git dirt out de graveyard and dat dirt, after dey speak on it, would make you go crazy.

> When dey wants conjure you, dey sneak round and git de hair combin' or de finger or toenail, or anything natural 'bout your body and works de hoodoo on it.

> Dey make de straw man or de clay man and dey puts de pin in he leg and you leg gwineter git hurt or sore jus' where dey puts de pin. Iffen dey puts de pin through de heart you gwineter die . . .

Dey make de charm to wear round de neck or de ankle and
dey make de love powder too out de love vine, what grow in
de wood. Dey bites de leaves and powders 'em. Dey sho'
works, I done try 'em.[128]

Among the materials used by the conjure doctor, goopher dust
(graveyard dirt) was believed to be partcularly potent. Red flan-
nel, useful for wrapping charms, bottles, pins, bones, reptiles,
scorpions, horse hair, roots, and herbs of various sorts made up
the root doctor's stock-in-trade. However, it was the spell and the
ritual invoked by the conjurer which gave the various items
power. It was believed that each charm had a spirit. Consequently
charms were moistened with liquor to strengthen their power by
strengthening their spirits.[129]

Even ordinary possessions—a knife, a hat, a shoe—could be
fixed by the conjurer's spell, so that the unsuspecting owner
would be conjured upon contact. One had to be extra careful in
disposing of worn clothing, nail clippings, cut hair, and washrags
lest they fall into the hands of an enemy. Their close contact with
the body made them dangerous instruments for conjure, as one
old root doctor from Georgia explained: "Duh haiah is one uh
duh mos powful tings yuh enemy kin git hold ub cuz it grow
neah duh brain an a han made outuh haiah kin sho affec duh
brain."[130]

The variety of illnesses, injuries, and misfortunes blamed on
conjure was endless. One especially gruesome and frequently
mentioned fix reportedly culminated with snakes or spiders roam-
ing up and down inside the victim's body. The conjurer supposedly accomplished this trick by putting the blood of a spider or
snake within the person and from this blood the spider or snake
would be spawned. Mental as well as physical illness was explained by conjure. "Wennebuh a pusson go crazy, wut is dat but
conjuh?" asked Fred Jones, an elderly informant for the Georgia
Writers' Project. The point of his rhetorical question was supported by two early analysts of conjure: "insanity on the planta-

tion was often laid to 'conjuration' and consequently took in the patient the form that the belief in conjuration would naturally give it."[131]

A central tenet of conjure was that any spell worked by a conjurer could be removed only by a conjurer; a medical doctor was useless. Even the conjure doctor could be effective only if he was called before the "hand" had done irreversible harm. If called in time, the root doctor took several steps to effect a cure. First he determined whether the illness was due to conjure or not. A small piece of silver was commonly used in diagnosis: if it turned black when placed in the patient's mouth or hand, he had been conjured. Once established that the patient had been conjured, the next step was to discover where the trick had been hidden and to identify the party who had ordered the conjuring done. Then the conjurer cured the patient by destroying or nullifying the power of the charm. Since most conjurers were also herbalists, medicinal potions, salves, and leaf effusions were usually part of the magical ritual. The final step in the cure, if the patient wished it, was to get revenge by turning the charm against the one who sent it. It was said that if you discovered a trick and burned it, the sender would burn, and that if you threw it into water, he would drown. At any rate, the sender could be repaid in kind, and any client of a conjurer had to take that risk into account and live with the fear of retribution.[132]

The reasons for which slaves sought the conjurer's assistance were not all so deadly serious. Affairs of the heart, for example, supplied the conjurer with a great deal of business. Henry Bibb was one of many slaves who turned to conjure to aid romance:

> One of these conjurers, for a small sum agreed to teach me to make any girl love me that I wished. After I had paid him, he told me to get a bull frog, and take a certain bone out of the frog, dry it, and when I got a chance I must step up to any girl whom I wished to make love me, and scratch her somewhere on her naked skin with this bone, and she would be certain to love me, and would follow me in spite of herself; no

matter who she might be engaged to, nor who she might be
walking with.

Bibb, not surprisingly, failed in his first attempt but decided to
try again. Seeking out another conjurer, he was advised to get a
lock of hair from any girl and wear it in his shoes and the girl
would then love him above anybody else. Unfortunately, the girl
Bibb asked for a lock of hair refused to cooperate. "Believing that
my success depended greatly upon this bunch of hair," Bibb explained, "I grasped hold of a lock . . . which caused her to
screech, but I never let go until I had pulled it out. This of course
made the girl mad with me, and I accomplished nothing but
gained her displeasure."[133]

Marital peace was preserved, according to Aunt Irene, a former
slave from Alabama, by conjurers who sold "hush water in a jug.
Hush water was jes' plain water what dey fixed so if you drink it
you would be quiet an' patient. De mens would git it to give to
dey wives to make 'em hush up."[134] Conjurers also sold
talismans—good-luck charms to ward off sickness, misfortune, or
another's animosity.

The ability to tell fortunes was another supernatural skill possessed by some slave conjurers (though not all conjurers were
fortune-tellers or vice versa.) William Wells Brown, although
skeptical (at least in hindsight), went to an old soothsayer in St.
Louis named Frank, who predicted the escape from slavery which
Brown was contemplating: "Whether the old man was a prophet,
or the son of a prophet, I cannot say; but there is one thing
certain, many of his predictions were verified. I am no believer in
soothsaying; yet I am . . . at a loss to know how Uncle Frank
could tell so accurately what would occur in the future. Among
the many things he told was one which was enough to pay me for
all the trouble of looking him up. It was that I *should be free*! He
further said, that in trying to get my liberty I would meet with
many severe trials. I thought to myself any fool could tell me
that!"[135] One can't help wondering what influence Uncle Frank's

prediction had upon Brown's determination to brave those "severe trials" in his eventual escape from slavery. More than a few slaves were skeptical about the power of conjurers, especially after a charm failed to work. But even then a quick-witted conjurer might save face by blaming the dissatisfied customer for failing to follow instructions. In the story of a trick doctor related by Puckett, a slave received a hand which would enable him to "cuss out" hs master without being harmed. The slave tried it and received a terrible beating for his insolence. When he went back to the conjurer to complain, he was informed, "I gi' you a runin' han'! (a charm which would give the possessor swiftness . . .) Why did'nt yer run?"[136]

A failed charm might lead a slave to lose faith in that particular charm, or in the conjurer who supplied it, without destroying his belief in conjure as such. Doubts were tempered by the prevalence of belief. Jacob Stroyer, for example, confessed: "I held the idea that there were such things, for I thought the majority of the people believed it, and that they ought to know more than could one man."[137]

Trouble might inspire in an unbeliever a willing suspension of disbelief. This seems to have been the case with Frederick Douglass, who prided himself on being above conjure. "I had a positive aversion to all pretenders to 'divination.' It was beneath one of my intelligence to countenance such dealings with the devil as the power implied." But when Douglass was bedeviled by Covey, the slave breaker, he accepted a root which Sandy the local conjurer told him would prevent Covey or any other white man from whipping him.[138] In some individuals, such as Douglass, conjure stirred ambivalence—what the intellect denied, the emotions and the imagination affirmed, or, as one folklorist astutely observed, "Practices are more enduring than theories."[139]

The simple fact is that slave conjurers kept their credibility and their authority because their power worked. Whatever explanation the modern observer offers—outright poisoning, probable coincidence, psychosomatic suggestion, or psychic phenomenon—

some became sick and some were cured by conjure. Undoubtedly the conjurers' knowledge of both medicinal and poisonous herbs, his astuteness in judging human nature, and the sound practical advice he gave accounted for a good deal of his success. Still, the magical words he spoke and the esoteric rites he performed, the imaginative world of power which he represented and the folk traditions he bore, were important to slave culture and should not be lightly dismissed.[140]

Despite skeptics and charlatans, the conjurer's reputation, on some plantatins at least, reached legendary proportions. The tale of one remarkable conjurer named Dinkie was told by William Wells Brown. Dinkie held everyone on the plantation, white or black, in his power. Able to come and go at his pleasure, he never worked. "No one interfered with him . . . Dinkie hunted, slept, was at the table at meal time, roamed through the woods, went to the city, and returned when he pleased. Everybody treated him with respect," even the white ladies who sought him out for love potions and forecasts of romance. When a new overseer, unfamiliar with Dinkie's status, tried to force him to work in the fields, Dinkie, by some secret means, set him straight. His power, it was rumored, came from his being in league with Satan. Whatever the source of his power, it was clear to all that Dinkie was his own master.[141]

The conjurers' exploits, like those ascribed to Dinkie, were discussed with awe and, one suspects, a good deal of embellishment and enjoyment in the quarters. According to one former slave, the children on his plantation liked to play conjure man in a game called hoodoo doctor.[142] A figure to be feared, the conjurer became also a folk character, and stores which told of his resourcefulness, independence, and power were a source of vicarious pleasure to slaves whose own independence and power were so severely restricted.

Nothing challenged the credibility of the conjurer as much as his claim that he could conjure white folks. Whether whites were susceptible to conjure was problematic, as the testimony of ex-slaves reveals. Some ex-slaves argued that only blacks could be conjured. One claimed, for instance: "They had in those days a Hoodoo nigger, who could hoodoo niggers, but could'nt make ole master stop whipping him, with the hoodooism." A clear-cut explanation for the immunity of whites was that whites did not believe in conjure and you had to believe in it for conjure to work.[143] On the other hand, many slaves believed that conjure would work against whites; at least, they tried to prove it. Hoodoo doctors frequently were asked "to save the slave from punishment, to enable him to escape the 'patrolers,' or, in the case of a runaway, to enable him to return home without suffering from his master's anger." In order to "soften the master's heart and sooth his anger," slaves were given roots to chew. Using a jack, fortune-tellers predicted whether a slave would receive a whipping or not. Powders and charms were placed in or near the big house to improve the white folks' disposition.[144] Eugene Genovese has noted several cases of conjured whites in the antebellum South. That whites did succumb to conjure is not surprising given the similarity of their own folk beliefs and also the probable influence of slave folklore upon white children.[145]

One of the arguments advanced by C. C. Jones for the conversion of the slaves to Christianity was the danger that "superstitions brought from Africa" might be used to turn the slaves dangerously against their masters. "On certain occasions they [slaves] have been made to believe that while they carried about their persons some charm with which they had been furnished, they were *invulnerable*. . . . They have been known to be so perfectly and fearfully under the influence of some leader or conjurer or minister, that they have not dared to disobey him in the least particular; nor to disclose their own intended or perpetrated crimes, in view of inevitable death itself . . . "[146] The historical precedent Jones had in mind was no doubt the Denmark Vesey Conspiracy of 1822, in which the conjurer Gullah (or Cooter) Jack had great influence over the conspirators, who called him the "little man who can't be shot, killed or taken." According to a witness at his trial, Jack gave his recruits "some dry food, consisting of parched corn and ground nuts, and said eat that and nothing else on the morning [the rebellion] breaks out, and when you join us as we pass put into your mouth this crab-claw and you can't then be wounded . . . "[147]

The countercultural nature of conjure was implied by the belief that conjure was African. To be sure, hoodoo combined African and European magical lore. It is significant, however, that both slaves and whites repeatedly connected conjure with Africa. Over and over again hoodoo doctors were described as "African-born" or as "pure Africans." Sandy the conjurer was described by Frederick Douglass as a "genuine African" whose magical powers were inherited from the East. William Wells Brown reported that Dinkie was "a full blooded African and reportedly descended from a king in his native Africa." A former Georgia slave, named Thomas Smith, cited the ability of Aaron to turn his rod into a serpent before Pharaoh as an example of the magical expertise of Africa. "Dat happen in Africa de Bible say. Ain' dat show dat Africa wuz a lan uh magic powah since de begginnin uh history? Well duh descendants ub Africans hab duh same gif tuh do unnatchal ting." Black folk in coastal Georgia and the Sea Islands preserved numerous stories about the miraculous ability of their African-born ancestors to fly back to Africa when they were mistreated on the plantations of America. William Adams, ex-slave from Texas and himself a conjurer, felt that "De old folks in dem days knows more about de signs dat de Lawd uses to reveal His laws dan de folks of today. It am also true of de cullud folks in Africa; dey native land." The prevalence of the idea that conjure was African in origin and that Africans were especially powerful conjurers indicates that slaves thought of hoodoo as their own separate tradition. Whites might be susceptible to conjure, but almost never were they conjurers.[148]

Revenge against overseers and masters was a clear theme in the folktales and ghostlore told by slaves to one another and to their children. In these tales ghosts, witches, and conjurers redressed the wrongs which the slaves could not. The following stories from Edisto Island, South Carolina, surely must have appealed to the slaves' frustrated sense of justice:

> [a slave] wen' to a witch man. When his master 'mence to whip him, eve'y cut he give de man, his [master's] wife way off at home feel de cut. Sen' wor' please stop cut lick de man. When he [master] got home, his wife was wash down wid blood.

> His master beat him so sevare, so de man went to a witch. De witch said, 'Never min'! you go home. Tomorrow you will see me.' When de man got up in de mornin', de white man was jus' as happy as happy can be; but de more de sun goes down, he commence ter sleep. At de same time he call to his Negro, 'Tommorrow you go an' do such an' such a tas'. Given' out his orders kyan hardly hol' up his head. As soon as de sun was down, he down too, he down yet. De witch done dat. He [witch] come but he stay in his home an' done dat.[149]

In yet another example, recorded shortly after the Civil War, a conjurer and his son take revenge upon an overseer:

> dey goes to de overseer's house, an' give de sign an' slip t'rough de keyhole. Den dey unbar de door on de inside an' take out de overseer an' his son, widout deir knowin' it; an de conjeror tetch de overseer wid his switch an' he turns to a bull, an' tetch de overseer's son an' he turns to a bull-yerlin.' Den de conjeror mounts de bull an' de boy he mounts de bull-yerlin, an' sets off a long way over de creek to blight a man's wheat what de conjeror had a spite agin."[150]

In these stories—as in the tales of Jack, Brer Rabbit, or High John—the slaves could identify with the protagonist and vicariously enjoy their exercise of power over whites. With their emphasis on revenge, the stories also served as muted protests for the slaves who did not dare to complain overtly about the injustice of their situation.

Then, too, the world of conjure answered deeply felt needs within the slaves' own community, where white control inhibited the free outward expression of social conflict. For example, masters limited fighting among slaves in order to protect their human property from serious damage and to preserve order on the plantation. In addition, the common burden of slavery itself tended to create group solidarity, as did Christian fellowship, which prohibited fighting, backbiting, and animosity between "brothers and sisters in Christ." The very closeness of the quarters necessitated a degree of tolerance while at the same time exacerbating personal tensions. Given these constrictions, conjure served as a perfect vehicle for expressing and alleviating anger, jealousy, and sheer ill will among slaves. When unable to settle disputes openly, the slaves turned to the secret system of conjure.[151] Primarily, conjure was a method of control: first, the control which comes from knowledge—being able to explain crucial phenomena, such as illness, misfortune and evil; second, the control which comes from the capacity to act effectively—it was "a force . . . by which mankind can (or thinks he can) achieve almost every desired end . . . "; third, a means of control over the future through reading the "signs"; fourth, an aid to social control because it supplied a system whereby conflict, otherwise stifled, could be aired.

The pervasiveness of conjure in the quarters suggests a problem: What was the relationship of conjure to Christianity, of the conjurer to the slave preacher? The practice of conjure was, at least in theory, in conflict with Christian beliefs about the providence of God, and indeed one way of relating conjure to Christianity was to make the former the realm of the devil, in effect creating a balance of good and evil. Willis Easter recited a song his mother had taught him "to keep from bein' conjure" which illustrates this point:

> Keep 'way from me, hoodoo and witch, Lead my path from de porehouse gate; I pines for golden harps and sich, Lawd, I'll jes' set down and wait. Old Satan am a liar and conjurer, too—If you don't watch out, he'll conjure you.

Another former slave put it this way: "I'm a believer, an' dis here voodoo an' hoodoo an' sper'ts ain't nothin' but a lot of folks outten Christ."[152]

And yet conjure was not always employed for evil. Puckett noted that conjurers in the twentieth century were all very religious. Closer to the slavery period, Herron and Bacon observed that the source of the conjurers' power was not well defined. One informant stated, "I have always heard that those doctors sold themselves to the Devil before they were given the power." Another reported that all the conjure doctors she had heard of claimed "a special revelation from God." Some conjurers saw nothing strange in calling upon God to assist their cures. (While it is an intriguing possibility, I have found no evidence of conjurers who were also ministers.) The conflict between Christianity and conjure was more theoretical than actual. Even those slaves who condemned conjure as evil did not deny its reality. Moreover, among black folk there was a refusal to dichotomize power into good and evil—a refusal which Herskovits and others see as African. In the slave community the power to heal and the power to harm resided in one person, the conjurer; in Africa these powers resided in any one of the gods who had to be propitiated in order to avoid misfortune and illness. There is an amoral quality to conjure which makes it stray outside norms of good and evil. Whether it was good or bad, one had to respect power that worked. In a world of practical power, good was power which worked *for* you, bad was power which turned *against* you. The primary categories were not good and evil but security and danger. Therefore an unequivocal rejection of conjure was not only unnecessary but foolhardy. To be safe, one kept on the right side of all spiritual power.

Moreover, Christian tradition itself has always been attuned to special gifts (charisms) of the Spirit as they are manifested in prophecy, healing, and miracles. As a result, Christianity, especially on the popular level, has a certain tendency to appropriate and baptize magical lore from other traditions. In an important sense, conjure and Christianity were not so much antithetical as complementary. Discussing the differences between magic and religion, M. J. Field gives a succinct statement of this complementary relationship in her book on witchcraft in West Africa, *Search for Security*:

> Classical anthropology distinguishes between religion and magic by saying that religion involves a deity whom man implores, magic involves forces which man commands . . . It may be added, first that religion usually postulates a deity who is good and who demands goodness, whereas magic is of two kinds, good and bad. Furthermore, a deity generally has at his disposal a diversity of blessings and punishments, whereas each special magic is directed to one narrowly circumscribed end [;] . . . magics, unlike deities, make no moral demands and, above all, will operate automatically and inexorably. . . . Magic, or, as it is more often called in West Africa, 'medicine,' always involves concrete apparatus . . . and a ritual in which the apparatus is handled. There is no activity in life which cannot be assisted by medicine.

Conjure could, without contradiction, exist side by side with Christianity in the same individual and in the same community because, for the slaves, conjure answered purposes which Christianity did not and Christianity answered purposes which conjure did not.[153]

6
Religion, Rebellion, and Docility

White folk's got a heap to answer for the way they've done to colored folks! So much they won't never *pray* it away![1]

THE tendency of Christianity to support the established order has long been noted and criticized by some. It has been alleged that Christianity, with its otherworldly, compensatory emphasis, is a religion particularly fitted for slaves. And as we have seen, missionaries from the colonial S.P.G. to the antebellum advocates of plantation missions labored long and hard to convince masters that this was so. Yet temporal rulers—from provincial governors in the late Roman empire, to medieval kings and emperors, down to presidents of modern states—have had abundant opportunity to ponder the disruptive implications of a religious conscience owing ultimate allegiance to a "higher authority" than their own. Clerical and civil leaders have appealed for centuries to the sayings of Jesus— "My kingdom is not of this world," "Blessed are the meek," "Render to Caesar the things that are Caesar's, to God the things that are God's"—to validate obedience to authority. Yet Christians individually and in groups have disagreed, sometimes violently, with their rulers, ecclesiastical and political, about what was legitimately Caesar's and what God's. Revolutionary interpretations of the Bible by such slaves as Vesey and Turner were proof to American slaveholders that slave Christianity could become a double-edged sword.

As early as 1774 American slaves were declaring publicly and politically that they thought Christianity and slavery were incompatible. In that year the governor of Massachusetts received "The Petition of a Grate Number of Blacks of this Province who by divine permission are held in a state of slavery within the bowels of a free and Christian Country." The petitioners protested that "we have in common with other men a natural right to our freedoms without being deprived of them by our fellowman . . . There is a great number of us sencear . . . members of the Church of Christ . . . Bear ye onenothers Bordens How can the master be said to Beare my Borden when he Beares me down with the Have [Heavy] chanes of slavery and operson [oppression] against my will . . . how can the slave perform the duties of a husband to a wife or parent to his child . . . [?]"² In arguing for their freedom, these New England slaves combined the political rhetoric of the Revolution with appeals to the claims of Christian fellowship. Most slaves had to keep publicly silent about their attitudes, but in private they condemned the hypocrisy of Christian slave-owners. Frederick Douglass, who himself composed a bitterly ironic attack on slaveholding Christianity as an appendix to his *Narrative*, claimed that "Slaves knew enough of the orthodox theology of the time to consign all bad slaveholders to hell."³ And Charles Ball recorded that in his experience, slaves thought that heaven would not be heaven unless slaves would be avenged on their enemies. "A fortunate and kind master or mistress, may now and then be admitted into heaven, but this rather as a matter of favour, to the intercession of some slave, than as a matter of strict justice to the whites, who will, by no means, be of an equal rank with those who shall be raised from the depths of misery in this world." Ball concluded that "The idea of a revolution in the conditions of the whites and blacks, is the cornerstone of the religion of the latter . . ."⁴

The slaves' notion of a future reversal of the conditions of whites and blacks was also noticed by Emily Burke, a white observer commenting on slave life in Georgia, " . . . they believe, and I have myself heard them assert the same, that in the life to come there will also be white people and black people; but then the white people will be slaves, and *they* shall have the dominion over them. I never saw a negro a Universalist; for they all believe in a future retribution for their masters, from the hand of a just God." One former slave implied that slaves had already lived through Hell: "in them days it was hell without fires," but slave-holders faced eternal punishment. "This is one reason why I believe in a hell. I don't believe a just God is going to take no such man [a sadistic master] as that into his kingdom." Escaped slave John Anderson asserted: "Some folks say slaveholders may be good Christians, but I can't and won't believe it, nor do I think that a slaveholder can get to heaven. He may possibly get there, I don't know; but though I wish to get there myself, I don't want to have anything more to do with slaveholders either here or in heaven." The same view was stated in a more humorous manner in a story which, according to Lewis and Milton Clarke, slaves delighted in telling one another: "The master called the slave to his sick bed. 'Good-bye Jack; I have a long journey to go; farewell.' 'Farewell massa! pleasant journey; you soon be dere, massa—*all de way down hill!*' " Another anecdote popular among the slaves pointed ol' massa's soul in the same direction: A slave named George was informed by his master that he was to be buried in a good coffin and placed beside his master's earthly remains in the same vault with the white folks. George's response to this news was mixed: "I like to have good coffin when I die," but "I fraid massa, when de debbil come take your body, he make mistake, and get mine."[5]

On a more serious plane, the slaves' confidence in the ultimate condemnation of slaveholders was supported by manifestations of their masters' guilt. John Brown recalled his master's deathbed attempt to save his soul:

> There was my old master Thomas Stevens. Ever so many times before his time was come. But though he . . . recovered from his illnesses, in his frights he sent for us all and asked us to forgive him. Many a time he would exclaim, that he wished 'he'd never seen a nigger.' I remember his calling old Aunt Sally to him and begging and praying of her to get the devil away from behind the door, and such like.

Brown goes on to generalize: "It is a common belief amongst us that all the masters die in an awful fright, for it is usual for the slaves to be called up on such occasions to say they forgive them for what they have done. So we come to think their minds must be dreadfully uneasy about holding slaves . . . All this may seem to be trifling, but it is the truth . . . and I only give what I have myself experienced." Brown's observation is certainly not "trifling." For slaves to perceive their master's guilt-filled dread and to see him begging for their prayers and forgiveness vindicated their belief in final retribution and demonstrated not only their moral superiority to whites but also a serious measure of psychological and emotional control over them.[6]

In the slaves' moral judgement, ministers in particular were deserving of condemnation. "The ministers used to tell us not to be disorderly on taking the sacrament," observed James Sumler. "I thought he was disorderly himself, for he kept slaves." Contempt for ministers was well deserved, according to slave testimony. William Humbert, fugitive slave from Charleston, South Carolina, recalled for example:

> I have seen a minister hand the sacrament to the deacons to give the slaves, and, before the slaves had time to get home, living a great distance from church, have seen one of the same deacons, acting as patrol, flog one of the brother members within two hours of his administering the sacrament to him, because he met the slave . . . without a passport, beyond the time allowed him to go home. My opinion of slavery is not a bit different now from what it was then: I always hated it from childhood. I looked on the conduct of the deacon with a feeling of revenge. I thought that a man who would administer the sacrament to a brother church member and flog him before he got home, ought not to live.[7]

William Wells Brown caustically described a young minister, named Sloan, "who had been at the South but a short time, and it seemed his whole aim was to please the slaveholders, especially my master and mistress. He was intending to make a visit . . . and he not only tried to please them, but I think he succeeded admirably. When they wanted singing, he sung; when they wanted praying he prayed; when they wanted a story told, he told a story. Instead of his teaching my master theology, my master taught theology to him." Alienation from ministers of this sort made it impossible for slaves to find fellowship in church with whites, as David West, who had belonged to a mixed Baptist church in Virginia before he fled slavery to Canada, sadly recalled. West wished the members of his old church well, but, he warned, "there will be a time when all will be judged. . . . I have often tried to love my minister and brethren in Pokaron church, but when I heard them say, 'Do unto others as ye would that others should do unto you,' and saw what they were doing to their own brethren in Christ, I thought . . . 'Who then can be saved?' " One freedman revealed the chasm between minister and slave when he stated matter-of-factly: "We couldn't tell NO PREACHER NEBER how we suffer all dese long years. He know'd nothin' 'bout we."[8]

Slaves distinguished the hypocritical religion of their masters from true Christianity and rejected the slaveholder's gospel of obedience to master and mistress. Ex-slave Douglas Dorsey reported that after the minister on his plantation admonished the slaves to honor their masters, whom they could see, as they would God, whom they could not see, "the driver's wife who could read and write a little" would say that the minister's sermon "was all lies." Lunsford Lane recounted an incident when a "kind-hearted clergyman . . . who was very popular with the colored people" made the mistake of preaching "a sermon to us in which he argued from the Bible that it was the will of Heaven from all eternity that we should be slaves, and our masters be our owners, [and] many of us left him . . . "[9] From the other side of the pulpit, Charles Colcock Jones recalled a similar reaction to a sermon he gave before a slave congregation in 1833:

> I was preaching to a large congregation on the *Epistle of Philemon*: and when I insisted upon fidelity and obedience as Christian virtues in servants and upon the authority of Paul, condemned the practice of *running away*, one half of my audience deliberately rose up and walked off with themselves, and those that remained looked any thing but satisfied, either with the preacher or his doctrine. After dismission, there was no small stir among them; some solemnly declared 'that there was no such an Epistle in the Bible'; others, 'that they did not care if they ever heard me preach again!' . . . There were some too, who had strong objections against me as a Preacher, because I was a *master*, and said, 'his people have to work as well as we.'[10]

According to Lewis and Milton Clarke, slaves believed that there existed somewhere a real Bible from God, "but they frequently say the Bible now used is master's Bible," since all that they heard from it was "Servants, obey your masters."[11]

Some slaves' inner rejection of "white folks religion" was expressed outwardly by their rejection of their masters' denomination. The slaves of a mean master named Gooch, according to Moses Roper, figured that their master was such "a bad sample of what a professing Christian ought to be" that they refused to "join the connexion [Baptist] he belonged to thinking they must be a very bad set of people" and joined instead the Methodist Church.[12]

Nowhere is the slaves' rejection of the master's religion clearer than in their refusal to obey moral precepts held up to them by whites, especially commands against stealing. While white preachers repeatedly urged "Don't steal," slaves just as persistently denied that this commandment applied to them, since they themselves were stolen property. Josephine Howard demonstrated how the structure of white morality could collapse when examined from the slaves' point of view: "Dey allus done tell us it am wrong to lie and steal, but why did de white foks steal my mammy and her mammy? Dey lives clost to some water, somewheres over in Africy, and de man come in a little boat to de sho' and tell dem he got presents on de big boat . . . and my mammy and her mammy gits took out to dat big boat and dey locks dem in a black hole what mammy say so black you can't see nothin'. Dat de sinfulles' stealin' dey is." Charles Brown, a fugitive slave from Virginia, claimed that he had expressed the same argument to his master's face: "I told my master one day—said I, 'You white folks set the bad example of stealing—you stole us from Africa, and not content with that, if any got free here, you stole them afterward, and so we are made slaves.' " According to George Womble, who had been a slave in Georgia, "slaves were taught to steal by their masters. Sometimes they were sent to the nearby plantations to steal chickens, pigs and other things that could be carried away easily. At such times the master would tell them that he was not going to mistreat them and that he was not going to allow anyone else to mistreat them and that by taking the above mentioned things they were helping him to be more able to take care of them."[13]

The practical justification for stealing was stated succinctly by former slave Rachel Fairley, "How could they help but steal when they didn't have nothin'? You didn't eat if you didn't steal." But in Henry Bibb's view, it was not simply need which justified a slave in taking his master's goods—it was a matter of the worker's right to the fruits of his labors: "I did not regard it as stealing then, I do not regard it as such now. I hold that a slave has a moral right to eat and drink and wear all that he needs, and that it would be a sin on his part to suffer and starve in a country where there is a plenty to eat and wear within his reach. I consider that I had a just right to what I took, because it was the labor of my hands." Other slaves concluded that it was not morally possible for one piece of property to steal another, since they both belonged to the same owner. The slaves' own moral code, however, was careful to distinguish between "taking" from the master and "stealing" from another slave, which was regarded as a serious wrong. "They think it wrong to take from a neighbor but not from their masters . . . a slave that will steal from a slave is called *mean as master*. This is the lowest comparison slaves know how to use: 'just as mean as white folks.' "[14]

Lying and deceit, normally considered moral vices, were virtues to slaves in their dealings with whites. The slaves on his plantation, noted William Wells Brown, "were always glad to shirk labor and thought that to deceive whites was a religious duty." Addressing "the good people who read this confession," John Brown explained in his narrative to readers who might not understand the ethical system by which slaves lived: "In fact, we felt we were living under a system of cheating and lying and deceit, and . . . did not see the wrong of it, so long as we were not acting against one another. I am sure that, as a rule, any one of us who would have thought nothing of stealing a hog, or a sack of corn, from our master, would have allowed himself to be cut to pieces rather than betray the confidence of his fellow slave . . . " The principle "Us against them"—the in-group use of indirection and the development of masks to conceal true feelings—was essential to the slaves' own moral system. As plantation missionary Charles Colcock Jones observed, "the Negroes are scrupulous on one point, they make common cause, as servants, in *concealing* their faults from their owners."[15]

"Puttin' on ol' massa" could involve hiding one's true feelings while simulating the opposite: "When the white folks would die the slaves would all stand around and 'tend like they was crying but they would say 'They going going on to hell like a damn barrel full of nails,'" according to a former slave. Jacob Stroyer recalled that when his former master's corpse was carried home, "all the slaves were allowed to stop at home that day to see the last of him, and to lament with mistress. After all the slaves who cared to do so had seen his face, they gathered in groups around mistress to comfort her; they shed false tears, saying 'Never mind, missus, massa gone home to heaven.' While some were saying this, others said, 'Thank God, massa gone home to hell.'" Infrequently, the slaves let the mask drop and revealed their true feelings about whites. Ex-slave Martha Jackson recalled one example: "dey sarn't down in de woods and all over de plantation er lookin' fer de niggers to come to de Big House 'cause dey overseer was dead. En here dey comes a-shoutin' and a-clappin' de han's and a-holl'rin sumpin' awful:

> "Ole John Bell is de'd en gone
> I hopes he's gone to hell!"

'En dat was de onles' time I's ever seen dem niggers happy on dat plantation 'tel atter s'render."[16]

White missionaries to slaves and freedmen before and immediately after the war observed that the disregard slaves held for the

morality preached by slaveholding Christians amounted to antinomianism. Bishop William Capers put his finger on the basis of the
slaves' antinomian attitude when he ramarked that "the prevalent
conceit that sin is sin for white men not negroes . . . [held] a fond
control over them." Charles Colcock Jones stated matter-of-factly
that among the slaves "antinomianism is not uncommon, and at
times, in its worst forms." Jones went on to explain, echoing the
same point made by Capers:

> Sometimes principles of conduct are adapted by church mem-
> bers at so much variance with the Gospel that the 'grace of
> God is turned into lasciviousness.' For example, members of
> the same church are sacredly bound by their religion not to
> reveal each others sins, for that would be backbiting and in-
> juring the brotherhood. And again, that which would be an
> abominable sin, committed by a church member with a
> worldly person, becomes no sin at all if committed with
> another church member. The brethren must 'bear one
> another's burdens and so fulfil the law of Christ.'[17]

Another plantation missionary, Thomas D. Turpin, stationed
on the May and New River Mission in coastal South Carolina
reported that the Christian slaves in his area had developed a
heterodox system of penance to expiate sin. Sinners were indicted
by church leaders, and, if found guilty, were punished according
to the degree of seriousness of their sin. There were three levels of
punishment. "If the crime was of the first magnitude, the perpe-
trator had to pick up a quart of benne seed [a small straw-colored
seed] . . . poured on the ground . . . and if of the second, a quart
of rice; and if of the third, a quart of corn; and . . . they also had
high seats and low seats . . . " To Turpin these slaves held "in-
correct views relative to those who ought to be punished." For
example, "it was also a rule among them never to divulge the
secret of stealing; and if it should be divulged by any one member, that one had to go on the low seat or pick up the benne
seed," that is, endure the punishment appointed for sins of the
first magnitude. Jones' and Turpin's descriptions support Capers'

insight that slaves viewed sin differently than did whites: what seemed antinomianism to white clergymen was in the slave's own system of moral judgment a primary value—to protect one another by not revealing the "sins" of ones fellow slaves.[18]

The alienation of black Christians from the moral norms of white Christianity was revealed also by missionaries who wrote reports, after the war, about the "immoral piety" of the freedmen. The experience of Charles Stearns is illustrative. Try as he might, Stearns found he could not convince the freedman to accept his moral code as essential to Christianity:

> I have known whole platoons to arise, and leave their seats and not return to the place of worship, when stealing was touched upon in the mildest manner. And it is a common remark among them, 'we would go and hear Mr. S. [tearns] preach much oftener, if he would leave off preaching against lying and stealing, and preach the gospel.' . . . They were always ready to hear about God, and living with him in heaven, but seldom wished to hear of their duties to each other. After the close of the meeting, I was waited upon at my house by a deputation of the brethren, who gravely informed me that my sermon had given great offense, and the people were determined to abandon the Sunday school and meeting, if I persisted in talking about such worldly matters. When I informed them that I could not desist from denouncing the sins they were guilty of, one of them persuasively said, 'Now Mr. S., if you must talk about stealing, why not call us together on Monday and tell us about it, and let us have a good heavenly time on Sunday, in worshipping the God we all love so much.' . . . It matters not what sin they may be guilty of, their confidence in their acceptance with God is unshaken . . . I have never seen one yet, professing to be a Christian, who was troubled with any doubts upon the subject of his acceptance with God. They said, 'God is not like man, and he is not going to punish us for every little sin.'[19]

The fact which Stearns failed to appreciate was that the freedmen's distaste for moralistic preaching was directly rooted in their experience of the dichotomy between Christianity and the practice of Christian slaveholders. Recently freed blacks were unwilling to listen to another white man preach to them about moral duty. Moreover, Stearns suggests that the freedmen, at least those whom he observed, were less concerned about the sins they committed than about God's acceptance of them as believers, an acceptance assured in their experience of conversion. Slaves could be stubborn in their assurance of election, as the following story retold by Olmsted indicates:

> A slave, who was 'a professor,' plagued his master very much by his persistence in certain immoral practices, and he requested a clergyman to converse with him and try to reform him. The clergyman did so, and endeavored to bring the terrors of the law to bear upon his conscience. 'Look yeah, massa,' said the backslider, 'don't de Scriptur say, 'Dem who believes an is baptize shall be save?' 'Certainly,' the clergyman answered; and went on to explain and expound the passage: but directly the slave interrupted him again. 'Jus you tell me now, massa, don't de good book say dese word: 'Dem as believes and is baptize, shall be save;' 'want to know dat.' 'Yes but—' 'Dat's all I want to know, sar; now wat's de use o' talkin' to me? You aint a goin to make me bleve wat de blessed Lord says, an't so, not ef you tries forever.' The clergyman again attempted to explain, but the negro would not allow him, and as often as he got back to the judgement-day, or charging him with sin, and demanding reformation, he would interrupt him in the same way. 'De Scriptur say, if a man believe and be baptize he shall—he *shall* be save. Now, massa minister, I *done* believe and I *done* baptize, and I shall be save suah. —Dere's no use talkin, sar.'[20]

In the area of sexuality, too, slave mores sometimes diverged from the norm preached by white Christians, but, as Frances Butler Leigh observed, that did not mean they had none. "The negroes had their own ideas of morality, and held to them very strictly; they did not consider it wrong for a girl to have a child before she married, but afterwards were extremely severe upon anything like infidelity on her part." The testimony of several freedmen before the American Freedmen's Inquiry Commission in 1863 supports Mrs. Leigh's assertion. Robert Smalls, for instance, reported that "the majority" of young slave women had premarital sex but did not regard it as evil. Once they joined the church, however, they stopped "promiscuous intercourse with men" and "very few lawful married women" engaged in extramarital affairs, according to Smalls.[21]

While some slaves rejected the moral system preached by the master and his preachers, others devoted themselves to a life of virtue, in which they developed both a sense of personal dignity and an attitude of moral superiority to their masters—an attitude that could simultaneously support compliance to the system of slavery and buttress the slave's own self-esteem. William Grimes's righteousness, for example, led him to take a surprising attitude toward his master. When punished for something he had not done, Grimes adopted a stance which seems to be a classic case of accommodating the status quo:

> It grieved me very much to be blamed when I was innocent, I knew I had been faithful to him, perfectly so. At this time I was quite serious, and used constantly to pray to my God. I would not lie nor steal. . . . When I considered him accusing me of stealing, when I was so innocent, and had endeavored to make him satisfied by every means in my power, that I was so, but he still persisted in disbelieving me, I then said to myself, if this thing is done in a green tree what must be done in a dry? I forgave my master in my own heart for all this, and prayed to God to forgive him and turn his heart.[22]

Grimes is, of course, alluding to the sacrifice of Christ and identifying himself with Jesus, the archetypal "Suffering Servant," who spoke the words concerning green and dry wood on his way to death on Calvary. From this morally superior vantage point Grimes is able to forgive his master. Note, however, the element of threat in the question: "if this thing is done in a green tree [to the innocent] what must be done in a dry [to the guilty]?" Those who are guilty, those who persecute the innocent, will be judged and punished. The threat of judgment becomes more explicit

when it is recalled that the full context of the words that Grimes
quotes is a prophecy of destruction:

> Daughters of Jerusalem, weep not for me, but weep for your-
> selves, and for your children. For behold, the days are coming,
> in which they shall say, Blessed are the barren, and the
> wombs that never bare, and the paps which never gave suck.
> Then shall they begin to say to the mountains, Fall on us; and
> to the hills, Cover us. For if they do these things in a green
> tree, what shall be done in the dry? [Luke 23:28–31]

Whether one marvels at Grimes's attitude as saintly or as neurotic
depends upon one's own religious views, but the significant aspect of this incident is Grime's view of himself—what it meant for
him, a slave, to feel moral authority over his master, to forgive his
master, to have the leverage of moral virtue by which to elevate
his own self-worth. A similar attitude was revealed by Solomon
Bayley, who belonged to the same Methodist class meeting with
the man who was attempting to sell Bayley's wife and infant
daughter. The slave admitted that it was extremely difficult "to
keep up true love and unity between him and me, in the sight of
God: this was a cause of wrestling in my mind; but that scripture
abode with me, 'He that loveth father or mother, wife or children,
more than me, is not worthy of me'; then I saw it became me to
hate the sin with all my heart, but still the sinner love; but I
should have fainted, if I had not looked to Jesus, the author of my
faith . . . " The attitude which Bayley strove to achieve is as old in
the Christian tradition as "Father forgive them for they know not
what they do" and as recent as Martin Luther King's articulation
of "soul force" and "redemptive suffering." A similar impulse lay
behind the comment of Mary Younger, a fugitive slave who escaped to Canada: "if those slaveholders were to come here, I
would treat them well, just to shame them by showing that I had
humanity." This assertion of one's humanity in the very teeth of
slavery's dehumanizing power was perhaps involved in Grimes's
and other slaves' adherence to moral virtue—an attitude which
might otherwise have seemed merely servile.[23]

At the same time, it is clear that this superior moral righteous-ness did support the slave system, as both William Grimes and Josiah Henson attested. Grimes confessed that:

> My conscience used sometimes to upbraid me with having done wrong, after I had run away from my master and arrived in Connecticut; and . . . I went up on a high mountain and prayed to the Lord to teach me my duty, that I might know whether or not I ought to go back to my master. Before I came down I felt satisfied, and it did seem to me that the Lord heard my prayers, when I was a poor wretched slave, and delivered me out of the land of Egypt, and out of the house of bondage; and that it was His hand, and not my own artfulness and cunning, which had enabled me to escape . . . [24]

The anomaly of Grimes's feeling guilt over running away from his master pales in comparison with the punctilious devotion to duty of another slave, Josiah Henson. As a trusted overseer, Henson was commissioned by his master to transport a score of slaves from Maryland to Kentucky. On the journey Henson and his charges traveled by boat on the Ohio River, and passing along the Ohio shore, they "were repeatedly told . . . that [they] were no longer slaves but free men, if [they] chose to be so. At Cincinnati crowds of coloured people gathered round us, and insisted on our remaining with them." Out of a sense of duty and pride, Henson "sternly assumed the captain, and ordered the boat to be pushed off into the stream" and back into slavery! Later Henson rebelled, fled to Canada, and lived to regret what he came to call his "unpardonable sin."[25]

Many slaves who remained in bondage contemplated a different escape: "I was a member of the First Baptist Church, I heard the white minister preach, and I thought within myself, I will seek a better world—here I am in bondage, and if there is a better world above, where I shall not be pulled and hauled about and tor-mented, as I am in this, I will seek it," recalled Henry Atkinson. It would be simplistic, however, to imterpret the consolation that Atkinson found in his religion as merely compensatory otherworldliness. When opportunity arose, this same Henry Atkinson sought a successful escape from slavery in this world as well. For those who saw no chance of escape, "trustin in the Lord" helped to stave off despair. "Trustin' was de only hope of de pore black critters in dem days. Us jest prayed for strength to endure it to de end. We didn't 'spect nothin' but to stay in bondage 'til we died," acknowledged Delia Garlic, who survived slavery in Virginia, Georgia, and Louisiana. More pointedly, an anonymous former slave, speaking not only for himself but for many, admitted: "As I look back over it now, I don't wonder that I felt as I did. I just gave up all earthly hopes and thought all the time about the next life." Accommodationist? No doubt it was that. Certainly, the religion of the slaves could support accommodation to the system of slavery. The experience of Govan Littlejohn was not unique: "My ma teach me to fight nothing in dis world but de devil." Religious symbols which might have been incendiary to some slaves were smothered by the skeptical realism of others, such as Charles Davenport, who scoffed: "De preachers would exhort us dat us was de chillen o' Israel in de wilderness an' de Lord done sent us to take dis land o' milk and honey. But how us gwine-a take land what's already been took?" Accommodationist, compensatory, antirevolutionary these views were, but perhaps they need to be pondered from the perspective of those who endured the experience and lived to tell it. Angered by latter-day critics of slave docility, a former slave remarked: "I have heard a heap of people say they wouldn't take the treatment what the slave took, but they woulda took it or death. If they had been there they woulda took the very same treatment."[26]

The effect of religion upon the attitudes, motivation, and action of slaves was complex. While some sought escape in the world beyond, others saw escape on this earth as a religious quest, sanctioned and directed by divine providence. (Nor were these alternatives always contradictory.) John Atkinson, who successfully fled slavery from Norfolk, Virginia, to Canada, likened the decision to escape to the experience of conversion. "A man who has been in slavery knows, and no one else can know, the yearnings to be free, and the fear of making the attempt. It is like trying to get religion, and not seeing the way to escape condemnation." The simile is suggestive of the capacity of religious symbols to support slaves in the act of rebellion by flight. The decision to escape, like the experience of conversion, might involve a prolonged struggle, an emotional and psychological "wrestling" which is suddenly overcome in the experience of "coming through." The threatening visions of Hell and Satan paralleled the anticipated perils of flight, pursuit, and possible capture. In both experiences the goal was freedom, physical or spiritual, and success depended not solely upon one's own efforts but upon the providence of God. Confidence in the providence of God helped some slaves to bridge the gap of fear separating the yearnings to be free from the attempt to become so. Fugitive slave John Thompson described the escape of three friends, "very religious persons, one of them being a Methodist preacher," who were certain of success because they "had full confidence in the surety of the promises of God." Thompson also spoke of his own decision to escape as a conversion experience. William and Ellen Craft preceded their journey to freedom with a prayer and a timely reminder of biblical precedent:

> When the time had arrived for us to start, we blew out the lights, knelt down, and prayed to our Heavenly Father mercifully to assist us, as he did his people of old, to escape from cruel bondage; and we shall ever feel that God heard and answered our prayer. Had we not been sustained by a kind, and I sometimes think special, providence, we could never have overcome the mountainous difficulties . . . [27]

Religious faith sometimes sustained the decision of slaves to flee or to revolt. Slave rebelliousness should not be thought of exclusively in terms of acts such as arson, sabotage, flight or revolt, for religion itself, in a very real sense, could be an act of rebelliousness—an assertion of slave independence, which sometimes required outright defiance of the master's command. G.W.

Offley stated that when slaves in Queen Ann's County, Maryland, experienced religion at a Methodist revival around 1830, "they would disobey their ungodly masters and would go to meetings nights and Sundays." Offley also claimed that he learned from his mother and father the potentially revolutionary doctrine "that God is no respecter of persons, but gave his son to die for all, bond or free, black or white, rich or poor," and that God protects those whom he chooses to sanctify for some task. To illustrate this last belief, Offley recounted the story of Praying Jacob, a tale which applies the lesson "Render unto Caesar the things that are Caesar's render unto God the things that are God's" to the master-slave relationship:

> [Praying Jacob] was a slave in the state of Maryland. His master was very cruel to his slaves. Jacob's rule was to Pray three times a day, at just such an hour of the day; no matter what his work was or where he might be, he would stop and go and pray. His master has been to him and pointed his gun at him, and told him if he did not cease praying he would blow out his brains. Jacob would finish his prayer and then tell his master to shoot in welcome—your loss will be my gain—I have two masters, one on earth and one in heaven— master Jesus in heaven, and master Saunders on earth. I have a soul and a body; the body belongs to you, master Saunders, and the soul to Jesus. Jesus says men ought always to pray, but you will not pray, neither do you want to have me pray. . . . Sometimes Mr. S. would be in the field about half drunk, raging like a madman, whipping the other slaves; and when Jacob's hour would come for prayer, he would . . . kneel down and pray, but he [Saunders] could not strike the man of God."[28]

Offley's story of Praying Jacob, no less than William Wells Brown's story of the conjurer Dinkie, extols the independence of a slave who stands up to his master and does so with impunity because he is protected by supernatural power. In the case of Praying Jacob, however, it is not the force of conjure but the protective care of God for his elect, which shields the slave from the white man's whip and gun.[29]

When the master's will conflicted with God's, slaves faced a choice which was simultaneously an opportunity to assert their own free will and to act virtuously, even heroically, in the context of Christianity, in which disobedience to white authority, no matter the consequence, could seem morally imperative. When Thomas Jones, for example, grew concerned about the state of his soul, his master told him to stop moping about, forbade him to attend prayer meetings, and ordered him to stop praying. In spite of repeated and severe whippings, Jones persisted in attending Methodist class meetings and refused to promise that he would abandon prayer. Eli Johnson claimed that when he was threatened with five hundred lashes for holding prayer meetings, he stood up to his master and declared, "In the name of God why is it, that I can't after working hard all the week, have a meeting on Saturday evening? I'll suffer the flesh to be dragged off my bones . . . for the sake of my blessed Redeemer." Fugitive slave James Smith, while still enslaved in Virginia, joined the Baptist Church and felt a call to preach to his fellow slaves. To prevent him from preaching, his master kept him tied up all day on Sundays and, when he proved intransigent, flogged him as well. Nevertheless, Smith kept up his ministry as best he could and later reported that "many were led to embrace the Saviour under his preaching."[30]

The husband of Candus [Candace?] Richardson, ex-slave from Franklin County, Mississippi, stole off to the woods to pray, "but he prayed so loud that anybody close around could hear," and so was discovered and punished. The fact which Mrs. Richardson proudly stressed was that "beatings didn't stop my husband from praying. He just kept on praying and it was his prayers," she explained to W.P.A. interviewers, and "a whole lot of other slaves that cause you young folks to be free today." Beatings did not stop slaves from praying, and these prayers were symbols of resistance, symbols whose power was not underestimated by the planters. A contraband slave interviewed in Columbus, Kentucky, in 1862 told a white missionary from the North: "When I was a slave my master would sometimes whip me *awful*, specially when he knew I was praying. He was determined to whip the Spirit out of me, but he could never do it, for de more he whip the more the Spirit make me *content* to be whipt . . . " That contentment, it may be said, stifled outward political resistance, but it may also be argued that it represented a symbolic inward resistance, a testing of wills and a victory of the spirit over the force of brutality.[31]

Prayer was such an effective symbol of resistance because both masters and slaves believed in the power of prayer. Hence the desperate need of some masters and mistresses for slaves to pray for the success of the Confederacy, and hence their anger when slaves dissembled or refused outright to do so. As A.M. French preceptively observed after listening to scores of slave testimonies in South Carolina:

> The prayers of the poor slaves, are proven to have had great value, in the minds of their Master, in scores of ways. They argued, and begged, coaxed and threatened, broke up meetings, punished, to make them pray 'fo' de confederates.' It is proven to have been so from the fact that so many refer to it, as a known fact in so many incidental ways; for instance— 'Massah say, we pray for de war, say we shouldn't, mus' pray for de 'fed'rates. We pray mo', pray harder. Den dey wouldn't let we hab meetin's, broke up de meetin's, but didn't broke our hearts, we pray mo' and mo', in de heart, night and day, and wait, for de Lord . . . Oh we pray for de Lord to come, to hasten his work' . . . . A deeply pious ex-slave said . . . 'I pray dat God bless you, and gib you success! Massah angry, but mus' pray for de comin' ob de Lord, an' his people.' Another said, 'I knew God would bless you, an' give victory, I feel it when I pray. Massah angry 'cause I pray for de North, can't help it mus' pray for the whole worl'. Massah say, 'No! Pray for de 'fed'rates.' But I knew God would bless de North.[32]

W.B. Allen, former slave from Georgia, remembered the time when he was a boy and his white folks asked him "to pray to God . . . to hold the Northern armies back" and he "told them flat-footedly that, while I loved them, and would do any reasonable praying for them, I could not pray against my conscience:

that I not only wanted to be free, but I wanted to see all the Negroes freed!" Some of Allen's outspokenness may have derived from his knowledge that the South was losing the war. Nevertheless, he was shouting in public what had been repeated in the dead of night in the private place of prayer which the slave claimed as his own. Less frank, but just as firm as Allen, was a slave woman named Maria from Raleigh, North Carolina, who described her mistress's failure to persuade her to pray for the South:

> On our plantation, when the war was going on, there was a great revival, and mistress called the colored people together and told them to pray—to pray mightily that the enemy may be driven back. So we prayed and prayed all over the plantation. But 'peared like de more de darkies prayed, de more nearer de Yankees come. Then the missus said, 'stop all this praying for the enemies, I won't have it. I believe they are praying for the enemies to come.' So there was no more praying where mistress could hear it ... One day my mistress came out to me. 'Maria, M'ria ... what *does* you pray for?' 'I prays, missus, that de Lord's will may be done.' 'But you mustn't pray that way. You must pray that our enemies may be driven back.' 'But, missus, if it's de Lord's will to drive 'em back, den they will go back.'[33]

In prayer, religious slaves kept in touch with what Paul Radin has described as "an inner world" where they could "develop a scale of values and fixed points of vantage from which to judge the world around them and themselves." In this inner, religious world the primary value and fixed point was the will of God. And in opposition to the slaveholder's belief, the slave believed that slavery was surely contrary to the will of God. John Hunter, a fugitive from slavery in Maryland, attested to this belief: "I have heard poor ignorant slaves, that did not know A from B, say that they did not believe the Lord ever intended they should be slaves, and that they did not see how it should be so." Lydia Adams asserted, "I've been wanting to be free ever since I was a little child. I said to them I didn't believe God ever meant me to be a slave . . . " From sermons he heard in a Methodist church, Francis Henderson concluded "that God had made all men free and equal, and that I ought not to be a slave . . . "[34] In this view, to trust in God's providence was to believe in the deliverance of the slaves. Since slavery was against the will of God, and since God's will could not be frustrated forever, it followed that the slaves would be freed, even though the when and the how might remain unknown. Was there not precedent in God's emancipation of Israel from Egypt? With this hope slaves consoled themselves in times of despair and found enough purpose to endure the enormity of their suffering. Polly, a slave of Barbara Leigh Smith Bodichon, eloquently expressed to her mistress the meaning she derived from religion: "we poor creatures have need to believe in God, for if God Almighty will not be good to us some day, why were we born? When I heard of his delivering his people from bondage I know it means the poor African." When Fredrika Bremer questioned a slave about enduring the conditions of slavery, she received this answer, "We endeavor to keep ourselves up as well as we can . . . what can we do unless we keep up a good heart. If we were to let droop, we should die!" A contraband in Beaufort, S.C., explained to a missionary why belief was essential to her life:

> O missus! I could not hab-libbed had not been for de Lord—neber! Work so late, and so early; work so hard, when side ache so. Chil'en sold; old man gone. All visitors, and company in big house; all cooking and washing all on me, and neber done enough. Missus neber satisfied—no hope. Noting, noting but Jesus, I look up. O Lord! how long? Give me patience! patience! O Lord! Only Jesus know how bad I feel; darsn't tell any body, else get flogged. Darsn't call upon de Lord; darsn't tell when sick. But . . . I said Jesus, if it your will, I will bear it.[35]

Clayborn Gantling, born a slave in Dawson, Georgia, in 1848, recalled the sight of slaves "sold in droves like cows . . . white men wuz drivin' 'em like hogs and cows for sale. Mothers and fathers were sold and parted from their chillun; they wuz sold to white people in diffunt states. I tell you chile, it was pitiful, but God did not let it last always. I have heard slaves morning and night pray for deliverance. Some of 'em would stand up in de fields or bend over cotton and corn and pray out loud for God to help 'em and in time you see He did." David Smith, in Baltimore, turned to God when he was threatened by his master with sale to the Deep South. Smith viewed God's power to free him from sin as a pledge of His power to free him from slavery: "I knew very well, if God was able to deliver me from the corrupt influence of the world and the power of Satan, that he was able to deliver me from this slave-holder. Yet I was like so many others, I did not see by what method he would secure my deliverance. Still with child-like simplicity I trusted him . . . " Smith saw his trust validated when he was purchased and manumitted by a kind sister-in-law of the master who threatened to sell him.[36]

Slaves prayed for the future day of deliverance to come, and they kept hope alive by incorporating as part of *their* mythic past the Old Testament exodus of Israel out of slavery. The appropriation of the Exodus story was for the slaves a way of articulating their sense of historical identity as a people. That identity was also based, of course, upon their common heritage of enslavement. The Christian slaves applied the Exodus story, whose end they knew, to their own experience of slavery, which had not ended. In identifying with the Exodus story, they created meaning and purpose out of the chaotic and senseless experience of slavery. Exodus functioned as an archetypal event for the slaves. The sacred history of God's liberation of his people would be or was being repeated in the American South. W. G. Kiphant, a Union Army chaplain with the 10th Iowa Veterans who worked among the freedmen in Decatur, Alabama, wrote disapprovingly in 1864 of the emphasis that Exodus received in the slaves' religion: "There is no part of the Bible with which they are so familiar as the story of the deliverance of the children of Israel. Moses is their *ideal* of all that is high, and noble, and perfect, in man. I think they have been accustomed to regard Christ not so much in the light of a *spiritual* Deliverer, as that of a second Moses who would eventually lead *them* out of their prison-house of bondage."[37]

The story of Israel's exodus from Egypt helped make it possible for the slaves to project a future radically different from their present. From other parts of the Bible, especially the prophetic and apocalyptic books, the slaves drew descriptions which gave form and, thus, assurance to their anticipation of deliverance. The troublesome question, according to Aunt Ellen, a freedwoman in North Carolina, had not been *if* the slaves would be free, but *when*: "When we used to think about it, it 'peared like de Judgement, sure to come, but a powerful step off." As that "powerful step" loomed closer with the beginning and progress of the war, slaves turned, as had generations of Christians before them in time of crisis, to the biblical promises of God for reassurance. Thomas L. Johnson recalled that in Richmond those blacks who could read "believed that the eleventh chapter of Daniel referred directly to the war."

> We often met together and read this chapter in our own way. The fifth verse would perplex many of our company and then verses 13–15 would be much dwelt upon, for though the former verses spoke of the apparent victory of the South, these latter verses set forth the ultimate triumph of the North, for did it not say: 'For the King of the North shall return and shall set forth a multitude greater than the former. . . . so the King of the North shall come and cast up a mound and take the most fenced cities, and the arms of the South shall not withstand.' Thus we eagerly grasped at any statements which our anxiety, hope, and prayer concerning our liberty led us to search for, and which might indicate the desirable ending of the great War.[38]

Old Testament prophecies of the destruction of Israel's enemies easily and naturally fit the slaves' desire that whites suffer just retribution for the brutality of slavery. Biblical prophets had spoken in images violent enough to suit the most vengeful feelings. Mary Livermore, a New England governess on a Southern plantation, was astonished by the prophetic terms which Aggy,

the normally "taciturn" housekeeper, used to express her outrage
at the beating her master had given her daughter:

> Thar's a day a-comin'! Thar's a day a-comin' . . . I hear de
> rumblin' ob de chariots! I see de flashin' ob de guns! White
> folks' blood is a-runnin' on de ground like a riber, an' de
> dead's heaped up dat high! . . . Oh, Lor'! hasten de day when
> de blows, an' de bruises, an' de aches, an' de pains, shall come
> to de white folks, an' de buzzards shall eat 'em as dey's dead in
> de streets. Oh, Lor'! roll on de chariots, an' gib de black
> people rest an' peace. Oh, Lor'! gib me de pleasure ob livin'
> till dat day, when I shall see white folks shot down like de
> wolves when dey come hongry out o' de woods![39]

Not all slaves took solace in religion. Some slaves would not
accept belief in a supposedly just God who could will or permit
slavery. If God was all-just and all-powerful, why did the innocent suffer and injustice reign? was a question which devastated
faith in the minds of some slaves. "I pretended to profess religion
one time," recalled one. "I don't hardly know what to think about
religion. They say God killed the just and unjust; I don't understand that part of it. It looks hard to think that if you ain't done
nothing in the world you be punished just like the wicked. Plenty
folks went crazy trying to get that straightened out." Nor did all
slaves distinguish true Christianity from that practiced by their
masters: for them it remained a white man's religion. Daniel Alexander Payne, A M F. bishop, discussed the origins of slave unbelief in a statement written in 1839:

> The slaves are sensible of the oppression exercised by their
> masters; and they see these masters on the Lord's day wor-
> shipping in his holy sanctuary. They hear their masters pro-
> fessing Christianity; they see their masters preaching the gos-
> pel; they hear these masters praying in their families, and they
> know that oppression and slavery are inconsistent with the
> Christian religion; therefore they scoff at religion itself—mock
> their masters, and distrust both the goodness and justice of
> God. Yes, I have known them even to question his existence.
> I speak not of what others have told me, but of what *I have*
> *both seen and heard from the slaves themselves.*[40]

The experience of Frederick Douglass may be added to that of Payne. Douglass spoke of "the doubts arising . . . partly from the sham religion which everywhere prevailed" under slavery, doubts which "awakened in my mind a distrust of all religion and the conviction that prayers were unavailing and delusive." Charles C. Coffin questioned a freedwoman named Nellie in Savannah in 1864 about her religious belief. She admitted: " . . . it has been a terrible mystery, to know why the good Lord should so long afflict my people, and keep them in bondage, —to be abused, and trampled down, without any rights of their own, —with no ray of light in the future." Though she had refused to despair, she reported of others: "Some of my folks said there wasn't any God, for if there was he wouldn't let white folks do as they have done for so many years . . . " John Dixon Long maintained that working as a minister in the South he met with unbelief among slaves "who suspect the Gospel to be a cheat, and believe the preachers and the slaveholder to be in a conspiracy against them."[41] There is no way of knowing how many slaves were doubters, agnostics, or atheists, but it is clear that some saw Christianity as meaningless, a sham, and a white man's religion—a fact which should temper generalizations about the piety of all slaves.

Two poles of behavior, accommodation and rebelliousness, have been the foci for discussion about slave personality and slave-master relationship. Slave testimony indicates that Christianity supported both, influencing some slaves to accept and others to rebel against their enslavement. But these were not the only alternatives. Religion, especially the revivalistic, inward, experientially oriented religion to which many slaves and masters adhered had an egalitarian tendency which occasionally led to moments of genuine religious mutuality, whereby blacks and whites preached to, prayed for, and converted each other in situations where the status of master and slave was, at least for the moment, suspended. In the fervor of religious worship, master and slave, white and black, could be found sharing a common event, professing a common faith and experiencing a common ecstasy. "I have

witnessed . . . many a season of refreshing in which master, mistress, and slave alike participated, and seen them all rejoice together," remarked H. J. Harris, a Methodist missionary to Mississippi plantations after 1839. On the Frierson plantation, in
Sumter County, South Carolina, the front yard of the big house
was set aside for the slaves' Sunday worship. Black preachers
were always invited to conduct these services, according to former
slave Irving Lowery. A table covered with a white cloth on which
lay a Bible was set up to serve as a pulpit, and chairs were
arranged for the slave congregation. Overlooking the yard was the
piazza, or gallery, of the big house where white families sat and
watched the services. In Lowery's words:

> No white preacher was ever allowed to stand behind that
> table, though some of them very much desired to do so. That
> long piazza was usually filled with devout [white] worshippers
> and the seats below with zealous colored Christians . . . .
> Sometimes when the old preacher would warm up to his
> subject . . . the audience would break forth in shouts of joy
> and praise. While some colored sister would be jumping out
> in the audience some of the white ladies were known to act in
> a similar manner in the piazza.[42]

Occasionally religious mutuality between white and black Christians included personal recognition and respect. Reverend C. C.
Jones, for example, felt that he was put to shame by the sincerity
and eloquence of the prayers said by Dembo, a native African and a
member of Jones's Midway Church: "I can never forget the prayers
of *Dembo* . . . . There was a depth of humility, a conviction of
sinfulness . . . an assurance of faith . . . a flowing out of love, a
being swallowed up in God, which I never heard before nor since;
and often when he closed his prayers, I felt as weak as water, and
that I ought not to open my mouth in public, and indeed knew not
what it was to pray." On the other side of the racial line, William
Wells Brown acknowledged that he had "the greatest respect" for
"the Christian zeal" of one planter in his area, Dr. John Gaines, "a
truly pious and conscientious man, willing at all times to give of his

means . . . in spreading the Gospel." Henry Clay Bruce allowed that some white ministers "were good men and preached reasonable sermons giving good advice, spiritually and morally, and were beloved by their colored congregations. I remember one whose name was W. G. Cooper, who was so well admired by his colored flock that they raised forty-five dollars and presented him a suit of clothes, when he went to conference, and sent a petition to have him returned to that charge." When the white pastor of Mount Olive Baptist Church in Harris County, Georgia, failed to appear for service on one Sunday during the war, he was replaced by Uncle Sol Mitchell without "a shadow of an objection to the negro slave's occupying the pulpit," recalled Parthenia Hague, a white Southern woman, who added that all joined in the service and that she personally had "never knelt with more humble devotion and reverence than on that Sabbath morning."[43]

At the core of the evangelical piety shared by slave and master was the conversion experience. Sometimes slaves were instrumental in the conversion of whites and vice versa. Elijah Marrs, worried over the state of his soul, was cutting corn stalks in a field one day with one of his young masters. Many years later Marrs still remembered the role played by this young master in his conversion: "He looked at me, and he saw that I was sin sick. He, being a Christian, took me in hand and told me that I was a sinner, and that Jesus Christ died to save sinners, and all I had to do was to believe that Jesus Christ was able to save. He told me about hell and its horrors. From morning to evening he talked. I prayed the best I could after I left him." A week later Marrs "was struck with conviction" and shortly afterward "professed faith in Christ."[44]

A more dramatic instance of religious reciprocity between slave and master was recounted by a former slave named Morte:

> One day while in the field plowing I heard a voice . . . I looked but saw no one . . . Everything got dark, and I was unable to stand any longer . . . With this I began to cry, Mercy! Mercy! Mercy! As I prayed an angel came and touched me, and I looked new . . . and there came a soft voice

saying, 'My little one, I have loved you with an everlasting love. You are a chosen vessel unto the Lord' . . . I must have been in this trance more than an hour. I went on to the barn and found my master waiting for me . . . I began to tell him of my experiences . . . My master sat watching and listening to me, and then he began to cry. He turned from me and said in a broken voice, 'Morte I believe you are a preacher. From now on you can preach to the people here on my place . . . But tomorrow morning. Sunday, I want you to preach to my family and my neighbors' . . . The next morning at the time appointed I stood up on two planks in front of the porch of the big house and, without a Bible or anything, I began to preach to my master and the people. My thoughts came so fast that I could hardly speak fast enough. My soul caught on fire, and soon I had them all in tears . . . I told them that they must be born again and that their souls must be freed from the shackles of hell.[45]

Unfortunately, we don't know what Morte thought about the significance of his power, spiritual and momentary though it may have been, over his master. Nor do we know what his fellow slaves thought when they saw Morte breaking up the rocky ground of the white folks' hearts. However, the spectacle of a slave reducing his master and his master's family and friends to tears by preaching to them of *their enslavement* to sin certainly suggests that despite the iron rule of slavery, religion could bend human relationships into some interesting shapes.

Slave religion has been stereotyped as otherworldly and compensatory. It was otherworldly in the sense that it held that this world and this life were not the end, nor the final measure of existence. It was compensatory to the extent that it consoled and supported slaves worn out by the unremitting toil and capricious cruelty of the "peculiar institution." To conclude, however, that religion distracted slaves from concern with this life and dissuaded them from action in the present is to distort the full story and to simplify the complex role of religious motivation in human behavior. It does not always follow that belief in a future state of

happiness leads to acceptance of suffering in this world. It does
not follow necessarily that a hope in a future when all wrongs will
be righted leads to acquiescence to injustice in the present. Religion had different effects on the motivation and identity of different slaves and even dissimilar effects on the same slave at different
times and in different circumstances.

To describe slave religion as merely otherworldly is inaccurate,
for the slaves believed that God had acted, was acting, and would
continue to act within human history and within their own particular history as a peculiar people just as long ago he had acted
on behalf of another chosen people, biblical Israel. Moreover,
slave religion had a this-worldly impact, not only in leading some
slaves to acts of external rebellion, but also in helping slaves to
assert and maintain a sense of personal value—even of ultimate
worth. The religious meetings in the quarters, groves, and "hush
harbors" were themselves frequently acts of rebellion against the
proscriptions of the master. In the context of divine authority, the
limited authority of any human was placed in perspective. By
obeying the commands of God, even when they contradicted the
commands of men, slaves developed and treasured a sense of
moral superiority and actual moral authority over their masters.

In the role of preacher, exhorter, and minister, slaves experienced status, achieved respect, and exercised power, often circumscribed but nonetheless real. In the peak experience of conversion,
slaves felt raised from death to life, from sorrow to joy, from
damnation to election. The conversion experience equipped the
slave with a sense of individual value and a personal vocation
which contradicted the devaluing and dehumanizing forces of
slavery. In the prayer meetings, the sermons, prayers, and songs,
when the Spirit started moving the congregation to shout, clap,
and dance, the slaves enjoyed community and fellowship which
transformed their individual sorrows. That some slaves maintained their identity as persons, despite a system bent on reducing
them to a subhuman level, was certainly due in part to their
religious life. In the midst of slavery, religion was for slaves a
space of meaning, freedom, and transcendence.

Conclusion:
Canaan Land

Shout the glad tidings o'er Egypt's dark sea
Jehovah has triumphed, his people are free!
FREEDMEN'S HYMN

THE profound joy with which slaves celebrated their long-awaited Day of Jubilee was tempered by the memory of past suffering, the awareness of present uncertainty, and the anticipation of future trouble. Though slavery had ended, its legacy of oppression remained, rendering freedom less than complete. As contraband slave Brother Thornton warned the refugees at Fortress Monroe, Virginia, Canaan Land was still off in the distance:

> We have been in the furnace of affliction, and are still, but God only means to separate the dross, and get us so that like the pure metal we may reflect the image of our Purifier, who is sitting by to watch the process. I am assured that what God begins, he will bring to an end. We have need of faith, patience and perseverance, to realize the desired result. There must be no looking back to Egypt. Israel passed forty years in the wilderness, because of their unbelief. What if we cannot see right off the green fields of Canaan, Moses could not. He could not even see how to cross the Red Sea. If we would have greater freedom of body, we must free ourselves from the shackles of sin, and especially the sin of unbelief. We must snap the chain of Satan, and educate ourselves and our children . . .[1]

Gazing back at their lives in slavery, former slaves affirmed that they had trusted in the Lord and that the Lord had delivered them. Like the children of Israel of old, they had lived through Egypt and Exodus and the experience had constituted them a peculiar, a chosen, people. This identity was to remain—in the midst of the chaos, disappointment, and disaster of Reconstruction—a bedrock of hope for freed black Christians as it had been for them as slaves. As the one institution which freed blacks were allowed to control, the church was the center of social, economic, educational, and political activity. It was also a source of continuity and identity for the black community. In their churches, black worshipers continued for decades to pray, sing, preach, and shout as they or their parents had during slavery.

We are fortunate that the former slaves were not silent about their religious faith and that they left their testimony as a legacy for their children and for any who wish to understand it. The history of slave religion is the story of the faith of a people, a people whose lives were marked by their trust in the Lord. This quality of trusting faith was summed up simply by a ninety-year-old ex-slave interviewed in the 1930s toward the end of her life. When asked, "Are all your people dead?" Maria Jenkins replied, "De whole nation dead . . . De whole nation dead—Peggy dead—Toby dead—all leaning on de Lord."

Notes

Preface

1. For a discussion of the neglect of black Church history and an enumeration of areas for exploration in the context of general American Church history, see Robert T. Handy, "Negro Christianity and American Church Historiography," in *Reinterpretations in American Church History*, edited by Jerald C. Brauer (Chicago: University of Chicago Press, 1968), pp. 91–112.
2. Daniel J. Boorstin, *The Americans: The National Experience* (New York: Random House, Vintage Books, 1965), pp. 196–97.
3. John W. Blassingame, *The Slave Community* (New York: Oxford University Press, 1972) and *Slave Testimony* (Baton Rouge: Louisiana State University Press, 1977); Eugene D. Genovese, *Roll, Jordan, Roll: The World the Slaves Made* (New York: Pantheon, 1974); Lawrence W. Levine, *Black Culture and Black Consciousness* (New York: Oxford University Press, 1977); see also C. Vann Woodward, "History from Slave Sources," *American Historical Review*, Vol. 79, No. 2 (April 1974), pp. 470–81; and Sterling Stuckey, "Through the Prism of Folklore: The Black Ethos in Slavery," in *Black and White in American Culture*, edited by Jules Chametzky and Sidney Kaplan (New York: Viking Press, 1971), pp. 172–91.

Chapter 1

1. For estimates of the volume of the slave trade see Philip D. Curtin, *The Atlantic Slave Trade: A Census* (Madison: University of Wisconsin Press, 1969). Curtin's figures have been challenged as excessively low by J. E. Inikori, "Measuring the Atlantic Slave Trade," *Journal of African History*, Vol. 17, No. 2 (1976), pp. 197–223.
2. The classic statement on African cultural influence in the New World is still Melville J. Herskovits, *The Myth of the Negro Past* (Boston: Beacon Press, 1958). A handy but too brief overview is Roger Bastide, *African Civilisations in the New World* (New York: Harper & Row, Harper Torchbooks, 1971). An important recent

contribution is Sidney W. Mintz and Richard Price, *An Anthropological Approach to the Afro-American Past: A Caribbean Perspective* (Philadelphia: Institute for the Study of Human Issues, ISHI Occasional Papers in Social Change, No. 2., 1976).

3. Gomes Eannes De Azurara, *The Chronicle of the Discovery and Conquest of Guinea*, translated by Charles R. Beazley and Edgar Prestage, 2 vols. (London: Hakluyt Society, Series I, Vols. 95 and 100, 1896-1899). See Vol. 95, pp. 39-85, and Vol. 100, p. 288; also Louis B. Wright, *Gold, Glory, and the Gospel* (New York: Atheneum, 1970), pp. 24-31.

4. Thomas Winterbottom, *An Account of the Native Africans in the Neighbourhood of Sierra Leone*, 2 vols., 1st publ. 1803 (London: Frank Cass & Co., 1969), 1: 231. Archibald Dalzel, *The History of Dahomey*, 1st publ. 1793 (London: Frank Cass & Co., 1967), p. vi. C. K. Meek describes a similar adaption in twentieth-century Nigeria: "the Koran is their fetish no less than the village idol, stone, or tree; to swear falsely on the Koran would mean certain death; while to drink the ink with which the Koran texts are written is a cure for every ill" (C. K. Meek, "The Religions of Nigeria," *Africa*, Vol. 14, July 1943, p. 107). See the description of interesting admixtures of Muslim and traditional beliefs among the Wolof in *The Wolof of Senegambia*, by David P. Gamble (London: International African Institute, 1957), pp. 64-72. Fortes and Dieterlen comment: "Where, as in Northern Nigeria and Ghana, Islam is propagated by missionaries, its development may be similar to that of Christianity in its early stages in Europe. Traditional beliefs will fuse with modern teaching in the tribal setting" (M. Fortes and G. Dieterlen, eds., *African Systems of Thought* [London: Oxford University Press, 1965], p. 30).

5. John Barbot, *A Description of the Coasts of North and South Guinea* (London, 1732), pp. 80, 104.

6. Ralph M. Wiltgen, S.V.D., *Gold Coast Mission History, 1471-1880* (Techny, Ill.: Divine Word Publications, 1956). Owerri, or Warri, is in southern Nigeria, in Ibo country. John Adams described an audience with the king of Warre: "On entering the . . . palace, we were much surprised to see placed on a rude kind of table, several emblems of the catholic religion, consisting of crucifixes, mutilated saints and other trumpery. Some of these were . . . of brass and others of wood. On inquiring how they came into their present situation, we were informed, that several black Portuguese missionaries had been at Warre, many years since, endeavouring to convert

the natives into Christians; and the building in which they performed their mysteries, we found still standing. A large wooden
cross, which had withstood the tooth of time, was remaining . . . in
one of the angles formed by two roads intersecting each other. We
could not learn that the Portuguese had been successful in making
proselytes . . . " (John Adams, *Sketches Taken During Ten Voyages
to Africa Between the Years 1786 and 1800*, reprint [New York:
Johnson Reprint Co., 1970], p. 31). Barbot, pp. 183, 305, 377–78.
According to Barbot, the island of Fernando Po had two parishes in
St. Anthony Town, each served by a black priest, one ordained in
Lisbon, the other in St. Tome. Ibid., p. 400; William Smith, *A New
Voyage to Guinea*, 1st publ. 1744 (London: Frank Cass and Co.,
1967), p. 25. See also Barbot, p. 157, on Gold Coast mulatto Chris-
tians. Nzinga Mbemba was baptized, according to Wiltgen, "on
May 3, 1491, along with six of his noblemen." His son, Prince
Henrique, was sent to Rome, where Pope Leo X nominated him as
bishop in 1518. See Wiltgen, pp. 11, 14–15. For the story of
Nzinga Mbemba, Dom Affonso I, see Basil Davidson, *The African
Slave Trade* (Boston: Little, Brown & Co., 1961), pp. 117–62;
Georges Balandier, *Daily Life in the Kingdom of the Kongo* (New
York: World Publishing Co., Meridian Books, 1969), pp. 244–63;
and J. Van Wing, *Etudes Bakongo*, 2nd ed. (Brussels: Desclee de
Brouwer, 1959), pp. 19–43. See also *Europeans in West Africa,
1450–1560*, edited by John W. Blake, 2 vols. (London: Hakluyt
Society, 1942), pp. 31–32.

7. Some detailed studies of the origins of slaves are Curtin, *Atlantic
Slave Trade*; Melville J. Herskovits, "On the Provenience of New
World Negroes," *Social Forces*, 12 (December 1933): 247–62;
Walter Rodney, "Upper Guinea and the Significance of the Origins
of Africans Enslaved in the New World," *Journal of Negro History*,
54 (October 1969): 327–45; W. Robert Higgins, "The Geographi-
cal Origins of Negro Slaves in Colonial South Carolina," *The South
Atlantic Quarterly*, 70 (Winter 1971): 34–47; Marion D. Kilson,
"West African Society and the Atlantic Slave Trade, 1441–1865,"
in *Key Issues in the Afro-American Experience*, edited by Nathan I.
Huggins, Martin Kilson, and Daniel M. Fox (New York: Harcourt,
Brace, Jovanovich, 1971), pp. 39–53; *Documents Illustrative of the
History of the Slave Trade to America*, edited by Elizabeth Donnan, 4
vols. (Washington, D.C.: Carnegie Institution Publication No. 409,
1930–1935).

8. Problems confront anyone attempting to describe the African reli-

gious heritage of American slaves. Among these is the question of the historicity of "traditional" African cultures. Can it be assumed that African cultures and religions have not changed since the close of the Atlantic slave trade a century ago? To simply use current ethnological accounts of African religions without taking into account the possibility of change is methodologically questionable. Due to pressures from without—intensified Muslim and Christian missions, European imperialism, Western technology and education—and the growth of African nationalism during the late nineteenth and twentieth centuries, African traditional religions have changed and continue to do so. For some cases in point see James Boyd Christensen, "The Adaptive Functions of Fanti Priesthood," in *Continuity and Change in African Cultures*, edited by William R. Bascom and Melville J. Herskovits (Chicago: University of Chicago Press, 1959), pp. 257–78; John C. Messenger, Jr., "Religious Acculturation Among the Anang Ibibio," in *Continuity and Change in African Cultures*, pp. 279–99. Besides external pressures to change, there are also indigenous processes of change within traditional African societies themselves, changes that scholars of African religions have come to recognize. See T. O. Ranger and I. M. Kimambo, eds., *The Historical Study of African Religion* (Berkeley: University of California Press, 1973). On the other hand, it might be suspected that religion, particularly religious myth and ritual might be among the most conservative elements of culture. Further complicating the issue is a second but related problem, that of sources for writing the history of nonliterate cultures. For investigations of oral sources for the history of African peoples, see Jan Vansina, *Oral Tradition: A Study for Historical Methodology* (London: Routledge & Kegan Paul, 1965); Daniel F. McCall, *Africa in Time Perspective* (New York: Oxford University Press, 1969). Written sources contemporaneous with the slave trade are travel accounts compiled by chroniclers, explorers, trading-company representatives, missionaries, and travelers. These European descriptions of "Guinea" are often marred by ethnocentric bias, but as a genre they do give a general, if distorted and fleeting, view of some elements of religious belief and practice in West Africa during the centuries of the slave trade. When correlated with later anthropological accounts, some of the distortion and confusion can be neutralized (though it would be naive to assume that some modern accounts of African religions do not also suffer from bias). Another written source is the slim body of narratives by enslaved Africans educated in Europe or America. See *Af-*

rica Remembered: Narratives by West Africans from the Era of the
Slave Trade, edited by Philip D. Curtin (Madison: University of
Wisconsin Press, 1968).

9. Geoffrey Parrinder, West African Religions, 2nd rev. ed. (London:
Epworth Press, 1961), pp. 13–25; John S. Mbiti, Concepts of God
in Africa (New York: Praeger, 1970); Edwin W. Smith, ed., African Ideas of God (London: Edinburgh House, 1950), pp. 224–97.

10. William Bosman, A New and Accurate Description of the Coast of
Guinea (London, 1705), p. 368a. See also Barbot, p. 340. Many
travel accounts note West African belief in a supreme deity. See
William Smith, A New Voyage to Guinea, 1st publ. 1744 (London:
Frank Cass & Co., 1967), pp. 143, 237; John Matthews, A Voyage
to the River Sierra-Leone, 1st publ. London, 1788 (London: Frank
Cass & Co., 1966), p. 65; Winterbottom, p. 222.

11. Parrinder, p. 15; R. S. Rattray, Ashanti (London: Oxford University
Press, 1923), p. 144; T. J. Bowen, Adventures and Missionary Labours in Several Countries in the Interior of Africa from 1849 to 1865,
1st publ. 1857 (London: Frank Cass and Co., 1968), pp. 206–7.

12. E. Bolaji Idowu, Olodumare, God in Yoruba Belief (London: Long-
mans, Green & Co., 1962), p. 52; M. J. Field, Religion and Medicine of the Ga People (London: Oxford University Press, 1937), pp.
4–6, 10, 40, 61–62; Daryll Forde and G. I. Jones, The Ibo and
Ibibio-Speaking Peoples of South-Eastern Nigeria (London: Oxford
University Press, 1950), p. 25; P. Amaury Talbot, The Peoples of
Southern Nigeria, 3 vols. (London: Oxford Unversity Press, 1926),
2: 40–43; John H. Weeks, Among Congo Cannibals (London:
Seeley, Service & Co., 1913), pp. 246–48; John H. Weeks, Among
the Primitive Bakongo (London: Seeley, Service & Co., 1914), p.
276; Melville J. Herskovits, Dahomey: An Ancient West African
Kingdom, 2 vols. (Evanston, Ill.: Northwestern University Press,
1967), 2: 101–5; John M. Jantzen and Wyatt MacGaffey, eds., An
Anthropology of Kongo Religion (Lawrence, Kans.: University of
Kansas Publications in Anthropology, No. 5, 1974), pp. 35, 71.

13. Rattray, Ashanti, pp. 87–91; A. B. Ellis, The Tshi-Speaking Peoples,
1st publ. London, 1887 (Chicago: Benin Press, 1964), pp. 176–95;
Parrinder, pp. 7–12. Herskovits explains: "a vodu is thought of by
the Dahomeans as something which is localized, and that a spirit,
while . . . existing everywhere in space, must also have definite
places to which it can be summoned, where it can be commanded by
the proper formulae to aid its worshippers, and from which it can go
forth to achieve those things desired of it" (Dahomey, 2: 171). See

the "Extrait de queleques textes sur les ⟨⟨fetiches⟩⟩," in Pierre
Verger, *Notes sur le culte des orisa et vodun* (Dakar: Memoires de
l'Institut Francais d'Afrique noire, No. 51, 1957), pp. 33–70. The
Ewe term *vodũ* or *vodun* is used in Haiti to refer to "the gods" and is
applied to Afro-Haitian religion in general as "voodoo." The Yoruban term *orisha* is used in Afro-Brazilian *candomblé* and Afro-Cuban
santeria to refer to "the gods." See Verger, *Notes*, pp. 27–32,
"Definition des orisa et vodun."

14. Peter Morton-Williams, "An Outline of the Cosmology and Cult
Organization of the Oyo Yoruba," in *Peoples and Cultures of Africa*,
edited by Elliott P. Skinner (Garden City, N.Y.: Doubleday, 1973),
pp. 654–77; Robert Farris Thompson, *Black Gods and Kings* (Bloomington: Indiana University Press, 1976), Chap. 2, p. 2.

15. Parrinder, pp. 75–94; A. B. Ellis, *The Yoruba-Speaking Peoples*
(London, 1894), pp. 93–106; A. B. Ellis, *The Ewe-Speaking
Peoples*, 1st publ. London, 1890 (Oosterhout, N. B., Netherlands:
Anthropological Publications, 1966), pp. 139–52; Ellis, *Tshi*, pp.
119–48; Herskovits, *Dahomey*, 2: 170–200. Herskovits offers a
brief and useful description of Dahomean cults: "Thus each pantheon has its associated priesthood and its initiated devotees; each
cult-group subjects its candidates for membership to a period of
initiation during which cicatrizations are given . . . During their seclusion all novitiates [novices] learn the particular dance steps which
are distinctive of the cult to which they are vowed; their emergence
from the cult-houses is marked by special ceremonials; and when
they emerge, they are resurrected beings, with new names, each
speaking a language which was not the one spoken when entering . . . " (*Dahomey*, 2: 170). The practice of initiation into a cult
group of the devotee, who is then prepared for possession by the
gods upon ritual occasions, is an important element of African religious life carried to the New World, where, as we shall see, it has
endured to the present. For the phenomenon of spirit possession in
Africa, see M. J. Field, "Spirit Possession in Ghana," in *Spirit Mediumship and Society in Africa*, edited by John Beattie and John
Middleton (London: Routledge & Keagan Paul, 1969), pp. 3–13;
Pierre Verger, "Trance and Convention in Nago-Yoruba Spirit Mediumship," in *Spirit Mediumship and Society in Africa*, pp. 50–66;
Verger, *Notes*, pp. 71–73, 95–108; M. J. Field, *Religion and Medicine of the Ga*, pp. 100–9; William Bascom, *The Yoruba of Southwestern Nigeria* (New York: Holt, Rinehart & Winston, 1969), p.
78.

16. Janzen and MacGaffey, pp. 34–38; K. A. Busia, "The Ashanti," in *African Worlds*, edited by Daryll Forde (New York: Oxford University Press, 1954), p. 191; Barbot, pp. 309–10; Ellis, *Tshi*, pp. 34–118; Verger, *Notes*, pp. 522–24; Rattray, *Religion and Art in Ashanti* (London: Oxford University Press, 1927), pp. 5–6.

17. The best general treatment is Benjamin Ray, *African Religions* (Englewood Cliffs, N.J.: Prentice-Hall, 1976).

18. W. T. Harris and Harry Sawyer, *The Springs of the Mende Belief and Conduct* (Freetown: Sierra Leone University Press, 1968), p. 15.

19. M. J. Field, *Religion and Medicine of the Ga*, p. 197; Parrinder, pp. 115–27; Herskovits, *Dahomey*, 1: 194–238.

20. Ellis, *Yoruba*, pp. 128–29; Idowu, pp. 194–95; Weeks, *Bakongo*, p. 115; Geoffrey Parrinder, *West African Psychology* (London: Lutterworth Press, 1951), pp. 115–29.

21. Field, *Religion and Medicine of the Ga*, p. 197.

22. M. Fortes and G. Dieterlen note that "death alone is not a sufficient condition for becoming an ancestor entitled to receive worship." A proper burial is "the *sine qua non*" (*African Systems of Thought*, p. 16); Parrinder, *West African Religion*, p. 107; Herskovits, *Dahomey*, 1: 352–402; Harris and Sawyer, pp. 30–33; Rattray, *Religion and Art in Ashanti*, pp. 149–66; Ellis, *Ewe*, pp. 159–60; Weeks, *Bakongo*, pp. 266–75; M. J. Field, *Search for Security*, 1st publ. 1960 (New York W. W. Norton & Co., 1970), p. 49.

23. Rattray, *Ashanti*, pp. 92–108; Samuel Johnson, *The History of the Yorubas* (London: Routledge & Kegan Paul, 1921), pp. 29–30; C. K. Meek, "The Religions of Nigeria," *Africa*, 14 (July 1943), 111; Verger, *Notes*, pp. 507–10.

24. Barbot noted, "The priests . . . are look'd upon as able physicians, being well skill'd in the knowledge of herbs and plants, which they administer where there is occasion, and are therefore much respected" (Barbot, p. 135); see Field, *Religion and Medicine of the Ga*, pp. 110–34; T. Adeoye Lambo, *African Traditional Beliefs: Concepts of Health and Medical Practice* (Ibadan, Nigeria: Ibadan University Press, 1963).

25. Travel accounts are replete with incidents of the use of what Europeans called "ju-jus, gris-gris," and "fetishes." See also Ellis, *Yoruba*, pp. 117–18; Ellis, *Ewe*, pp. 91–95; Ellis, *Tshi*, pp. 98–109; Wing, pp. 324–425; Harris and Sawyer, pp. 66–72; Weeks, *Bakongo*, pp. 232–44.

26. Bosman, p. 148.

27. Field, *Religion and Medicine of the Ga*, pp. 135–60, 200; see the sec-

tion on "Witchcraft and Sorcery" in Fortes and Dieterlen, pp. 21 ff.; Parrinder, *West African Religion*, p. 152; H. Debrunner, *Witchcraft in Ghana*, 2nd ed. (Accra: Presbyterian Book Depot, 1961); Rattray, *Religion and Art in Ashanti*, pp. 167–70; Bosman, pp. 149–51.

28. Idowu, pp. 7–9; 77–80; Parrinder, *West African Religion*, pp. 137–50; William Bascom, *Ifa Divination* (Bloomington: Indiana University Press, 1969); Verger, *Notes*, pp. 568–70. Bosman noted a simpler form of divination by use of "a sort of wild Nuts; which they pretend to take up by guess and let fall again; after which they tell them, and form their Predictions from the numbers falling even or odd" (Bosman, p. 152).

29. Alfred Metraux, speaking of Dahomean religion in *Voodoo in Haiti* (New York: Schocken Books, 1972), p. 30; John Storm Robert, *Black Music of Two Worlds* (New York: Praeger, 1972), p. 6; Herskovits, *Dahomey*, 2: 114–16; Verger, *Dieux d'Afrique* (Paris: Paul Hartmann, 1954), p. 165.

30. Pierre Verger, *Dieux d'Afrique*, p. 9.

31. J. F. Ajayi, *Christian Missions in Nigeria, 1841–1891* (Evanston, Ill.: Northwestern University Press, 1965), pp. 4–5.

32. Donald Hogg, "The Convince Cult in Jamaica," Yale University Publications in Anthropology, No. 58, in *Papers in Caribbean Anthropology*, compiled by Sidney W. Mintz (New Haven: Department of Anthropology, Yale University, 1960), p. 4. Compare Hogg's statement with that of Herskovits' describing the place of the *winti* in Paramaribo, Dutch Guiana: " . . . a winti may at the same time be both a good and an evil spirit. The fact is that the logic of the Negroes of Paramaribo holds that no spirit is either good or evil in the absolute sense. This concept of the absence of a spirit which is wholly good or completely evil enters here in a more subtle way. For while it generally follows that a spirit is friendly if it is worshipped, unfriendly if it is neglected, and evil if it has been sent to do evil, a spirit may be temperamentally as inconstant as human beings are inconstant" (Melville J. Herskovits, *New World Negro*, [n.p., Minerva Press, Funk and Wagnalls, 1969], p. 288).

33. Hogg, pp. 12–13.

34. George Eaton Simpson, *Religious Cults of the Caribbean* (Rio Piedras, Puerto Rico: Institute of Caribbean Studies, University of Puerto Rico, 1970), p. 202; Orlando Patterson, *The Sociology of Slavery: An Analysis of the Origins, Development and Structure of Negro Slave Society in Jamaica* (Rutherford, N.J.: Fairleigh Dickinson University Press, 1969), pp. 198–202.

35. Arthur Ramos, *The Negro in Brazil* (Washington, D.C.: Associated Publishers, 1939), pp. 1-14, 80-82; Donald Pierson, *Negroes in Brazil* (Carbondale, Ill.: Southern Illinois University Press, 1967), pp. 6-7. The terms *macumba* and *candomblé* were originally applied to African dances in Brazil and were later extended to Afro-Brazilian religious cults and ceremonies, though in southern Brazil, Uruguay, and Argentina, *candomblé* still refers to dance. The major studies (not yet translated into English) of *candomblé*: Nina Rodrigues, *Os Africanos no Brasil*, 3rd ed. (Rio de Janeiro: Companhia Editora Nacional, 1945); Arthur Ramos, *O Negro Brasileiro* Vol. 1, *Ethnographia Religiosa*, 2nd rev. ed. (Rio de Janeiro: Companhia Editora Nacinal, 1940); Edison Carneiro, *Candombles da Bahia* (Rio de Janeiro: Tecnoprint Grafica, 1957); Roger Bastide, *Les Religions Afro-Brésiliennes* (Paris: Presses Universitaires de France, 1960); and Verger, *Notes*.

36. Verger, "Yoruba Influence in Brazil," *ODU, Journal of Yoruba and Related Studies*, No. 1 (January 1955), p. 4; Bastide, *African Civilisations*, pp. 105-9, 115-17; for a "geography" of the "nations" of *candomblé*, see Bastide, *Religions Afro-Brésiliennes*, pp. 241-305.

37. For a convenient list of the principal *Nago-Gege* gods, their cult objects, foods, days, and colors, see Pierson, pp. 282-83. For a description of temples, hierarchy, and cult organization, see Etienne Ignance, "Le fétichisme des negres du Bresil," *Anthropos*, Band/ Tom. 3 (1908): 894-98; Melville J. Herskovits, "The Social Organization of the Candomble," in *The New World Negro*, pp. 226-47; Ramos, pp. 84-86; Edison Carneiro, "The Structure of African Cults in Bahia," *Journal of American Folklore*, Vol. 53, No. 210 (1940), pp. 271-78. For praises and songs to the gods, see Verger, *Notes*. Occasionally the *pae de santo* or *mae de santo* are called by the Yoruban terms *babalorisha* and *iyalorisha*. See the detailed description of "Initiations et Etat de Transe" in Verger, *Notes*, pp. 71-108; also the account of a *filhas de santo* recorded in Pierson, pp. 263-70; and Herskovits, "The *Panan*, an Afrobahian Religious Rite of Transition," in *New World Negro*, pp. 217-26.

38. For an extensive description of the gods in Brazil, as well as a discussion of myths, praises and songs, and excerpts from earlier observers, see Verger, *Notes*.

39. Simpson, "The Shango Cult in Trinidad," in *Religious Cults of the Caribbean*, pp. 11-22, 112-13; Melville J. Herskovits and Frances S. Herskovits, *Trinidad Village* (New York: Alfred A. Knopf, 1947), pp. 17-23; William Bascom, *Shango in the New World* (Aus-

tin: University of Texas, Occasional Publications, 1972), pp. 3–4, 10, 12.

40. Bascom, *Shango*, p. 13; Bascom, "Yoruba Acculturation in Cuba," in *Les Afro-Americains* (Dakar: Mémoires de l'Institut Francais d'Afrique Noire, No. 27, 1952), pp. 166–67. The classic studies of Afro-Cuban religious cults are Fernando Ortiz, *Hampa Afro-Cubana: Los Negros Brujos* (Madrid: Editorial-America [1906]); Lydia Cabrera, *El Monte* (Havana: Ediciones CR, 1954).

41. Bascom, "The Focus of Cuban Santeria," in *Peoples and Cultures of the Caribbean*, edited by Michael M. Horowitz (Garden City, N.Y.: Doubleday, Natural History Press, 1971), pp. 520–27.

42. Bascom, "The Yoruba in Cuba," *Nigeria*, Vol. 37, No. 37 (1951), p. 17; Bascom, "Two Forms of Afro-Cuban Divination," in *Acculturation in the Americas, Proceedings and Selected Papers of the XXIXth International Congress of Americanists*, 3 vols., edited by Sol Tax (Chicago: University of Chicago Press, 1952), 2: 169–79.

43. For tables charting the identification of African gods and Catholic saints, see Ignace, pp. 901–2; Pierson, pp. 306–8; Bastide, *Religions Afro-Brésiliennes*, pp. 362–96. See Herskovits, "African Gods and Catholic Saints in New World Negro Belief," in *New World Negro*, pp. 321–29. Herskovits notes "that in Dahomey itself, among those natives of the city of Abomey who are members of the Catholic Church, this same identification is made between Xevioso and Santa Barbara" (Ibid., p. 326). See also Bascom, "Yoruba in Cuba," pp. 14–15.

44. Herskovits and Herskovits, *Trinidad Village*, pp. 329–33; Alfred Metraux, *Voodoo in Haiti* (New York: Schocken Books, 1972), p. 83; Harold Courlander, *The Drum and the Hoe* (Berkeley: University of California Press, 1960), p. 318; Simpson, *Religious Cults of the Caribbean*, pp. 237–44, 248–49.

45. Simpson, pp. 37–45, 92.

46. Herskovits, *New World Negro*, p. 226*n*; Octavio Da Costa Eduardo comments that "heathen instruments, i.e., unbaptized ones, can bring on possession by evil spirits"; Octavio Da Costa Eduardo, *The Negro in Northern Brazil: A Study in Acculturation*, Monographs of the American Ethnological Society, Vol. 15 (New York: J.J. Augustin, 1948), p. 96.

47. Michel Laguerre, "An Ecological Approach to Voodoo," *Freeing the Spirit*, Vol. 3, No. 1 (1974), p. 11.

48. Quoted by Metraux, pp. 34–35.

49. *L'Essai sur l'Esclavage et Observations sur l'Etat Present des Colonies*, quoted by Simpson, p. 234.
50. "Introduction" to Metraux, p. 10; Simpson, pp. 235–37.
51. Metraux, pp. 25–57, 86–88; Courlander, pp. 317–31.
52. Courlander, pp. 21–22, 29; Metraux, pp. 120–21; Laguerre, pp. 11–12.
53. Philip D. Curtin, *Two Jamaicas* (Cambridge: Harvard University Press, 1955), pp. 32–35; Martha Warren Beckwith, *Black Roadways: A Study of Jamaican Folk Life* (Chapel Hill: University of North Carolina Press, 1929), pp. 157–74; Patterson, pp. 210–15; Edward Bean Underhill, *The West Indies: Their Social and Religious Condition* (London, 1862), pp. 194–201.
54. Simpson, p. 169.
55. Simpson, pp. 69, 140–52, Herskovits and Herskovits, *Trinidad Village*, pp. 199–209.
56. Metraux, pp. 146–53; Herskovits, *Life in a Haitian Valley* (New York: Alfred A. Knopf, 1937), pp. 199–218; Ramos, *Negro in Brazil*, pp. 91–92; Verger, *Notes*, p. 507; Da Costa Eduardo, p. 122.
57. Herskovits, "The Southernmost Outposts of New World Africanisms," in *New World Negro*, p. 212; Bastide, "L'Axexe," in *Les Afro-Americains*, pp. 105–10; Da Costa Eduardo, p. 121; Pierson, p. 287; Patterson, p. 204; Simpson, p. 202; Beckwith, pp. 70–87.
58. Herskovits, *New World Negro*, pp. 268–75, 315–19; Silvia W. De-Groot, *Djuka Society and Social Change* (Assen, Netherlands: Koninklejhe Van Gorcum & Co., 1969), pp. 27–29; Jean Hurault, *Africains de Guyane* (Paris: Editions Mouton, 1970), pp. 29–33, 36; Herskovits, "Note sur la divination judiciaire par le cadavre en Guyane Hollandaise," in *Les Afro-Americains*, pp. 187–92.
59. Charles Leslie, *A New History of Jamaica*, cited in Patterson, pp. 196–97.
60. Parrinder, *West African Psychology*, pp. 38–40, 52–54, 61–62, 64; Bascom, *Yoruba of Southwestern Nigeria*, pp. 71–72; Parrinder, *West African Religion*, p. 114.
61. Octavio Da Costa Eduardo, pp. 109–10.
62. *Akra* corresponds to the Akan term *'kra*; *yorka* is a Kalinda Indian term. Herskovits, *New World Negro*, pp. 268–75, 315–19; De Groot, pp. 27–29; Hurault, *Africaines de Guyane*, pp. 29–33.
63. Herskovits, *New World Negro*, pp. 305–14; De Groot, pp. 23–25.
64. Patterson, pp. 187–92; Curtin, *Two Jamaicas*, pp. 23–41; Beckwith, pp. 85–156.

65. Pierson, pp. 254–58; Ignace, pp. 900–1; Simpson, pp. 22–23, 121–23, 169–72, 177–78.
66. Herskovits and Herskovits, *Trinidad Village*, pp. 199–209, 327; Simpson, pp. 53–54, 91, 147–52; see also Walter Mischel and Frances Mischel, "Psychological Aspects of Spirit Possession," *American Anthropologist*, 60 (1958): 246–60, a psychological study of the importance of drumming to spirit possession in *shango*; George Eaton Simpson, *Cult Music in Trinidad* (Folkways Ethnic Library Album No. FE 4478, 1961).
67. Morton Marks, "Uncovering Ritual Structure in Afro-American Music," in *Religious Movements in Contemporary America*, edited by Irving I. Zaretsky and Mark P. Leone (Princeton, N.J.: Princeton University Press, 1974), pp. 60–116.
68. Simpson, p. 169.
69. Melville J. Herskovits and Frances S. Herskovits, *Afro-Bahian Religious Songs* (Library of Congress Music Division, Recorded Sound Section, Album L-13; recorded 1941–42).
70. Bastide, *Religions Afro-Brésiliennes*, pp. 76–78; Bastide, *African Civilisations*, pp. 91–93; Da Costa Eduardo, pp. 104–7.
71. Pierson, p. 239. In a footnote to the same page, Pierson states: "It is also reported that on at least two occasions representatives of African chiefs arrived in Bahia from Ajuda, with which port Bahian officials were maintaining direct commercial relations." Harry Johnston notes that "Between 1850 and 1878 about four thousand to six thousand Brasilian 'emancipados' settled at Lagos and Wydah, and a few went to Angola" (*The Negro in the New World*, 1st publ. 1910 [New York: Johnson Reprint, 1969], p. 98n). See also Pierre Verger, "Influence du Bresil au Golfe du Benin," in *Les Afro-Americains*, pp. 11–104.
72. Bastide, *Religions Afro-Brésiliennes*, p. 64.
73. Ibid.; Pierre Verger, "Le culte des Vodouns d'Abomey aurait-il été apporte à S. Luiz do Maranhão par la mère du roi Ghézo?," *Les Afro-Americains*, pp. 157–60.
74. Mintz and Price, p. 29; Bascom, "Yoruba Acculturation in Cuba," pp. 166–67.
75. "Maroon" comes from the Spanish *cimarrón*, a word for runaway domestic animals that have become wild. For treatments of maroon societies see Bastide, *African Civilisations*, pp. 46–71; Richard Price, ed., *Maroon Societies* (Garden City, N.Y.: Doubleday, Anchor Books, 1973). In 1663 Portuguese Jews who had emigrated to Dutch Guiana sent their slaves to hide in the forests when the tax

collector came around to levy taxes. The slaves neglected to return. (Bastide, *African Civilisations*, p. 50.)

Chapter 2

1. *The Poems of Phillis Wheatley*, edited by Julian D. Mason, Jr. (Chapel Hill: University of North Carolina Press, 1966), p. 7.
2. Benjamin Bussey Thatcher, *Memoir of Phillis Wheatley* (Boston, 1834; New York, 1834), p. 13.
3. Charles Ball, *Fifty Years in Chains* (New York: Dover Publications, 1970), p. 265; reprint of *Slavery in the United States: A Narrative of the Life and Adventures of Charles Ball, A Black Man* (New York, 1837).
4. Ball, *Fifty Years*, p. 263.
5. Ibid., p. 219. Ball also describes the native Africans as "revengeful, and unforgiving," as well as feeling "indignant at the servitude that is imposed upon them."
6. *Memoir of Mrs. Chloe Spear: A Native of Africa . . .* (Boston, 1832), p. 17.
7. Fredrika Bremer, *The Homes of the New World*, 2 vols. (New York, 1853), 2: 484–85.
8. Leonard L. Haynes, Jr., *The Negro Community Within American Protestantism, 1619–1844* (Boston: Christopher Publishing House, 1953), pp. 32–33.
9. *Drums and Shadows*, Georgia Writers' Project, Works Projects Administration, reprint (Garden City, N.Y.: Doubleday, Anchor Books, 1972), pp. 136–37, 154; Charles Lyell, *A Second Visit to the United States of America*, 2 vols. (New York, 1850), 1: 266; "Autobiography of Omar ibn Said, Slave in North Carolina, 1831," *American Historical Review*, Vol. 30, pp. 787–95, especially pp. 793–94; for more information on Bilali and Old Tom, see Lydia Parrish, *Slave Songs of the Georgia Sea Islands* (New York: Creative Age Press, 1942), pp. 24–27.
10. Charles Colcock Jones, *The Religious Instruction of the Negroes in the United States* (Savannah, Ga., 1842), p. 125; *Drums and Shadows*, p. 134.
11. Octavio Da Costa Eduardo, pp. 46, 123.
12. For Herskovits' views, see *The Myth of the Negro Past* (Boston: Beacon Press, 1958); for Frazier's position, see *The Negro Church in America* (New York: Schocken Books, 1964), pp. 1–19, *The Negro*

Family in the United States (Chicago: University of Chicago Press, 1966), pp. 3–16, and *The Negro in the United States*, rev. ed. (New York: Macmillan, 1957), pp. 3–13. Other important comments on the debate can be found in *Afro-American Anthropology: Contemporary Perspectives*, edited by Norman E. Whitten, Jr. and John F. Szwed (New York: The Free Press, Macmillan, 1970). Also useful is Thomas Richard Frazier, "Analysis of Social Scientific Writing on American Negro Religion," 1967 Columbia University Ph.D. dissertation. A cogent attack on Herskovits' methodology is M. G. Smith's article, "The African Heritage in the Caribbean," in *Caribbean Studies: A Symposium*, edited by Vera Rubin (Seattle: University of Washington Press, 1957), pp. 34–46. Smith's attack is followed by a defense of Herskovits by George E. Simpson and Peter B. Hammond on pp. 46–53 of the same volume.

13. Herskovits, *Myth*, pp. xxviii–xxix, 20–32.
14. Ibid., pp. 6–9, 15–17.
15. Ibid., pp. 53–87, 122.
16. Ibid., pp. 86–105, 293.
17. Ibid., pp. 105–9, 293–94. The queen mother of the Dahomean king Glele was sold into slavery in Brazil during Glele's minority by his uncle, the regent. Upon Glele's accession he tried to find his mother, unsuccessfully.
18. Ibid., pp. 77–81, 294–96. Support for Herskovits' assertion that African speech patterns underlay the pidgin English of the slaves is presented by J. L. Dillard, *Black English: Its History and Usage in the United States* (New York: Random House, Vintage Books, 1973), pp. 39–138.
19. Herskovits, *Myth*, p. 296.
20. Ibid., pp. 141–42, 296–98.
21. Ibid., pp. 298–99. I have taken pains to outline Herskovits' position because I agree with Daniel Crowther that it is important "to direct attention to what Herskovits actually wrote, rather than to the sometimes naive, sometimes malicious misinterpretations of his position in secondary or tertiary sources" (quoted by Whitten and Szwed, p. 38).
22. Frazier, *Negro Family*, p. 7.
23. Frazier, *Negro Church*, pp. 1–16.
24. Ibid., pp. 1–2.
25. Ibid., pp. 2–3.
26. Frazier, *Negro Family*, pp. 7–8.
27. Frazier, *Negro Church*, p. 6.
28. Frazier, *Negro in the U.S.*, p. 3.

29. Ibid., p. 14.
30. Ibid., p. 21.
31. Herskovits, *Myth*, p. 207.
32. Arthur Huff Fauset, *Black Gods of the Metropolis* (Philadelphia: University of Pennsylvania Press, 1944), pp. 98–106.
33. Herskovits, *Myth*, p. xxiv.
34. Ibid.
35. The New Testament speaks of the Holy Spirit as a comforter and advocate, e.g., John 14:26.
36. Herskovits, *Myth*, pp. 232 35.
37. Ibid., p. 17.
38. Mark 1:8. I will return to the issue of spirit possession below. Here I only wish to stress the difference in the theologies reflecting the experience of possession by water spirits and baptism by the Holy Spirit.
39. See Charles A. Johnson, *The Frontier Camp Meeting* (Dallas, Texas: Southern Methodist University Press, 1955), pp. 56–62, and the description by Barton W. Stone of the scene at the Cane Ridge Meeting of 1801 quoted by Sidney Ahlstrom in *A Religious History of the American People* (New Haven: Yale University Press, 1972), pp. 434–35.
40. Frederick Morgan Davenport, *Primitive Traits in Religious Revivals* (New York: Macmillan, 1917), pp. 92–93, cited by Herskovits, *Myth*, pp. 230–31.
41. Herskovits, *Myth*, p. 231.
42. Hortense Powdermaker, *After Freedom* (New York: Atheneum, 1969), pp. 259–60; Herskovits, *Myth*, pp. 227–28.
43. John D. Long, *Pictures of Slavery in Church and State* (Philadelphia, 1857), p. 159.
44. Cited by Ulrich Bonnell Phillips, *American Negro Slavery* (Baton Rouge: Louisiana State University Press, 1966), pp. 316–17.
45. John Leland, *The Virginia Chronicle* (1790), p. 13, cited by Herbert S. Klein, *Slavery in the Americas, A Comparative Study of Virginia and Cuba* (Chicago: The University of Chicago Press, 1967), p. 120. For an extended description of black participation in a nineteenth-century camp meeting, see Fredrika Bremer, *Homes of the New World*, 1: 306–17.
46. Frederick Law Olmsted, *The Cotton Kingdom*, 2 vols. (New York, 1861), 1: 310–11. For a modern analysis of this old tradition of preaching style, see Bruce Rosenberg, *The Art of the American Folk Preacher* (New York: Oxford University Press, 1970).

47. Olmsted, *Cotton Kingdom*, 1: 312–13. I am not claiming that this style of preaching or ecstatic response was unique to black Christians in nineteenth-century America.

48. Erika Bourguignon, "Ritual Dissociation and Possession Belief in Caribbean Negro Religion," in *Afro-American Anthropology*, edited by Whitten and Szwed, p. 88.

49. K. Stewart, cited by I. M. Lewis, *Ecstatic Religion* (Baltimore, Md.: Penguin Books, 1971), p. 65.

50. Bourguignon, pp. 91–92.

51. *God Struck Me Dead: Religious Conversion Experiences and Autobiographies of Negro Ex-Slaves* (Social Science Source Documents No. 2, Fisk University Social Science Institute, Nashville, Tenn., 1945, mimeographed copy), p. 153.

52. Robert Anderson, *From Slavery to Affluence: Memoirs of Robert Anderson, Ex-Slave*, edited by Daisy Anderson Leonard (Steamboat Springs, Colo.: The Steamboat Pilot, 1927), pp. 24–26, 31.

53. Morgan Godwin, *The Negro's and Indian's Advocate* (London, 1680), cited by Dean J. Epstein, "African Music in British and French America," *The Musical Quarterly*, Vol. 59, No. 1 (1973), pp. 79–80.

54. John Sharpe, "Proposals for Erecting a School, Library and Chapel at New York," New York Historical Society, *Collections* (1880), p. 341, cited by Epstein, p. 80.

55. Alexander Hewatt, *An Historical Account of the Rise and Progress of the Colonies of South Carolina and Georgia* (London, 1779), 2: 100, 103, cited by Epstein, p. 81.

56. Sir Charles Lyell, *A Second Visit to the United States*, 1: 269–70.

57. John F. Watson, *Methodist Error . . .* (Trenton, N.J., 1819), pp. 28–31, cited by Eileen Southern, ed., *Readings in Black American Music* (New York: W.W. Norton & Co., 1971), pp. 62–64; see also Don Yoder, *Pennsylvania Spirituals* (Lancaster: Pennslvania Folklore Society, 1961), pp. 27–28.

58. Southern, *Readings*, p. 62.

59. Frederick Law Olmsted, *A Journey in the Seaboard Slave States* (New York, 1856), p. 449.

60. Daniel Alexander Payne, *Recollections of Seventy Years*, 1st publ. 1886 (New York: Arno Press and the New York Times, 1969), pp. 253–55.

61. Ibid., pp. 254–56.

62. John A. Lomax and Alan Lomax, *Folk Song U.S.A.* (New York: Duell, Sloan & Pearce, 1947), p. 335.

63. George E. Simpson, cited by Harold Courlander, *Negro Folk Music U.S.A.* (New York: Columbia University Press, 1963), p. 196; see Chapter 2, p. 37, for Simpson's description of "laboring in the spirit." Courlander comments: "The Jamaican revivalists have over-laid and disguised the African elements in their worship, and hold themselves aloof from the so-called African cults such as the Cumina. Nevertheless, they form a bridge between the ring shout in the United States and the openly acknowledged African-style cult activi-ties of the West Indies and, of course, Africa itself," pp. 196–97.

64. [William Francis Allen, Charles Pickard Ware, Lucy McKim Garrison], eds., *Slave Songs of the United States*, 1st publ. 1867 (New York: Peter Smith, 1951), pp. xii–xiv; see also, for more detailed descriptions of the ring shout, W. F. Allen, "The Negro Dialect," *Nation*, 1 (December 14, 1865): 744–45, reprinted in Bruce Jackson, ed., *The Negro and His Folklore in Nineteenth-Cen-tury Periodicals* (Austin: University of Texas Press, 1967), p. 79; and H. G. Spaulding, "Under the Palmetto," *Continental Monthly*, 4 (August 1863): 188–203, reprinted in Bernard Katz, ed., *The So-cial Implications of Early Negro Music in the United States* (New York: Arno Press and The New York Times, 1969), pp. 4–8; and Thomas Wentworth Higginson, *Army Life in a Black Regiment*, 1st publ. 1869 (Boston: Beacon Press, 1962), p. 17.

65. Courlander, *Negro Folk Music*, pp. 195–96; see also Eileen South-ern, *The Music of Black Americans: A History* (New York: W.W. Norton & Co., 1971), pp. 161–62.

66. Lorenzo Dow Turner, *Africanisms in the Gullah Dialect*, reprint (New York: Arno Press and The New York Times, 1969), p. 202. The Kaaba is "the small stone building at Mecca which is the chief object of pilgrimage of Mohamammmedans." *Sauwata*, derived from Arabic, means to run until exhausted.

67. *Drums and Shadows*, p. 133.

68. Ibid., p. 171. There were also variations of the ring shout called Rocking Daniel, Flower Dance and Down to the Mire, used in religious settings, described by Davenport, pp. 54–55, and by Cour-lander, p. 201.

69. "The shout is a fusion of two seemingly irreconcilable attitudes to-ward religious behavior. In most of Africa, dance, like singing and drumming, is an integral part of supplication . . . In the Euro-Chris-tian tradition, however, dancing in church is generally regarded as a profane act. The ring-shout in the United States provides a scheme which reconciles both principles. The circular movement, shuffling

steps, and stamping conform to African traditions of supplication, while by definition this activity is not recognized as a 'dance.' However, if one violates the compromise by going too far, he has committed an irreverent act" (Courlander, p. 195). To cross one's feet is to dance and would violate decorum.

70. Charles Stearn, *Narrative of Henry Box Brown* (Boston, 1849), pp. 17-18; Samuel Miller Lawton, "The Religious Life of South Carolina Coastal and Sea Island Negroes," Ph.D. dissertation, George Peabody College for Teachers, 1939, pp. 143-44; Higginson, pp. 205-206.

71. Letter to *Dwight's Journal of Music* (November 8, 1862), reprinted in Katz, p. 10.

72. Cited by Southern, *Music of Black Americans*, p. 200.

73. I will return to the theology of the spirituals and their role in slave religion in a subsequent chapter.

74. Ibid., pp. 172-224; Marshall Sterns, *The Story of Jazz* (New York: New American Library, Mentor, 1958), pp. 92-103. The specific debate over African vs. European origins for the Negro spirituals has used up even more ink and paper than the discussion over Africanisms in American culture generally. There is no need to review here the huge amount of literature on the spirituals. For a recent treatment of this issue, with references to the literature, see Part 1 of John Lovell's *Black Song: The Forge and the Flame* (New York: Macmillan, 1972). On the subject of early collections of Negro spirituals, reference has already been made to Katz; Higginson; and Allen, McKim and Ware. See also Southern's collection of *Readings in Black American Music*, which reprints accounts of slave song, as does Bruce Jackson's *Negro and His Folklore*. See also an important article by Alan Lomax, "The Homogeneity of African-Afro-American Musical Style," in *Afro-American Anthropology*, edited by Whitten and Szwed, pp. 181-201 in which Lomax applies cantometrics (a technique invented by him and Victor Grauer for measuring traits of song performance) to compare African and Afro-American styles of singing. Disagreeing with those who find little African influence in Afro-American spirituals, Lomax says that "Cantometric analysis points conclusively in another direction—that the main traditions of Afro-American song, especially those of the old-time congregational spiritual—are derived from the main African song style model. European song style did influence the African tradition in America in regard to melodic form and, of course, tex-

tual content. In most other respects. Afro-American song has hewed
to the main dynamic line of the principal African tradition" (p. 197).
75. The fullest published account of the history of voodoo is Robert
Tallant's *Voodoo in New Orleans* (London: Collier-Macmillan,
1962), which draws upon most of the earlier sources. I am indebted
to an unpublished seminar paper done for the Yale History Department by Charles Hegler, who compared voodoo in New Orleans to
vaudou in Haiti. For an encyclopedic treatment of hoodoo belief and
practice, see Newbell Niles Puckett, *The Magic and Folk Beliefs of
the Southern Negro*, 1st publ. as *Folk Beliefs of the Southern Negro*
(Chapel Hill: University of North Carolina Press 1926; New York:
Dover, 1969); and Henry M. Hyatt, ed., *Hoodoo-Conjuration-
Witchcraft-Rootwork* (Washington, D.C.: American University
Bookstore, 1970); see also Jackson, especially his appendices, where
he lists nineteenth-century periodical articles on Negro folklore; and
the "Ethnology and Folklore" column which appeared frequently in
issues of the *Southern Workman* from 1894 to 1900.
76. A. B. Ellis, "On Vodu-Worship," *The Popular Science Monthly*, 38
(November 1890–April 1891): 651–58.
77. Tallant, pp. 19–22; Lyle Saxon, Edward Dreyer, and Robert Tallant, compilers, *Gumbo Ya-Ya* (Cambridge, Mass.: Riverside Press,
1945; New York: Johnson Reprints Corporation, 1969, p. 225).
78. Tallant, p. 67.
79. Tallant, p. 111. In Haiti and Africa, *Legba*, the messenger between
man and gods, enables divine-human communication to take place
and receives the first praise and offerings at the liturgical rites. In
this sense, he opens the way.
80. Ibid. Puckett notes, "in New Orleans a red ribbon was worn about
the neck in honor of 'Monsieur Agoussou' . . . which demon especially loved that color" (Puckett, p. 221).
81. Helen Pitkin, *An Angel by Brevet* (Philadelphia, 1904), pp. 6, 182–
212; cited by Puckett, pp. 192–96.
82. Courlander, *The Drum and the Hoe*, p. 321.
83. Tallant, pp. 44–105; George W. Cable, "Creole Slave Songs," *The
Century Magazine*, 31 (April 1886): 807–28, reprinted in Katz, pp.
47–68.
84. Hegler, pp. 13–14; the three accounts are J. W. Buel, *Metropolitan
Life Unveiled*, an anonymous account entitled *Souvenirs de l'America*
and C. D. Warner, *Studies in the South and West*. Buel and Warner
are quoted at length by Tallant, as is the anonymous account by

Henry Castellanos in *New Orleans As It Was* (New Orleans, 1895), pp. 91–96.
85. Zora Neale Hurston, *Mules and Men*, 1st publ. 1935 (New York and Evanston, Ill.: Harper & Row, 1970), pp. 239–60; see also Herskovits' comments on Hurston's initiation experience in *Myth*, pp. 245–49.
86. The unique ambience of New Orleans is demonstrated by such institutions as the Mardi Gras Carnival and the Place Congo, a square in the city, where slaves were permitted to gather on Sunday afternoons to dance, sing, and drum. Place Congo was in existence until approximately 1843. For a description of Place Congo and the dances performed there, see Cable, "The Dance in Place Congo," *The Century Magazine*, 31 (February 1886): 517–32, reprinted in Katz, pp. 32–47.
87. Mary A. Owen, "Among the Voodoos," *Proceedings of the International Folk-Lore Congress*, 1891 (London, 1892), p. 240.
88. It was not uncommon for conjurers throughout the South to advertise themselves as New Orleans–trained.
89. The role of the conjurer and conjuring during slavery will be discussed in a succeeding chapter.
90. Herskovits, *Myth*, p. 249.
91. Cited in *Gumbo Ya-Ya*, p. 250.
92. Puckett, p. 320.
93. Ibid., p. 315.
94. *Gumbo Ya-Ya*, p. 557.
95. Castellanos, p. 94.
96. Puckett, p. 201.
97. Mary Owen, p. 230.
98. Cited by Puckett, pp. 232–34.
99. Ruth Bass, "Mojo," *Scribner's Magazine*, 87 (1930): 83–90, reprinted in *Mother Wit from the Laughing Barrel: Readings in the Interpretation of Afro-American Folklore*, edited by Alan Dundes (Englewood Cliffs, N.J.: Prentice-Hall, 1973), pp. 385–86.
100. Ibid., pp. 386–87.
101. Ibid.; see also Edward L. Pierce, "The Freedmen at Port Royal," *Atlantic Monthly*, 12 (September 1863): 303.
102. Loudell F. Snow, "I Was Born Just Exactly with the Gift," *Journal of American Folklore*, 86 (July–September 1973): 277.
103. Ruth Bass, "Little Man," in Dundes, p. 394.
104. *Drums and Shadows*, p. 184.
105. Bass, "Little Man," p. 395; Puckett, pp. 104–7; Susan Showers,

NOTES TO PAGES 85–97   343

"A Weddin' and a Buryin' in the Black Belt," *New England Magazine*, 18 (1898): 478–83.

106. *Drums and Shadows*, p. 128; Frances Butler Leigh, *Ten Years on a Georgia Plantation Since the War* (London, 1883), p. 77.

107. Puckett, pp. 257, 319, 381; *Drums and Shadows*, pp. 117, 121, 178; Herskovits, *Myth*, p. 237.

108. The victim of a hag or witch "may gain possession of the tormentor's skin and sprinkle it with pepper and salt, so that it cannot be used." The *Southern Workman* printed a story "of a hag who finds her skin on the doorstep thus doctored, and after trying it on several times and finding it smarts and burns, she dances wildly about crying 'O Skinny, Skinny, Skinny, don't you know me?' " "Hags and Their Ways," *Southern Workman*, 23 (February 1894): 27.

109. Klein, p. 101; an analogous New World example of the amenability of Catholicism to syncretism with "pagan" beliefs is the Virgin of Guadalupe, whose shrine was built on the site of the most important shrine to Tonantzin, Aztec goddess and mother of the gods.

110. Herskovits, *Myth*, p. 120.

111. Guion G. Johnson, *A Social History of the Sea Islands*, p. 127; see Herskovits, *Myth*, p. 117.

112. Curtin, *Atlantic Slave Trade*, pp. 88–89; C. Vann Woodward, "Southern Slaves in the World of Thomas Malthus," in his collection of essays *American Counterpoint* (Boston: Little, Brown & Co., 1971), p. 82.

113. Woodward, pp. 83–84.

114. Curtin, cited by Woodward, p. 82.

115. Woodward, pp. 84–86.

116. Ibid., pp. 87–89. It should also be noted that "the phenomenal rate of increase among Afro-Americans in the South" occurred "against the background of an unparalleled rate of increase among the white population of the United States as a whole . . . " (p. 89).

117. Ibid., p. 102.

Chapter 3

1. Gomes Eannes De Azurara, *Chronicle*, 1: 50–51.

2. Ibid., I, 81–82, 84–85.

3. Cited in Marcus W. Jernegan, "Slavery and Conversion in the American Colonies," *American Historical Review*, Vol. 21, No. 3 (April 1916), p. 508.

4. Ibid.

5. In 1682 John Barbot unfavorably compared Protestant efforts to convert the slaves in America with those of Catholics: "In this particular, I must say, the *Roman* catholicks of the *American* plantations are much more commendable . . . ." (Barbot, *Description of Guinea*, pp. 270–71). Bishop Berkeley in 1731 stated: "It must be owned our reformed planters with respect to the natives and the slaves, might learn from the Church of Rome how it is [to] their interest and duty to behave. Both French and Spaniards, take care to instruct both them and their Negroes in the Popish religion, to the reproach of those who profess a better." Quoted by Charles Colcock Jones, *The Religious Instruction of the Negroes in the United States* (Savannah, Ga., 1842), p. 28. In the North American colonies it does not appear that the Catholics were any more proficient than the Protestants at converting slaves. See the comments by John Carroll quoted on p. 112.
6. Barbot, p. 271.
7. Ibid.
8. Helen Tunnicliff Catterall, ed., *Judicial Cases Concerning American Slavery and the Negro*, 4 vols. (Washington, D.C.: The Carnegie Institution, 1926), I, 55*n*.
9. Jernegan, p. 506. In spite of colonial legislation, some slaveholders were still wary that baptism would free their slaves, so in 1729 several appeals were sent to England on the subject. The Crown-Attorney and Solicitor-General ruled in agreement with the colonial legislatures (Charles Vernon Bruner, "The Religious Instruction of the Slaves in the Ante-bellum South," Ph.D. dissertation, George Peabody College of Teachers, 1933, p. 35).
10. Frank J. Klingberg, *An Appraisal of the Negro in Colonial South Carolina: A Study in Americanization* (Washington, D.C.: The Associated Publishers, 1941), p. 7.
11. Ibid., p. 6.
12. Jernegan, p. 508, 508*n*. Peter H. Wood, in an excellent study of slavery in colonial South Carolina, states that the clergy's "insistence upon the Fourth Commandment . . . conflicted directly with the Negroes' brief hours for rest and fraternization on the one hand and with their meager chance for self-sufficiency and betterment on the other." Thus, he holds, clergymen were in the position of arguing "increasingly for removing . . . these vestiges of black autonomy." See Peter H. Wood, *Black Majority: Negroes in Colonial South Carolina from 1670 through the Stono Rebellion* (New York: Alfred A. Knopf, 1974), pp. 138–39.

13. Quoted by Edgard Legare Pennington, *Thomas Bray's Associates and Their Work Among the Negroes* (Worcester, Mass.: The American Antiquarian Society, 1939), pp. 38–39.

14. Cited by Jones, *Religious Instruction*, p. 28.

15. Le Jau to the Sec. of the S.P.G., March 22, 1708/9, printed in *The Carolina Chronicle of Dr. Francis Le Jau, 1706–1717*, edited by Frank J. Klingberg (Berkeley and Los Angeles: University of California, 1956), p. 55.

16. [Edmund Gibson], *A Letter of the Lord Bishop of London* . . . (London, 1727), p. 14. See also the sermon of William Fleetwood, Bishop of Asaph, delivered in 1711 before the S.P.G. in London, reprinted in Klingberg, *Anglican Humanitarianism*, pp. 203–4.

17. Morgan Godwin, *The Negro's and Indian's Advocate, Suing for Their Admission into the Church: Or A Persuasive to the Instructing and Baptizing of Negro's and Indians in our Plantations* (London, 1680). Godwin argued that "Atheism and Irreligion were the true Parents" of the notion that slaves are *"no Men"* (Godwin, p. 3).

18. Cotton Mather, *The Negro Christianized: An Essay to Excite and Assist that Good Work, the Instruction of Negro Servants in Christianity* (Boston, 1706), pp. 4–6; Godwin, p. 9.

19. Peter Kalm, *Travels Into North America*, 2nd ed., reprinted in Vol. 13 of *A General Collection of the Best and Most Interesting Voyages and Travels*, edited by John Pinkerton (London, 1812), p. 503.

20. Klingberg, *Anglican Humanitarianism*, p. 217. Secker's whole sermon is reprinted in Klingberg.

21. Le Jau to the Sec. of the S.P.G. September 18, 1711, *Carolina Chronicle*, p. 102.

22. *Historical Collections Relating to the American Colonial Church*, edited by William Stevens Perry, 4 vols. (Hartford, Conn., 1870) 1: 315.

23. Gibson, *Letter*, p. 11.

24. Le Jau to the Sec., S.P.G., June 13, 1710, *Carolina Chronicle*, p. 76.

25. Thomas Secker, Sermon before the S.P.G., 1740/1, reprinted in Klingberg, *Anglican Humanitarianism*, p. 223.

26. Winthrop D. Jordan, *White Over Black; American Attitudes Toward the Negro, 1550–1812* (Baltimore, Md.: Penguin Books, 1969), p. 191.

27. Perry, 1: 301.

28. Quoted by Frederick Dalcho, *An Historical Account of the Protestant Episcopal Church in South Carolina* (Charleston, 1820), pp. 336–37.

29. Cited in [Charles Frederick Pascoe], *Classified Digest of the Records of the Society for the Propagation of the Gospel in Foreign Parts 1701–1892* (London, 1893), pp. 12, 30, 28.

30. Hugh Jones, *The Present State of Virginia* (1724), quoted by Pennington, p. 32.

31. Perry, 1: 325.

32. Perry, 1: 267, 277–78.

33. Perry, 1: 261–327; 4: 190–229, 292, 304–7.

34. Perry, 1: 344. I have found no evidence that the proposal was accepted.

35. Cotton Mather, *Magnalia Christi* (1702), quoted by Jernegan, p. 513*n*; Cotton Mather, *Life of John Eliot*, quoted by Jernegan, p. 513.

36. Richard Baxter, *Christian Directory*, quoted by Jones, p. 7; *Athenian Oracle* (1705), quoted by Lorenzo Johnston Greene, *The Negro in Colonial New England* (New York: Atheneum, 1968), pp. 259–60.

37. Greene, p. 257; see also pp. 265–66.

38. Ibid., p. 267.

39. Ibid., pp. 278–79. Hopkins had six or seven black members in his church in 1772, while Stiles had seventy blacks in a congregation of over five hundred (Greene, p. 269). For the full story of Hopkins' scheme, see Leonard I. Sweet, *Black Images of America, 1784–1870* (New York: Norton, 1976), pp. 23–26.

40. Greene, pp. 280–89.

41. Thomas E. Drake, *Quakers and Slavery in America* (New Haven: Yale University Press, 1950), p. 6.

42. Ibid., pp. 9–10.

43. Ibid., p. 11. The Germantown Quakers' remonstrance is reprinted in H. Shelton Smith, Robert T. Handy, and Lefferts A. Loetscher, eds., *American Christianity*, 2 vols. (New York: Charles Scribner's Sons, 1960), 1: 181–82.

44. Jernegan, p. 513; Henry J. Cadbury, "Negro Membership in the Society of Friends," *Journal of Negro History*, Vol. 21, No. 2 (April 1936), pp. 172–73; Thomas E. Drake, "Joseph Drinker's Plea for the Admission of Colored People to the Society of Friends, 1795," *Journal of Negro History*, Vol. 32, No. 1 (January 1947), p. 111.

45. Le Jau to the Sec., S.P.G., Feb. 1, 1709/10, *Carolina Chronicle*, p. 69; Le Jau to Sec., June 13, 1710, ibid., p. 77.

46. John Carroll, "Report for the Eminent Cardinal Antonelli Concerning the State of Religion in the United Stated of America," in *Documents of American Catholic History*, John Tracy Ellis, ed., 2 vols.

(Chicago: Henry Regnery Company, Logos paperback edition, 1967), 1: 148–49. For my comments on differences between the religious experience of black Catholics and black Protestants, see Chapter 5.

47. Roger Baudier, *The Catholic Church in Louisiana* (New Orleans, 1939), p. 75; John T. Gillard, *Colored Catholics in the United States* (Baltimore, Md.: The Josephite Press, 1941), pp. 64–67.

48. Gillard, pp. 65–67; V. Alton Moody, *Slavery on Louisiana Sugar Plantations;* reprinted from *The Louisiana Historical Quarterly* (April 1924), pp. 90–92.

49. A sense of the difficulties and meager successes of the S.P.G. missionaries may be gained from reading the abstracts of their letters prepared by the society itself. An abstract of a letter dated June 4, 1737, and written by Lewis Jones, missionary to South Carolina, is instructive: "That since his last of the 3rd of June 1735, he had baptized thirtynine Children, one of whom was a *Mulatto*, and another a *Negro*, but his Number of Communicants doth not exceed twenty; and once in five Weeks he preaches at one place, and once in six Weeks at another place in his extensive Parish very remote from the Church; that the pious Zeal of the venerable Society, and of his worthy Diocesan for promoting Christian Knowledge among the *Negroes* meets with but a cold Reception from them, but he had himself a *Negroe* Girl of seven Years of Age, that reads very prettily in the New Testament, and a *Negroe* Boy of five Years of Age, that spells well, and is apt to learn." Klingberg, *Appraisal of the Negro*, p. 68.

50. *Carolina Chronicle*, p. 76.

51. Klingberg, *Appraisal of the Negro*, p. 12.

52. Jones *Religious Instruction*, p. 10.

53. Klingberg, *Appraisal of the Negro*, p. 105.

54. Pennington, pp. 29–30.

55. Klingberg, *Appraisal of the Negro*, pp. 69–70.

56. Pennington, pp. 29–30.

57. Klingberg, *Appraisal of the Negro*, p. 114.

58. Ibid., pp. 106–7.

59. Pennington, p. 31.

60. Klingberg, *Appraisal of the Negro*, p. 119.

61. Pennington, pp. 74–75; Faith Vibert, "The Society for the Propagation of the Gospel in Foreign Parts: Its Works for the Negroes in North America Before 1783," *Journal of Negro History*, Vol. 18, No. 2 (April 1933), p. 176.

62. Ottolenghe to the Reverend Mr. Smith, Dec. 4, 1751, quoted in

James B. Lawrence, "Religious Education of the Negro in the Colony of Georgia," *Georgia Historical Quarterly*, Vol. 14, No. 1 (March 1930), p. 48.
63. Quoted by Lawrence, p. 52.
64. See Jordan, pp. 210–11. James Gignillat, a Huguenot minister in Santee, S.C., "said that the Roman Catholic Priests Christened all the Negroes that went into their midst" and "that he was willing to do the same," a policy which the S.P.G. did not adopt. See Klingberg, *Appraisal of the Negro*, p. 24n; Wood, p. 143.
65. Gibson, *Letter*, pp. 17–18.
66. Klingberg, *Appraisal of the Negro*, p. 24n.
67. Klingberg, *Anglican Humanitarianism*, p. 217.
68. Perry, 1: 327.
69. Klingberg, *Appraisal of the Negro*, p. 56.
70. *Carolina Chronicle*, p. 121. In February 1713 Le Jau gave an account of a Christian slave who had been so brutally punished for losing a load of rice that he committed suicide. Le Jau interpreted epidemics and other disasters as God's punishment for such cruelty. See Vibert, p. 178; Klingberg, *Appraisal of the Negro*, p. 19.
71. Francis Varnod, to the S.P.G., 1724, quoted by Klingberg, *Appraisal of the Negro*, p. 56.
72. Perry, 5: 48; Pennington, pp. 64–78; Klingberg, *Appraisal of the Negro*, p. 5n.
73. Pennington, p. 25.
74. Pennington, pp. 42–43. Apparently about two hundred blacks from Norfolk and Princess Anne counties gathered one Sunday during church and chose leaders for a plot; when discovered, four of the leaders were executed. See Jerome W. Jones, "The Established Virginia Church and the Conversion of Negroes and Indians, 1620–1760," *Journal of Negro History*, Vol. 46, No. 1 (January 1961), pp. 12–23.
75. Klingberg, *Appraisal of the Negro*, pp. 46–47.
76. Ibid., p. 89.
77. Ibid., p. 16.
78. *Carolina Chronicle*, pp. 76–77, 120.
79. Pennington, pp. 44–45.
80. Ibid., p. 25.
81. For interesting suggestions on the acculturation of slaves, see Chapters 2, 3, and 5 in Gerald W. Mullins, *Flight and Rebellion: Slave Resistance in Eighteenth-Century Virginia* (New York: Oxford University Press, 1972), and Herskovits' Introduction to *Accultura-*

tion in the Americas, edited by Sol Tax (New York: Cooper Square Publishers, Inc., 1967), pp. 55–57; see also Chapter 2 of this book.

82. Klingberg, *Anglican Humanitarianism*, pp. 122–23. See also Jordan, p. 212. Christianizing a slave made him less alien and, to a degree, more like the white colonist. While slaveholders and Christian missionaries, with the exception of the Friends, continually emphasized that this likeness involved no equality on any level but the spiritual, the admission of spiritual equality opened the way for religious reciprocity, always conditioned by the situation of slavery but nonetheless real.

83. "The Dawn of the New Day" is the title of Woodson's second chapter in *The History of the Negro Church* (Washington, D.C.: Associated Publishers, 1945).

84. Quoted by Jones, *Religious Instruction*, p. 34.

85. Cited in Jordan, p. 213.

86. Cited by Edwin Scott Gaustad, *The Great Awakening in New England* (Chicago: Quadrangle Books, 1957), p. 35.

87. Green, p. 276. For a similar reaction, see Perry, 3: 357.

88. Charles Chauncy, *Seasonable Thoughts on the State of Religion in New England* (Boston, 1743), quoted by Jordan, p. 212.

89. For an account of the spread of the revival in the South, see Wesley M. Gewhehr, *The Great Awakening in Virginia, 1740–1790* (Durham, N.C.: Duke University Press, 1930), Chapter X, "The Evangelicals and Slavery"; see also John B. Boles, *The Great Revival, 1787–1805* (The University Press of Kentucky, 1972).

90. Jones, *Religious Instruction*, pp. 37–38.

91. Cited in George William Pilcher, "Samuel Davies and the Instruction of Negroes in Virginia," *The Virginia Magazine of History and Biography*, Vol. 79, No. 3 (July 1966), p. 300.

92. Gewhehr, p. 237.

93. Edwin Scott Gaustad, *Historical Atlas of Religion in America* (New York: Harper & Row, 1962) pp. 9–13, 74–75; Jones, *Religious Instruction*, pp. 39–40; Joseph B. Earnest, *The Religious Development of the Negro in Virginia* (Charlottesville, Va.: The Michie Company, 1914), p. 48.

94. Jones, *Religious Instruction*, pp. 40, 53; W.E.B. Du Bois, *The Negro Church* (Atlanta, Ga.: Atlanta University Press, 1903), pp. 19–20.

95. Jones, *Religious Instruction*, p. 53; William Warren Sweet, *Story of Religion in America* (New York: Harper, 1930), p. 420; William Warren Sweet, *Religion in the Development of American Culture, 1765–1840* (New York: Charles Scribner's Sons, 1952), p. 279.

96. David Benedict, *A General History of the Baptist Denomination in America* (New York, 1848), p. 739.

97. I am indebted to Susan Solomon for her unpublished seminar paper, "Evangelicalism and Moralism in the 18th Century South," Yale University, 1969, in which she describes the different catechetical attitudes of Anglicans and Evangelicals toward the slaves; John Thompson, *The Life of John Thompson, A Fugitive Slave* (Worcester, Mass., 1856), pp. 18–19. For an example of the influence of conversion upon a planter's attitude toward his slaves' religious life, see Louis Morton, *Robert Carter of Nomini Hall* (Williamsburg, Va.: Colonial Williamsburg Inc., 1941), pp. 239–42.

98. Jernegan, p. 515.

99. Luther P. Jackson, "Religious Development of the Negro in Virginia, From 1760 to 1860," *Journal of Negro History*, Vol. 16, No. 2 (April 1931), p. 176; Jernegan, p. 515; Robert B. Semple, *A History of the Rise and Progress of the Baptists in Virginia* (Richmond, 1810), p. 355; Virginia Writers' Project, *The Negro in Virginia* (New York: Hastings House, 1940), p. 103; Lemuel Burkitt and Jesse Read, *A Concise History of the Kehukee Baptist Association* (Halifax [N.C.], 1803), pp. 258–59.

100. Semple, p. 128; Garnett Ryland, *The Baptists of Virginia, 1699–1926* (Richmond, Va.: Virginia Baptist Board of Missions and Education, 1955), p. 155.

101. Walter H. Brooks, "The Evolution of the Negro Baptist Church," *Journal of Negro History*, Vol. 7, No. 1 (January 1922), p. 103; Benedict (1850), p. 779.

102. J. H. Spencer, *History of Kentucky Baptists*, 2 vols. (n.p., 1886) 2: 654–55.

103. *Acts and Proceedings of the General Assembly of the Presbyterian Church in the U.S.A. in the Year 1801* (Philadelphia, 1801), p. 15; Edgar W. Knight, "Notes on John Chavis," *The North Carolina Historical Review*, Vol. 7, No. 3 (July 1930), pp. 326–45.

104. Woodson, *History of the Negro Church*, p. 47; Jackson, "Religious Development," pp. 184–85.

105. John Spencer Bassett, *Slavery in the State of North Carolina*, Johns Hopkins Studies in Historical and Political Science, Series XVII, No. 7–8 (Baltimore, Md.: Johns Hopkins Press, 1899), pp. 57–58.

106. John Rippon, *The Baptist Annual Register*, 1790–1793 (n.p., n.d.), p. 105.

107. Jones, *Religious Instruction*, p. 58; W. Harrison Daniel, "Virginia

Baptists and the Negro in the Antebellum Era," *Journal of Negro History*, Vol. 56, No. 1 (January 1971), pp. 2–3.

108. Ibid.

109. Donald G. Mathews, *Slavery and Methodism; A Chapter in American Morality* (Princeton, N.J.: Princeton University Press, 1965), pp. 64, 64*n*, 65, 65*n*.

110. Robert E. Park, "The Conflict and Fusion of Cultures with Special Reference to the Negro," *Journal of Negro History*, Vol. 4, No. 2 (April 1919), p. 120; Benedict [1850 ed.], p. 664; James M. Simms, *The First Colored Baptist Church in North America* (Philadelphia, 1888), pp. 36–39.

111. Jones, *Religious Instruction*, pp. 139–40; see also Richard C. Wade, *Slavery in the Cities* (New York: Oxford University Press, 1964), pp. 160–73.

112. Jackson, "Religious Development," p. 195*n*; Daniel, p. 4.

113. Jackson, "Religious Development," pp. 227*n*, 227–31.

114. Semple, pp. 114–15.

115. Walter H. Brooks, "The Priority of the Silver Bluff Church and Its Promoters," *Journal of Negro History*, Vol. 7, No. 2 (April 1922), pp. 172–75, 182–83; I.E. Bill, *Fifty Years With the Baptist Ministers and Churches of the Maritime Provinces of Canada* (Saint John, N.B., 1880), pp. 19–26.

116. Rippon, pp. 332–35.

117. Ibid., p. 545; Brooks, "Priority of Silver Bluff," pp. 184–90.

118. Rippon, pp. 340–41; Benedict, p. 740.

119. Rippon, pp. 263, 342, 540–41; Benedict, p. 741.

120. For the story of several other African Baptist churches, see Jackson, "Religious Development," pp. 188–92.

121. Leah Townsend, *South Carolina Baptists, 1670–1805* (Florence, S.C.: The Florence Printing Company, 1935), p. 258.

122. See Appendix, "Methodist Rules Concerning Slavery," in Mathews, pp. 293–99; Jackson, "Religious Instruction," p. 173*n*; Gewehr, pp. 244–48.

123. *The Journal and Letters of Francis Asbury*, edited by Elmer T. Clark, J. Manning Potts, and Jacob S. Payton, 3 vols (Nashville, Tenn.: Abingdon Press, 1958), 2: 151, 284, 591.

124. Earnest, p. 52; among the Presbyterians, David Rice and, among the Baptists, John Leland and David Barrow were prominent antislavery evangelicals. See Gewehr, pp. 238–39. See also Andrew E. Murray, *Presbyterians and the Negro—A History* (Philadelphia: Presbyterian Historical Society, 1966); W. Harrison Daniel, "Vir-

ginia Baptists and the Negro in the Early Republic," *The Virginia Magazine of History and Biography*, Vol. 80, No. 1 (January 1972) pp. 65–69.

125. Jones, *Religious Instruction*, p. 48; Jackson, "Religious Development," p. 196.
126. Ulrich B. Phillips, *Plantation and Frontier Documents: 1649–1863*, 2 vols. (Cleveland, Ohio: Arthur H. Clark, 1909) 2: 93; "Eighteenth Century Slave Advertisements," *Journal of Negro History*, Vol. 1, No. 2 (April 1916), pp. 202–4. Narratives of fugitive slaves frequently spoke of the decision to escape in terms of a religious conversion. Perhaps this was more than literary convention.
127. Jackson, "Religious Development," pp. 172–73.
128. Mullin, pp. 149, 158–60. Mullin argues that Gabriel's rebellion had less religious overtones than did either Vesey's or Turner's.
129. Department of Education, *Special Report of the Commissioner of Education* (Washington, D.C.: Government Printing Office, 1871), pp. 307, 383.
130. Robert W. Fogel and Stanley L. Engerman, *Time on the Cross* (Boston: Little, Brown & Company, 1974), pp. 24–25; Philip D. Curtin, "The Slave Trade and the Atlantic Basin," in *Key Issues in the Afro-American Experience*, edited by Nathan I. Huggins, Martin Kilson, and Daniel M. Fox, 2 vols. (New York: Harcourt, Brace, Jovanovich, 1971), 1: 93.
131. Jones, *Religious Instruction*, p. 64.

Chapter 4

1. Jones, *Religious Instruction*, p. 176.
2. *Proceedings of the Meeting in Charleston, S.C., May 13–15, 1845, On the Religious Instruction of the Negroes* (Charleston, S.C., 1845), pp. 6–7.
3. Jones, *Religious Instruction*, p. 79; Luther P. Jackson, "Religious Instruction of Negroes, 1830–1860, With Special Reference to South Carolinia," *Journal of Negro History*, Vol. 15, No. 1 (January 1930), p. 84.
4. Lewis M. Purifoy, Jr., "The Methodist Episcopal Church, South and Slavery, 1844–1865," (Ph.D. dissertation, University of North Carolina, Chapel Hill, 1965), pp. 127–28; Jones, *Religious Instruction*, p. 69; *Second Annual Report of the Missionary to the Negroes in Liberty County, Ga.* (Charleston, 1835), p. 11.

NOTES TO PAGES 155-164   353

5. Jones, *Religious Instruction*, pp. 70–72, 77–79.
6. James Stacy, *History of Midway Church* (Newman, Ga. [1899]), pp. 168–70.
7. *Proceedings of the Charleston Meeting, May 13–15, 1845* (Charleston, S.C., 1845), pp. 6–7.
8. Jones, *Religious Instruction*, pp. 221–22.
9. Ibid., pp. 97–99.
10. Quoted by Bruner, pp. 112–13.
11. Jones, *Religious Instruction*, pp. 86, 192; *Third Annual Report, Liberty County Association* (1836), pp. 14–15.
12. Jones, *Religious Instruction*, p. 80.
13. Mathews, p. 72.
14. *Fifth Annual Report, Liberty County Association*, p. 23.
15. Purifoy, p. 124.
16. Cited by Charles Deems, *Annals of Southern Methodism for 1856* (Nashville, Tenn., 1857) p. 207.
17. Bruner, p. 110.
18. *Third Annual Report, Liberty County Association*, p. 20.
19. R. Q. Mallard, *Plantation Life Before Emancipation* (Richmond, Va., 1892), p. 117.
20. Jones, *Religious Instruction*, pp. 68, 72, 79–80, 82–83; 230–31; see also Thomas S. Clay, *Detail of a Plan for the Moral Improvement of Negroes on Plantations* (n.p., 1833).
21. Jones's *Catechism* quoted by Mason Crum, *Gullah: Negro Life in the Carolina Sea Islands* (Durham, N.C.: Duke University Press, 1940), pp. 204–5.
22. See 'A Narrative of the Conspiracy and Intended Insurrection, Amongst a Portion of the Negroes in the State of South Carolina in the Year 1822," in *The Trial Record of Denmark Vesey*, edited by John Oliver Killens (Boston: Beacon Press, 1970), pp. 11, 14, 46, 95–97, 159; Richard C. Wade, in "The Vesey Plot: A Reconsideration," *Journal of Southern History*, 30 (May 1964): 143–61, has argued that the conspiracy existed only in the minds of white citizens. Even if this were so, which I doubt, reports of the plot had a very real effect on white attitudes about slave religion. See Killens, pp. xix–xxi.
23. Killens, *Trial Record*, pp. 13–14, 61, 64, 76–78; Vincent Harding, "Religion and Resistance Among Antebellum Negroes, 1800–1860," in *The Making of Black America*, edited by August Meier and Elliott Rudwick, 2 vols. (New York: Atheneum, 1969), 1: 186.
24. "Verbatim Record of the Trials in the Court of Oyer & Terminer of

Southampton County, Held Between 31 August and 21 November 1831 . . . " in Henry Irving Tragle, *The Southampton Slave Revolt of 1831: A Compilation of Source Material* (New York: Random House, Vintage Books, 1973), p. 222. Gray's "Confession" goes into vivid detail about Turner's visions and religious ideas, but it is difficult to say how much is Turner and how much is Gray.

25. Jones, *Religious Instruction*, pp. 215–16.

26. Quoted by Crum, pp. 204–5.

27. Jones, *Religious Instruction*, p. 241; *Proceedings of the Charleston Meeting*, pp. 33, 42; Donald G. Mathews, "Charles Colcock Jones and the Southern Evangelical Crusade to Form a Biracial Community," *Journal of Southern History*, Vol. 41, No. 3 (August 1975).

28. Blassingame, ed., *Slave Testimony*, p. 411.

29. Ibid, p. 435.

30. Ibid, p. 420; see for example, William Wells Brown, *Narrative of William W. Brown, A Fugitive Slave* (Boston, 1848), pp. 37–38, 80; Lunsford Lane, *Narrative of Lunsford Lane* (Boston, 1848), pp. 12–14.

31. George P. Rawick, ed. *The American Slave: A Composite Autobiography*, 19 Vols. (Westport, Conn.: Greenwood, 1972) Vol. 4, *Texas*, pt. 1, p. 281.

32. Charles Nordhoff, "The Freedmen of South-Carolina," in *Papers of the Day*, edited by Frank Moore (No. 1, 1863), pp. 6–7, written at Port Royal, March 20, 1863.

33. *Third Annual Report, Liberty County Association*, p. 7; Mathews, p. 68; Charles Sackett Sydnor, *Slavery in Mississippi* (New York: D. Appleton-Century Company, 1933), p. 61, citing Olmsted, *The Cotton Kingdom*, 2: 81–82; John Roles, *Inside Views of Slavery on Southern Plantations* (New York, 1864), p. 43.

34. Jones, *Religious Instruction*, p. 192.

35. Whitemarsh B. Seabrook, *An Essay on the Management of Slaves* (Charleston, 1834), pp. 14, 21.

36. Seabrook, pp. 15, 18, 23.

37. Seabrook, pp. 20, 22.

38. *Eighth Annual Report, Liberty County Association* (1843), p. 12.

39. Joe Gray Taylor, *Negro Slavery in Louisiana* (Baton Rouge, La.: Louisiana Historical Association, 1963), p. 139; Oscar H. Darter, *The History of Fredericksburg Baptist Church, Fredericksburg, Virginia* (Richmond, Va.: Garrett and Massie, 1959), p. 127; *Minutes of the Dover Baptist Association . . . 1850* (Richmond, 1850), p. 11.

40. Purifoy, p. 161; Jones, *Religious Instruction*, p. 85; Mathews, p. 75.

41. Crum, pp. 210, 229.
42. Mathews, p. 81; see also Crum, p. 201.
43. Cited by Guion Griffis Johnson, *Antebellum North Carolina: A Social History* (Chapel Hill, N.C.: University of North Carolina Press, 1937), p. 543.
44. Jones, *Religious Instruction*, pp. 78–79; Liberty County, Ga., in 1830 had a population of 1,544 whites and 5,729 blacks.
45. Jackson, "Religious Instruction," pp. 95, 103; Purifoy, pp. 151–52. For example, "the Virginia Annual Conference . . . between 1858 and 1860 showed an increase in the number of missions from four to seventeen and an increase in Negro membership in missions of 1,661, whereas, the net gain in Negro membership for the entire Conference was only 648," because missions "had been established to take over . . . Negro membership" (Purifoy, 155*n*).
46. Long, *Pictures of Slavery*, pp. 20–21.
47. *Proceedings of the Charleston Meeting*, p. 56; Jones, *Religious Instruction*, p. 127.
48. *Tenth Annual Report, Liberty County Association*, (1845) pp. 24–25; see also W. G. Hawkins, *Lunsford Lane*, 1st publ. Boston, 1863 (Miami, Fla.: Mnemosyne Publishing Company, 1969), p. 65; Jones, *Religious Instruction*, p. 129.
49. Jones, *Religious Instruction*, p. 114.
50. Jackson, "Religious Development," p. 217–18.
51. Jones, *Religious Instruction*, pp. 94–95; *Tenth Annual Report, Liberty County Association* (1845) p. 10; James B. Sellers, *Slavery in Alabama* (University, Ala.: University of Alabama Press, 1950), pp. 299–300; Noah Davis, *A Narrative of the Life of Rev. Noah Davis* (Baltimore, Md., 1859), p. 27; Jeremiah Bell Jeter, *The Recollections of a Long Life* (Richmond, Va., 1891), pp. 105, 211.
52. Jackson, "Religious Development," pp. 203–5.
53. *Proceedings of the Charleston Meeting*, pp. 50, 70; Nehemiah Adams, *A South-Side View of Slavery*, 3rd ed. (Boston, 1855), p. 54; Jackson, "Religious Development," pp. 200–2, 230, 230*n*, 232.
54. Quoted by J. Carleton Hayden, "Conversion and Control: Dilemma of Episcopalians in Providing for the Religious Instruction of Slaves, Charleston, South Carolina, 1845–1860," *Historical Magazine of the Protestant Episcopal Church*, Vol. 40, No. 2 (June 1971), p. 143.
55. Church minute books and records constitute a genre of evidence not yet fully exploited by historians of slavery. See comments by Michael Mullin, ed., *American Negro Slavery: A Documentary History* (New York: Harper & Row, 1976), pp. 271–73; see also "Records of the

Forks of Elkhorn Baptist Church, Kentucky, 1800–1820," excerpted by William Warren Sweet, ed., *Religion on the American Frontier, The Baptists, 1783–1830: A Collection of Source Material* (Chicago: University of Chicago Press, 1931); W. Harrison Daniel, "Southern Protestantism and the Negro, 1860–1865," *The North Carolina Historical Review*, Vol. 41, No. 3 (July 1964), pp. 338–59; Kenneth K. Bailey, "Protestantism and Afro-Americans in the Old South: Another Look," *Journal of Southern History*, Vol. 41, No. 4 (November 1975), pp. 451–72. A valuable source for manuscript church minutes is the Historical Commission of the Southern Baptist Convention located in Nashville, Tenn.

56. *Minutes of the Dover Baptist Association . . . October 8, 1796* (Richmond, Va., 1797).

57. Z. T. Leavell and T. J. Bailey, *A Complete History of Mississippi Baptists*, 1 (Jackson, Miss., 1904): 40.

58. Reprinted in Sweet, *Religion on the American Frontier*, pp. 320–24.

59. See, for example, Wheeler's (Wheeley's) Baptist Church Minutes, 1790–1798, entry for September 1793 and entry for July 1837 in Flat River Primitive Baptist Church Records, 1786–1938. Manuscripts in the Southern Historical Collection, UNC Library, Chapel Hill, N.C.; *Minutes of Black Creek Baptist Church* (Virginia), February 24, June 22, 1792, and *Minutes of the South Quay Baptist Church* (Virginia), August 1780, both cited by W. Harrison Daniel, "Virginia Baptists and the Negro in the Early Republic," *Virginia Magazine of History and Biography*, Vol. 80, No. 1 (January 1972), p. 63.

60. George W. Purifoy, *A History of the Sandy Creek Baptist Association* (New York, 1859), pp. 76, 83–84.

61. *Minutes of the Virginia Portsmouth Baptist Association . . . 1793* (Norfolk, Va., n.d.), p. 4.

62. Flat River Primitive Baptist Church Records, Nov. 1790 entry.

63. Flat River Church Records.

64. Flat River Church Records, July 1795 and Aug. 1800 entries.

65. Welsh Neck Baptist Church Minutes, 1738–1932, typescript, South Caroliniana Library, University of South Carolina; excerpted in Mullins, ed., *American Negro Slavery*, pp. 278–80.

66. Ibid.

67. Jones, *Religious Instruction*, pp. 94–95; *Proceedings of the Charleston Meeting*, 1845, p. 70.

68. *Minutes of the Portsmouth Baptist Association*, 1794, 1797, 1800, 1801, 1821–25, 1829, 1838; Luther P. Jackson, *A Short History of*

NOTES TO PAGES 189-200

the Gillfield Baptist Church, Petersburg, Va., (Petersburg, Va.: Virginia Printing Co., 1937), pp. 5–15.

69. William B. Sprague, *Annals of the American Baptist Pulpit* (New York, 1860), pp. 251–64; Rev. James M. Simms, *The First Colored Baptist Church in North America* (Philadelphia, 1888), p. 46–78, *Minutes of the Sunbury Baptist Association, 1830* (Savannah, Ga., 1830), p. 7.

70. Simms, pp. 93–98, 102–3; Rev. E. K. Love, *History of the First African Baptist Church* (Savannah, Ga., 1888), pp. 10–11.

71. Simms, pp. 96, 112–14.

72. Love, pp. 12–13.

73. Love, pp. 14–15.

74. Love, pp. 16–24.

75. Love, pp. 20–21, 23–24.

76. Love, pp. 21–22.

77. *Minutes of the Sunbury Baptist Association . . . 1836* (Savannah, Ga., 1836), p. 9; *Minutes of the Sunbury Baptist Association . . . 1837* (Savannah, Ga., 1837), p. 6; Love, p. 30.

78. Charles Hays Rankin, "The Rise of Negro Baptist Churches in the South Through the Reconstruction Period" (Master of Theology thesis, New Orleans Baptist Theological Seminary, 1955), pp. 36–38.

79. Reprinted in Lewis G. Jordan, *Negro Baptist History, U.S.A., 1750–1930* (Nashville, Tenn.: The Sunday School Publishing Board, National Baptist Convention, n.d.), pp. 103–4.

80. *Minutes of the Dover Baptist Association, 1830 . . . 1831 . . . 1843 . . . 1851 . . . 1860*; Benedict, 1850, p. 662; Henry L. Swint, ed., *Dear Ones at Home: Letters From Contraband Camps* (Nashville, Tenn.: Vanderbilt University Press, 1966), p. 155.

81. *Minutes of the Virginia Portsmouth Baptist Association . . . 1851* (Richmond, 1851), p. 19.

82. J. Lansing Burrows, ed., *American Baptist Register For 1852* (Philadelphia, 1853) pp. 70–74; Emily P. Burke, *Reminiscences of Georgia*, (n.p., 1850), p. 34; Simms, pp. 63–64.

83. Sir Charles Lyell, *A Second Visit to the United States of North America*, 2: 14–16.

84. Benedict, 1850 ed., p. 813.

85. Hosea Holcombe, *A History of the Rise and Progress of the Baptists in Alabama* (Philadelphia, 1840), pp. 110–11; Sellers, pp. 300–1, 396–97; Benedict, 1850, p. 756. Offered his freedom by the Alabama Association, Phillips refused to accept, possibly because the

association wanted to send him as missionary to Africa; B. F. Riley, *History of the Baptists in the Southern States East of the Mississippi* (Philadelphia, 1898), pp. 318–19.

86. Benedict, 1850, pp. 771–72; Patrick H. Thompson, *History of Negro Baptists in Mississippi* (Jackson, Miss., 1898), pp. 24–28.

87. H. E. Sterkx, *The Free Negro in Ante-Bellum Louisiana* (Rutherford, N.J.: Fairleigh Dickinson University Press, 1972), pp. 261–66; Charles Hays Rankin, "The Rise of Negro Baptist Churches in the South Through the Reconstruction Period" pp. 35–36.

88. Lewis G. Jordan, pp. 106–8; Tennessee Historical Records Survey Project, Works Progress Administration, *Inventory of Church Archives of Tennessee: Tennessee Baptist Convention, Nashville Baptist Association* (Nashville: Tennessee Historical Records Survey, 1939), pp. 19–20; J. H. Spencer, *History of Kentucky Baptists*, 2 vols. (n.p., 1886), 2: 653–61; Benedict, 1850, pp. 813–15.

89. David Smith, *The Biography of Rev. David Smith* (Xenia, Ohio, 1881), p. 23–33.

90. Deems, *Annals of Southern Methodism for 1856*, pp. 212–13; James A. Handy, *Scraps of African Methodist Episcopal History* (Philadelphia: A.M.E. Book Concern, n.d.), pp. 70, 78.

91. John W. Blassingame, *Black New Orleans, 1860–1880* (Chicago: University of Chicago Press, 1973), pp. 13–14; Joe Gray Taylor, *Negro Slavery in Louisiana*, p. 146; Frank C. Tucker, *The Methodist Church in Missouri, 1798–1939* (Nashville, Tenn.: Parthenon Press, 1966), p. 55; J. Beverly F. Shaw, *The Negro in the History of Methodism* (Nashville, Tenn.: Parthenon Press, 1954), pp. 42–43; Fredrika Bremer, *Homes of the New World*, 2: 234–38.

92. E. A. Andrews, *Slavery and the Domestic Slave-Trade in the United States* (Boston, 1836), p. 37; Long, *Pictures of Slavery*, p. 361; Edenton M.E. Church Records, 1811–, Edenton, N.C., Ms. Southern Historical Collection U.N.C. Minutes of January 1815, April 1827, April 1828, July 1828, September 1829, February 1830, June 1830, and November 1830, when "On motion resolved that the col. Brethren be permitted to take seat in the Quarterly Meeting Conference but on no case to have a vote"; Methodist Episcopal Church, South, Minutes of Quarterly Conference Stokes Circuit, Ms. Southern Historical Collection, U.N.C. Minutes for November 1831. For instances of two black Methodist congregations (one in Kentucky, the other in Virginia) worshiping separately from white members of the same church, see Catterall, 1: 263, 468.

93. Walter Brownlow Posey, *The Presbyterian Church in the Old South-*

west, 1778–1838 (Richmond, Va.: John Knox Press, 1952), pp. 83–84; Ernest Trice Thompson, *Presbyterians in the South, 1607–1861* (Richmond, Va.: John Knox Press, 1963), 1: 442–43; Winfred Ernest Garrison and Alfred T. De Groot, *The Disciples of Christ, A History* (St. Louis, Mo.: Bethany Press, 1948), pp. 468–74; Minnie J. Smith, ed., *Records of the Moravians in North Carolina, 1838–1847* (Raleigh, N.C.: State Department of Archives and History, 1964), 9: 4678–80, 4733–36, 4790–92, 4821–25, 4839–55, 4876, 4913–15, 4954–56; Kenneth G. Hamilton, ed., *Records of the Moravians in North Carolina 1848–1851* (Raleigh, N.C.: State Department of Archives and History, 1966) 10: 5269–71, 5396–98, 5510–12, 5616–18.

94. A. M. Chreitzberg, *Early Methodism in the Carolinas* (Nashville, Tenn., 1897), p. 158–59.

95. Du Bois, *The Negro Church*, p. 29; Ahlstrom, *A Religious History of the American People*, p. 698.

Chapter 5

1. Rawick, ed., *The American Slave: A Composite Autobiography*, Vol. 5, *Texas Narratives*, pt. 4, p. 198. *The American Slave* is the published version of sixteen typescript volumes of interviews with ex-slaves prepared by the Federal Writers' Project in 1936–38. These volumes are Vols. 2–17 in Rawick's edition. Vols. 18 and 19 consist of two volumes of interviews done by Fisk University's Social Science Division in 1929–30, entitled *Unwritten History of Slavery* and *God Struck Me Dead*, respectively. Vol. 1 of the series is Rawick's own introduction to the set, entitled *From Sundown to Sunup: The Making of the Black Community*. With regard to "steal away," Dorothy Scarborough reported that she was told by Dr. Boyd, head of the Baptist Publication Society (Negro), various incidents in the history of old slave songs. "For example, he said of the familiar old spiritual, *Steal Away*, that it was sung in slavery times when the Negroes on a few plantations were forbidden to hold religious services. That was because the masters were afraid of gatherings which might lead to insurrections . . . So the Negroes would gather in a cabin and hold their service by stealth" (Dorothy Scarborough, *On the Trail of Negro Folk-Songs* [Cambridge, Mass.: Harvard University Press, 1925], pp. 22–23.

2. John B. Cade, "Out of the Mouths of Ex-Slaves," *Journal of Negro*

History, 20 (July 1935), 329. Another common notion was that slaves would occupy the "kitchen" of heaven and would continue there to serve their white masters as on earth. See Rawick, 3, *South Carolina*, pt. 3, p. 20, for an example.

3. Rawick, 6, *Alabama*, p. 398; Cade, p. 329.

4. Rawick, 8, *Arkansas*, pt. 1, p. 35; see also *God Struck Me Dead* (Philadelphia: Pilgrim Press, 1969), pp. 134–35. I have used the Pilgrim Press edition of *God Struck Me Dead* throughout.

5. Moses Grandy, *Narrative of the Life of Moses Grandy*, 2nd ed. (Boston, 1844), pp. 35–36; Rawick, 7, *Mississippi*, p. 24 Henry Bibb, *Narrative of the Life and Adventures of Henry Bibb* (New York, 1849), reprinted in *Puttin' On Ole Massa*, edited by Gilbert Osofsky (New York: Harper & Row, 1969), pp. 123–25; Rawick, 17, *Florida*, p. 166; Fisk University, *Unwritten History of Slavery: Autobiographical Accounts of Negro Ex-Slaves* (Washington, D.C.: NCR Microcard Editions, 1968), p. 60. This edition is used throughout.

6. Cade, pp. 330–31; Rawick 6, *Alabama*, p. 433; Fisk, *Unwritten History*, p. 150.

7. Rawick, 16, *Tennessee*, p. 34. Rawick, 1, *From Sundown to Sunup*, pp. 42–45, citing Mintz on pp. 43–44. Rawick argues that the pots recall similar vessels used in religious ceremonies in West Africa and the Caribbean to hold water and sacred objects. I find his theory unconvincing. For other comments on this custom, see Rawick, 16, *Alabama*, p. 40; 8, *Arkansas*, pt. 1, p. 295; Scarborough, p. 23. I would add one more tentative explanation. Perhaps the overturned pot is a fragmentary reflection of an emblem for the West African god Eshu Elegba. According to E. Bolaji Idowu, one of Eshu's emblems is "an earthenware pot turned upside down, with a hole in its middle." As noted above, in Africa, in Brazil and in the Caribbean it is obligatory to begin worship with an offering to Eshu-Elegba in order to ensure that the order and decorum of the service is not disturbed. Could it be that the overturned pot among slaves in the United States was a customary symbol of the *despacho* of Eshu whose full meaning had been lost? Idowu, p. 85. See also Alan Dundes, Preface to *Mother-Wit*, pp. xiii–xiv.

8. B. A. Botkin, ed., *Lay My Burden Down: A Folk History of Slavery* (Chicago: University of Chicago Press, 1945), p. 27. Botkin's is a collection of excerpts from the Federal Writers' Project interviews.

9. *God Struck Me Dead*, p. 76; Cade, p. 329.

10. Peter Randolph, *Sketches of Slave Life or, Illustrations of the Peculiar Institution* (Boston, 1855), pp. 30–31.

11. Rawick, 4, *Texas*, pt. 2, pp. 6–7.

12. Rawick, 4, *Texas*, pt. 1, p. 199.

13. Rawick, 8, *Arkansas*, pt. 1, p. 9; Fisk, *Unwritten History*, p. 131; Rawick, 16, *Tennessee*, p. 49; Jacob Stroyer, *My Life in the South* (Salem, Mass., 1898), p. 25; Cade, p. 330; Rawick, 6, *Alabama*, p. 416; 13, *Georgia*, pt. 4, p. 192.

14. Norman R. Yetman, ed. *Voices from Slavery* (New York: Holt, Rinehart & Winston, 1970), pp. 45–46. An excellent selection of FWP interviews, given (unlike Botkin) in their entirety. The book includes an article on the history of the collection of the narratives.

15. Fisk, *Unwritten History*, pp. 20, 86, 105, 149; Rawick, 8, *Arkansas*, pt. 2, p. 128; 3, *South Carolina*, p. 80: Yetman, p. 56.

16. *God Struck Me Dead*, pp. 87–88.

17. Robert Anderson, *From Slavery to Affluence*, p. 23; Rawick, 4, *Texas*, pt. 2, p. 170: Yetman, p. 335.

18. Mary Boykin Chesnut, *A Diary From Dixie*, edited by Ben Ames Williams (Boston: Houghton Mifflin Company, 1949), pp. 148–49; John Thompson, *The Life of John Thompson: A Fugitive Slave* (Worcester, Mass., 1856), p. 43; *American Missionary*, 6, (June 1862), 129.

19. Harry Smith, *Fifty Years of Slavery* (Grand Rapids, Mich., 1891), p. 38; see a similar account in Rawick, 17, *Florida*, pp. 243–44.

20. Thompson, pp. 18–19.

21. Anderson, p. 22; Fisk, *Unwritten History*, p. 108; "We got most of our outside news Sunday at church," claimed Adeline Jackson. Rawick, 3, *South Carolina*, pt. 3, p. 3; Robert Falls, in Rawick, 16, *Tennessee*, p. 14; 13, *Georgia*, pt. 3, pp. 28, 158, 168–69, 266; Arthur Singleton, *Letters From the South and West* (Boston, 1824), p. 75; Olmsted, *Journey in the Seaboard States* (New York, 1859), p. 454. Susan Dabney Smedes, *A Southern Planter* (New York, 1890), p. 106.

22. Rawick, 13, *Georgia*, pt. 3, p. 252; 6, *Alabama*, p. 3; 13, *Georgia*, pt. 3, p. 282; 16, *Tennessee*, p. 45. See also I. E. Lowery, *Life on the Old Plantation* (Columbia, S. C., 1911), pp. 112–14.

23. Northup, pp. 213–21; Lowery, pp. 64–66; Rawick, 3, *South Carolina*, p. 3; Frederick Douglass, *The Life and Times of Frederick Douglass* (rev. ed., 1892; London: Collier-Macmillan, 1962), pp. 145–47; Stroyer, p. 45.

24. Rawick, 17, *Florida*, p. 252; Stroyer, pp. 46–47; Joseph Holt Ingraham, *The South-West: By A Yankee*, 2 vols. (New York, 1835), 2: 55–56.

25. John Anderson, *The Story of the Life of John Anderson* (London, 1863; Freeport, N.Y.: Books for Libraries Press, 1971), p. 130; W[illia]m Wells Brown, *My Southern Home* (Boston, 1880; New York: Negro Universities Press, 1969), p. 97.
26. Blassingame, ed. *Slave Testimony*, p. 643; Burke, *Reminiscences of Georgia*, p. 245; Smith, p. 166; Roper, pp. 63–64.
27. Rawick, 13, *Georgia*, pt. 3, pp. 252–53; 17, *Florida*, p. 245; 4, *Texas*, pt. 1, p. 228; 3, *South Carolina*, pt. 3, p. 19; for a detailed and interesting account of a baptismal service soon after slavery ended, see 3, *South Carolina*, pt. 3, pp. 108–10.
28. Rawick, 12, *Georgia*, pt. 2, p. 227.
29. Ulrich Ronnell Phillips and James David Glunt, *Florida Plantation Records from the Papers of George Noble Jones,* (St. Louis; Missouri Historical Society, 1927), p. 31; Rawick, 12, *Georgia*, pt. 2, p. 227.
30. Lunsford Lane, *Narrative of Lunsford Lane* (Boston, 1842), p. 11.
31. Rawick, 4, *Texas*, pt. 1, p. 293; Brown, *My Southern Home*, p. 46; Rawick, 8, *Arkansas*, pt. 2, p. 128; 4, *Texas*, pt. 1, pp. 206–7; Fisk, *Unwritten History*, p. 107; John Anderson, p. 10; Olmsted, *Seaboard Slave States*, p. 449. Priscilla "Mittie" Munnikhuysen Bond, MS Diary, 1858–1865 (Louisiana State University), entry Saturday, January 4, 1862; Lowery, pp. 58–63.
32. Benjamin Drew, *The Refugee: A North-Side View of Slavery* (Boston, 1856), p. 131; *Gumbo Ya-Ya*, p. 239; Blassingame, *Slave Testimony*, p. 139–40; Stroyer, p. 16.
33. Rawick, 17, *Florida*, pp. 16–17; 6, *Alabama*, p. 284; Olmsted, *Seaboard Slave States*, p. 449; Frances Anne Kemble, *Journal of a Residence on a Georgia Plantation in 1838–1839* (London, 1863), pp. 139–43; Arthur Singleton, p. 77; Randolph, pp. 13–14; Rawick, 16, *Tennessee*, p. 45; see also *God Struck Me Dead*, p. 78; Olmsted, *Cotton Kingdom*, 1: 43–45; Rawick, 16, *Ohio*, p. 116; 16, *Maryland*, p. 9; 13, *Georgia*, pt. 3, pp. 61, 282; 4, *Texas*, pt. 1, p. 271; *Gumbo Ya-Ya*, p. 244; Charles Emery Stevens, *Anthony Burns; A History* (Boston, 1856; New York: Arno Press and The New York Times, 1969), p. 167.
34. [Charles Raymond,] "The Religious Life of the Negro Slave," *Harper's New Monthly Magazine*, 27 (1863), 678; Rawick, 13, *Georgia*, pt. 3, p. 330; Long, pp. 19–20.
35. Fisk, *Unwritten History*, p. 59; Rawick, 4, *Texas*, pt. 2, p. 9.
36. Rawick, 4, *Texas*, pt. 2, p. 44; Henry Clay Bruce, *The New Man: Twenty Nine Years a Slave, Twenty Nine Years a Free Man* (York, Pa., 1895), p. 73; Drew, p. 83.

37. Blassingame, *Slave Testimony* p. 643. Rawick, 17, *Florida*, pp. 214–15; Fisk, *Unwritten History*, p. 132.

38. James L. Smith, *Autobiography of James L. Smith* (Norwich, Conn., 1881) reprinted in *Five Black Lives* (Middletown, Conn.: Wesleyan University Press, 1971), p. 165.

39. Rawick, 6, *Alabama*, p. 390; Fisk, *Unwritten History*, p. 25; Drew, p. 91; Randolph, p. 26; Kemble, pp. 67, 199–200; see also Fisk, *Unwritten History*, pp. 73, 109; Bruce, p. 72; Duncan C. Heyward, *Seed From Madagascar* (Chapel Hill: University of North Carolina Press, 1937), pp. 198–99; see also Smedes, p. 79.

40. Fisk, *Unwritten History*, p. 46; Rawick, 4, *Texas*, pt. 2, p. 51; Yetman, p. 335. Olmsted observed a funeral in Richmond, Va., at which the black preacher "held a handkerchief before him as if it were a book, and pronounced a short exhortation as if he were reading from it." *Cotton Kingdom*, 1: 44.

41. Yetman, p. 95; Raymond, pp. 485, 677; see also Rawick, 6, *Alabama*, p. 52; Charles Augustus Murray, *Travels in North America During the Years 1834, 1835, 1836*, 2 vols. (New York, 1839), cited in Katherine M. Jones, ed., *The Plantation South* (Indianapolis, Ind.: Bobbs-Merrill Company, 1957), pp. 35–36.

42. Olmsted, *Seaboard Slave States*, pp. 450–51; David Macrae, *The Americans at Home*, 2 vols. (Edinburgh, 1870), 2: 108; see also *God Struck Me Dead*, pp. 74, 84.

43. *American Missionary*, 12 (February 1868), 29.

44. George H. Hepworth, *The Whip, Hoe, and Sword or the Gulf Department in '63* (Boston, 1864), pp. 165–68.

45. *American Missionary*, 8 (April 1864), 100.

46. A. M. French, *Slavery in South Carolina and the Ex-Slaves; or, The Port Royal Mission* (New York, 1862), p. 131.

47. Bruce Rosenberg, *The Art of the American Folk Preacher* (New York: Oxford University Press, 1970) is the most detailed analysis of this tradition; see also William H. Pipes, *Say Amen Brother! Old-Time Negro Preaching* (New York: William-Frederick Press, 1951); Whitelaw Reid, *After the War: A Tour of the Southern States 1865–1866*, edited by C. Vann Woodward (New York: Harper & Row, 1965), p. 521.

48. Olmsted, *Cotton Kingdom*, 2: 104; *American Missionary*, 13 (February 1869): 28.

49. Douglass, *Life and Times*, pp. 90–92, 94; Kemble, pp. 102–3; *Letters and Diary of Laura M. Towne*, 1862–1884, edited by Rupert Sargent Holland (Cambridge, Mass.: Riverside Press, 1912), pp.

144–45; C. C. Jones, Jr., *Negro Myths from the Georgia Sea Coast* (Boston, 1888), p. 159; Simms, *the First Colored Baptist Church in North America*, p. 19.

50. Rawick, 13, *Georgia*, pt. 3, p. 97; Yetman, p. 36; see also 6, *Alabama*, p. 433.

51. Carter G. Woodson, *Education of the Negro Prior to 1861*, p. 221; Macrae, 2: 113; [Elizabeth Ware Pierson, ed.,] *Letters From Port Royal, 1862–1868* (Boston, 1906; New York: Arno Press and the New York Times, 1969), p. 65; see also Macrae, 1: 229–30; 2: 108, 111–16; and *American Missionary*, 7 (April 1863): 91; (September 1863), 208; (October 1863), 231; and passim.

52. Sir Charles Lyell, *A Second Visit to the U.S.*, 1: 203, 271; Olmsted, *Cotton Kingdom*, 2: 70–71; Frederick Douglass, *Narrative of the Life of Frederick Douglass* (Boston, 1845; Garden City, N.Y.: Dolphin Books, Doubleday & Company, 1963), p. 41; Elijah P. Marrs, *Life and History of the Rev. Elijah P. Marrs* (Louisville, Ky., 1885; Miami, Fla.: Mnemosyne Publishing Co., 1969), p. 12; Rawick, 14, *North Carolina*, pt. 1, p. 95; see also Grandy, p. 36; *American Missionary*, 11 (September, 1867): 194–95.

53. *Third Annual Report, Liberty County, Georgia, Association* (1836), p. 4; William H. Heard, *From Slavery to the Bishopric* (Philadelphia: A.M.E. Book Concern, 1924), pp. 31–32; *American Missionary*, 10 (September, 1866): 197.

54. Macrae, 2: 95; *American Missionary*, 6 (June 1862): 138; 11 (March 1867): 65; 14 (May 1870): 103; 8 (April 1864): 105; 7 (April 1863): 81.

55. *American Missionary*, 12 (January 1868): 9; 14 (September–October 1870): 194, 221; Long, p. 288.

56. Harold Courlander, *Negro Folk Music, U.S.A.* (New York and London: Columbia University Press, 1963), p. 35. The interpretations of the spirituals which I have found most persuasive are those of Lawrence Levine, "Slave Songs and Slave Consciousness: An Exploration in Nineteenth-Century Social History, edited by Tamara K. Hareven (Englewood Cliffs, N.J.: Prentice-Hall, 1971), pp. 99–130; H. H. Proctor, "The Theology of the Songs of the Southern Slave," *Southern Workman*, Vol. 36, Nos. 11, 12 (November–December 1907), pp. 584–92, 652–56; John Lovell, Jr., "The Social Implications of the Negro Spiritual," *Journal of Negro Education*, 8 (October 1939): 634–43; reprinted in *The Social Implications of Early Negro Music in the United States*, Bernard Katz, ed. (New York: Arno Press and The New York Times, 1969), pp. 127–37;

Le Roy Moore, Jr., "The Spiritual: Soul of Black Religion," *American Quarterly*, Vol. 23, No. 5 (December 1971), pp. 658–76.

57. Smith, pp. 162–63.

58. Harris Barrett, "Negro Folk Songs," *The Southern Workman*, Vol. 41, No. 4 (April 1912), pp. 238–45.

59. Jeannette Robinson Murphy, "The Survival of African Music in America," *Popular Science Monthly*, 55 (New York 1899): 660–72, reprinted in Bruce Jackson, ed., *The Negro and His Folklore*, pp. 328–29.

60. See "Marcel," [W. F. Allen] "The Negro Dialect," *Nation* 1 (December 14, 1865): 744–45, reprinted in Bruce Jackson, ed., *The Negro and His Folklore*, pp. 78–81; Robert Gordon, "Negro 'Shouts' from Georgia," *The New York Times Magazine*, April 24, 1927, reprinted in Dundes, ed., *Mother Wit*, pp. 447–48. Gordon explains: "Not all spirituals were shouted. But whenever spirituals were sung they demanded a certain rhythmic movement of the body. This might be confined on formal occasions to a mere swaying backward and forward; it might on other occasions include a tapping of the feet or a patting of the hands; if opportunity offered, it might extend to real shouting." See also "The Negro Spiritual," *The Carolina Low-Country*, Augustine T. Smyth et al. [The Society for the Preservation of the Spirituals] (New York: Macmillan Company, 1931), p. 198; *Slave Songs of the United States*, pp. xv–xvi.

61. J[ames Miller] McKim, "Negro Songs," *Dwight's Journal of Music*, 19 (August 9, 1862): 148–49, reprinted in Katz, ed., *Social Implications of Early Negro Music*, p. 2.

62. Fisk, *Unwritten History*, p. 142.

63. Douglass, *Life and Times*, pp. 159–60.

64. Thomas Wentworth Higginson, *Army Life in a Black Regiment* (Boston, 1869; Boston: Beacon Press, 1962), pp. 217–18.

65. William A. Sinclair, *The Aftermath of Slavery* (Boston: Small Maynard & Company, 1905), p. 15.

66. Macrae, *The Americans at Home*, 2: 100.

67. Booker T. Washington, *Up From Slavery* (New York, 1901), reprinted in *Three Negro Classics* (New York: Avon Books, 1965), p. 39.

68. And "Making a way out of no-way," Zora Neale Hurston, in "High John de Conquer," *The American Mercury*, 57 (1943): 450–58, reprinted in Dundes, ed., *Mother-Wit*, p. 543.

69. Levine is using Mircea Eliade's concept of the sacred. See Levine, "Slave Songs and Slave Consciousness," pp. 114–15, and Mircea

Eliade, *The Sacred and the Profane* (New York: Harper & Row, 1961).

70. Vincent Harding, "The Uses of the Afro-American Past," *The Religious Situation*, 1969, edited by Donald R. Cutter (Boston: Beacon Press, 1969), pp. 829–40. George Pullen Jackson has demonstrated the similarity of verses and tunes in a significant number of black and white spirituals. See Jackson, *White Spirituals in the Southern Uplands* (Chapel Hill: University of North Carolina Press, 1933), pp. 274–302; *White and Negro Spirituals* (New York: J. J. Augustin Publisher, 1943), pp. 146–227, 306–25; *Spiritual Folk Songs of Early America* (Locust Valley, N. Y.: J. J. Augustin Publisher, 1953), pp. 169–240.

71. *Slave Songs*, p. 13.

72. Higginson, pp. 216–17. He felt that this may have been a "modification" of an old camp-meeting hymn.

73. *Slave Songs*, p. 36.

74. Macrae, 2: 97.

75. Higginson, p. 205.

76. [Charlotte Forten] "Life on the Sea Islands," *Atlantic Monthly*, 13 (May 1864): 589.

77. Marcel [W. F. Allen]"The Negro Dialect," in Jackson, *Negro and His Folklore*, p. 78.

78. Higginson, p. 212; *Slave Songs*, pp. 14, 84.

79. *Slave Songs*, p. 13; Macrae, 2: 102.

80. Fisk, *Unwritten History*, p. 21.

81. *Slave Songs*, pp. 4–5; Smith, p. 162.

82. Interview with Lorenzo Ezell in Rawick, 4, *Texas*, pt. 2, p. 26.

83. Eliza Frances Andrews, *The War-Time Journal of a Georgia Girl* (New York: D. Appleton & Company, 1908), p. 90; *Slave Songs*, p. 72, Higginson, p. 207.

84. *Slave Songs*, p. 57.

85. Ibid., p. 95.

86. [Forten] "Life on the Sea Islands," p. 594.

87. Higginson, p. 203.

88. *Slave Songs*, pp. 12, 55; Higginson, pp. 206, 212, 216–17.

89. *Slave Songs*, pp. 30–31.

90. Fisk, *Unwritten History*, p. 20.

91. Macrae, 2: 102; *Slave Songs*, p. 55.

92. *Slave Songs*, p. 2.

93. Higginson, p. 210; *Slave Songs*, p. 15; J. Ralph Jones, "Portraits of Georgia Slaves," *The Georgia Review*, Vol. 21, No. 1 (Spring 1967), p. 128.

94. *Slave Songs*, pp. 10–11
95. Ibid., p. 94.
96. *Slave Songs*, p. 101; Higginson, p. 209.
97. Higginson, p. 203.
98. *Slave Songs*, p. 12.
99. Stroyer, pp. 40–41.
100. Higginson, p. 207; *Slave Songs*, pp. 69, 105.
101. *Slave Songs*, p. 53; see Revelation, 6:12–13.
102. *Slave Songs*, pp.. 25, 43, 73.
103. Andrews, *War-Time Journal*, p. 90.
104. Frances Butler Leigh, *Ten Years on a Georgia Plantation Since the War* (London, 1883), p. 254; Gordon, "Negro Spirituals," *Carolina Low-Country*, p. 201. Leigh, writing in 1867, noted: "A negro must dance and sing, and as their religion, which is very strict in such matters, forbids secular dancing, they take it out in religious exercise, call it 'shouting,' and explained to me that the difference between the two was, that in their religious dancing they did not 'lift the heal' (*Ten Years*, p. 59).
105. Macrae, 2: 105; see also Hepworth, pp. 164–65.
106. *American Missionary*, 10 (May 1866): 103; Macrae, 2: 105–7.
107. Rawick, 3, *South Carolina*, pt. 3, p. 81; see also Rawick, 16, *Tennessee*, pp. 7, 45–46.
108. W. E. Burghardt Du Bois, *The Souls of Black Folk* (Chicago, 1903; New York: Fawcett Publications, 1968), p. 141.
109. Marrs, p. 13; Stevens, *Anthony Burns*, p. 163; Henson, p. 30; see also Leonard Black, *The Life and Sufferings of Leonard Black* (New Bedford, 1847), pp. 20–21; Macrae, 2: 90–97.
110. Fisk, *Unwritten History*, p. 106; *God Struck Me Dead*, pp. 19, 45.
111. Letter from Liele is excerpted in Rippon's *Register*, pp. 332–33.
112. William R. Ferris, Jr., refers to the classical terminology, "sense of sin, purgation, union with God," in his discussion of "The Negro Conversion," *Keystone Folklore Quarterly*, 14 (Spring 1970): 35–51; *God Struck Me Dead*, p. 23.
113. Raymond, pp. 680–82; *God Struck Me Dead*, p. 78; see also Jones, *Religious Instruction*, pp. 125–26; Macrae, 2: 90–97; Fisk, *Unwritten History*, pp. 74, 112; *American Missionary*, 10 (May 1866): 113–14.
114. *God Struck Me Dead*, pp. 18, 45–46; and passim; Randolph, pp. 25–26; see also *American Missionary*, 8 (May 1864): 127.
115. Ibid., Epilogue.
116. See Introduction to *God Struck Me Dead*, pp. xvii–xix.
117. John T. Gillard, *Colored Catholics in the United States* (Baltimore,

Md.: Josephite Press, 1941), p. 95; Roger Baudier, *The Catholic Church in Louisiana* (New Orleans: n.p., 1939), p. 433; for a different evaluation of the success of Catholic missionaries among Louisiana slaves, see Taylor, *Negro Slavery in Louisiana*, pp. 134–35; V. Alton Moody, *Slavery on Louisiana Sugar Plantations* (reprinted from *The Louisiana Historical Quarterly*, April 1924), pp. 90–93.

118. Gillard, p. 106; *Gumbo Ya-Ya*, p. 242; Olmsted, *Cotton Kingdom*, 2: 35–36.

119. Some might consider the Healy brothers, James, Alexander, and Patrick, to have been the first Negro priests in the United States, but as Gillard notes: "While it was generally known that the Healy brothers were colored, they were not known as Negro priests in the sense that the term is usually taken"—i.e., they did not minister among black people (Gillard, p. 185). For another view, see Albert S. Foley, *God's Men of Color* (New York: Farrar, Straus, 1955).

120. Harriet Martineau, *Retrospect of Western Travel*, 2 vols (New York, 1838), 1: 259; Harrison A. Trexler, *Slavery in Missouri, 1804–1865* (Baltimore, Md.: Johns Hopkins Press, 1914), p. 86; see also James M. Phillippo, *The United States and Cuba* (London, 1857), p. 310.

121. Pierre Landry, "From Slavery to Freedom," unpublished memoirs, cited by Charles Bathelemy Rousseve, *The Negro in Louisiana* (New Orleans: Xavier University Press, 1937), p. 39. Landry later converted to Methodism, became a minister and, during Reconstruction, a state senator.

122. See Foley, pp. 32–51, and Richard, Cardinal Cushing's Foreword, pp. v–vi.

123. *American Missionary*, 12 (October 1869): 227; 13 (March 1870): 62; see Gillard, *Colored Catholics*. A case could be made, of course, that in hemispheric perspective the majority of Afro-Americans are Catholics. The history of black Catholics in the United States has yet to be written.

124. Rawick, 17, *Florida*, p. 136.

125. Leonora Herron and Alice M. Bacon, "Conjuring and Conjure-Doctors," *Southern Workman*, 24 (1895): 117–18, 193–94, 209–11, reprinted in *Mother Wit from the Laughing Barrel*, edited by Alan Dundes—see p. 360 for quotation. Herron was a librarian and Bacon a teacher at Hampton Institute. In writing this pioneering article they used a series of essays about conjure written in 1878 by Hampton students. See also Puckett, *Magic and Folk Beliefs*, pp.

200–6. Most conjurers were male, but C. C. Jones, Jr., claimed that old women had a monopoly on conjuring along the coast of Georgia and the Carolinas. *Negro Myths from the Georgia Coast* (Boston and New York, 1888), pp. 151–52. I have found no confirmation of his contention. However, most witches—in keeping with the almost universal custom—were female.

126. A point discussed by Elliott Jacob Gorn in a superb analysis of conjure which has heavily influenced my comments. See " '. . . No White Man Could Whip Me': Folk Beliefs of the Slave Community," M.A. thesis, Folklore, University of California, Berkeley, 1975; Herron and Bacon, pp. 362–64.

127. Herron and Bacon, p. 364; Puckett, *Magic and Folk Beliefs*, pp. 222–24.

128. Rawick, 4, *Texas*, pt. 2, pp. 64–65.

129. Puckett, *Magic and Folk Beliefs*, pp. 233–34.

130. Georgia Writers' Project, *Drums and Shadows*, p. 36.

131. Rawick, 13, *Georgia*, pt. 3, p. 344; Georgia Writers' Project, *Drums and Shadows*, p. 25; Herron and Bacon, p. 365.

132. Herron and Bacon, p. 367.

133. Bibb, p. 30.

134. Rawick, 6, *Alabama*, p. 322.

135. Brown, *Narrative*, pp. 90–92.

136. Puckett, pp. 208–9.

137. Stroyer, p. 54.

138. Douglass, *Life and Times*, pp. 136–39.

139. Puckett, p. 571.

140. The effectiveness of a love potion offered for sale by one New Orleans conjurer was augmented by advice to "gib de 'oman ebbything she laks and lots up hit—nebber cross her en make er mad . . . Show her all de time dat she's de onliest 'oman you wants"—Puckett, "Race Pride and Folklore," *Opportunity*, Vol. 4, No. 39 (1966), pp. 82–84, reprinted in Dundes, *Mother Wit*, pp. 6–7.

141. Brown, *My Southern Home*, pp. 68–81; Blassingame, *Slave Community*, p. 49.

142. Rawick, 6, *Indiana*, pp. 47–49. Former slave from Tennessee, speaking of his own children who imitated his cousin a conjurer.

143. Fisk, *Unwritten History*, p. 46; Rawick, 13, *Georgia*, pt. 3, p. 216. For examples of the view that whites could be conjured, see Rawick, 11, *Arkansas*, pt. 7, pp. 20–21; 6, *Alabama*, pp. 169, 223; Puckett, *Magic and Folk Beliefs*, p. 275. For denials that whites

could be conjured, see Rawick, 7, *Oklahoma*, p. 204; 11, *Missouri*, pp. 250–51. Many whites, of course, believed in conjuration and formed, e.g., in New Orleans, a large part of the conjurers' clientele.

144. Herron and Bacon, p. 361; Puckett, p. 276; Bibb, pp. 26–27.
145. Genovese, *Roll, Jordan, Roll*, pp. 217–18; Blassingame, *Slave Community*, pp. 48–49.
146. Jones, *Religious Instruction*, p. 128.
147. *Trial Record of Denmark Vesey*, pp. 77–78; 7; also pp. 15–16, 63. I have noted above the aspects of conjure involved in Gabriel's Insurrection.
148. Douglass, *Life and Times*, p. 137; Brown, *My Southern Home*, pp. 10–11; Georgia Writers' Project, *Drums and Shadows*, pp. 25–26, 31, 76, 88, 143, 146–48; Genovese, *Roll, Jordan, Roll*, pp. 217–18.
149. Elsie Clews Parson, *Folk Lore of the Sea Islands, South Carolina* (Cambridge, Mass., and New York: American Folklore Society, 1923) pp. 61–63, reprinted in *A Documentary History of Slavery in North America*, Willie Lee Rose, ed. (New York: Oxford University Press, 1976) pp. 249–50.
150. Thaddeus Norris, "Negro Superstitions," *Lippincott's Magazine*, 6 (July 1870); 90–95, reprinted in *The Negro and His Folklore*, edited by Bruce Jackson.
151. C. C. Jones, Jr. *Negro Myths*, pp. 157–58; Herron and Bacon, p. 360.
152. Rawick, 4, *Texas*, pt. 2, p. 3; 6, *Alabama*, pp. 36–37.
153. Herron and Bacon, p. 366; Norman E. Whitten, Jr., "Contemporary Patterns of Malign Occultism Among Negroes in North Carolina," *Mother Wit*, edited by Dundes, p. 414; M. J. Field, *Search for Security: An Ethno-Psychiatric Study of Rural Ghana.* ([Evanston, Ill.:] Northwestern University Press, 1960), p. 40; Puckett, *Magic and Folk Belief*, pp. 565–67, 573–74; Gorn, p. 35. As noted above, Denmark Vesey's conspiracy was one outstanding example of the compatibility of Christianity and conjure represented, respectively, by the class leaders of the A.M.E. Church of Charleston and Gullah Jack Pritchard. In the twentieth century, Puckett states that he was acquainted with several conjurer-ministers, *Magic and Folk Beliefs* (p. 565). A fascinating story from the late nineteenth century demonstrating the power of conjure over an educated black minister and his congregation is told by Jeannette Robinson Murphy, a white Southern woman interested in preserving the old

spirituals and folklore of former slaves. See "The Survival of African Music in America," *Popular Science Monthly*, 55 (New York, 1899): 1660–672, reprinted in Jackson, pp. 333–34.

Chapter 6

1. Henry L. Swint, ed., *Dear Ones at Home: Letters from Contraband Camps* (Nashville, Tenn.: Vanderbilt University Press, 1966), p. 124.
2. Petition cited by St. Clair Drake, *The Redemption of Africa and Black Religion* (Chicago: Third World Press, 1970), pp. 23–24
3. Douglass, *Life and Times*, p. 41.
4. Ball, pp. 221–22; also see Rawick, 4, *Texas*, pt. 1, p. 281.
5. Burke, *Reminiscences of Georgia*, p. 47; *God Struck Me Dead*, p. 161; Anderson, p. 129; Lewis and Milton Clarke, *Narratives of Lewis and Milton Clarke* (Boston, 1846), pp. 113–14, 118–19.
6. John Brown, *Slave Life in Georgia*, edited by L. A. Chamerovzow (London, 1855), pp. 203–4.
7. Drew, pp. 68, 234–35.
8. William Wells Brown, *Narrative*, p. 34; Drew, pp. 62–63; A. M. French, *Slavery in South Carolina and the Ex-Slaves; or, The Port Royal Mission* (New York, 1862), p. 127.
9. Rawick, 17, *Florida*, p. 98; Lunsford Lane, pp. 20–21.
10. *Tenth Annual Report, Liberty County Association* (1845), pp. 24–25.
11. Lewis and Milton Clarke, p. 105.
12. Moses Roper, *A Narrative of the Adventures and Escape of Moses Roper*, 3rd ed. (London, 1839), p. 62.
13. Rawick, 4, *Texas*, pt. 2, p. 163; Drew, p. 247; Rawick, 13, *Georgia*, pt. 4, p. 185.
14. Rawick, 8, *Arkansas*, pt. 2, p. 259; Bibb, p. 166; Lewis and Milton Clarke, p. 119; see also Stroyer, pp. 57–59; Henson, p. 25; Douglass, *Life and Times*, pp. 104–6; Drew, p. 247.
15. William Wells Brown, *My Southern Home*, p. 52; John Brown, *Slave Life in Georgia*, edited by F. N. Boney (first published 1855; reprinted Savannah: The Beehive Press, 1972), pp. 71–72; Jones, *Religious Instruction*, p. 130.
16. Stroyer, p. 29; Rawick, 6, *Alabama*, p. 223.
17. Capers cited in Mathews, p. 76; Jones, *Religious Instruction*, p. 126.
18. Thomas Turpin, *Christian Advocate and Journal*, 8 (January 31, 1834), cited in Crum, *Gullah*, pp. 219–20.

19. Charles Stearns, *The Black Man of the South and the Rebels* (New York, 1872), pp. 355, 373–74, 381.
20. Olmsted, *Seaboard Slave States*, pp. 123–24.
21. Frances Butler Leigh, *Ten Years on a Georgia Plantation Since the War* (London, 1883), p. 164; Smalls' testimony is cited by Herbert G. Gutman, *The Black Family in Slavery and Freedom, 1750–1925* (New York: Pantheon Books, 1976), p. 63. See Gutman, pp. 61–74, for extended comment on sexual mores among slaves before and after marriage.
22. William Grimes, *Life of William Grimes* (New Haven, Conn., 1855); reprinted in *Five Black Lives*, pp. 198–99.
23. Solomon Bayley, *A Narrative of Some Remarkable Incidents in the Life of Solomon Bayley* (London, 1825), pp. 25–26; Drew, p. 181; see also *God Struck Me Dead*, p. 40.
24. Grimes, in *Five Black Lives*, pp. 83–84; see also interview with Charity Bowery in *The Emancipator*, April 5, 1848, reprinted in Blassingame, ed. *Slave Testimony*, pp. 261–67.
25. Henson, pp. 46–48.
26. Drew, p. 55; Rawick, 6, *Alabama*, p. 131; *God Struck Me Dead*, p. 83; Rawick, 3, *South Carolina*, pt. 3, p. 105; Yetman, p. 75; Fisk, *Unwritten History*, p. 148.
27. Drew, p. 29; John Thompson, pp. 75–78; William and Ellen Craft, *Running a Thousand Miles for Freedom* (London, 1860); reprinted in *Great Slave Narratives*, edited by Arna Bontemps (Boston: Beacon Press, 1969), p. 292.
28. G. W. Offley, *A Narrative of the Life and Labors of Rev. G. W. Offley* (Hartford, Conn., 1860); reprinted in *Five Black Lives*, 134–35.
29. For the story of Dinkie see Chapter 5, p. 282.
30. Thomas Jones, *Narrative of a Refugee Slave: The Experience of Thomas Jones* (Springfield, Mass., 1854), pp. 20–27; Drew, pp. 269–70; "The Lost Is Found," *Voice of the Fugitive* (January 15, February 26, March 11, April 22, June 3, 1852); reprinted in Blassingame, ed. *Slave Testimony*, pp. 276–78.
31. Rawick 6, *Indiana*, pp. 158–59; *American Missionary* [ser. 2] 7 (February 1863): 38.
32. A. M. French, pp. 133–34.
33. J. Ralph Jones, "Portraits of Georgia Slaves," *Georgia Review*, 21 (Summer 1967): 272; *American Missionary*, [ser. 2] 11 (May 1862): 102.
34. Radin, Foreword, *God Struck Me Dead*, p. vii; Drew, pp. 80, 111, 237–38.

NOTES TO PAGES 310–320 373

35. Barbara Leigh Smith Bodichon, *An American Diary, 1857–8*, edited by Joseph W. Reed, Jr. (London: Routledge & Kegan Paul, 1972), p. 65, diary entry of 12 December 1857; Bremer, *Homes of the New World*, 1: 291; *American Missionary* [ser. 2] 6 (June 1862): 138.
36. Rawick, 17, *Florida*, p. 142; David Smith, *Biography of Rev. David Smith* (Xenia, Ohio, 1881), p. 12.
37. W. G. Kiphant, Letter of May 9, 1864, Decatur, Ala., A.M.A. Archives, Amistad Research Center, Dillard University, New Orleans.
38. *American Missionary* [ser. 2] 11 (May 1867): 102; Thomas L. Johnson, *Twenty-Eight Years a Slave* (Bournemouth, England: W. Mate & Sons, 1909), pp. 29–30.
39. Mary A. Livermore, *My Story of the War* (Hartford, Conn., 1889), pp. 260–61.
40. Fisk, *Unwritten History*, p. 38; Douglas C. Strange, "Document: Bishop Daniel Alexander Payne's Protestation of American Slavery," *Journal of Negro History*, 52 (January 1967): 63.
41. Douglass, *Life and Times*, p. 135; Charles Carleton Coffin, *The Boys of '61; or Four Years of Fighting* (Boston, 1886), p. 415; Long, p. 127; for a discussion of Douglass' religious scepticism see William L. Van Deburg, "Frederick Douglass: Maryland Slave to Religious Liberal," *Maryland Historical Magazine* 69 (Spring 1974): 27–42.
42. W. P. Harrison, *The Gospel Among the Slaves* (Nashville, Tenn., 1893), p. 287; Irving E. Lowery, *Life on the Old Plantation* (Columbia, S.C., 1911), pp. 70–71, cited by Crum, p. 190.
43. *Tenth Annual Report, Liberty County Georgia Association* (1845), p. 32; Brown, *My Southern Home*, p. 3; Bruce, pp. 71–72; Parthenia Antoinette Hague, *A Blockaded Family* (Boston, 1889), pp. 10–11.
44. Elijah P. Marrs, *Life and History of Rev. Elijah P. Marrs* (Louisville, Ky., 1885), p. 14.
45. *God Struck Me Dead*, pp. 15–18.

Conclusion

1. *American Missionary*, Vol. 6, No. 2 (February 1862), p. 33.

Index

Christmas, slaves' celebration of, 224
Church discipline: and slave treatment, 171, 181–82; and slave marriage, 183–87
Clark, Gus, 214
Clark, Susan H., 242
Clarke, Lewis, 292, 295
Clarke, Milton, 292, 295
Clarke, Richard, 117
Clay, Thomas S., 170
Coffin, Charles C., 314
Coker, Daniel, 203–4
Coke, Thomas, 143–44
Confraternities (cofradias), 87–88
Conjure and conjurers, 33, 75, 80–86, 275–88
Conversion experience, 132–33, 266–71, 316–17
Conversion of slaves: cultural barriers to, 100, 121; in the eighteenth century, 148–49; as justification of enslavement, 96–98; opposition of masters to, 98–103; 107–8; and rebellion, 145–47
Convince cult (Jamaica) 16–17
Cooper, Rev. W.G., 316
Cotes, Rev. William, 124
Courlander, Harold, 71
Cox, John, 197
Craft, Ellen, 305
Craft, William, 305
Cult Initiation: in Africa, 10; in Jamaica, 29; in U.S., 73
Cumina cult (Jamaica), 17, 36
Curry, James, 230
Curtin, Philip D., 89–90

Dahomey, 6, 10, 15, 18, 20, 26–27, 75–77
Damballa-wedo, 23–24, 75, 76, 77, 79
Dance, and African religious influence, 15, 35–37, 61–62, 66–74. See also Ring-shout
Dangbe, 76
Daniels, Julia Francis, 223
Davenport, Carey, 167
Davenport, Charles, 304
Davenport, Frederick Morgan, 60
Davies, Samuel, 129–30

Davis, Minerva, 229
Davis, William, 228
Dawson, Anthony, 234
Decoudry, Israel, 188
Dede, Sanite, 79
Dembo (slave), 315
Dicey (slave), 185–87
Dickie, Rev. Adam, 125
Divination: in Africa, 10–11, 15; in Cuba, 20, 22, 23
Djuka, 42. See also Bush Negroes
Dorsey, Douglas, 294
Doughty, Charles, 206
Douglass, Frederick, 166, 238, 241, 247–48, 281, 284, 291, 314
Dover Baptist Association (Va.), 171–72, 181, 197
Drums and Shadows, 85
Du Bois, W.E.B., 209, 266
Duncan, Jonathan, 206
Dupee, George W., 201

Early, John, 160
Easter, Willis, 286
Edmundson, William, 110
Edwards, Anderson, 218, 232
Edwards, Jonathan, 128
Egungun society, 13, 30
Eliot, John, 108, 109
Ellis, Harrison W., 207
Ellis, Mary, 77
Erskine, George M., 207
Eshu-Elegba, 19, 20, 23, 24, 37–39, 77
Evangelicalism, 148
Evans, Henry, 135
Ewing, Mathew, 234
Ewing, "Uncle" Tom, 232
Exodus story, and slaves, 311–12

Fairley, Rachel, 296
Fauset, Arthur Huff, 56
Ferrill, Loudon, 201
Fetish. See Charms
Field, M.J., 12, 288
Fitzpatrick, Sarah, 225
Flat River Primitive Baptist Church, Person County, North Carolina, 184–85
Flint River Baptist Association (Ala.), black churches within, 199–200